800
23

Witold Rodzinski

The Walled Kingdom

A History of China from Antiquity to the Present

THE FREE PRESS
A Division of Macmillan, Inc.
New York

The Free Press
A Division of Macmillan, Inc.
866 Third Avenue, New York, N.Y. 10022

Printed in the United States of America

printing number

1 2 3 4 5 6 7 8 9 10

Library of Congress Cataloging in Publication Data

Rodzinski, Witold.
  The walled kingdom.

  Bibliography: p.
  Includes index.
  1. China—History, I. Title.
DS736.R63 1984   951   84-8035
ISBN 0-02-926870-2

Contents

List of Maps 7

Preface 9

1. The Rise of Ancient Chinese Civilization 11
2. The Establishment of a Centralized Monarchy 40
3. The Period of Division 67
4. The Restoration of the Empire: the Sui
   and T'ang Dynasties 86
5. The Sung Dynasties and the Northern Invaders 112
6. Mongol Rule and Ming Restoration 138
7. China Under Manchu Rule 164
8. The Opium Wars and the Taiping Revolution 180
9. The Problems of Modernization and Further
   Foreign Aggression 208
10. Imperialism and China, 1895–1901 229
11. The 1911 Revolution and the Rule of the
    Militarists, 1901–18 248
12. China in the First Post-war Years, 1919–24 274
13. The 1925–7 Revolution 294
14. The Chinese Communists and the Kuomintang
    Dictatorship, 1927–37 318
15. The War with Japan, 1937–45 345
16. The Victory of the Chinese Revolution, 1945–9 373
17. People's China: In Search of a Future, 1949–65 392
18. The 'Cultural Revolution' and Its
    Aftermath, 1966–82 416

Suggested Reading 435
Chronological Table of Dynasties 437
Index 439

List of Maps

1. Europe and China in the nineteenth century   12
2. The Yang-shao and Lung-shan cultures   14
3. Shang, thirteenth century BC   18
4. Western Chou, ninth century BC   24
5. Eastern Chou, *c.* 600 BC, the Spring and Autumn period   28
6. Eastern Chou, *c.* 300 BC, the Warring States period   30
7. The Ch'in Empire   41
8. The Han Empire, *c.* 100 BC   47
9. The Three Kingdoms, *c.* AD 230   68
10. Period of Division, *c.* 500   76
11. The T'ang Empire, *c.* 750   92
12. The Five Dynasties and Ten Kingdoms, *c.* 955   113
13. Northern Sung, *c.* 1100   116
14. Southern Sung, *c.* 1180   124
15. Mongol Rule. Kubilai's Empire   139
16. The Ming Empire, *c.* 1600   146
17. T'ai-p'ing T'ien-kuo   187
18. The Ch'ing Empire, *c.* 1893   209
19. The foreign powers and China (up to 1906)   218
20. China in 1983   430–1

Preface

There are innumerable problems involved in attempting to present a brief survey of four thousand years of Chinese history, but undoubtedly one of the most troublesome is determining the proportions of space to be devoted to modern and contemporary history and to the earlier ages. In the present work over half of the material deals with the years 1840–1982, and such a decision must be regarded as debatable, for other, different solutions were also possible. It was, at least partially, a subjective choice, in that I have continued to maintain for well over forty years an interest in the events taking place on the current Chinese political arena. Nonetheless, from the 1950s on, and the writing at that time of a doctoral dissertation on a subject connected with the years 1945–9, the feeling that contemporary and modern Chinese history simply cannot be properly understood without delving into the earlier past, perhaps even more so than in the case of most other countries, has grown constantly. In connection with this by no means original conclusion, I have devoted a good part of the past thirty years to the study of Chinese civilization from its beginning to the nineteenth century, and the results of this, such as they may be, are largely reflected in the first seven chapters of this book.

In the earlier sections I have paid some attention to various aspects of Chinese cultural development, while the chapters devoted to modern, and in particular to post-1949, events are concerned primarily with political history. I have already dealt with the entire period up to 1949 at greater length in a two-volume history. The two chapters on People's China in the years 1949–82 have been especially written for the present work, in spite of the reservations felt and expressed in print as to the advisability of doing just this. Nor have they vanished after the deed was done, and the conclusions drawn in these chapters should be considered tentative and subject to future emendation. The reasons for this are clear; much of the most pertinent historical material is still unavailable, and the events are too close to be viewed in proper perspective.

A final remark on transcription. Admittedly, the new 'pinyin' transcription, advocated by the PRC, will one day come into universal use. For the present, the simplified Wade-Giles used in this work seems preferable. It is employed in almost all the surveys referred to in the Suggested Reading, and in practically all the books listed in their bibliographies.

Warsaw
February 1983

1. The Rise of Ancient Chinese Civilization

The Beginnings

The history of China reaches back almost four thousand years. While civilization took shape in China obviously later than in Mesopotamia, Egypt or India, it is the only one which has continued uninterruptedly from its earliest beginnings, retaining many features of its ancient past. This singular continuity of evolution has been acknowledged and remarked upon by every student of the subject, and there is almost universal agreement that it constitutes one of the most outstanding characteristics of the Chinese historical process, endowing it with a unique nature.

The greater part of China in its present boundaries, and the basin of the Yellow River in particular, have shown signs of habitation by man and his immediate predecessors from a remote age. The most famous archaeological find was made in 1927 in Chouk'outien when remnants of Peking Man were unearthed. This species, living around 500,000 years ago, was a hominid, who hunted and gathered food for his subsistence, and was able to manufacture very crude stone implements. He was also capable of using fire. More recently, in 1963, remnants of an even older and more primitive hominid were discovered in Lant'ien (Shensi). Modern Chinese historians appear to go on the polycentric assumption that Homo sapiens in China could have developed directly from Peking Man. Nevertheless, a distinct gap exists between these finds and remnants, dating back 50,000 years, of what were undoubtedly already representatives of modern man. However, for the Neolithic period, traces of human activity have been found in practically all parts of China, and it seems certain that Neolithic man was the direct ancestor of the modern Chinese. There is little doubt at present that from this era on, the development of man in East Asia was indigenous. Moreover, this process took place

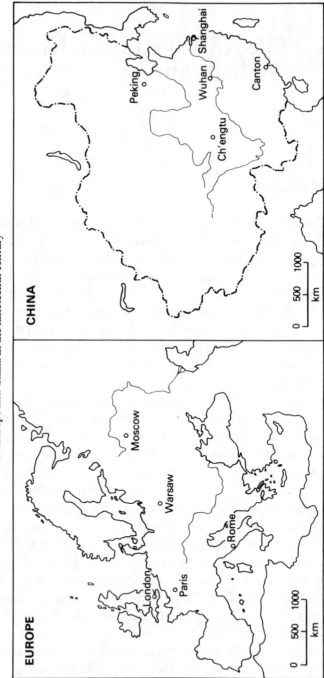

1. Europe and China in the nineteenth century

in an area largely cut off from other centres of ancient civilization by formidable geographical obstacles – deserts, mountains, jungles, and the immense expanse of the Pacific. Hence, the once fashionable Western theories regarding the foreign origins of Chinese civilization can be safely discarded. Thus the relative isolation in which this civilization was to take shape became one of its marked features. The Chinese were bound, almost inevitably, to regard their own country as the only extant civilization, as Chungkuo – the Middle Kingdom (the centre of the civilized world) – a view which profoundly affected their thinking throughout the ages.

Chinese archaeologists, whose work has been instrumental in revealing their country's past and holds almost boundless prospects for the future, have ascertained the existence of a number of early cultures in most parts of China. The two best known are the Yang-shao and Lung-shan. The first, named after a site in Honan, spread mostly over a wide range of territory in North China, and reveals the existence of a sedentary population using improved stone and bone implements, engaged in agriculture with millet as the main crop. At least two animals, pigs and dogs, had already been domesticated. The Yang-shao is renowned for its very fine red painted pottery, produced without the use of a potter's wheel. Some of the items found are clearly prototypes of ware which continued to be produced during the future millennia. Anthropologically, the people of this culture can be viewed as the ancestors of the modern North Chinese. It has been regarded as a period of transition from stone to metal, and dated from 3000 to 2000 BC.

The sites of the Lung-shan (Shantung) culture have yielded a quite different type of equally fine, but unpainted lustrous black ware, manufactured with the aid of the potter's wheel. While no signs of the use of metal have been found, this culture, considered more advanced than the Yang-shao, was also the product of a sedentary agricultural population. Domestication of animals had increased to include horses, sheep and cattle, while the cultivation of silk can also be said to reach back to this early era. Lung-shan sites extend from Shantung to Chekiang; it has been placed in the first half of the second millennium BC, and can be considered to be the direct predecessor of the Shang, the first historical Chinese civilization.

13

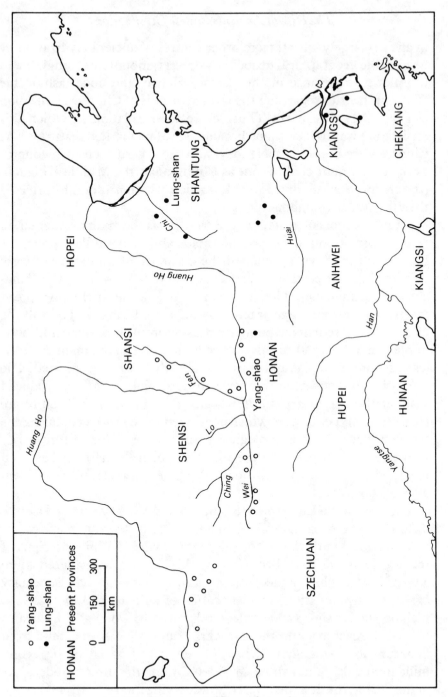

2. The Yang-shao and Lung-shan cultures

Mythology and Traditional Chinese History

Chinese mythology, although poorer in some respects than that of other peoples, does show how the ancient Chinese sought to explain the origins of their own civilization. A sequence of numerous mythical sovereigns, each of whom was said to have reigned for many millennia, is followed by a group of culture heroes to whom the main elements in the formation of Chinese culture were attributed. The most famous of these was assuredly Huang Ti – the Yellow Emperor – from whom the rulers of the Shang and Chou period claimed to be descended. It is the period of this early mythical empire, reigned over by Huang Ti's progeny and also by the model rulers Yao, Shun and Yü, that was later to be extolled by traditional Chinese history as the Golden Age in which the arts of civilization and the proper forms of government and morality were established. Thus the early tribal society of the third and second millennia BC was endowed with traits characteristic of a later age. But while anachronistic, this reconstruction of the past did observe a strict historical sequence and showed the first signs of that boundless concern which the Chinese were always to devote to their own history.

Yü, renowned for his laborious task of flood control, was regarded as the founder of the first traditional dynasty, the Hsia, whose dates were said to be 2205 to 1766 or 1989 to 1557 BC, depending on the chronology employed. The problem of the historicity of the Hsia has often been debated and remains a tantalizing one. There are no written records from this era, and no archaeological culture has been identified thus far with the Hsia. In traditional writing the history of this dynasty is presented almost solely by a list of rulers. However, there is little of the mythological in this account, the span of the reigns is normal, and the very aridity of this material speaks rather in favour of Hsia's historicity. It is probable that they represented a tribal confederacy in the middle reaches of the Yellow River, and the advanced level of Shang civilization leads one to presuppose the existence of a fairly highly developed predecessor. It should be noted also that the ancient Chinese were firmly convinced that they were the descendants of this dynasty, referring to themselves for many centuries as 'all the Hsia'. There seems to be a good chance that future archaeological exploration will help to throw light on this fascinating problem.

In this period the struggle by the scattered peasant communities to master the land in North and Northwest China continued. Immense effort was involved in this task, and the concentration on the development of agriculture constituted the prime factor differentiating the Chinese tribes from their ethnically similar neighbours. This was but an early stage of the most significant feature of Chinese history, since its fundamental nature was that of a continuously expanding agrarian society. From the 'cradle' of the Yellow River region, it was the peasant-agriculturist who was to be the principal bearer of Chinese civilization, extending his cultivation of the soil to ever new terrains, and simultaneously raising his skill to still higher levels.

The centuries preceding the establishment of the Shang dynasty also saw the growth of social differentiation within the rural communities with the emergence of a tribal aristocracy. Thus the transition to a class society had been made. The nature of this early society is not easy to classify. Chinese Marxist historians have sought to apply the pattern of sequential socioeconomic formations by postulating the necessity of the existence of a stage of slave society. Paradoxically, this somewhat schematic approach actually causes its proponents to proclaim europocentric views. Moreover, its fundamental error lies in the assumption that Mediterranean societal development was typical and hence obligatory for other parts of the world, thus disregarding the history of Europe itself, where, as is well known, the Slav and Germanic tribes accomplished a transition to feudalism without going through a Mediterranean type of slave society, which was actually an exception and not a rule. One can sympathize with the patriotic sentiments designed to show that Chinese history fully conforms to a universal pattern; nonetheless they seem redundant and have produced much wasted effort in periodization controversies over the past fifty years. Attention has been drawn to this problem primarily because even recent People's Republic of China publications continue to repeat the myth of a slave society in ancient China.

Shang Society

Although doubts had been cast on its historicity by hypercritical Chinese historians of the 1920s, there is not the slightest doubt at present that the existence of the Shang dynasty is fully attested by archaeological and literary data. What remains problematical is the time of its establishment and duration of its span; traditionally, it was said to have existed from 1766 to 1122 BC. These dates may be out by more than a century, while the first reliably determined date in Chinese history is 841 BC.

The political history of the Shang is practically as meagre as that of the Hsia. However, the list of thirty rulers, contained in the work of the great Han historian Ssu-ma Ch'ien, has been corroborated almost in its entirety by archaeological finds. The dynasty actually consisted of a number of small communities dominated by the strongest city-state, the Shang. Its area, which varied during its existence, centred on Honan, extending to Hupei, Shantung and Shansi. The capital was moved several times, probably due to floods of the Yellow River, and its last was Yin near Anyang. Hence the dynasty is also known as the Yin or Shang-Yin.

Shang society continued to be composed primarily of peasant communities ruled and exploited by a tribal nobility which acknowledged the supremacy of a hereditary monarchy. While partially town-dwelling, the nobility remained basically a warrior caste with a monopoly on bronze weapons and chariots. It employed its military strength for campaigns aimed at extending the scope of Shang rule, and extorting tribute from subjugated adjacent tribes. The Shang nobles also used their chariots to satisfy their great passion for hunting.

The monarchy was already an evolved institution with a rudimentary bureaucracy of officials. The Shang king held considerable power and also played a significant religious role. The succession of rulers was usually from brother to brother. The nobility also performed sacerdotal functions which perhaps explains why a separate priestly caste did not emerge in this era.

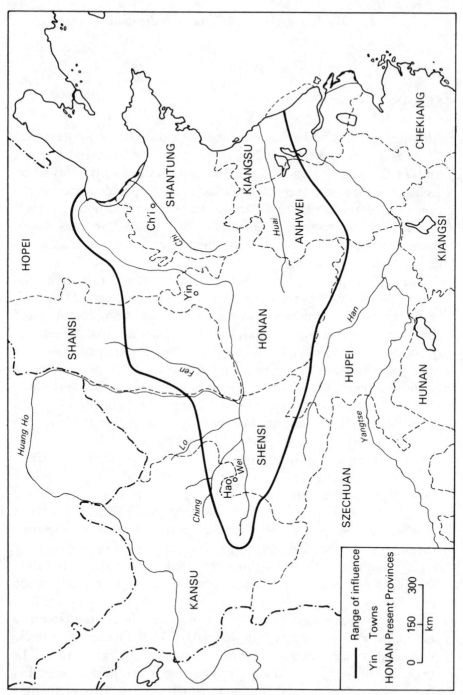

3. Shang, thirteenth century BC

The Shang towns, on which archaeological exploration has provided much data, contained a large artisan population, engaged in numerous crafts, and dependent on the nobility and royal court. Its social status is not clear but, in any case, agriculture remained the dominant field of production, and even the possible existence of slave-craftsmen does not justify the aforementioned attempts to classify the Shang as a slave society. The discovery of huge numbers of victims buried in the royal tombs, often adduced as an argument to prove this point, actually demonstrates just the opposite. They were clearly captives, brought in by the numerous foraging expeditions, while the barbarous fate they met only shows that in view of the low economic level there was little possibility of using them in social production.

The level of development by the Shang towns should not disguise the fact that the economy was fundamentally based on an agriculture which was still largely Neolithic in its implements and technique. Bronze, the outstanding innovatory trait of Shang civilization, was much too precious to be used for agricultural tools, which remained of stone and wood. The living conditions of the peasants had also remained much the same as in the past, in contrast to the palaces of the king and the nobility. Cereal cultivation, the range of which was basically similar to that of the preceding Lung-shan culture, was the principal domain of agriculture. The Shang had also proportionately more livestock than was true of later periods, as demonstrated by the reckless profusion of their animal sacrifices. It was in connection with the requirements of agriculture that the Shang evolved a calendar, dividing the year into 12 or 13 months of 29 to 30 days each, as well as a cyclical system of ten-day periods.

Shang Culture

Excavation of Shang sites, especially of Yin, led also to the discovery of great quantities of the most invaluable data – the oracle bones from what were probably the royal archives. Over 100,000 of these have been found and around half published. The inscriptions on them, longer as a rule than the very brief ones found on Shang bronzes, have provided the basic source material on Shang civilization. The bones had been used for divination by the method of scapulimancy, the cracks produced by touching them with a heated object provided the answer to the question posed. The inscriptions contain both the question and answer. The study of the oracle bones, a well-established discipline dating from the beginning of the present century, has led to the identification of over 1500 characters of the 5000 tabulated thus far.

It is completely clear that the language of the oracle bones is Chinese, while the script is already sufficiently sophisticated to presuppose an earlier stage of development of at least a few centuries. Thus, being the longest employed script in the world, though obviously not the oldest, Chinese writing constitutes a vital factor in the continuity of Chinese civilization. The Shang inscriptions reveal all the principal characteristics of this form of writing, and future development rested primarily in the enrichment of the vocabulary and hence in the increase of the number of extant characters.

While Chinese writing has a number of drawbacks, the difficulty of mastering it fully being the most apparent one, the attractiveness of its graphic form has affected the Chinese throughout the ages and its aesthetic quality has been intimately bound up with the development of Chinese art. Its terse, lapidary nature has also had an overwhelming impact on the shaping of Chinese literature. The Chinese script, due to its semi-algebraic nature, has played a crucial role in maintaining the country's cultural unity. Although as a result of expansion the spoken dialects have come to differ to the point of being as disparate tongues as the Romance or Slav languages, the conceptual nature of the character has remained unchanged. Moreover, during the many centuries the gap between colloquial and literary Chinese also increased immeasurably. Nonetheless, an educated Chinese has always been able to avail himself of the literature of almost any period, something no European can do with his own ancient literature, assuming that he possesses one.

As the first people on Chinese soil known to have acquired the use of metal, the Shang showed an uncanny mastery of this medium, and the work of their bronze casters is one of the glories of world civilization. Earlier speculation on the foreign origins of bronze can be disregarded, since it seems clear that in this case the development is as indigenous as that of the Chinese script. While the craftsmen also manufactured bronze weapons and equipment for chariots and horses, it is the ritual vessels which deserve special attention. The casting is unsurpassed, the beauty, vigour and boldness of conception unparalleled, and thus the unknown Shang masters produced true works of genius. Over fifty types of ritual vessels are known; they were employed primarily in connection with sacrifices and regarded also, due to the high cost of the metal, as objects of great intrinsic value. A glance at any reproduction of the Shang bronzes will show that the vessels were so richly ornamented with geometric and zoomorphic designs, that one might think that their makers suffered from a horror of empty space. In actual fact, both the shape and the decoration of the bronzes were largely based on earlier prototypes in wood, and especially on pottery.

The religion of the Shang took mainly the form of nature and fertility cults, as well as of ancestor worship practised by the nobility. A supreme being was also recognized whose worship was the king's prerogative. The nature cults embraced a number of local divinities, including the spirits of mountains and rivers. Human sacrifice was a fairly common practice, especially in connection with the worship of royal ancestors; it was to disappear only much later during the Chou era. The animistic elements inherent in the beliefs of the Shang were to survive, especially in the rural areas, up to modern times in the shape of popular cults. Although affected later both by Buddhism and religious Taoism, the influence of the cults remained considerable and was combined with ancestor worship, when it ceased to be a privilege of the nobility and became the most important general practice. This perhaps accounts for the fact that no single religion ever became dominant in China, while the great majority of the people maintained a specifically eclectic and mundane approach to matters of religion.

The Establishment of the Chou Dynasty

The five centuries of Shang rule were brought to an abrupt and dramatic end by an invasion from the west. This was undertaken by the Chou tribe whose capital, Hao, was now located in eastern Shensi. A vassal of the Shang, the Chou were a settled, agricultural people on a similar, though perhaps somewhat lower, level of civilization, also possessing already bronze weapons and using chariots. Ethnically, they differed little, if at all, from the Shang. During the two generations preceding the invasion, the Chou had strengthened their state appreciably, especially during the reign of Wen Wang, and, availing themselves of the dissatisfaction of other tribes with oppressive Shang rule, were able to form an alliance with them against the latter. Four different dates can be cited, again depending on the chronology favoured, for the onslaught against the Shang – 1122, 1111, 1066 and 1028.

The expedition was led by Wen Wang's son, Wu Wang, and the last Shang ruler, Chou Hsin, portrayed as the epitome of all evil, was quickly and decisively defeated. It should be noted that Chieh, the last sovereign of the Hsia, was pictured in almost identical terms; hence the stereotype in traditional Chinese historical writing of the bad last ruler of a fallen dynasty harks back to the earliest era. Nevertheless, the rapid initial victory notwithstanding, the Chou needed over twenty years to establish their rule firmly. For this purpose they set up their own garrisons in various strategic locations which, like 'islands in the sea' – Maspero's felicitous phrase – were to dominate the sparsely settled countryside. Simultaneously, most of the conquered territory was divided into over one hundred fiefs, granted primarily to members of the Chou royal family and clan and those tribal chiefs who had supported the Chou. Chou Hsin's son was left in control of some of the original Shang lands.

Shortly thereafter, however, a revolt of the Shang, supported by some of the Chou royal family, took place. This was suppressed by the Duke of Chou, regent for his nephew, Ch'eng, the thirteen-year-old son of Wu Wang. Afterwards, additional fiefs were granted and much of the Shang population resettled. The Duke of Chou who, along with Wen Wang and Wu Wang, was to be regarded subsequently as a paragon ruler of antiquity, established also an auxiliary capital in Loyang, more advantageously located to control the subdued territory. In area, the Chou realm was larger than the Shang, extending probably from Liaoning to the Yangtse, and from Kansu to the sea.

During its initial period the Chou monarchy was more effectively organized than its precursor, with the vassals rendering homage for their fiefs, paying tribute and serving with the military forces. Only the Chou ruler was entitled to use the term 'wang' – king – and its concomitant, the Son of Heaven, which also implied his supreme religious function. A hierarchical structure of the nobility was formed, and the beginnings of a bureaucracy of officials, both in the royal government and in the fiefs, established.

Although the downfall of the Shang signified the emergence of a new ruling class – the Chou nobility – it seems likely that the nature of Chinese society remained basically unaltered. The great bulk of the population was to be found in the village communities, dominated by the walled towns of the Chou nobility and their adherents. The system of landholding in this era still remains to be definitely elucidated. It is possible to assume that the village communities did adhere at this time to the well-field system, a subject of much controversy among historians. The system is said to have implied communal cultivation of the land, the ownership of which was vested, theoretically at least, in the hands of the monarch. The name was derived from a division of the land into nine squares, a picture of this resembling the Chinese character for the word 'well'. The peasants cultivated the eight outer plots in rotation, while offering the crops of the inner one as tribute to their local lord. In addition, all the community members were subject to labour service (corvée). The degree of their dependence on the nobility, while varying, would seem to have been considerable, in some ways almost akin to serfdom. However, they were not slaves, since what slavery there was during the Chou period was restricted primarily to domestic slavery. Thus, if the Shang can be regarded as proto-feudal, then the Chou can be safely classified as an early stage of Chinese feudalism, employing this term in the sense of a mode of production and the form in which exploitation of the basic producers, the peasants, was effectuated. The political structure of the Chou era clearly and unambiguously deserves to be referred to as feudal; confusion ensues when some historians, who restrict the meaning of this term to political phenomena, see in the creation of a centralized, absolute monarchy, beginning with Ch'in and Han, an end to feudalism in China. In reality, in its socioeconomic sense, it was to be present up to the middle of the twentieth century.

During the first centuries of Chou rule the overall level of the economy, and of agriculture in particular, did not undergo any

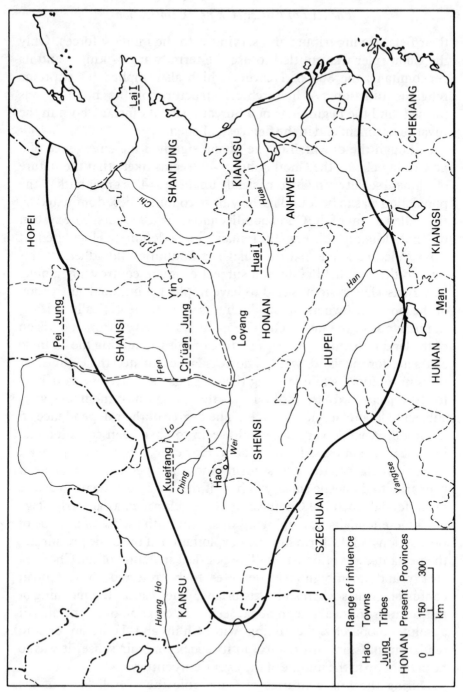

4. Western Chou, ninth century BC

significant change. The Chou continued to develop the crafts which had flourished under the Shang, Chou bronzes being especially plentiful and a valuable source of historical data due to their inscriptions, appreciably longer than those of their predecessors. In general, elements of both the Chou and Shang culture were fused into a new entity, without a distinct break in continuity, but it was the Chou era which was to witness the firm emergence of most of the features of civilization considered to be typically 'Chinese'.

There is marked paucity of reliable data on the political history of Western Chou, i.e., the period up to 770 BC, when the capital was shifted eastwards. A major concern of the rulers was the struggle they waged against the semi-nomad tribes living in North and Northwest China, as well as in many locations in the Chou domain itself. Many of the latter, called Ti, I and Jung, probably did not differ ethnically from the Chinese, and were ultimately subjugated and assimilated, a process which was to continue for many centuries during the expansion of China southward.

By the ninth century BC the Chou monarchy became progressively weaker, and its authority was challenged by the local feudal rulers, bent on expanding their own domains and enhancing their power. In 841 BC, the first firmly attested date in Chinese history, a revolt drove Li Wang, a particularly oppressive monarch, from his throne. The ultimate crisis of Western Chou occurred during the reign of Yu Wang who, having alienated his vassals by his inane method of pleasing his favourite concubine, deprived himself of their aid and perished when attacked by a nomad tribe in 771 BC. His successor, P'ing Wang, was forced to abandon the destroyed capital, Hao, and establish himself in Loyang. But in the subsequent period, known as Eastern Chou, the power and influence of the monarchy sank rapidly into insignificance; the rulers turned into *rois fainéants*, while their domain became reduced ultimately to a sorry scrap of land around the capital. The political fate of the country was to be determined by the feudal states, struggling for its mastery.

Eastern Chou

The Eastern Chou period covers the time span from the transfer of the capital to Loyang to the unification of all China by the Ch'in (770–221 BC). Chinese historians have also traditionally divided it into two sub-periods – the Spring and Autumn (722–481) and the Warring States (403–221). Both names are those of well-known works, to be referred to later. Generally speaking, Eastern Chou was an era of crucial change in practically all respects, full of dramatic events, which also witnessed an unprecedented and unparalleled flourishing of Chinese thought.

One of the decisive factors affecting development in this period was the introduction of iron, possibly in the seventh century. Casting was employed practically from the outset, and iron began to be used on a large scale for the manufacture of agricultural tools and weapons. The new implements, along with the use now of the iron-tipped plough, brought about what has been called a true agricultural revolution. Iron tools also greatly facilitated further irrigation and flood control, and a number of famous projects, some of them still functioning to the present day, were engineered during this period. The marked increase of agricultural production also gave rise to a population growth. Some authors estimate that by the fifth century the population of the Chinese lands could have already reached the impressive figure of 20 to 25 million.

The economic upsurge also resulted in the growth of trade, the increase in the number and size of towns and of artisan production. In step with these changes, the use of money in the economy became more prevalent, and coinage was introduced, first in the shape of miniatures of tools, then in that of the famous copper cash. Gold and silver were also used but usually only by weight. Although the general effect of these transformations was quite significant, it should be borne in mind that the country as a whole still persisted in conditions of a natural economy.

The impact of economic growth revealed itself in far-reaching changes in societal structure. By the fourth century, the old village community had definitely fallen apart, and the direct control of most of the land by the great aristocratic clans had also largely disappeared. As a result, land was turned into alienable private property, and the great majority of the members of the earlier rural communities became either free peasant landholders or tenants on the remaining noble estates. There is no way of determining, due to the lack of sufficient data, what the proportions between these two categories were. It is possible to maintain that the new social relations were perhaps somewhat less oppressive but, nonetheless, the peasants still remained subject to corvée, an increasing burden in connection with the large irrigation projects and the construction of military defence works, and also, from the sixth century on, to taxation by the state.

Transformations also took place within the ruling class itself. While the nobility still held all political power, the great aristocratic clans underwent a process of disintegration. The abandonment of primogeniture in respect to landed property had as its consequence the breaking up of estates and, ultimately, the emergence of numerous groups of landless or impoverished nobility. Its representatives were later to play a crucial role in the cultural and political life of the country. The growth of trade had brought the merchants, basically a new class, into much greater prominence. However, they were distrusted and looked upon with contempt by the landowning aristocracy and as a result found themselves at the bottom of the hierarchical structure of Chou society. This was said to be composed of four groups: (1) 'shih' – nobles (later scholar-officials), (2) 'nung' – peasants, (3) 'kung' – artisans, and (4) 'shang' – merchants.

The principal feature of political development in the Spring and Autumn period was the struggle for dominance between the rulers of the separate states composing the Chou realm, in whose hands all effective power already rested. Warfare between them was almost endemic, and its result was the steady expansion of the stronger and the disappearance by annexation of the weaker ones. Only fourteen of the less than 100 states were of any significance and, of these, four – Ch'in, Chin, Ch'i and Ch'u – were to be the most active in the ensuing strife. One of the main sources of conflict was the desire to gain control of the country's central area, largely present Honan, in which the Chou royal domain was also located. Simultaneously, as the

27

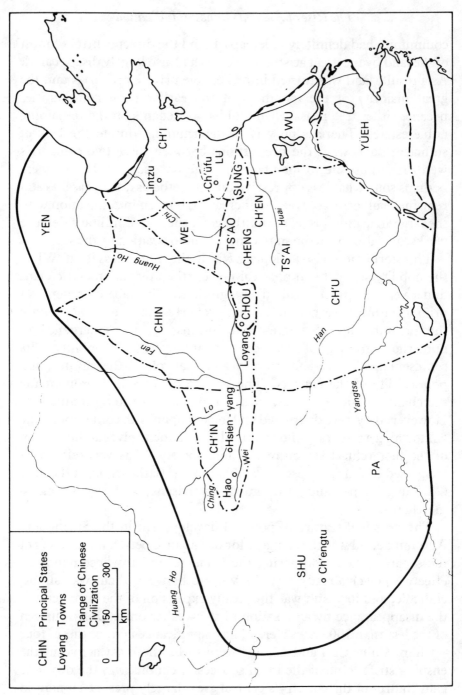

5. Eastern Chou, *c.* 600 BC, the Spring and Autumn period

states expanded, conquering and assimilating the lands and people which had originally separated the 'islands in the sea', their borders met, thus giving rise to new causes for friction.

Of the four states mentioned above, Ch'i was the first to rise to prominence in the seventh century, after having reduced most of Shantung to its rule. It was able to utilize its considerable economic resources – good land, salt, iron, trade – and during the reign of Duke Huan (685–643) had introduced a number of important reforms, sponsored by his famous advisor, Kuan Chung. Thus, Ch'i could take upon itself the task of leading a league of Chou states against their current greatest threat, the state of Ch'u. The creation of this league, which existed loosely for the next two centuries, also showed that the Chou monarchy had really lost all political power, since this rested in the hands of the hegemon, the league's leader. Although the leadership of the league was advantageous, it was also onerous, and Ch'i was unable to retain it for long. After a short lapse of time, the hegemony passed to Duke Wen of Chin; the story of his tumultuous life was familiar to every literate Chinese for over two thousand years due to its compelling account in the *Tso Chuan* ('the Tso chronicle'). Chin's territory embraced most of Shansi and neighbouring parts of Shensi, Honan and Hopei. A well-organized state, Chin kept the league leadership for over a century, in almost constant conflict with its main rival, Ch'u. Later, in the fifth century, it was greatly weakened by internal struggles, which ultimately led to its partition into three new states – Chao, Han and Wei.

Ch'u, the largest of the contending states, was centred on the middle reaches of the Yangtse and the area of the Han; later it extended from Szechuan to the sea. Ethnically heterogeneous, since the basic population was probably composed of non-Chinese Man tribes, while the ruling class was Chinese by descent or acculturation, Ch'u, regarded as 'semi-barbarian' by the Chou states, had, in fact, a unique and interesting culture. The torturous struggle of Chin and Ch'u ultimately weakened both fatally. Ch'u was then engaged in conflict with two peripheral coastal states – Wu and Yüeh – both also ethnically non-Chinese at the outset. Wu's territory covered all of Kiangsu and northern Anhwei. Having crushingly defeated Ch'u, it assumed the hegemony in 482 BC. However, shortly thereafter, in 473, it was to be in turn vanquished by its southern neighbour, Yüeh,

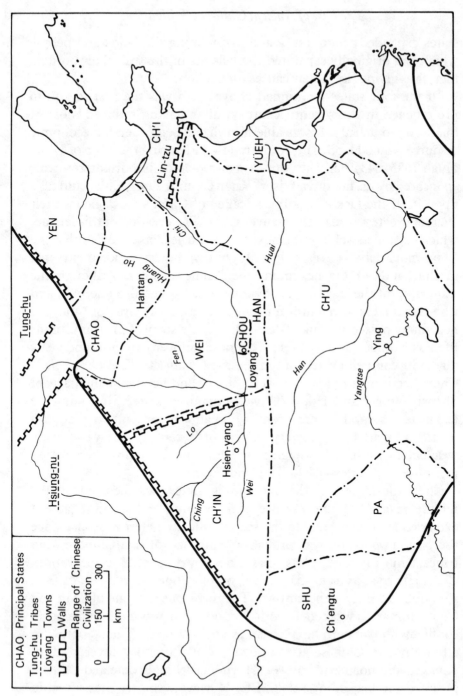

6. Eastern Chou, c. 300 BC, the Warring States period

whose area covered most of Chekiang.

Warfare in the Spring and Autumn era was waged primarily by the nobles and their retainers and its scale was relatively modest. Chariots, accompanied by infantry, were still the main arms, and military operations were generally conducted according to set rules, at times quixotically chivalrous. All this was to change radically in the ensuing Warring States period. The armies grew immensely in size; vast peasant levies were sent into battle as infantry, accompanied by cavalry which completely replaced the chariots. The employment of cavalry reflected the influence of the northern nomads and also brought about a change in clothing, from robes to tunic and trousers. The aim of military campaigns was now to attain the physical annihilation of enemy forces, and the master in this new mode of warfare proved to be the frontier state of Ch'in.

After the disaster of Western Chou in the eighth century, Ch'in had taken over the former Chou lands in Shensi. Here it expanded its strength in constant struggle with neighbouring nomad tribes, and by the beginning of the fourth century BC became the most active contestant in the striving for power, taking full advantage of its excellent strategic and easily defensible location. After gaining territory which made further eastward and southward expansion much more feasible, Ch'in annexed the states of Pa and Shu, embracing the greater part of Szechuan, thus further improving its strategic position and securing necessary resources.

The reforms put into effect by Shang Yang, the minister of Duke Hsiao (361–338), are said to have led to a further strengthening of Ch'in's capacity for warfare. As an application in practice of Legalist theories in their formative period, the reforms stipulated the establishment of an administration on a territorial basis to replace the rule of the clan aristocracy, the introduction of a severe penal code and of a system of collective responsibility with compulsory spying and denunciation, the marked enhancement of the position of the military, the confirmation of private landownership, the encouragement of the development of agriculture and the attracting of new settlers. Simultaneously, total hostility was demonstrated towards anything smacking of culture. While after the death of Duke Hsiao, Shang Yang himself suffered a dire fate – he was torn apart by five horses and his entire family exterminated – the reforms took their course and assuredly helped to convert Ch'in into the most ruthless, despotic and militarist state among the Seven Great Martial States (Ch'in, Ch'u, Ch'i, Han, Wei, Chao and Yen) still left on the blood-besplattered arena of struggle for the mastery of the Middle Kingdom.

From 312 BC on, Ch'in systematically proceeded on its road of conquest, annexing ever more territory 'as a silkworm devours mulberry leaves', to use Ssu-ma Ch'ien's eloquent phrase, which almost no author can resist quoting. Mass terror and cruelty were its preferred weapons. While addiction to the use of multiples of the word 'wan' – ten thousand – is common throughout all Chinese history, and hence gross exaggeration often results, it would seem that in the instance of Ch'in, the figures relating to some of the massacres its forces perpetrated, such as the extermination in 260 BC of the entire 400,000-strong captive Chao army, were close to the truth. The Ch'in were the Assyrians of East Asia – without the bas-reliefs. The name of 'the ferocious beast of Ch'in' was fully deserved.

Chou Culture

No other period in Chinese history has given rise to such a wealth of philosophical thought as the Eastern Chou. The reason for this might well lie in the character of the era, the political and social crisis exemplified by continuous warfare and the downfall of so many states, which impelled men to question the unsatisfactory present and to seek ways and means of overcoming its difficulties. This would go far towards explaining the nature of ancient Chinese thought, since it was primarily concerned with social and political problems and man's role in resolving them. It was thus basically a humanistic philosophy, in which morals and ethics were seen to be of key importance in attaining an improvement in the conditions of society. Due to this absorption in the questions of the current moment, the philosophers of the Chou era paid, on the whole, scant attention to anything relating directly to metaphysics or religion.

It stands to reason to begin a brief account of Chou thought with the man whose views were to prove of fundamental importance in the shaping of the Chinese world outlook. Confucius (Latinization of K'ung fu-tzu – Master K'ung) was born in 551 BC in Lu (Shantung) of an impoverished noble family, which claimed descent from the ancient Shang rulers. There is a paucity of reliable data on his life, which later became the subject of much myth-making. After holding some minor posts in his own state of Lu, he spent years wandering from court to court seeking, and failing to find, a ruler willing to put his concepts into practice. At a certain stage disciples began to gather around him, and he spent his last years at home, continuing to teach his numerous pupils. He died in 479 BC, having been an object of devotion and veneration for his followers, but the qualities which they ascribed to him were, in effect, the attributes of the superior man he himself advocated in his teachings.

Confucius made no claim of originality for his views, calling himself but a transmitter and not a creator. This might well have been true, since most of his ideas, almost completely devoid of metaphysical or religious speculation, were drawn from the heritage of the earlier Chou era. It was this source that Confucius utilized for presenting his views of a model society, to be based on the Golden Age of antiquity. At least three reasons can be adduced for this harking back to the past – Confucius' own genuine attachment to it, derived partially from his own background, the strength of conservative tradition in general, and in the state of Lu in particular, and the stamp of orthodox authority which would thus be affixed on his teaching.

According to him, in the Golden Age, just as Nature and Heaven followed a set way – the Tao – so man adhered to his proper place in society and observed all customary rites. Proper relations within the patriarchal family, the basic social unit, were of prime importance, and could be applied with equal effect to the state, which is only the family writ large. Thus, the virtue and benevolence of the patriarchal ruler could bring about the well-governed society, so sadly lacking in Confucius' own turbulent times. However, the remedy was to be found not only in this repeatedly advocated return to a glorious past, but also in the cultivation, by means of education, of proper moral and ethical principles. It was with this in mind that Confucius presented the image of what the 'chün-tzu' – the superior man – should be like. He was to be upright, righteous, loyal, forgiving and tolerant, cultured, a follower of the rites, and, above all, humane. The possession of these attributes, and not descent, which Confucius himself ignored in accepting his disciples, was to determine who could qualify as the superior man, fit for participation in ruling. Hence, the most significant aspect of his teaching was this elaboration of a moral and ethical code of behaviour for the ruling class. But it was his role as the country's first known educator which does more to assure Confucius of his place in Chinese history, while his obvious love of learning and knowledge, as expressed so aptly in the opening phrase of the Analects, can still arouse respect and admiration today.

There are no writings which can be traced to Confucius. Tradition, based on Mencius, ascribes to him the edition of the *Ch'un ch'iu* ('The Spring and Autumn Annals'), the dry-as-dust chronicle of Lu covering the years 722–481. He has also been credited with compiling both the Book of Songs and the Book of History. This is quite improbable, but it is certain that he was well acquainted with both of them. The only extant work on his views is the *Lun yü*, ('The Analects'), which contains his sayings and anecdotes regarding him; it was compiled by his disciples, or their followers. It was they who continued to propagate Confucius' views, but during the two centuries after his death, the Confucian school was but one of many. The transformation of Confucianism – a term of European origin – into a form of state ideology was to occur much later, and in the process Confucius' original ideas were to be distorted to an appreciable degree.

It was well over a hundred years before Confucius' views found a brilliant propagator in the person of Mencius (371–289). Born in Tsou (also Shantung), Mencius' background and career resembled that of Confucius in many ways. However, the crisis of Chou society had deepened profoundly during the time separating the two men, and this undoubtedly affected Mencius' interpretation of the Master's teachings. In some respects, his views may be regarded as somewhat less conservative; he emphasized very strongly the concept of *vox populi, vox dei* (although by people he meant the nobility), and developed still further the Mandate of Heaven theory, an early Chou creation, according to which a worthless ruler could and should be removed from power, but, of course, only by the action of his ministers or equals. Simultaneously, the class essence of

Confucianism is quite apparent in Mencius' view that society is made up of only two groups, those who work with their brawn, and those who work with their mind. The former are to support and be ruled by the latter. However, he also stressed the need for the ruler to show concern for the people's welfare, considering this to be an indispensable element of good government.

Most authors regard Mencius' views on the essential goodness of human nature as his most original contribution. For him this served as the starting point for emphasizing the need for cultivation, by means of education, of all the virtues extolled by Confucius, in order to preserve and develop this initial goodness. He lauded Confucius to the skies and, as the Plato – or St Paul if one prefers – of the Confucian creed, he engaged in vitriolic and biased polemics against its enemies, which probably aided in bringing about its ultimate triumph. His writings, eloquent and persuasive, were also compiled by his disciples and became, in time, a basic component of the Confucian canon, as one of the Four Books.

The most outstanding philosopher of the fourth century BC was Hsün Ch'ing (*fl.* 298–238), customarily classified as a Confucianist. However, there are numerous aspects of his work which could be considered as more closely linked with Taoism or Legalism. His views are said to contain materialist and agnostic elements; this may be due to his treatment of Heaven as a purely natural phenomenon. His assessment of human nature was exactly the opposite to that of Mencius, but he stressed that its initial evilness could be transformed by education.

Of the 'Hundred Schools' said to have flourished in the Eastern Chou era, Taoism was the only one which, along with Confucianism, was destined to survive the catastrophe of Ch'in rule. The earliest work of this school was the *Tao te ching* ('The Way and the Power') attributed to Lao Tzu. Everything regarding even the existence of such a person, supposedly living in the sixth century BC, is highly debatable, and most modern scholars consider that the work originated in the fourth century. The book, a very brief text, is probably, apart from the Analects, the most famous Chinese classic, translated many times into most European languages. The philosophy expressed in it can be viewed as a protest against the evils of society, and the solution offered is a withdrawal, which would make possible the attainment of harmony with the Tao. But this is not the Confucian Tao, concerned with society, but rather, as Needham has it, the Order of Nature. Concomitant with this is the guiding principle of 'wu wei', which implies 'doing what is natural'. In his vision of the perfect society, Lao Tzu reverted to an even remoter past, to the primitive community preceding the Golden Age of the Confucians, splendidly depicting its supposed glories in his last chapter.

The authorship of the subsequent significant Taoist work is ascribed to Chuang Chou (*c*. 360–280) who, at least, was a historical, although almost unknown, person. The *Chuang-tzu* is a gem, full of marvellous, wise parables and allegories, regarded by many as the finest work in Chinese literature. While in accord with the fundamental ideas of the *Tao te ching*, the *Chuang-tzu* puts still more stress on the relativity of all aspects of life, and contains probably more elements of mysticism. This did not prevent Taoism from serving a useful role in the rise of early science, since the Taoist contemplation of nature was not merely a passive one. As a philosophical school of considerable coherence, it maintained its attractiveness for many centuries for members of the Chinese upper classes, affording them a mode of escapism from the stultifying conformism of orthodox Confucianism. Perhaps the greatest merit of Taoism, bound up with its approach to nature, is to be found in the far-reaching inspiration it furnished for Chinese culture, its poetry and particularly its painting.

In the period preceding Ch'in unification it was the school of Mo Ti (*c*. 480–397) which offered the greatest challenge to Confucianism. Mo Ti's views, preserved in a series of essays incorporated in the *Mo-tzu*, and regarded by some authors as containing materialist elements, were based fundamentally on a utilitarian approach to all social problems. It was this utilitarianism which coloured his vision of the perfect society, causing him to decry the extravagant rites, of which the Confucians were so enamoured, and, more importantly, to oppose the ruinous warfare of the feudal lords, which he castigated as wasteful and murderous. This, however, was not a completely pacifist creed, for Mo Ti did approve of defensive warfare, and his followers became famous for their skill in conducting it.

The core of Mo Ti's philosophy lay in the doctrine of Universal

Love which, if applied generally, could do away with the main sources of social conflict and war. This was considered to be a broader and more effective approach than that of the Confucians, with their emphasis on family relations and individual virtues. Mo Ti also sought the sanction of antiquity and of religion for his views, but he reached back to an even earlier age, the Hsia, which made it possible for him to give full play to his imagination. The appeal to religion was rather restrained; he neither offered Heaven nor threatened with Hell, as Fitzgerald aptly noted. Mo Ti sought to base his creed on reason, and his followers were later to be the pioneers in the development of logic and dialectics. The Mohists formed a well-organized and disciplined sect, which exercised considerable influence until it disappeared in the Ch'in holocaust. There was probably no possibility for the existence of such an outspoken humanitarian doctrine, with its strong democratic overtones, under the conditions of a despotic, centralized monarchy.

The school which did much to bring precisely such a monarchy into being was that of the Legalists, whose views have already been partially noted in connection with Shang Yang's reforms in Ch'in. Although influenced by other trends of thought, the Legalists, never a coherent group, were by far the most consistent exponents of *Realpolitik*, with a strong aversion to all other views and practically all aspects of culture. Their vision of society called for the establishment of a ruthlessly authoritarian monarchy, ruling, with the aid of draconic laws, a dispirited people, crushed into blind obedience. The fundamental aim was to bring into existence a powerful militarist state with the resources necessary for pursuing a policy of constant expansion. Thus the only things which mattered, according to the Legalists, were the related tasks of building up invincible military forces and the encouragement of agriculture.

The clearest exposition of the Legalist credo can be found in the work of Han Fei (*c.* 280–233), a disciple of Hsün Ch'ing. In cogently argued essays, preserved as the *Han-fei-tzu*, he displayed a thoroughly Machiavellian approach to politics, advocating the steps necessary to enhance the absolute power of the ruler, and the legal measures required for ensuring this goal. Simultaneously, Han Fei contemptuously rejected the appealing to the sanction of antiquity, favoured by almost all the other schools of thought. Another disciple

37

of Hsün Ch'ing, Li Ssu, was to become the chief minister of the first Ch'in emperor, and contributed mightily to putting the Legalist theories into practice. Ironically, both men paid with their lives for serving the monstrously rapacious state, whose growth they had aided in different ways.

A brief mention must be made of at least one more of the Hundred Schools – the Naturalists. This name refers to two early materialist concepts, the dualist theory of negative and positive principles – 'yin' and 'yang' – considered to be the fundamental source of all natural phenomena, and the theory of the Five Elements (wood, metal, fire, water and earth), seen as the essential mechanism of permutations in the world of nature and man. Both views were purportedly combined into one theory, later to be incorporated as a vital component part of the Confucian world outlook, by Tsou Yen (*c.* 350–270), regarded by Needham as the real founder of all Chinese scientific thought.

A considerable number of works of fundamental significance in the history of Chinese letters originated in the Chou era. One of the earliest, perhaps the most important, and assuredly the best known and most enjoyable, is the *Shih ching* ('The Book of Odes' or 'The Book of Songs'), the first anthology of Chinese poetry. The 305 poems, dating from the tenth to the seventh century BC, range in subject matter from love songs and folk motifs to more ponderous dynastic paeans and ritual hymns. They provide an invaluable insight into early Chinese society, although some European historians, such as Granet, have imposed their own preconceptions on the material derived from this source. The verses were rhymed and set to music, lost many centuries ago. Arthur Waley's rendition is splendid and masterful; it is both interesting and worthwhile to compare it with the translation of the great Swedish scholar, Bernhard Karlgren. The Odes, cherished and memorized by countless generations, for a profound knowledge of them was the hallmark of a civilized being, became a basic part of the Chinese Classics.

The next collection of poems, the *Ch'u t'zu* ('Elegies of Ch'u'), come from the fourth century. Its authorship is sometimes ascribed to the first Chinese poet known by name, Ch'ü Yüan (*c.* 343–280). Considered the greatest poet of ancient China, Ch'ü Yüan, a noble of the state of Ch'u, whose tragic life ended in suicide, was undoubtedly the creator of the *Li sao* ('The Lament'), a richly imaginative, autobiographical poem, reflecting the specific culture of Yangtse-based Ch'u.

The *Shu ching* ('The Book of History' or 'The Book of Documents') is the earliest collection of historical material, pertaining to the early Chou period and to preceding eras. It is composed mostly of speeches and proclamations, and its authenticity has been the cause of much controversy. A considerable part of it, accepted as authentic for many centuries, was proven without a doubt to be a forgery. Nonetheless, the genuine parts are of inestimable value, although, due to the archaic and extremely concise nature of its language, it is a difficult text to utilize. It was also included in the category of the Five Classics, together with the *I ching* ('The Book of Change'), a work devoted to divination, and the *Li chi* ('The Book of Rites'), a text dating from the second century BC dealing with rites and ceremonies, the aforementioned Spring and Autumn Annals and the Book of Odes.

The *Tso Chuan* ('The Tso Commentary'), while regarded traditionally as a commentary to the *Ch'un ch'iu* is, in fact, an original work, dating from the end of the fourth century. It covers the years 722–468 and constitutes not only the principal source for this period, but also the most important historical text of the entire Chou era. It is full of fascinating details and well-told anecdotes, a truly vivid work, especially when compared with the insufferably dull and dreary Spring and Autumn Annals. On the whole, it can be considered reliable, which cannot be said of the other famous works, the *Kuo yü* ('Conversations from the States') dealing with the same epoch, and the *Chan kuo ts'e* ('The Intrigues of the Warring States'), which dates from the period to which its name has been given. In both instances much of the material is derived from the historical romances already current, but both, especially the latter, make interesting reading, and capture the flavour of life in these dramatic and momentous years.

2. The Establishment of a Centralized Monarchy

The Ch'in Unification of China

Ch'in's inexorable drive for mastery was to enter its final stage shortly after the accession to the throne in 246 BC of the fourteen-year-old King Cheng. During the first years of his reign, power lay in the hands of the chief minister, Lü Pu-wei, a wealthy merchant and reputedly his natural father, and a policy of relative moderation was followed. However, after Lü's disgrace and dismissal in 237 BC, a group of Legalist ministers assumed office, and the campaigns against the other states were quickly resumed, in which all the previous ruthlessness was once again fully employed. Simultaneously, Ch'in skilfully benefited from the utter inability of its enemies to compose their differences and combine their forces to meet the threat from the west. The end came rapidly – Han was destroyed in 230, Chao in 228, Wei in 225, Ch'u in 223, Yen in 222, and Ch'i in 221. All of China lay prostrate before the Ch'in.

The question of how to rule the conquered lands was among the first to be resolved. The Chou precedent of distributing fiefs was rejected; instead, Ch'in's administrative system was extended to the entire country. Thirty-six commanderies (increased later to 42) were established, each of which was composed of a number of districts or prefectures. A military and a civilian governor were appointed to rule each commandery, with a third official acting as supervisor. Thus a new, large and non-hereditary bureaucratic structure, both central and local, was set up, completely subject to the autocratic emperor, forming the fundamental pattern of the despotic, centralized monarchy, which was to be maintained for over two thousand years. Cheng now adopted a new title, that of Ch'in Shih Huang-ti – the First Emperor of the Ch'in. It was hoped that a line of successors, indicated numerically in a similar fashion, would rule over this

7. The Ch'in Empire

realm for ten thousand generations.

Other features prevailing in Ch'in, such as the principle of private landownership, were also extended to the whole country. The population of the conquered states was completely disarmed, the weapons melted down, and the metal utilized for the casting of gigantic statues and bells. Reputedly, 120,000 aristocratic families from other states were deported and resettled in Shensi near the Ch'in capital, Hsien-yang. A number of measures of standardization of the coinage, weights and measures, length of axles and, most important of all, of the Chinese script, were introduced. At the same time, Shih Huang embarked on a grandiose rebuilding of his capital, where an immense palace was erected, along with 270 other residences. An equally monstrously large and elaborately furnished mausoleum was constructed. This still awaits the archaeologist's spade, but it is in this vicinity that the fascinating discovery of the life-size statues of Ch'in warriors was made in 1974. A vast number of forced labourers – 700,000 according to Ssu-ma Ch'ien – was pressed into work on these megalomaniacal projects.

In line with Legalist theory, the consolidation of political power called for full thought control as well. It was with this in mind that in 213 BC Li Ssu proposed, and Shih Huang approved, the notorious plan for the proscription and destruction of all the writings considered to be subversive, which culminated in the Great Burning of Books. Since the list had included the Odes, the Book of History, most historical chronicles, and practically the totality of extant literature, the loss to Chinese culture was irreparable. Those who had cherished this heritage fared no better; around 460 scholars were executed, probably buried alive.

Territorial expansion was pursued by the new empire as relentlessly as domestic consolidation. At the outset, campaigns were directed against the nomadic Hsiung-nu (almost surely the ancestors of the Huns), whose newly formed tribal confederation ruled the steppes and deserts from Liaoning to the Pamirs. A 300,000-strong army, led by the talented Meng T'ien, expelled them from the Ordos area in northern Shensi. It was also against the Hsiung-nu that the celebrated Great Wall was constructed. Actually, already extant fortification lines were expanded and linked up to stretch from Kansu to the sea, a distance of 1400 miles. The building of the wall was the task of Meng T'ien's army and of forced labourers and convicts. Shipped there by the hundreds of thousands, they perished in numbers almost as large. In the future, the Great Wall did somewhat hamper nomad invasions but it served even more, as Lattimore observed, to demarcate the Chinese agricultural population from the nomadic way of life.

Large-scale military operations were also conducted in the south during the years 221–214 BC against the state of South Yüeh, the population of which was ethnically either Thai, Mon-Khmer, or Vietnamese (Yüeh = Viet). The 500,000-strong Ch'in army encountered much resistance, but ultimately the area, covering much of present Kwangtung, Kwangsi and North Vietnam, was conquered. Four new commanderies were established here, and a policy of mass colonization pursued.

Shih Huang's military campaigns and building projects consumed immense resources and rapidly brought about a ruination of the economy. According to Ssu-ma Ch'ien, the burden of taxes and corvée increased twenty- to thirty-fold; the peasantry was also being bled white by military service. Thus, discontent, exacerbated by the government's draconic laws which provided for twelve forms of capital punishment, became widespread, and a profound crisis gripped the entire country already in the last years of his reign.

The First Emperor of the Ch'in died in 210 BC. The problem of his personality has remained controversial and topical to the present day. During the 'cultural revolution' of 1966–76 this despotic tyrant, responsible for the death of countless hundreds of thousands of his countrymen, was extolled, not by chance, as a great progressive statesman. In reality, the image is rather that of a ferociously cruel, paranoically suspicious and prodigiously credulous man of average ability, 'with the face of a jackal and the heart of a wolf'. Eberhard quite correctly considers the chief minister, Li Ssu, to be the truly great personality of the Ch'in unification.

An elaborate conspiracy by Li Ssu and the chief eunuch, Chao Kao, which included the famous scene of hiding Shih Huang's death by having the carriage bearing his corpse followed by a cart of rancid fish, brought about the elimination of the crown prince, and the enthronement of a more pliable younger son to reign as the Second Emperor. However, power rested in the hands of Chao Kao, and

Ch'in rule became even more oppressive, with terror affecting the entire country. Nonetheless, within a year a revolt led by two peasants, Ch'en Sheng and Wu Kuang, broke out in Anhwei. The uprising, which can be considered the first of a long series of peasant rebellions constituting a characteristic feature of Chinese history, quickly spread, and the insurgent forces posed a threat to the Ch'in capital itself, only to be defeated soon by the superior Ch'in army. But other revolts took place simultaneously, in which many members of the old aristocracy also participated, and Ch'in rule collapsed in most of East and Central China to be replaced, in most cases, by a restoration of the former states.

In the ensuing struggle against Ch'in, two leaders emerged, destined to bring about its complete downfall, and then to contend for the mastery of the Middle Kingdom – Liu Pang and Hsiang Yü. A petty official of peasant origin, Liu Pang was a crafty, shrewd and stubborn individual, endowed with considerable political acumen and the capacity for dealing with men. He had become an outlaw, having contravened the severe, but ultimately self-defeating Ch'in law. Hsiang Yü was descended from an old aristocratic military family of Ch'u. An excellent soldier, of imposing stature, strength and bravery, cruel, arrogant and selfish, he soon rose to be the chief leader of the principal insurgent army. In 207 BC Hsiang Yü led his forces against the main Ch'in army; having forced it to surrender, he then had it totally massacred. In the meantime, Liu Pang had achieved the conquest of the Ch'in homeland, displaying much moderation in his policy towards its population. However, when Hsiang Yü, with his much larger army, also entered 'the land within the passes', he had the Ch'in royal family exterminated, its treasures looted, and Shih Huang's palaces and all of Hsien-yang put to the torch.

The inevitable confrontation between Liu Pang and Hsiang Yü was temporarily postponed, for the former, being in a weaker position, agreed to become the king of Han, ruling over the Han River area in southern Shensi and Szechuan, while Hsiang Yü established himself as the hegemon king, the strongest ruler in East China. Nevertheless, the conflict between the two men soon erupted, turning into a savage five-year-long struggle, known as the war between Han and Ch'u, which laid waste to much of East and Central China. It ended in Hsiang Yü's defeat and suicide, the superior general having been overcome by a leader politically more astute. The turbulent events of these years are marvellously narrated by Ssu-ma Ch'ien.

In 202 BC Liu Pang ascended the imperial throne offered him by his generals to become the first ruler of the Han dynasty, destined to remain in power, with a brief interruption, for four centuries. Although the Ch'in regime had been crushed thoroughly, much of its heritage was preserved, above all the concept of a centralized autocratic monarchy. The restoration of the state of affairs preceding the Ch'in unification was no longer possible, since the previous states had been effectively destroyed and the old aristocracy almost totally exterminated in the ensuing warfare. Hence a new ruling class was to participate in the establishment and consolidation of the Han dynasty.

Western Han

The problems facing the new dynasty and its ruler, Liu Pang (most commonly referred to, as were all Han emperors, by his posthumous name of Kao-tsu), were truly daunting. The country was in chaos and the economy a shambles. Hence the restoration of normal conditions had to be the prime task. The huge armed forces were quickly demobilized, and the soldiers resettled on the land. A number of measures to encourage agricultural production were taken, of which the most important was the reduction of the burdens borne by the peasants. In 197 BC the land tax was set at one-fifteenth of the harvest, and later lowered to one-thirtieth. The poll tax was also diminished, and both were but a fraction of what the Ch'in had extorted from the people.

The results were not long in coming. During the first seven decades of Han rule agricultural production increased markedly; it also made possible the rapid growth of population which, by the end of the first century BC, had risen to a figure close to 60 million. The development of agriculture was aided by a considerably greater use of iron tools and an expansion of irrigation. Other domains of the economy also progressed. This was particularly true of textiles; Han silks were of high quality, as attested by numerous archaeological finds.

The government established by Kao-tsu retained many features of the Ch'in administration, while abandoning some of its predecessor's barbarous severity. Nonetheless, it differed in one essential respect since the Han ruler, convinced that the Ch'in had collapsed due to the lack of sufficient supporters, granted fiefs to his key generals and members of his clan. The country was thus divided into two areas, one ruled directly by the central government, the other composed of fiefs. Very quickly, however, Kao-tsu turned against his erstwhile comrades in arms, including the brilliant strategist, Han Hsin, to whom he owed his victory, depriving them of their kingdoms and, in most cases, their lives, later on restricting the fiefs to the Liu family. Although attracted to his native locality, he ultimately chose Ch'ang-an (the present Sian) as the capital, since from Shensi 'one could hold the Empire by the throat'. The dual nature of the administration established by Kao-tsu did cause some trouble for his successors, as evinced by the Revolt of Seven Kings in 154 BC. But this was rapidly suppressed and subsequently the power of the local rulers was whittled down still more. Ultimately, in 127 BC, the ingenious method of stipulating that all the sons should participate in inheriting a fief was applied, and the problem resolved itself almost completely.

An outstanding feature of the early Han period was the formation of a new ruling class, composed primarily of landowners of plebeian descent, in many cases Kao-tsu's former followers. Avid for wealth, these parvenu families were quick to build up large landed estates, and the forms of exploitation of the peasants applied by them remained basically unaltered during the next two millennia of Chinese feudalism. The estates were either run with the help of hired labour or, more commonly, the land would be let out to tenants. However, the peasants, the bulk of whom had, by this time, become small landholders, were subject not only to this type of exploitation, but also to the no less onerous burdens imposed upon them by the state. The taxes they paid constituted the major part of the government's revenue; they continued to be subject to the corvée in various forms and remained the primary source of manpower for the armed forces. Most sources agree that their reward for all these contributions to Han society was a vegetating and impoverished existence, often verging on the brink of ruin and starvation.

The availability of plentiful cheap peasant labour was one of the two

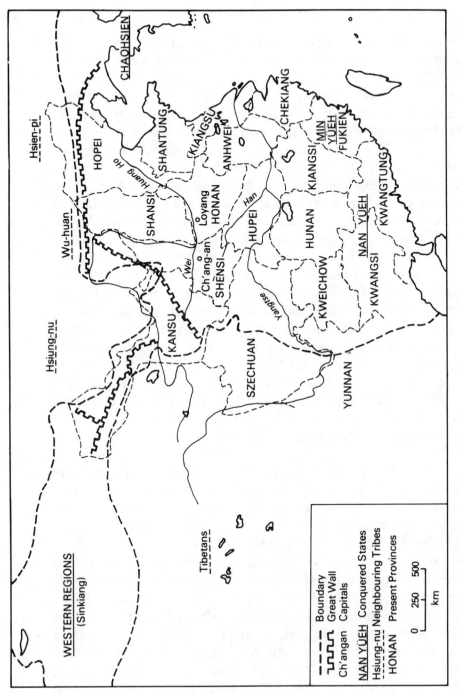

8. The Han Empire, *c*. 100 BC

principal reasons why slavery, also in the Han era, never developed on a large scale, as it did in the Roman Empire at precisely the same time. The other rested in the intensive, gardening-like nature of Chinese agriculture which rendered the use of slaves questionable. Thus slavery remained restricted primarily to domestic service, with some slaves employed also in government-operated mines and crafts. According to Wilbur, the total number of slaves never exceeded one per cent of the population in the Western Han period.

An indispensable element in the consolidation of the Han monarchy was the establishment of a smoothly functioning governmental structure. This was largely accomplished by an appropriate elaboration of the official bureaucracy, partially modelled on the Ch'in, to serve the needs of both the central and local administration. By the first century BC, the bureaucracy numbered around 130,000 officials, not an excessive figure in relation to the size of the population. The officials were selected on the basis of recommendation, with the initial steps leading to the examination system also being taken during this period. The overwhelming majority came from large landowner families; this feature was to remain practically constant throughout the entire imperial era and was of prime significance, since it effectively assured the political domination of this class, helping it to survive for countless generations, in spite of changes of dynasties and other vicissitudes of fate.

While not as sophisticated as that to be developed by later dynasties, such as the T'ang, the main outlines of imperial government were shaped by the Han, although it remained still largely personal, concentrating on catering directly to the requirements of the monarch and the court. The political role of the chief minister was usually considerable, although this depended mostly on the personality of the individual monarch who could rule alone quite despotically. A great degree of similarity characterized both the central and local administration which, in any case, did not reach down lower than the district capital. This left the countryside largely free of direct rule and control by superior authority, since, in Reischauer's words, 'the government thus was a relatively small, highly centralized body that floated on a sea of isolated peasant communities'.

The resurgence of Confucianism during the Western Han era resulted from the debacle, actually somewhat superficial, suffered by Legalism, discredited by its association with the Ch'in tyranny. Thus, in spite of his contempt for scholars, which he did not hesitate to demonstrate in a most outright fashion, Kao-tsu turned, of necessity, to the Confucianists when about to organize his administration, having grasped the lesson taught him by his chamberlain, Lu Chia, that an empire can be conquered, but not ruled, on horseback. But the ideology which the Confucianists who were to serve the Han represented was a far cry from the ethical teachings of Confucius and Mencius. As propagated by perhaps its most eminent spokesman, Tung Chung-shu (179–104 BC), this credo was a mélange of older philosophical views with the 'yin-yang' and Five Elements theories, the latter being interpreted in a metaphysical fashion, implying an interdependence between natural phenomena and human existence, thus providing a fertile breeding ground for innumerable superstitions.

The progress of Confucianism was slow but steady. The Ch'in edict against Confucian literature was repealed in 191 BC, and sanction granted for its reconstruction and renewed study. During the next two generations the Confucianists penetrated into the top stratum of the bureaucracy, becoming also the foremost educators. In the Imperial University, founded in 124 BC (50 students at the outset but 3000 a century later), it was the Confucian canon which formed the basis of its curriculum and a thorough knowledge of it became a prerequisite for entry into officialdom. In respect of the art of ruling, the concept which the Confucianists stressed perhaps the most pertained to the paternalistic role, in the Mencian vein, of a properly ordered government. The objective effect of such an approach, regardless of whether its proponents were fully conscious of it, would be the reduction of social tension between the ruler and his subjects, between the exploiters and the exploited.

A neglected arrow wound caused the death of Kao-tsu in 195 BC. His son Hui (194–188) succeeded him, but all power rested in the hands of the dowager empress Lü, a formidably indomitable and unbelievably cruel woman. She remained the real sovereign until her death in 179 BC, having placed her kinsmen in all the key posts. Her rule was the first instance of a consort family seeking to aggrandize itself. However, after her death, the Lius, with the help of Kao-tsu's old followers, carried out a successful coup, and exterminated the rival Lü clan. The rein of Emperor Wen (179–157), a moderate and frugal ruler, witnessed the further growth of the country's prosperity and stability, and the accumulation of resources which made possible the aggressive policies to be pursued by his grandson, Emperor Wu (140–87 BC).

Wu-ti, probably the best-known Han ruler, apart from the dynasty's founder, was cast in the mould of the classical despot, resembling in some ways the First Emperor of the Ch'in. During his reign the Han empire underwent its greatest territorial expansion, while simultaneously a domestic social crisis grew more acute.

The first three decades of Emperor Wu's rule were largely dominated by one single issue, the struggle against the Hsiung-nu. These troublesome nomads had recovered completely from the defeats inflicted on them by the Ch'in, and regained the Ordos region. Under the rule of the able and ruthless Mei Tei (Mao Tun), the second ruler of their newly created empire, they posed a vital threat to the Han, incessantly raiding North China. In 201 BC, during one of his razzias, Mei Tei succeeded in surrounding Kao-tsu and his army, forcing the Chinese to conclude a humiliating treaty which provided for the regular payment of heavy tribute, mostly grain and silk, to the Hsiung-nu, and the conclusion of marriages between the two ruling houses. Nonetheless, in spite of the tribute, which Kao-tsu's successors continued to render, the Hsiung-nu did not cease their attacks. It was this danger which Wu-ti's government intended to eliminate, by smashing the Hsiung-nu and driving them north of the Gobi. After the failure in 133 BC of a scheme to capture the Hsiung-nu 'shan-yu' (emperor), an almost endless series of immensely costly campaigns was launched which, by 119 BC, did succeed in vanquishing the Hsiung-nu and forcing them northward. These results were achieved not only by the lavish use of human and financial resources – the armies used were huge, up to 100,000 strong – but perhaps primarily by the application of the nomads' mode of warfare, the use of mobile light cavalry. The Hsiung-nu never recovered from these blows and, after 58 BC, when their empire collapsed due to internal dissension, they no longer posed an urgent threat to the Chinese state.

It was in connection with the war against the Hsiung-nu that one of the most interesting episodes of Han history was to occur. In 138 BC Chang Ch'ien, a court official, was dispatched on a mission to the Indo-European-speaking Yüeh-chih, who earlier had been defeated and driven westwards by the Hsiung-nu. The plan was to persuade them to join the Chinese in an attack on their common enemy. Captured by the Hsiung-nu, the intrepid Chang Ch'ien managed to escape ten years later, and ultimately made his way to the Yüeh-chih, by now conquering Bactria (present Afghanistan), to find them completely indifferent to the Han scheme. Taken prisoner once more during his return trip, Chang Ch'ien again succeeded in evading his captors, returning to China after thirteen years, with his Hsiung-nu wife and one survivor out of his original 100 followers.

The significance of the above story rests in the fact that Chang Ch'ien's report on his adventures (Ssu-ma Ch'ien's version is based on the original) provided the first reliable knowledge relating to the lands he had visited, and served to inspire the westward expansion shortly to be undertaken. The conquest of the Kansu Corridor in 119 BC had now made this feasible. Another mission to Central Asia, led by the indefatigable Chang Ch'ien in 115 BC, furnished still more data, and campaigns launched in 104 and 102 led to the conquest of all the oasis states of present Sinkiang, placing the main trade routes, north and south of the T'ien Shan – the famous Silk Route – under firm Chinese control. While the mastery of the Western Regions, the Chinese name for this part of Central Asia, did lead to an increase of trade, the latter did not prove particularly advantageous, and the growth of cultural contacts with the West was indubitably of greater significance.

The expansionist policy was pursued during Emperor Wu's reign also in other directions, and some of the results obtained were to prove ultimately more important than the immensely costly wars against the Hsiung-nu. This is particularly true of the campaign in the south, begun in 119 BC, which led to the conquest of the state of South Yüeh – it had reasserted its independence after the fall of the Ch'in – and the permanent annexation of the area of present Kwangtung and Kwangsi. The independent states existing in Chekiang and Fukien were also subjugated, and thus almost the entire southern seaboard incorporated into the Han realm. A policy of deportation of the native population and large-scale colonization and migration of Chinese converted all these areas within a few centuries into Chinese-speaking ones. Han rule was also extended in 109 BC to North Korea, with three commanderies established there. One of these, Lo-lang, has provided very rich archaeological finds, illustrating various aspects of Han culture. The colony in Korea served as a bridgehead for the spread of Chinese cultural influence not only to all of Korea, but to Japan as well.

Territorial expansion, while seemingly increasing the might of the Chinese realm, brought in its train serious consequences, the ruin of the economy and the squandering of previously accumulated resources, thus leading to an almost insoluble financial crisis. A large variety of measures were introduced to deal with this crisis, among them the sale of titles, forcible taxation of large landowners, and especially of merchants, customarily discriminated against, and, probably the most important, the establishment of state monopolies in the production of iron and salt, previously in private hands. By these means a certain temporary alleviation of the crisis was achieved, but the untackled basic causes remained unresolved and were to re-emerge with ever greater force during the reigns of Wu-ti's successors.

The policies pursued by Emperor Wu's government, both foreign and domestic, were by no means approved wholeheartedly by all Han officials. This was shown clearly by the discussion, held in 81 BC, on the merits and disadvantages of the iron and salt monopolies. A passage from one of the speeches made during its course deserves to be quoted, since it furnished, unintentionally, a telling illustration of the true nature of Chinese feudal society, valid not only for the Han, but equally for other eras as well.

Those who live in high walls and spreading mansions, broad chambers and deep rooms, know nothing of the discomforts of one-room huts and narrow hovels, of roofs that leak and floors that sweat.

Those with a hundred team of horses tethered in their stables and wealth heaped in their storehouses, who hoard up the old and stow away the new, do not know the anxiety of facing days that have a beginning but no end, of weighing goods by the pennyworth . . .

Those who recline on soft couches or felt mats, with servants and attendants crowding about them, know nothing of the hardships of a cartpuller or a boathauler, straining up the hills, dragging against the current . . .

Those who sit in the place of authority and lean on their writing desks, examine criminal charges brought before them and scribble their decisions, know nothing of the terror of cangues and bonds, the pain of whips and rods.

The financial crisis to which Wu-ti's reign had given rise was, in reality, both the reflection and the cause of a still more important phenomenon – the social crisis. Its main manifestation was the steady growth of large landed estates at the expense of the peasants. The latter, debt-ridden due to increased taxation and in the hands of usurers, were impelled to sell their land, and often themselves and their families, becoming tenants, farm labourers or slaves. The reduction in the number of tax-paying landholders, in turn, worsened the government's financial position, since the large landowners were either exempt from taxation, or managed to swindle their way out of paying it. The continuous growth of the population, increasing the pressure on the land, undoubtedly exacerbated the situation still further. The census for AD 2 showed a figure of over 59 million, probably more than the entire Roman Empire. While the reliability of early Chinese censuses is open to question, since they were based on the number of households and conducted for fiscal purposes, thus leading to much evasion, the above is considered by most historians to be close to the truth.

The crisis produced by land concentration and the pauperization of the peasants was practically a cyclical, inherent feature of Chinese feudal society, leading often to a social revolution – a peasant rebellion and dynastic collapse. Although unable to find a solution, the Confucianists showed an awareness of these problems by stressing the need for a paternalistic concern for the people's welfare and the proper development of agriculture.

The Wang Mang Interlude

Against the background of the mounting social crisis the struggle for power within the ruling class itself also became more acute during the first century BC. It was waged primarily by rival coteries of officials, often linked to consort families, especially powerful if, as in the case of this period, the emperors were usually minors when placed on the throne. A special role was played in these conflicts by the eunuchs whose number, due to the flamboyant growth of the imperial harem, had greatly increased. Their rise to power, by no means restricted to the Han for it reappeared in the T'ang and Ming periods as well, was partially due to the fact that they were often employed by the emperor as an instrument of struggle against other cliques. Just as often the eunuchs were also successful in converting the ruler into their obedient puppet. Their propensity for self-enrichment and corruption seems to have been unlimited, but then all the accounts relating to them come from the brush of their bitter enemies, the scholar-officials, who hated them as well for their plebeian origin.

In the welter of court intrigue during the reigns of the last rulers of Western Han, all debauched and totally incapable, the Wang clan, related to one of the dowager empresses, rose to great eminence. Its most notable representative was Wang Mang, a remarkably able, scholarly, frugal and ambitious man, who succeeded in forming a strong faction of personal followers from the ranks of the highest officials. He claimed, sincerely, to be a fervent Confucianist, anxious to base his policies on the Confucian canon and the ways of antiquity, gaining thereby the support of a number of prominent Confucian scholars. By AD 1 Wang Mang was the *de facto* ruler of the empire, and eight years later he deposed the infant emperor, and, having staged an elaborate ceremony of renunciation of the throne by the latter, declared himself the First Emperor of the Hsin dynasty (usually rendered as 'New', but perhaps derived rather from Wang Mang's title – the marquis of Hsin). The short span of his dynasty – AD 9–23 – has deservedly drawn the attention of most historians, since it witnessed a remarkable attempt to deal with the country's growing social and economic crisis.

Wang Mang met the problems facing him head on. Already in AD 9 he proclaimed a series of reforms, the most important of which included a plan for declaring all land the property of the emperor, the prohibition of the sale and purchase of land, the confiscation of large estates and the distribution of land to the peasants. In accord with his archaizing tendencies, Wang Mang stated his intention to revive the well-field system. Private ownership of slaves was to be curtailed, and the slave trade prohibited. The state iron and salt monopolies were strengthened and new ones introduced. Stringent attempts to control coinage were made, and the currency depreciated. Government credit was also to be granted to peasants at a much lower rate of interest than that of the usurers.

The reforms introduced by Wang Mang were aimed at improving the government's financial position and, simultaneously, reducing social tension by alleviating the dire conditions of the peasants. They were countered by such a strong opposition from the great landowners and so sabotaged by his officials that within three years Wang Mang was forced to repeal the main measures pertaining to the land and slaves. The reforms could have perhaps succeeded if the emperor had been able, as intended, to refashion his officialdom. This, however, was not accomplished, and the corrupt bureaucrats, themselves of landlord origin, had no desire to implement measures adversely affecting their own class and families. What new revenue was raised found its way mostly into their pockets; hence neither the government nor the peasants were any better off, and the people's disaffection grew constantly against the background of near famine conditions.

Most of Wang Mang's reforms, except for the land 'nationalization', were not new but modelled on measures utilized in the past, particularly in the time of Emperor Wu. It is, of course, a preposterous anachronism to regard Wang Mang, as Hu Shih did, as 'the first socialist' in China. It would seem equally nonsensical to view his measures, as some modern Chinese historians maintain, as reactionary. They were, in effect, a noteworthy attempt to resolve the social crisis, while remaining within the framework of the feudal society. Herein, too, lay the basic cause of their failure.

Shortly after assuming the throne, Wang Mang also proceeded to inveigle himself in a conflict with the Hsiung-nu; some authors claim that he did so to draw attention away from the critical domestic situation. The war, which started in AD 10, quickly led to a disastrous defeat of Wang Mang's forces, the loss of the Chinese hold on the Western Regions, and placed a further strain on the already perilous condition of the Chinese economy. In addition, a number of natural calamities, including a catastrophe caused by the change in the course of the Yellow River in AD 11, gave rise to famine in many parts of the country. Peasant discontent soon turned into open revolt, although the uprisings, which started in AD 14, were initially still on a restricted, local scale. However, in AD 18, the activities of a Taoist secret society, the Red Eyebrows, converted the spontaneous movement into an organized rebellion, one of the largest and most important in Chinese history. From its place of origin in Shantung, the rebellion, whose principal leader was Fang Ch'ung, quickly spread to a large part of East China, with the insurgents attacking towns, killing landlords and government officials. The armies sent by Wang Mang against the Red Eyebrows were completely unable to cope with the rebels, and spent most of their time plundering the countryside themselves.

At this stage, the Liu clan, very widespread and exceedingly numerous, since polygamy, or rather concubinage, had been a constant feature of Chinese feudal society up to the twentieth century, although limited almost solely to the upper classes, now joined the battle against Wang Mang, whom they regarded as a usurper. Some of the Lius were also able to gain control of such peasant units as the Green Forest Army. The ablest general among them proved to be Liu Hsiu, a large landowner from eastern Honan, but it was Liu Hsüan who was proclaimed the new Han emperor. In the struggle against the Lius and the Red Eyebrows Wang Mang's forces were resoundingly defeated. By AD 23, a revolt broke out in Ch'ang-an, and Wang Mang, deserted by practically all his supporters, but still undaunted and confident that destiny would preserve him, took refuge in a tower. It was soon taken and Wang Mang, seated unperturbed on the throne, in his whole imperial regalia, was killed and beheaded.

Wang Mang's death did not signify an end to the devastating conflict. The Liu army occupied Ch'ang-an only to be driven out in AD 24 by the Red Eyebrows. The latter were then compelled by famine to abandon the ruined city and seek to return to their Shantung haunts. However, within the next three years, their forces were to be largely annihilated by Liu Hsiu's army. The defeat of the Red Eyebrows was, in some respects, symptomatic of Chinese peasant rebellions. The peasants were able to bring down a dynasty, but could think of nothing better than to replace it with a new one, and this would seem to have been an ever-present, built-in limitation. In this instance, the Red Eyebrows found a Liu within their own ranks to place on the throne; in other cases, peasant rebel leaders would proclaim themselves emperor. But almost always the upper classes were able to channel the peasant revolt for their own purposes, and it would be their representatives who would climb to power on the backs of the peasant forces.

In AD 25 Liu Hsiu proclaimed himself emperor after his rival Liu Hsüan had died, and embarked on a lengthy campaign to consolidate his rule and eliminate the many other contenders for power. While re-establishing the Han dynasty he also shifted the capital from Ch'ang-an – now a complete shambles – to Loyang in his native Honan. Hence the distinction, by analogy with the Chou, between the two Han eras – Western and Eastern – also referred to as Early and Later Han.

Eastern Han

It took ten years for Liu Hsiu, known as Emperor Kuang Wu (25–57) to gain complete victory. The methods followed in stabilizing the power of the new dynasty were to become a pattern for the future. The social crisis could now be alleviated, at least partially, since the calamitous warfare had markedly decreased the population, great landowners and peasants alike. Sufficient land was now available to satisfy the needs of the peasants, and large amounts of state land were distributed to them. At the same time, the tax burden was radically reduced and the land tax lowered from one-tenth to one-thirtieth. The bureaucracy, especially at the lower level, was also much compressed in size. As a result, due to the unremitting toil of the peasants, the economy recovered rapidly, and by the end of the first century AD the previous level of the period 60–50 BC had been reached once again. However, in spite of having been decimated, the great landowners were in a stronger position than at the beginning of Western Han, and the growth of great estates made considerable progress. It was advantageous to engage tenants on a large scale, since the estate owner paid the lowered taxes, while demanding at least half of the tenant's harvest. Some of the estates are said to have resembled fortified manors, with their own armed forces of retainers.

It does not seem that the growth in agricultural production was marked by any particular innovations in technique. What did occur in this period was the emergence of the northern part of the Great Chinese Plain (Honan, Hopei and Shantung) as the main economic area, primarily due to the massive destruction which the northwest, especially Shensi, had suffered.

The political development of the first century of the Eastern Han is unremarkable. The administration resembled that of its precursor, and the bureaucracy continued to be recruited almost exclusively from the great landowner families. The prestige of the Confucian scholar-officials rose still more, partially as a result of Kuang Wu's deliberate policies. The latent struggle for power at the court between cliques of officials, consort families and eunuchs was to rise to the surface during the subsequent century, particularly due to the fact that, after the first three rulers, all the following emperors were minors when placed on the throne. All the parties to the conflict seem to have been equally greedy for wealth and avid for power. The Liang family, by providing three empresses, became the effective ruler of the country by the middle of the second century, and its members accumulated a vast number of key posts. However, its rivals, the eunuchs, were able, due to their influence on a new emperor, to bring about its downfall, and the whole Liang clan was exterminated in 159. Such was the atmosphere prevailing at the court in the last decades of the Eastern Han. The domination of the eunuchs was bitterly opposed by most of the high officials, aided in their struggle by the turbulent students of the Imperial University, now 30,000 strong. A special association of officials and students, directed against the eunuchs, was created in 168, but it was speedily crushed by the latter. More than a hundred of its leaders were murdered, and the eunuchs continued to repress all opposition to their rule by the use of mass terror.

During the first century of their rule, the emperors of the Eastern Han reverted to the expansionist policies pursued during Emperor Wu's reign, seeking to recover the positions lost in the period of the Wang Mang interlude. The Hsiung-nu were still considered to be the principal enemy. However, they had been much weakened by a number of famines and internally divided as well. Simultaneously, they were now being attacked by their eastern neighbours, the Wu-huan and the Hsien-pi (the first probably proto-Tungusic, the second proto-Mongol), often acting as allies of the Chinese. These tribes were pure nomads, while the Hsiung-nu had become partly sedentary and increasingly dependent on trade with the Han empire. By 48, the division of the Hsiung-nu into a northern and southern group had become an accomplished fact. The southern Hsiung-nu surrendered to the Chinese, and many were settled in North China. The northern Hsiung-nu remained a rival of the Han in the Western Regions, but, in general, the Hsiung-nu problem had lost most of its urgency.

It was against this background that the reconquest of the Western Regions was undertaken. It is intimately associated with the activities of Pan Ch'ao (d. 102), the brother of the eminent historian Pan Ku. Beginning his mission in 73, he succeeded with much skill in restoring Han rule in Central Asia. By 91, all the petty states of the Tarim Basin, still mostly Indo-European speaking, had once more become Chinese vassals. Pan Ch'ao accomplished this task at a minimum cost for his government, employing local forces for his offensive operations, a perfect example of the classical Chinese theory of using 'barbarians' to fight 'barbarians'. He has also been regarded by some modern Chinese historians as 'a great diplomat', a rather odd conception of diplomacy, since one of his initial actions was the personally led and organized murder of his rival, the Hsiung-nu ambassador, and his whole suite, in the capital of one of the Western Regions kingdoms.

In 91 Pan Ch'ao was nominated the Protector General of the Western Regions, and in 97 he led an expedition across the Pamirs reaching the Caspian, the furthest point ever to be reached by the Chinese. A mission dispatched by him to establish contact with the Roman Empire came to nought, but the reconquest of the Western Regions did restore Chinese control of the Silk Route and led to

59

further fruitful contacts with the West. After Pan Ch'ao's retirement in 102, the Han position in Central Asia became progressively weaker, primarily due to the general political deterioration of the dynasty.

By the middle of the second century the endemic social crisis, which had been the principal cause of the collapse of Western Han, and of Wang Mang's dynasty as well, surfaced with full force. Once more the concentration of landownership led to a decrease in the number of peasant smallholders, and an increase of the tax burden on the remaining ones. Local peasant uprisings, all suppressed, started to spread from 126 on. At the same time, the monarchy's position was being steadily undermined by the appreciable growth in the influence of the great landowner families, which were becoming the dominant political force in the provinces, thus leading to a progressive decentralization of governmental authority.

In this situation the outbreak of a new peasant rebellion was sufficient to bring about the final downfall of the Eastern Han. Once again, the revolt was the work of a Taoist secret sect, the 'T'ai P'ing Tao' ('The Road of Universal Peace'). It was founded by Chang Chüeh, a faith healer, and its influence spread rapidly in East China, where it gained countless followers among the peasants. The movement, also called the Yellow Turbans from the distinguishing headdress of its adherents, was well organized into local units. The signal for a countrywide revolt was to be given by a rising in the capital, set for February 184. However, the plan was disclosed by a traitor, and over a thousand suspected participants were killed. This initial setback did not discourage the Yellow Turban leaders from launching the general uprising. Between March and November 184 the insurgents gained many successes, but the ruling landowner class, putting aside temporarily its own internal conflicts, mustered all its forces for a counterattack. The death of the principal leaders, Chang Chüeh and his two brothers, was followed by the defeat of the main Yellow Turban armies and a barbarous pacification of all the areas in North and East China affected by the revolt, in which many thousands were slain in practically every district. Nonetheless, the peasant rebellion kept on reappearing, in Szechuan also, where the Five Bushels sect, a movement analogous to the 'T'ai P'ing Tao', flourished. Twenty years were to pass before the landowners could consider the task of putting the peasants back in their place completed. But the memory of the Yellow Turbans remained vivid among the rural population for many centuries.

In the course of the Yellow Turban rebellion the authority of the central government collapsed totally. It was not the monarch and his court but the provincial generals, almost all from great landowner families who, in charge of their own personal armies, conducted the struggle against the peasants. In 189, two of these armies, led by provincial warlords, advanced on Loyang to participate in a coup aimed at ending the rule of the eunuchs. While the many previous attempts had failed, since the eunuchs were usually forewarned thanks to their excellent system of espionage, this time the conspiracy was successful, and terminated in the massacre of the entire 2000-strong eunuch establishment.

The Han realm disintegrated into complete anarchy with the provincial warlords fighting each other for the possession of the person of the emperor, and then for the throne itself. In 190, one of them, Tung Cho, dethroned the current ruler, replacing him with his brother, who nominally ruled till 220. But the Eastern Han had already received its deathblow and its further existence was a pure fiction. All power had been grasped by the generals, and a tragic and gloomy era in Chinese history of incessant warfare, untold suffering and of the country's dismemberment was about to begin.

Han Culture

The Han era was noteworthy not only for the consolidation and expansion of the Chinese empire. It was equally significant for the many-faceted flourishing of Chinese culture which became appreciably more widespread, encompassing a numerous ruling class and affecting the population as a whole. It is possible to maintain that the fundamental forms of national culture, founded on a common script and literature, and endowed with the capacity to survive no matter what the future had in store for the Middle Kingdom, were moulded precisely in this period. It is not by accident that the Chinese refer to themselves as 'Han jen' – men of Han.

The four centuries of Han rule could not possibly be said to rival the Chou in its richness and variety of philosophical thought. This might well have been the result of the progressive emergence of Confucianism, and its assumption of the position of a dominant state ideology. But the existence of a relatively stable society did favour the systematization of earlier views, the assembling of the remnants of antiquity in order to grasp the past in a comprehensive fashion. Hence it was not by chance that historical writing was to become the prime achievement and the splendid glory of the Han epoch.

It is perilously close to a truism to state that the Chinese have been almost uniquely concerned with history, seeing in it not only the main source of knowledge regarding the functioning of human society – the problems of which had been raised to the forefront by Chou philosophy – but viewing it also as providing a model for the present. However, in delving into the past, the Han historians read it through the prism of the present, and thus their reconstruction of antiquity, to which they ascribed the institutions of their own time, became of necessity anachronistic. Nonetheless, whatever their faults, it is they who preserved the fundamental knowledge of the past which, otherwise, would have been irretrievably lost to posterity.

The outstanding Han historical work and its author deserve special mention. Ssu-ma Ch'ien (145–90 BC), a descendant of a Ch'in aristocratic family, held the post of Grand Astrologer, as had his father, Ssu-ma T'an. It was the latter who devised and initiated the bold project of compiling a comprehensive history of China, but practically all of the famous *Shih chi* ('Records of the Historian') comes from the brush of the son. Ssu-ma Ch'ien was superbly prepared for this task. In his youth he had travelled very widely, and his reading was omnivorous, covering almost all extant literature, as well as materials from the Imperial Archives, which were open to him. In his role as a high court official he had gained a fine understanding of the mechanism of politics. His devotion to his work knew no bounds. Even a dreadful personal tragedy – the despotic Emperor Wu sentenced him, unjustly to be sure, to castration, to which he could have responded by the traditional Chinese gesture of protest (suicide) – did not weaken his determination to complete his project. Ssu-ma Ch'ien referred to his history in modest terms, as the systematization and representation of material available. In reality, it is not only the most important source for Chinese ancient history, but also one of the greatest works of Chinese letters. He often did incorporate ancient texts almost in their entirety, but this was not considered as plagiarism, rather as showing respect for the authorities made use of.

The *Shih chi* is an enormous work in 130 chapters, containing over half a million characters (the Peking 1972 edition is in ten volumes, 3322 pages), which, happily, has survived almost intact. The first twelve chapters are devoted to the basic annals of the emperors, from the earliest era to Wu-ti. The next ten contain chronological tables of various ruling houses. These are followed by eight essays on rituals, music, the calendar, astronomy, astrology, imperial rites, rivers and canals, and weights and measures. The subsequent thirty chapters take up the history of princely houses, while the last seventy are mostly biographical sketches, but also include essays on geography and neighbouring peoples. This mode of composition causes material relating to a given person or event to be dispersed in various sections; it might make a reader work more, but it does provide a stimulatingly kaleidoscopic impression. The *Shih chi*, while primarily a political history, is at the same time an incredibly rich source of information on practically all the domains of life in ancient China. Its influence on future historical writing was immense, while Ssu-ma Ch'ien's style was considered as the height of perfection in classical Chinese, and admired unreservedly by countless generations of all those in East Asia who could read Chinese. A major part of the *Shih chi* is available in English, French and Russian.

Another splendid Han historical work is the *Han shu* ('The History of the Early Han'). This project, meant to be a continuation of the *Shih chi*, was initiated by Pan Piao (3–54) but almost all of it, extended to cover the entire Western Han period, was written by his son, Pan Ku (32–92), Pan Ch'ao's elder brother. However, the work was not finished when Pan Ku died in prison, and the task of completing it was undertaken by his sister, Pan Chao (d. 116), a famous poetess and essayist in her own right. Almost half of the *Han shu*, the part dealing with the early Han period, is taken, practically verbatim, from the *Shih chi*. It is likewise a lengthy work of 100 chapters (those containing the Annals have been rendered into English by Dubs) and follows, in most respects, the construction of its predecessor. In covering only the history of a single dynasty, the

Han shu set the pattern for all the future Standard Histories, systematically produced during the next nineteen centuries.

The achievements in historical writing outshone by far the philosophical works of the Han era. There is little really worth noting in the eclectic synthesizing in which the Confucianists were engaged, in spite of the importance which their creed was assuming as the sole official orthodoxy. An interesting Taoist work did appear during the Western Han – the *Huai-nan tzu*. It was compiled at the court of Liu An (d. 122 BC), the ruler of Huai-nan, and is considered as characteristic of Taoist views in this period. The beginning of the transformation of Taoism from a philosophical creed to a popular religion, combining folk cults and innumerable other superstitions, also dates from this epoch. The latter had significant political overtones as well, as shown by the influence it had on the formation of such movements as the Red Eyebrows and Yellow Turbans.

The only eminent Han philosopher was Wang Ch'ung (27–97), referred to by Needham as 'the most atheistic and agnostic of all the Confucian rationalists'. An original and independently minded thinker, Wang Ch'ung fought against the ballast of superstitious ideas which were gaining an upper hand in Han Confucianism, in particular the concept that man's fate is linked with, and dependent on, the actions of Heaven. His essays, considered to be written in a brilliant style and clear language, were collected in the *Lun heng* ('Discourses Weighed in the Balance'), and his views could have formed a basis for the development of a scientific outlook, had the nature of Han society permitted this.

The rise to prominence of Han Confucianism was also the result of the strenuous efforts which the Confucian scholars had devoted to the reconstruction of the Classics. In this task high standards of critical scholarship were adhered to, and many of the texts established in this period became accepted versions. The Han scholars were noted for their scrupulousness in transmitting texts, and it was they who initiated the practice of clearly distinguishing commentaries from the text by the use of smaller sized characters. An important step in the study of the Chinese language was the appearance of the *Shuo wen* dictionary, compiled by Hsü Shen (d. AD 120). It listed over 10,000 characters, and employed the principle of distinguishing them according to radicals, of which 540 were recognized as against the 214 in use at present.

The prose style of Han literature was to be very highly regarded in later periods, especially the T'ang and Sung, when some of the foremost writers advocated a return to its simplicity, directness and expressiveness. In poetry, the main development was in the direction of the usage of an elaborately rich and exotic vocabulary, as exemplified by the lengthy works of Ssu-ma Hsiang-ju (179–147 BC), probably the most talented Han poet.

Numerous advances were made during the Han in the techniques of production, especially in agriculture, where drought-resistant rice was introduced, intertillage used, crop rotation applied, and hillsides utilized for planting vegetables and fruit trees. In general, Chinese technology in this era was equal, and in some ways superior, to that of the other main centres of civilization. Two of the most renowned Chinese inventions were also made at this time. The manufacture of paper was undoubtedly started, at the latest, in the first century AD, although it took more than a thousand years for this boon to mankind to reach Europe. It was, however, a mixed blessing for Chinese historians, since the gap between its invention and that of printing was too long, and its perishability caused relatively few manuscripts from this intermediate period to survive. A century after the invention of paper, the Chinese were already beginning to manufacture a form of proto-porcelain, thus opening the gate to one of their most brilliant artistic crafts.

Political turbulence, as exemplified by the sad fate of Ch'ang-an and Loyang, has been responsible for the irretrievable loss of probably the great majority of the finest examples of Han art. Nonetheless, both earlier archaeological exploration and especially discoveries made since 1949, such as those in Manch'eng and Mawangtui, have furnished much valuable material, and more can certainly be hoped for.

Some fine examples of stone sculpture have survived, but perhaps the best works in stone are the famous bas-reliefs from the Wu family tomb in Shantung (second century AD). The variety of topics is far-ranging, presenting an impression of Han customs. In Han decorative arts, one can now add to the renowned lacquer ware found in Lo-lang the magnificent specimens from Mawangtui. In bronze, the Shang and Chou tradition was continued in the manufacture of sacrificial vessels, but the Han products lack vitality and originality. However, the bronze mirrors of this period display masterful workmanship. Much use was also made of both gold and silver inlay.

The origins of painting are surely to be looked for in the Han epoch. Paintings on silk were already common, but unfortunately, very few of them, notably those known to have been in the imperial collections, have survived. Han architecture has fared no better than painting; in this case as well, literary accounts constitute the main source of knowledge. A slight idea can also be gained from clay models found in tombs. The imperial palaces, highly ornamented and coloured, glittering with precious stones and shining marble, must have been especially impressive. But the Chinese built in wood, and all these magnificent creations of the talented Han craftsmen were destined, like those of the Ch'in, to go up in smoke.

3. The Period of Division

The Three Kingdoms

The downfall of the Eastern Han, signifying the complete collapse of the centralized monarchy, ushered in one of the gloomiest and most tragic eras in Chinese history. During its span of almost four hundred years the division of the country was to be exacerbated by incessant incursions of nomad peoples into North China. However, in spite of the undeniable retrogression, caused by the immense devastation of the economy, the oft-drawn analogy with the fate of the Roman Empire is partially misleading, since Chinese civilization managed to survive and, although much altered, preserve its fundamental continuity.

The initial struggle of the provincial warlords, lasting for three decades from the entry of their army into Loyang in 190, led ultimately not to the establishment of a new dynasty, capable of ruling the entire country as the Han had done, but to the formation of three separate, rival states – Wei, Shu and Wu – known in Chinese history by the name of the Three Kingdoms. Largely due to the great popularity of the famous Ming novel, 'The Romance of the Three Kingdoms', and the innumerable tales and plays derived from it, the events of this period are among the best known to the Chinese themselves. It has thus been endowed with a somewhat romantic air which, in reality, its brutality and violence hardly justifies.

The most powerful of the Three Kingdoms was Wei; its territory embraced the greater part of the Yellow River area in North China, the country's main agricultural terrain, and its population, estimated at close to 29 million, was considerably larger than that of its rivals. It was founded by Ts'ao Ts'ao (155–220), perhaps the most relentlessly ruthless of the contestants for power, renowned for his brutal suppression of the Yellow Turban insurgents. Having successfully

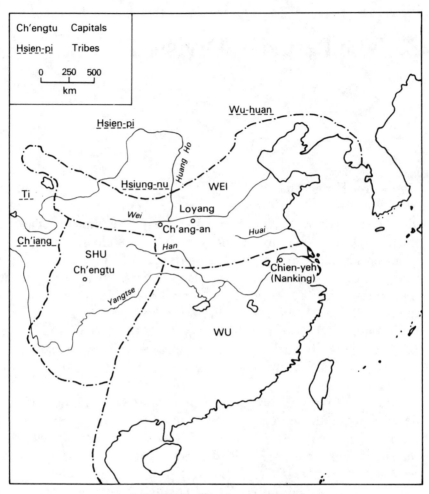

Hsien-pi

Wu-huan

Huang Ho

Ti

Hsiung-nu

WEI

Wei

Loyang

Ch'ang-an

Huai

Ch'iang

Han

SHU

Ch'engtu

Chien-yeh
(Nanking)

Yangtse

WU

9. The Three Kingdoms, *c.* AD 230

eliminated other warlords in North China, and consolidated his rule there, Ts'ao Ts'ao made a supreme bid to conquer the rest of the country. His attempt in 208 to cross the Yangtse was frustrated in the famous battle of Ch'ih-pi, in which his immense fleet was destroyed by his enemies' fireships, and most of his army slain. Ts'ao Ts'ao's plan for assuming the imperial throne was foiled by his unexpected death, and was put into effect by his son, Ts'ao Pei, in 221, when the last Han emperor was deprived of his fictitious position. However, the Ts'ao royal family was soon to face the growing strength of rival, great landowning clans in Wei, one of which, the Ssu-ma, successfully gathered all real power into its own hands. During its 64-year span of existence, the Wei government managed to bring about, mainly for the purpose of meeting its military requirements, a rehabilitation of agriculture. A large number of military and civilian agricultural colonies were established, a method already employed by Emperor Wu of the Western Han, which ultimately did result in a restoration and increase of agricultural production and the accumulation of needed reserves.

The kingdom of Shu or Shu Han was established by Liu Pei (161–223), an impoverished member of a collateral line of the Han imperial clan. Its principal area was Szechuan and southern Shensi; later on it was expanded southwards to include parts of Kweichow and Yünnan. Its population of perhaps 7.5 million made it the weakest of the Three Kingdoms, but the fertile Ch'engtu plain provided it with the necessary resources. Liu Pei, who had taken power in Shu in 214, proclaimed himself emperor in 221, after Ts'ao Pei's dethronement of the last Han ruler. His successes were in large measure due to his chief minister, Chu-ko Liang (181–234), one of the ablest men in Chinese annals, renowned for his brilliant strategy and political wisdom. After Liu Pei's death in 223, Chu-ko Liang continued to prop up the state, but his death in 234 was followed by its steady decline. In 263, the forces of Wei easily overcame the formidable natural obstacles, and conquered Shu, meeting with no resistance from its ruler, Liu Pei's inept son.

Wu's territory was the largest, stretching from the middle and lower reaches of the Yangtse to North Vietnam. However, this immense area was still very sparsely settled, and much of the population, thought to be over eleven million, consisted of non-

Chinese peoples. The founding of this state marked the beginning of the real development of the Yangtse Valley, stimulated also by the establishment of its capital in present Nanking. Wu's ruler, Sun Ch'üan (185–252), proclaimed himself emperor in 229.

Each of the Three Kingdoms, accurately described by Eberhard as condottiere states, considered itself to be the true heir of the Han empire, but, in effect, they all were not only smaller, but also much weaker politically, since in each case the central government was, to a great extent, at the mercy of the great landowner families. The ruinous warfare preceding their foundation was to be continued by them, with the result that the country's economy suffered almost irreparable damage. The formerly flourishing towns were practically all destroyed, while the population had declined drastically. The considerable progress made during the Han in the direction of a money economy was now cancelled out, with barter used almost universally, especially in the rural districts. There was no solution in sight to the social crisis, since ever greater numbers of free peasants had been deprived of their land and many of them were forced to become tenants on the increasingly prevalent great estates.

The Chin Dynasties and the Nomad Invasions

In 265, two years after the conquest of Shu, Ssu-ma Yen, the Wei general responsible for its accomplishment, dethroned the last monarch of the Ts'ao family, and proclaimed himself the First Emperor of a new dynasty – the Chin (or Tsin). Its history is one of the most unedifying of all, although by their very length, Chinese annals unfortunately furnish numerous other examples. Its sole feat was the conquest in 280 of Wu, thus accomplishing a reunification of China, which shortly proved to be of very short duration. Wu-ti – Ssu-ma Yen's posthumous honorific title – had at the same time gravely weakened the prospects of his dynasty by distributing appanages to at least fifteen of his sons (considering the size of his harem, reputedly ten thousand women, he might well have had many more) with the foreseeable consequences of future conflict.

The overall situation of the country remained calamitous; the census of 280 showed a population figure of only 16 million, and some authors see this as signifying a loss of 30 million, since the figure for 156 was 56 million. This seems most unlikely; although the drop in population was truly grievous, the disparity is most probably due to the effects of the social crisis referred to earlier, and the radical dimunition in the number of tax-paying peasant smallholders.

Shortly after Wu-ti's death in 289, the almost inevitable struggle for power among the Chin princes broke out. Its apogee was the Rebellion of the Eight Princes, which lasted from 291 to 306, and devastated the ruined country still more. In its course the contenders availed themselves of the aid of nomad auxiliaries, thus doubly facilitating the ensuing nomad deluge.

A large part of the nomad tribes destined to destroy Chinese rule in the north already resided in this area, playing a role strikingly similar to that of the Germanic tribes in the Roman Empire. Combined with that of their kinsmen from beyond the empire's frontiers, their strength proved to be overpowering when used against the weakened and corrupt government of the Chin. Chinese traditional historical writing refers to these tribes as the Five Hu – the Five 'Barbarian' Peoples. Among them were the Ch'iang and the Ti, both ethnically Tibetan, living mostly in Kansu and Shensi, engaged primarily in shepherding, and accustomed to fight as infantry. The Chieh and the Huns (the name now used for the Hsiung-nu), probably of Turkic stock, controlled a large part of Shansi, while the Hsien-pi, probably proto-Mongol, were busy infiltrating Hopei and Liaoning. The last three were cast in the traditional nomad mould, raising horses and cattle, and fighting as cavalry. Their military superiority over the Chinese lay precisely in this, since they were superb mounted archers, and most of North China formed a terrain in which their mode of warfare could be practised with relative ease. Although employed as frontier guards and auxiliary troops by the Chin, the nomads within the country were also the victims of considerable exploitation and oppression by the Chinese ruling class; this gave rise to much pent-up tension.

The first to rise against Chinese rule were the Huns, whose contacts with the Chinese had been the longest and most intimate. In 304, the Hun tribal chiefs proclaimed their leader, Liu Yüan, as king and rightful ruler of the empire. As a bearer of the former dynasty's family name, and claiming to be descended from it, Liu Yüan called his new state the Han, and in 308 assumed the title of emperor. With the aid of his tribal cavalry, at most 50,000 horsemen, he overran a large part of North China. His task was continued successfully by his son, Liu Ts'ung, who captured Loyang, while the Han general, Shih Le, a former slave, took Ch'ang-an in 316. In both instances the devastation and slaughter were indescribable, and the same was true of the better part of the north. Formerly the country's most highly developed region, it was now destined to undergo almost 150 years of total disruption and destruction under the iron heel of the nomad invaders. It was also to witness the rise of a large number of states – Chinese historians speak of sixteen – formed by the nomads. Ephemeral by nature, these creations resembled soap bubbles; some of them would be blown up to cover all of North China, and then would burst to disappear instantly without leaving a trace – except for ruin and death. The principal cause of this lay in the incessant, savage warfare which the nomad tribes waged against each other. At the same time they were always greatly outnumbered by the Chinese peasant population, and hence easily prone to being ultimately assimilated.

The nomad invasion of China was part of a great simultaneous expansion of these peoples, lasting from the fourth to the sixth century, which, in Goodrich's words, was their 'great period . . . in which they brought both China and the Roman Empire to their knees'. Much the same process was to be repeated by the Mongols in the thirteenth century. In both cases, a really satisfactory explanation still remains to be offered.

The loss of Ch'ang-an and Loyang, accompanied by the capture of two Chin emperors, put an end to this dynasty's sway in North China, but a member of the royal family succeeded in maintaining its rule over the rest of the empire. In 317 he established his capital in present Nanking, and hence the dynasty is referred to from this point on as the Eastern Chin, distinguishing it from the earlier period, known as Western Chin. The collapse of Chinese authority in the north was followed by probably one of the greatest migrations in the country's history. Some modern Chinese historians believe that a major part of the great landowner families fled with their many dependants to the Yangtse Valley. It was they who were to dominate the Eastern Chin government, and its political history during the century of its existence (317–419) also reflected to a large extent the practically constant conflict between them and the older landowner families of this region. After its initial consolidation, the Eastern Chin undertook relatively few attempts to reconquer the territory lost to the nomads, and those made later proved to be quite ineffective.

The newly arrived migrant population did contribute to a sizable increase in agricultural production, especially by the cultivation of new lands, and the economy, relatively untouched by warfare in contrast with the north, progressed steadily. However, the Eastern Chin rulers were as covetous and oppressive as their predecessors, and the social crisis soon gave rise to a number of peasant revolts. The most famous and largest of these, which was centred on eastern Chekiang, might be regarded as similar to the Yellow Turban movement, since its leader, Sun En, was said to be a prominent follower of the Five Bushels sect. During the rebellion, which lasted from 399 to 403, the insurgents, with some of the coastal islands as their main base, made skilful use of naval forces, at one point even sailing up the Yangtse with a fleet of 1000 junks and an army of reputedly 100,000 men, to threaten Nanking. Nevertheless, in spite of the strong support of the peasantry, the uprising was suppressed by the government forces led by Liu Yü, the future founder of the Sung dynasty. The methods used in pacifying the affected area were such that, according to the Annals, 'the people bitterly regretted the rule of the rebels'.

The state established by Liu Yüan lasted only until 329, to be superseded by another, of which Shih Le was the emperor. But the Huns demonstrated a special aptitude for mutual destruction, and by the middle of the fourth century their place as rulers of most of North China was taken by the Tibetans. The state founded by them, Earlier Ch'in, was the strongest and most extensive thus far, and its administration largely based on the Chinese model. It also posed the greatest threat to the Eastern Chin, since its ruler, Fu Chien, was determined to conquer the entire Middle Kingdom. In 383, an immense host, purportedly 900,000 men, cavalry and infantry – the former composed mostly of nomads, the latter largely of Chinese conscripts – advanced towards the Yangtse. When warned that the Great River would prove a formidable obstacle, Fu Chien supposedly replied: 'My army is so huge that if all the men in it throw their whips into the Yangtse this will suffice to cover it.' But even before reaching the Yangtse Fu Chien's troops were disastrously defeated in the decisive battle of the Fei River (Anhwei) by a much smaller Chin force. Treachery within his own camp was one of the causes, but the main one rested in the fact that the Chinese infantry, pressed into service by force, only too happily availed itself of an opportunity to flee. Allegedly half of Fu Chien's army was wiped out, and his empire disintegrated almost immediately. Thus, a nomad conquest of all China was to be postponed for 900 years. The fall of Earlier Ch'in was followed by further anarchic struggles for the control of North China. In 386 there were seven separate states in this area, in 400 – nine, in 415 – seven, in 425 – five. Finally, all the contenders were vanquished, and the unification of the north accomplished by the Toba.

The Northern and Southern Dynasties

The Toba (T'opa) tribe, considered to be ethnically either Turkic or Tungusic, made its first appearance in the middle of the fourth century, when its rulers established the small state of Tai in northern Shansi. The collapse of Fu Chien's empire enabled them to emerge as the main aspirant to power, having succeeded in forming a large confederation, said to include around 119 tribes of different origin. In 398, the Toba ruler proclaimed himself emperor of a state to be known as the Northern Wei. The nomads, a small minority in comparison with the Chinese peasant population, were always faced with two alternative policies in respect to the latter; they could drive away or exterminate the peasants and convert the land into pasturage, or seek to rule and exploit them by becoming a new ruling caste. The Toba rulers opted from the very outset for the second choice, but, in view of their own inexperience and incapacity, the setting up of an administration for this purpose could only be achieved with the aid of Chinese methods and Chinese officials. In the process of expanding their state they also refrained from dividing the conquered territory among the tribes, and established a unitary, Chinese-style admin-istration, while simultaneously preserving the structure of their tribal confederation.

The Northern Wei emperors obtained the willing collaboration of the Chinese landowner families, and this proved to be the key factor in the successful consolidation of their state. They have been praised by one modern Chinese author for 'drawing on the rich experiences in the administering of China'. Actually, on nearly every occasion during the next 1500 years, the Chinese landowners were only too happy, in their own class interest, to assist, if given the chance, the conquering northern nomads in exploiting and oppressing their own countrymen, the Chinese peasants.

After a series of campaigns, waged mostly against the states set up by the Mu-jung clan of the Hsien-pi, the rulers of Northern Wei succeeded by 439 in becoming the masters of all North China. Their ambition was to conquer the entire country, but all attempts to achieve this, the last serious one taking place in 507, were frustrated. Hence, for a century and a half, China was to remain divided into two empires, the Northern Wei and its successor states in the north, the Eastern Chin and the four dynasties following it in the south, the period being referred to as that of the Northern and Southern Dynasties.

Having become the rulers of the rich agricultural lands of North China, the Northern Wei emperors were soon faced with a threat to their state, posed by the powerful Jou-jan (Avar) nomad tribes. Acting like traditional Chinese rulers, and for identical motives, the Toba undertook numerous campaigns against the Avars in the years 407–49, at the same time repairing and extending the Great Wall. A better proof of their rapid sinification could not be found. This striking phenomenon was also revealed by the concern shown by Northern Wei for the proper development of agriculture. They were the initiators, clearly on the advice of their Chinese officials, of the ingenious system known as land equalization, which was to be applied for almost three centuries as an attempt to resolve this problem. The main provisions of this scheme stipulated the distribution of state land to the peasants – agricultural land for life tenure, orchard plots in perpetuity. The quantity involved, the first category being always much larger, differed, depending on the period. The land equalization system did not imply a breaking up of landed estates which were not affected by it; in fact, concentration of landownership continued apace. Nonetheless, its application resulted in helping to

75

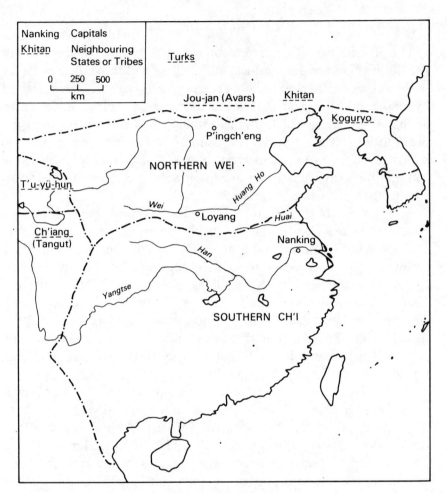

Nanking   Capitals

Khitan   Neighbouring
           States or Tribes

0   250   500

km

Turks

Jou-jan (Avars)   Khitan

P'ingch'eng

Koguryo

NORTHERN WEI

Huang Ho

T'u-yü-hun

Wei

Loyang

Huai

Ch'iang
(Tangut)

Nanking

Han

Yangtse

SOUTHERN CH'I

10. Period of Division, *c.* 500

maintain in existence a sufficient number of tax-paying peasant smallholders, and to bring about an increase in agricultural production. It was also closely bound up, throughout the entire period of its existence, with the functioning of a peasant militia, which furnished a large part of the Northern Wei armed forces, especially its infantry.

A further proof of the sinification of the Toba was offered in 493, when the capital was shifted from P'ingch'eng (T'atung, North Shansi) to Loyang, and a large number of measures, such as the adoption of Chinese as the official language, and of Chinese surnames by the Toba aristocratic families, the dynasty itself being renamed Yüan, and the prohibition of the use of the Hsien-pi language, dress and customs. All this pertained, however, primarily to the ruling stratum of Northern Wei; a fair part of the Toba nobility and people had remained faithful to the nomad way of life, and thus a source of conflict between them and their rulers was created.

After over a century of existence, the Northern Wei empire, having become almost completely sinified and dominated by the Chinese great landowning families, succumbed to internal stress, caused in part by the dual nature of its society, and, even more, by the re-emergence of the ever present social crisis. In 523 a two-year-long large-scale revolt of mostly nomad frontier troops, provoked by the rapacious greed of their commanders, almost toppled the dynasty. It was followed shortly by a widespread peasant uprising in Hopei, which weakened it still further. Both events, as well as conflicts within the imperial clan, helped to bring about the disintegration of Northern Wei into two separate states – Western Wei (534–57) and Eastern Wei (534–50) – in which power rested, in reality, in the hands of Chinese generals. In both cases, the Toba rulers were soon removed, and new dynasties founded – Northern Chou (557–81) taking the place of Western Wei, and Northern Ch'i (550–77) that of Eastern Wei. Sinification made still further progress, and most of the tribesmen, having ceased to be nomads, merged with the Chinese peasants. The Toba, as a people, simply disappeared. Thus, in contrast with Europe, in China the assimilation of the conquerors was far more thorough, and the Chinese character of the lands they had overrun and ruled preserved. This was due not only to the numerical superiority of the Chinese peasants, but also to the fact that they had become, as a consequence of the Han era, to a considerable degree the fundamental repository of Chinese culture.

The political history of Northern Chou and Northern Ch'i is a truly depressing chronicle of unmitigated evil deeds; the latter, in particular, would seem to have produced perhaps the most monstrously depraved rulers of the many similar ones who have afflicted the Chinese people throughout the ages. Their state was annexed by Northern Chou in 577, but the newly unified north was shortly to fall under the sway of a new dynasty – the Sui.

In respect to political development, the situation in the south did not differ appreciably. Liu Yü, the general responsible for crushing the Sun En uprising, put an end to the rule of Eastern Chin. His dynasty, the Liu Sung (420–79), was followed by three more – the Southern Ch'i (479–502), the Liang (502–57) and the Ch'en (557–89). The rise and fall of these regimes followed in all instances a similar pattern. Each was founded by a successful general and, having rapidly become the scene of incessant conflicts, mostly within the ruling family, fell victim to new contenders for the throne. The details are as sordid as those pertaining to the north, with murder on a mass scale, especially of the members of the previously ruling dynasty, as the preferred instrument of politics. Under these circumstances, the south was, in reality, ruled not so much by these reprehensible monarchs, as by the great landowning families. After the first century, the differences between those who had migrated from the north and the original landowners had largely disappeared, and the great families dominated the countryside completely, becoming a powerful closed oligarchy also in effective control of the bureaucracy. The economic position of these magnates was further strengthened by the rapid growth of their estates, which, according to some Chinese historians, began to show features of a manorial system. In any case, the number of tenants on their estates increased markedly, while, simultaneously, the ranks of the peasant smallholders were depleted still further. But these social changes took place against the background of a considerable general economic development of the south, which largely made up for the earlier regression and facilitated the restoration of a money economy. This was due primarily to the great growth of population which has been estimated to have increased fivefold in the years 280–464. Thus the first crucial steps in the shifting of the country's centre of economic gravity to the Yangtse Valley were taken in precisely this period.

Culture in the Period of Division

In contrast to its dismally wretched political history, the cultural developments of this era, particularly those connected with the rise of Buddhism, are of considerable interest and significance. Beginning probably with the first century AD, the influence of Buddhism penetrated slowly into China from the Western Regions, which, in this period, were a flourishing centre of this faith. Up to the third century Buddhism remained a small, insignificant sect, largely unnoticed since, according to Maspero, it was viewed as only an odd variety of Taoism. Its followers were mostly foreign merchants from Central Asia, and its initial propagators were also primarily foreigners. However, the overwhelming and universal crisis of Chinese society, which followed in the wake of the downfall of the Eastern Han, created a totally new situation, eminently conducive to the further spread of the new religion. It is only such a background which can explain, at least partially, why a foreign creed, with its advocacy of personal salvation, monasticism and celibacy, asceticism, mendicancy and general otherworldliness, all so utterly divergent from Chinese customs and tradition, as exemplified by Confucianism, was able to achieve relatively quickly an immense success, penetrating all aspects of Chinese life and assuming the position of the most influential religious ideology. The impact of Buddhism was undoubtedly the strongest foreign influence to have affected China up to the nineteenth century, and it has often been compared with that of Christianity in Europe. The analogy is only partially justified, although there were some striking resemblances, such as that of the Buddhist ritual to the meretricious pomp and pageantry of Roman Catholic worship. Luckily, Buddhism never attained in China the dominant position held by the Christian church in medieval Europe, although it also demonstrated the same tendency to become a state within a state.

It seems quite logical that Buddhism should have been destined to achieve its great successes first in North China, in the states of the unlettered nomad conquerors, since it was here that Chinese society had suffered its most grievous blows. On the whole, the nomad rulers looked on the growth of the Buddhist church with favour, and utilized it for establishing their own administration, a need partially created by the mass migration of the Confucian great landowner families. The spread of Buddhism was so rapid that by the middle of the fifth century, nine-tenths of the population of North China had purportedly become its followers. Inasmuch as the same process, although started somewhat later, was taking place in the south, it has been maintained that by 500 most of the country was already Buddhist; 3000 temples were said to exist, as well as a community of two million monks and nuns. Some authors believe that the protection granted to the Buddhist establishment by the rulers of both the north and south was largely derived from their appreciation of its social role, since its general otherworldly tenor and belief in personal salvation in a future reincarnation tended to shape an attitude of useful and malleable passivity to existence in the present. There were moments when the pendulum swung in the direction of persecution, most often provoked by Buddhism's Taoist and Confucian rivals. It should be stressed, however, that its scope was mild by European standards – no Albigensian crusades, no autos-da-fé, no Saint Bartholomew's Days – and usually had a distinct economic motivation, depriving the Buddhist church of some of its quickly and easily accumulated wealth, and secularizing some monks and nuns.

The first persecution took place in Northern Wei in 444, but almost immediately thereafter the Buddhist establishment recovered completely from its effects, and the Toba rulers, predominantly fervent Buddhists, heaped untold wealth on it, thus aiding it to become the largest single landowner in their realm. The Buddhist monasteries also quickly became a refuge for all those seeking to escape from the state's onerous burdens – taxation, corvée and military service – while their estates had no difficulty in finding tenants, since the peasants usually considered they would be oppressed less by the Buddhists than by the landowners. By the seventh century, the Buddhist establishment had become an economic power in the land, but its political influence, though great, remained limited. This was partly the result of the watchful policy pursued towards it by most of the rulers, and probably also of its loose organization, marked by the existence of different sects and tendencies. Simultaneously, the rise of Buddhism had by no means signified the total elimination of opposing creeds, a goal towards which, it should be added in fairness, it did not strive. Thus the continued presence and influence of Taoism and Confucianism also prevented the Buddhist church from attaining complete domination, while the coexistence of the three creeds probably helped to mould the noteworthy non-absolutist and eclectic approach of the Chinese to religious matters.

Before its entry into China, Buddhism had already, in its long history, undergone many changes and the formation of various tendencies. In general, the main form to be propagated in China was the Mahayana, a creed quite distinct from the original ethical teaching of Gautama, and much more akin to a new religion, richly endowed with a huge pantheon of Buddhas and Bodhisattvas, and, at the same time, with a complex metaphysical philosophy. Hence, Buddhism could appeal easily to different strata of the population, while its generally tolerant approach made it capable of assimilating concepts from rival creeds. In time, its sinification progressed to the point where it bore little resemblance to the original state.

The coming of Buddhism also opened the gates of the Middle Kingdom to Indian influence in the fields of philosophy, literature, mathematics, astronomy, and, in particular, art and architecture. The overall effect on Chinese culture was tremendous, but it should be stressed that this was a meeting of equals, of two mature civilizations, and hence differed profoundly from the influence exercised by China on Korea and Japan, in which of course Buddhism also played a vital role.

The simplest variant for obtaining personal salvation, perhaps the most fundamental element in Buddhism's appeal, came to be furnished by the sect advocating the worship of the Amitabha Buddha; it was to become the creed's predominant form. In the great wealth of Buddhist thought there was also room for a messianistic trend, the worship of the future Buddha, Maitreya, which, in time, became a part of the beliefs of secret societies, such as the White Lotus, often engaged in leading revolutionary peasant movements. But probably the most striking of the many schools to arise on Chinese soil was Ch'an, the furthest removed from orthodox Buddhism, and the most thoroughly Chinese. A subjective, iconoclastic sect, Ch'an, founded in the sixth century, gained much ground from the ninth century on. Its emphasis on inward enlightenment and its negative approach to ritual clearly revealed the strong influence of Taoism. Ch'an's greatest importance rested perhaps on its fruitful influence on Chinese art, particularly on painting. Goodrich has perceptively called it 'probably the finest flowering of Indian culture in China'.

The propagation of Buddhism necessitated the rendition into Chinese of its vast literature, thus giving rise to the many intriguing problems involved in translating an Indo-European language into Chinese. Ultimately, the difficulties did not prove insurmountable, but the marvellous remark of Kumarajiva (344–410) deserves to be recalled. He observed that 'translating Sanskrit into Chinese is like feeding a man rice chewed by another; it is not merely tasteless, it is nauseating'. This did not prevent him from translating 98 Buddhist sutras. As a result of the assiduous work of hundreds of others like him, the gigantic corpus of Buddhist literature was put into Chinese, and many early sutras are now known only in their Chinese version. Emperor Wu of the Liang, the munificent patron of Buddhism, had the entire Buddhist canon, the Tripitaka, published already in 517.

Many Chinese followers of the new religion were animated by the desire to travel to the land of its origin, and for the period 259–790 the names of 186 Chinese pilgrims have been recorded. But there were undoubtedly still more of these fearless men who did not hesitate to venture on the uniquely perilous route, traversing some of the world's most arduous terrain, and often paying with their lives for their faith. Fa-hsien is probably the best known among the earlier pilgrims. Departing in 399, he reached India by way of Central Asia and Afghanistan, and stayed there and in Ceylon until 413, studying, collecting scriptures and images, and visiting holy places. After a hazardous sea journey, which included a stay in Java, he reached Shantung in 414, with his cherished collection undamaged. Fa-hsien then spent his remaining years translating the material acquired, also leaving behind an invaluable account of his travels.

Neither the dominance of Confucianism in the Han era nor the rise of Buddhism had put an end to the further development of Taoist philosophical thought during the Period of Division. In the second half of the third century it was represented by a group of exceedingly talented men, referred to as the Seven Sages of the Bamboo Grove. These thinkers, among whom Hsi K'ang (232–62) was probably the most outstanding, were also known for their eccentricities, but these might well have been only a reflection of the chaotic conditions of the time and a form of protest against the hidebound, conformist nature of Confucianism. Simultaneously, some of them took part in formulating the ideas of what is called by some authors Neo-Taoism, a trend whose principal aim was to achieve a synthesis of Confucianism and Taoism. The Neo-Taoists were also famous for their profound commentaries on the Taoist classics. Such was the case, for example, of Wang Pi (226–49), in Fung Yu-lan's words 'one of the most precocious geniuses in the history of Chinese thought', who wrote on the *Tao te ching*.

The spread of Buddhism did have a great influence on a process mentioned earlier, the transformation of Taoism into a popular religion, since the Taoists borrowed most of the paraphernalia of their creed – its immense pantheon, its liturgy and canon – from their more successful rivals. The organization of the Taoist church was also modelled on the Buddhist establishment. It was to produce even more divergent sects. Its political significance, although it had, as seen, much influence among the peasants, was probably always less than that of the Buddhists. K'uo Ch'ien-chih (d. 432) is usually considered to have been most instrumental in organizing the church, while an earlier prominent Taoist, Ko Hung (253–333), is regarded by many authors as the principal founder of religious Taoism, which, it should be added, has practically nothing in common with the philosophy from which it claimed to be derived. He was also probably the greatest alchemist in China, since the Taoists persevered untiringly in their search for the elixir of immortality, incidentally contributing much thereby to the development of Chinese proto-science in many fields. Needham's monumental work deals exhaustively with this subject.

If, like the present writer, one may find it difficult to sense empathy for the religious aspects of Buddhism, one cannot refrain from admiration for its effects on the development of Chinese art. It would be possible to hazard the statement that Buddhism's greatest gift to Chinese culture rests precisely therein. This is particularly true of early Chinese Buddhist sculpture, some examples of which have deservedly been described as 'treasures of loveliness'. While the original iconography of Buddhist sculpture was obviously foreign, in time, just as the religion itself, it became sinified, and all the various influences merged into a purely Chinese art form which during its most splendid period – the sixth and seventh centuries – was unsurpassable and unmatched for its austere beauty. Such a judgement is based, however, only on a small part of the sculptures, mostly in stone, that have survived, in spite of the vandalism inspired by foreign collectors. Almost all the work in wood, and especially in bronze, of which there was a vast quantity, has vanished.

Two cave temples are the best-known sites for Buddhist stone sculpture. The earlier one, dating from 460 to 535, is located in Yün-kang (near T'atung) and composed of twenty giant caves, as well as many lesser ones, containing an imposing number of statues, many of monumental size. The later one, begun in the sixth century, is in Lung-men, near Loyang, and is even more impressive; its gigantic figures are known throughout the world. The style of the sculptures here is said to be already completely Chinese. Another famous centre of Buddhist religious art, of which there are many, especially in North China, is Tunhuang in Kansu. It is noted particularly for its great number of mural paintings, which are among the very few specimens of this art form to have survived. But Tunhuang was only a remote provincial outpost, and hence one can well imagine that the general level of Buddhist religious painting, especially the work done in the capitals, must have been much higher, probably as magnificent and outstanding as the sculptures.

Secular painting also made considerable progress in the Period of Division, especially at the Chin court in Nanking, which remained the country's cultural centre from the fourth to the sixth century. The most eminent painter of the Chin era was Ku K'ai-chih (*c.* 344–406), whose famous scroll in the British Museum is remarkable for its skilled portrayal of figures. The first attempt to formulate the canon of painting was the work of Hsieh Ho (*fl. c.* 500), and his Six Principles were to initiate a vast outpouring of art criticism which, especially for earlier periods, is often the sole source of knowledge. In the twin art of calligraphy, the writing of Wang Hsi-chih (321–79) was to be considered for many centuries as the acme of perfection.

Poetry during the Southern Dynasties remained basically a pastime of the great aristocratic houses, and its language is regarded by some specialists to be so artificial and allusive as to verge on the incomprehensible. The work of the greatest poet of this period, and one of the most prominent figures in the entire history of Chinese literature, T'ao Yüan-ming (T'ao Ch'ien, 375–427), is of a completely different sort, noted for its simplicity and beauty. Following his Taoist inclinations, he had retired early from an official post to spend his life on a small estate, to commune with nature and devote his time to art. Apart from his many verses, T'ao Yüan-ming also wrote the well-known satirical allegory 'The Peach Blossom Fountain'.

Inventiveness did not disappear altogether in this calamitous era. It is unfair not to mention the appearance of the humble wheelbarrow, since the brilliant idea of replacing one carrier by a wheel saved so much toil for future generations. A product which later was to be so intimately connected with the European conception of China – tea – was first introduced during this period in the south, and the custom of tea-drinking became nationwide by the eighth century.

4. The Restoration of the Empire: the Sui and T'ang Dynasties

The Sui Unification

In 581 Yang Chien, a prominent general of mixed Chinese and nomad origin, overthrew the Northern Chou ruler, massacred most of the Yü-wen royal family, and assumed the throne as the First Emperor of the new Sui dynasty (Wen-ti, 581–614). He lost relatively little time in embarking on his fundamental plan of reuniting the country. In 587 the state of Later Liang on the middle Yangtse was eliminated, and in 589 the conquest of the south was accomplished easily, since the Ch'en dynasty was weak and discredited, and its last indolent ruler offered practically no resistance.

Thus, after almost four centuries, a unified China became a reality once more, but the problems facing the new Sui dynasty were very complex, since the long Period of Division had given rise to considerable differences in the development of the various parts of the country in very many respects. The most urgent issue was the establishment of a truly strong, centralized government; it was largely resolved during the first years of Wen-ti's reign by an efficacious reorganization of the administration and the bureaucracy. These measures did not imply any basic alteration in the structure of power inasmuch as the ruling group continued to be composed, as it had been during the Northern Dynasties, of aristocratic landowning families, mostly of mixed origin (nomad and Chinese), similar to that of Wen-ti.

The need to restore the economy was no less pressing, and the new government devoted much of its efforts to this goal. The Sui continued to utilize the Northern Wei land equalization system, allocating even greater amounts of land to the peasants, in order to bring about an increase in agricultural production which would guarantee a permanent flow of greater revenue and the achievement of a stabilization of social conditions. The corvée labour which these peasants also had to render was utilized on a considerable scale for the construction of numerous large granaries, located mostly close to the capital, and for the expansion of the canal system which was initiated in Wen-ti's reign.

Success was not long in coming; the economy recovered rapidly and immense quantities of tax grain poured into the new granaries, while equally vast amounts of tax silk cloth filled the imperial storehouses. A marked growth of population also took place; the figure in 606 was 46 million. The Sui quickly became wealthy and able to accumulate impressive reserves which, at least during Wen-ti's rule, were not wasted, since he has been described not only as cunning and despotic but also as miserly.

The rapid domestic consolidation made it possible for the Sui to seek to reassert China's dominance in its relations with its neighbours. The most formidable of these was the newly formed empire of the Turks, stretching from the Khingan Range to the Caspian. This great power had, however, been recently weakened by a division into two parts, and Wen-ti's government happily applied the traditional Chinese policy, playing off the Western and Eastern Turkish states against each other. As a result, the initial steps aimed at recovering China's position in the Western Regions were already taken in the Sui period. Chinese sovereignty over North Vietnam was also restored in 605, and thus an image of an Imperial China, as the great power of East Asia, reappeared once again.

The short duration of the Sui dynasty has inclined many authors to compare its fate with that of the Ch'in; in both instances the overly ambitious means employed in effecting reunification are said to have been the cause of their downfall. But there was nothing in Wen-ti's reign that would seem to justify the analogy; the crisis was to come during his successor's rule.

The vicious palace intrigues, so characteristic of the Period of Division, did not bypass the Sui. Wen-ti died in 604, almost surely murdered on the order of his son, Yang Kuang, who then assumed the throne, and is known as Yang-ti (604–18). A highly gifted man, but clearly tainted with imperial megalomania, Emperor Yang also became a most controversial figure. He has been unsparingly censured for his enormities in Chinese traditional historical writing, while some Western authors see fit to exonerate him believing that, in his case, the stereotype of the 'bad, last ruler' has been mechanically and uncritically applied. The facts should determine which appraisal is closer to the truth.

Almost immediately upon taking power, Yang-ti embarked on a grandiose construction programme. This involved the rebuilding of Loyang, which he chose as his capital, on a lavish scale; 2 million men were employed on this project and transport of rare timber from the south was said to have cost the lives of countless thousands. The expenditures were then further increased by the reconstruction of Yangchow, his former residence as Viceroy of the South, in a similar fashion. In addition, Yang-ti had 1.2 million men dispatched in 607 to rebuild and enlarge the Great Wall; half of them are said to have died during this two-year-long task.

Still greater masses of forced labour were employed during Yang-ti's reign for the further extension of the canal system which ultimately linked Loyang with Hangchow, while a spur also led from the middle reaches of the Yellow River northwards to the region of Peking. The aims of this gigantic project were probably to facilitate both the transport of food to the capital and the movement of troops. Close to 5.5 million people are said to have been pressed into work on the canal construction, and thus all the nearby areas were stripped bare of manpower. Evasion was punished by death, and a police force of 50,000 acted as overseers, liberally using the whip and the cangue to enforce the required discipline. Some authors, especially those favouring the 'hydraulic society' theory, believe that the entire raison d'être of the centralized autocratic monarchy in China lay precisely in its ability to undertake such projects which, in view of the primitive technique, did involve the mobilization of 'a million men with teaspoons'. If so, then in the instance of Yang-ti's programme the matter had already been driven to its utmost extreme. The emperor himself added a note of extravagant absurdity when, upon the completion of the canal from Loyang to Hangchow, he hastened to travel on this section by boat with his entire entourage. His own vessel was a fabulous dragon boat, four storeys high and 220 feet long, and was followed by a cortège 200 li in length. Eighty thousand men were employed to tow the boats; 40 palaces were especially erected along the route, and food was requisitioned from all the neighbouring areas to nourish this swarm of imperial locusts. *Sapienti satis.*

While the above projects were ruinous enough and involved the consuming of the greater part of the reserves accumulated during Wen-ti's reign, they might not have, by themselves, brought on the regime's crisis. When, however, the tremendous burdens of costly and abortive warfare were added on, then even the seemingly limitless patience of the Chinese peasants with their oppressors did come to an end. The expansionist policies of the Sui were aimed in many directions. A campaign against the T'u-yü-hun tribe for the purpose of clearing and safeguarding the Kansu Corridor was concluded successfully. Expeditions against Champa (present central Vietnam) and Taiwan were also dispatched. But all these actions were of little significance when compared to Yang-ti's war of aggression against Korea, which was to seal the fate of the Sui. The nominal reason for waging it rested in the failure of the king of Koguryo (which embraced North Korea and Liaotung) to recognize Sui sovereignty and offer tribute. Mobilization began in 611 and, if the figures are true, the largest army in Chinese history before the twentieth century, 1,130,000 men, was sent towards the Korean frontier. A large number of warships and vast food supplies were also prepared, while hundreds of thousands of local inhabitants were impressed for transport. In the next year, the Chinese vanguard divisions attacked P'yongyang, the Koguryo capital, and meeting with undaunted Korean resistance, suffered a humiliatingly disastrous defeat. Three hundred thousand Chinese troops had crossed the frontier; only 2700 returned. The results of the second campaign in 613 were no better. During its course the first revolt against Yang-ti, led by a member of the imperial family, took place; it was suppressed quickly and over 30,000 people suspected of participation, most of them unjustly, were executed. Although the Koreans were now exhausted, Yang-ti's third campaign in 614 also ended in a fiasco.

The catastrophic defeat of the Chinese army in Korea emboldened the Eastern Turks. Having invaded northern Shansi they succeeded in surrounding Yang-ti and his whole army, and had to be bought off with a heavy tribute. This additional humiliation overfilled the cup; the Sui government was now bankrupt to boot, and 'the people swarmed like bees', which simply meant that rebellions broke out throughout the country, but especially in North and Northeast

China, the regions which had suffered the most as a result of the war in Korea. The majority of the insurgents were peasants and their numerous armed bands grew greatly in strength to become merged into two armies, one operating in Hopei, and the second attacking Loyang. In face of this crisis, Yang-ti seemingly lost his will to rule; in 616 he escaped to his beloved Yangchow, to seek his habitual solace in wine and women and await his doom. It came in the form of a silken cord with which he was strangled in 618 by trusted members of his own entourage.

The collapse of the Sui brought in its wake complete chaos quite similar to the situation created by the fall of the Ch'in. Throughout the country, former Sui generals and officials began their scramble for power, and, although it was the peasants who by their revolt had been responsible for bringing down the oppressive regime, once again it was not they who were to profit by its destruction.

The Rise of the T'ang Dynasty

The T'ang epoch is without a doubt one of the most important in Chinese history; many historians, both Chinese and Western, regard it also as probably the most glorious. It is abundantly clear that during its three centuries China was the largest, the richest, most powerful and civilized country in the world. It was also an era in which the idea of the integrity of China as a unified empire was firmly established for all posterity.

In the chaotic welter following the collapse of the Sui, it was the Li family from Shensi which emerged victorious. The Lis were quite representative of the great aristocratic families in the northwest, being of mixed Chinese and nomad origin. Ennobled during the Northern Chou, they were related also to the Sui royal family. In 617, Li Yüan, duke of T'ang, was the Sui military governor of T'aiyüan, and in an advantageous position to make a bid for supreme power. Having assembled a force said to have been 200,000 strong, he took Ch'ang-an, placing a Sui prince on the throne as a new emperor. The puppet was quickly put aside and in 618 Li Yüan became the first emperor of the T'ang (Kao-tsu, 618–26). Traditionally, his younger son, Li

Shih-min, has been portrayed as the real moving spirit of this entire episode; this view, however, has recently been discounted by modern historians who credit Li Yüan with achieving the rise to power.

There was a multitude of other contenders for the empire, as many former Sui generals and officials had followed the same path as the Lis. It took the T'ang almost ten years to consolidate their rule, employing a large arsenal of means ranging from military action to liberal conciliation. Throughout all these years they availed themselves also of the invaluable aid of the Eastern Turks, paid for by tribute. In 626, the ambitious Li Shih-min disposed of the heir apparent and another brother, and shortly thereafter compelled his father to abdicate. During his reign (T'ai-tsung, 627–49) he was to demonstrate those capabilities which have caused him to be regarded by many Chinese and Western historians as the ablest emperor in Chinese history. There is little doubt that T'ai-tsung was truly a highly talented man, a good general and a wise statesman. During his first years he also surrounded himself with outstanding ministers, whose advice he respected and followed. The great prestige of the dynasty was largely the accomplishment of his reign, although it was also to be upheld by the fortunate circumstance of a hundred years of domestic peace which ensued.

The difficulties of establishing a truly effective centralized state, derived from the disruptive heritage of the Period of Division, were legion, and borne out as well by the failure of the Sui. In solving the problems involved, the T'ang, while continuing some of the Sui measures, reached, in reality, further back to the Han. Rejecting one aspect of early Han rule – the grant of fiefs to members of the imperial family – the T'ang modelled their administration on the Han, although ultimately their bureaucracy and fundamental government structure became considerably more elaborate and sophisticated. The significance of the measures undertaken in this domain rests in the fact that the T'ang administration became, in turn, the basic pattern to be followed by all dynasties up to the twentieth century.

The government's structure was pyramidical, with the emperor, theoretically the absolute ruler, at the apex. The Imperial Chancellery, the Imperial Secretariat and the Department for State Affairs comprised the principal bodies of the central government. The Department supervised the six ministries: (1) officials, (2)

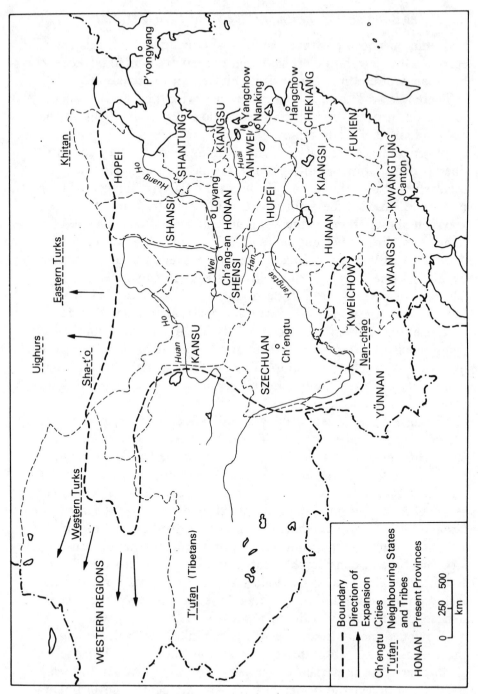

11. The T'ang Empire, c. 750

finances, (3) rites, (4) army, (5) justice and (6) public works. Nine other offices and five bureaus had the task of controlling other administrative matters and servicing the imperial court. An additional important institution was the Board of Censors whose function was to control and report on the actions of the officials. The country was divided for administrative purposes into 10 (later 15) large circuits, over 350 prefectures, 1500 counties, and around 16,000 districts. The county, ruled by a magistrate, constituted the lowest basic level to be manned by the central bureaucracy.

The partial utilization during the Han of the examination system had lapsed completely during the Period of Division when recommendations by the great families prevailed. It was set into motion once more by the T'ang and by the eighth century had become an important, though not the major, method for the recruitment of officials. However, the hereditary principle, by which sons of high officials could enter the bureaucracy without taking the examinations, remained in force and the fuller implementation of the examination system had to await the Sung. Western authors are inclined to regard it as one of the most significant aspects of Chinese historical development, and it is true that from the T'ang era onwards more and more of the bureaucracy was recruited by these means, and thus a large part of the country's most talented individuals were syphoned off into government service. Nonetheless, the examination system was fated, by its very nature, to become a conservative and stereotyped institution, serving ultimately to hamper future intellectual growth by its emphasis on Confucian orthodoxy. While theoretically the examinations were open to practically all comers, the bright peasant lad included, in reality, the lengthy and costly preparations needed to acquire the indispensable mastery of the Classics effectively continued to restrict entry into the bureaucracy to the landowner families.

The expansion of the examination system was accompanied by a corresponding growth of education, as exemplified by the restored Imperial University which, by the eighth century, had over 2000 students. Both phenomena were responsible for the re-emergence, after its eclipse during the Period of Division, of Confucianism, which once again was destined to become the dominant political ideology, systematically supported by all the T'ang rulers, regardless of their own religious predilections.

The lessons of history were not lost on the Early T'ang emperors; they were fully conscious of the fact that the principal cause of their predecessor's collapse had been peasant discontent. It was with this in mind, above all, that the first T'ang rulers, especially T'ai-tsung, implemented the land equalization policy on a larger scale than ever before. There was now a great quantity of abandoned land, and the plots allocated were also proportionately larger. New provisions made it possible for the peasant to reduce his taxes by performing more corvée, or vice versa. It is also probable that within the next two generations the stipulation that the land be returned fell into abeyance and it became the peasants' permanent property. It is quite likely that in the Early T'ang a major part of the peasantry, having received land, was composed of free smallholders. Thus not only was the social crisis alleviated, but the further existence of a numerous, free, tax-paying and corvée-rendering peasantry was guaranteed for the time being. This also made it possible to continue to base the state's armed forces on the militia system, of which the peasantry remained the backbone.

The above measures soon produced the desired results; agricultural production grew rapidly and the government's revenue increased proportionately, with taxation kept on a moderate level. Financial stability was to be maintained throughout most of the first century of T'ang rule. The conciliatory policy followed towards the peasants did not mean that the position of the landowners was affected adversely in any fashion. The landed estates of the great families, and of the Buddhist establishment, remained intact, and shortly the cyclical process of further concentration of landownership was to recommence, gathering momentum in the eighth century, and bringing in its wake, by the ninth century, the inevitable exacerbation of the social crisis.

The political stability of the Early T'ang contributed to improving still further the standing of the country's ruling class which, due to the traditions of the Northern Dynasties, assumed to a large degree an aristocratic nature. The T'ang nobility and the higher ranking officials were all exempt from taxation and, in fact, supported by the state. Hence, they were also the main beneficiaries of the economic prosperity created by the toil of the peasantry. The great wealth of this upper class and its lavish mode of life did serve to stimulate a further growth of the economy, especially of trade. The demand for luxury goods was said to be so heavy, that the roads leading to Ch'ang-an from all directions were simply clogged with merchant caravans.

In its composition, the T'ang ruling class was far from homogeneous; the position of the great aristocratic families of the northwest, associated with the Lis in their rise to power, was challenged by the elite landowner clans of East China, with their claim to be the true heirs of Chinese culture. In step with the growth of the bureaucracy and the implementation of the examination system, the landowning families most closely bound up with these processes became the main component of the ruling stratum.

The general upsurge of the economy in the Early T'ang period, generated by the growth of agricultural production, was also reflected in the further development of handicrafts, especially in the manufacture of silk, paper and porcelain. This was true, both in respect to the many state manufactories and the increasing number of private producers, now associated in guilds. The growth of domestic trade was further facilitated by the marked improvement of communications, and led to the rise of new trading communities. Foreign trade remained, however, largely under the control of foreign merchants, whose numerous colonies were to be found in the capital and the southern ports. Further urban development was a logical concomitant; it pertained, above all, to Ch'ang-an, the splendid checkerboard-like T'ang capital which, with its population of one million by the eighth century, was indisputably the largest and most civilized city in the world. It was noted for its cosmopolitan air, since many thousands of foreigners from various parts of Asia resided within its walls, treated with a tolerance assuredly derived from a sense of stability and self-confidence. It was indubitably the least xenophobic era in Chinese history.

The achievement of domestic consolidation was quickly utilized by the T'ang emperors for initiating a policy of territorial expansion. In this endeavour they were to prove to be infinitely more successful than the Sui, and the consequence was not disaster, but the creation of an empire still larger than the Han. Their foremost antagonists were the Eastern Turks, their former allies, who were powerful enough to launch in 624 an invasion which brought their horsemen almost to the gates of Ch'ang-an. However, a revolt by some of their subject tribes, the Uighurs in particular, greatly weakened them, and enabled T'ai-tsung to defeat them decisively in 627–8. As a result, the Eastern Turkish empire fell apart, the Ordos region and most of East Mongolia were annexed by the Chinese, while hundreds of thousands of Turkish tribesmen were resettled in North China. The Western Turks remained to be dealt with, and here the main bone of contention was mastery of the Western Regions. By 648 a series of campaigns, waged with the help of the Uighurs, led to the establishment of T'ang rule over this area. The renewal of Chinese control of the Silk Route brought about a marked increase in trade, but whether this proved advantageous to China is debatable. Silk cloth remained the main export item while primarily luxury goods were imported.

At the height of its power the T'ang empire claimed sovereignty over most of Central Asia, including the lands west of the Pamirs, such as Bukhara, Samarkand and Ferghana. In reality, the Chinese influence in this area was quite fragile, and the peoples subjected to T'ang rule, mostly Turkish tribes, fought incessantly, and ultimately successfully, to regain their freedom.

The westward expansion during the Early T'ang also led to significant contacts with Tibet, especially during the reign of its first unifier, Srong-btsan-sgam-po (617–50), whose marriage to Wen-chang, a T'ang princess, resulted in the introduction of some elements of Chinese culture into Tibet. The Tibetans were soon to become a military power and a dangerous threat to the Chinese position in Central Asia, but the truly critical phase in the relations between the two countries came in the middle of the eighth century.

During the reign of T'ai-tsung Chinese armies renewed their war of aggression against Korea and initially, in the years 644–6, they also met with little success. Only later, when allied with Silla, the state in Southeast Korea, were the Chinese able to achieve first the destruction of Paekche, in Southwest Korea, and later the conquest of Koguryo. This made it possible for Silla to unite all Korea in 678 and effectively preserve its independence, while paying lip service to Chinese suzerainty. Nonetheless, it was precisely this period which witnessed the striking impact of Chinese culture in all its aspects on Korea, whose civilization henceforth was almost a carbon copy of the Chinese. This was particularly true of political institutions which were modelled faithfully on those of the T'ang.

Earlier, Korea had been an intermediary in the transmission of Chinese culture to Japan, as shown in the instance of Buddhism which had become so important in both those countries. But during the first two centuries of T'ang rule, direct contact between China and Japan flourished unceasingly and resulted in an unparalleled flow of Chinese influence, whose effects were almost as far-reaching as in the case of Korea. Even today there is a much better chance of finding extant examples of T'ang art and architecture in Japan than in China. However, although so much of Chinese culture was transplanted, the Japanese did succeed in assimilating this great gift, while largely preserving the originality of their own civilization.

The first century of T'ang rule also saw the unfolding of closer relations with Persia, India, Ceylon and Southeast Asia, while Arab merchants were especially active in expanding trade with China on the southern maritime routes. Occasional contacts were made even with the Byzantine Empire. All this made possible the further enrichment of Chinese culture with new elements, while simultaneously such great Chinese inventions as paper now began their trek westward.

A concomitant result was the entry into China of new foreign religions, but none of these was to gain anything resembling the influence attained by Buddhism, since they remained basically restricted to the sizable colonies of foreign merchants. Zoroastrianism was linked with the Persians; Manichaeism had been brought in by the Syrians, but its importance increased considerably when the entire Uighur people became converted to this fascinating and severely dualistic creed. Nestorianism was propagated by both Syrians and Persians, while the Arabs were the main bearers of Islam. All these religions were able to benefit from the T'ang policy of complete toleration, which remained in effect for two hundred years, in such striking contrast with the contemporary history of the Mediterranean world.

The foundations of the T'ang empire had been laid so solidly during T'ai-tsung's reign that it was not to be appreciably affected by the turbulent political events of the subsequent half a century. His successor, Kao-tsung (650–83), proved to be a vacillating and ineffective ruler, and from 660 on real power rested in the hands of the Empress Wu. A former concubine of T'ai-tsung, Wu Chao, indisputably highly gifted, proved to be one of the most ruthless, unscrupulous and tyrannical rulers in the long history of the Middle Kingdom. After Kao-tsung's death she remained the unchallenged, absolute master of the empire, and having set aside the puppet-like rule of two of her own sons, she proclaimed herself in 698 the empress of a new dynasty, the Chou. It was to end in 705 when, at the age of eighty-two, she was finally forced to abdicate. A brilliant manipulator of factions within the ruling class, the appallingly cruel Wu Chao was unstinting in her use of terror against all opponents, real and imaginary. Her numerous victims included most of the Li imperial clan. As distinct from T'ai-tsung, who treated Buddhism with disdain, viewing it as a vulgar foreign sect devoted to deluding the masses with tricks, the Empress Wu was its fervent patron, probably not only because of her amorous predilection for Buddhist monks. As a result, the Buddhist establishment reached the height of its political and economic power during her rule. The attempts made in the years 1966–76, for obvious current requirements, to portray her as a very progressive statesman, representing the interests of the new bureaucratic landlord families against the old T'ang aristocracy, can be safely dismissed with the contempt they deserve.

After the removal of Empress Wu from power in 705, one of the former puppet emperors, Chung-tsung, was replaced on the throne, but history seemed to repeat itself since his consort, Empress Wei, also aiming at total power for herself, had him poisoned in 710. However, a coup soon organized by Li Lung-chi, the son of the second puppet emperor, Jui-tsung, led to her assassination and the extermination of her entire clan. In 712 Jui-tsung ceded the throne to his son, who as Emperor Hsüan-tsung (712–56) was to preside over what, on the surface, appeared to be the full restoration of the glory and prosperity of the T'ang empire.

Middle and Late T'ang

The cultural brilliance of Hsüan-tsung's reign, which has caused it to be called the Golden Age of T'ang civilization, served to conceal a process in which the basic principles that the empire had been founded upon were steadily undermined. While political stability had been restored after decades of murderous strife and corruption, the social crisis was to resurface once again with full force. The main cause rested in the breakdown of the land equalization system which, by the middle of the eighth century, had, in effect, ceased to function. Henceforth, as Twitchett has noted, no future dynasty succeeded in imposing the system of land allocation; it was to be undertaken again only after 1949. The collapse of this system was brought about primarily by the incessant spread of great estates which, by this same period, had acquired much of the best land and assumed a dominant position in the economy. Some authors maintain that the manorial system, whose roots rested in the Eastern Han, now really began to flourish and became a decisive feature of Chinese feudalism, at least to the Mongol conquest.

The growth of the rural population, increasing the pressure on the land and leading to a diminution in the size of the peasants' holdings, was a contributing element in bringing about the progressing deterioration of their economic position. The result of both these factors was the constant decrease in the number of tax-paying peasant smallholders; according to the 754 census, there were only 7.6 million tax-payers out of a total population of 52.8 million. A concomitant effect was the falling into abeyance of the peasant militia system which was gradually replaced by a mercenary professional army. By 742 this force, in which the number of nomad auxiliaries increased steadily, numbered 574,000, of which 490,000 were stationed on the frontiers. This constituted a much greater drain – a fivefold increase since 714 – on the government's financial reserves than the previous arrangement, at a time when its revenues from taxes on agriculture declined, while its expenditures, also in view of the luxurious extravagance of Hsüan-tsung's court, kept mounting. Thus a financial crisis was inevitably drawing close.

Conflicts within the ruling stratum had not disappeared with the renewal of political stability during the early part of Hsüan-tsung's reign, but were kept within bounds. However, during his last decades on the throne, Hsüan-tsung ceased to interest himself in the control of the government, and was content to delegate it to others. Thus, against the background of increasing strife of bureaucratic cliques, Li Lin-fu, a member of the imperial clan, was able to establish what amounted to his own dictatorship during the years 736–52. The policies followed during this period, especially the establishment of military governors in the frontier regions, were to have fatal consequences for the dynasty.

The strong position of the T'ang empire, as established by T'ai-tsung, also began to weaken during the last twenty years of Hsüan-tsung's reign. Undoubtedly the most important single event was the devastating defeat suffered in 751 by the T'ang army at the hands of the Arabs in the historic battle of Atlach (on the Talass River in North Kirghizia). As a result, Chinese rule in Central Asia collapsed like a house of cards, not to be restored for a millennium, and then by the Manchus at that. In the southwest, the state of Nan-chao, ethnically mostly Thai, inflicted a severe defeat in the same year on the T'ang forces and remained a threat to Szechuan for the next century. The northeast now began to be troubled by a new group of nomad tribes, the Khitan, who within the next two centuries were to prove their mettle as truly dangerous enemies of Chinese rule in this region. It was this deterioration of the empire's position which had led not only to the changes in the army's structure mentioned above, but also to the substantial increase in power of the military governors on the frontiers. The latter, becoming 'a tail too big to wag', soon proved to be a much greater danger to the rule of the T'ang than to the external enemies.

By the early 750s An Lu-shan, an illiterate former slave of Turkish and Sogdian origin, and now a general in command of three districts in the northeast, had become the most powerful of the military governors. A cunning, grotesquely obese man, he had, as a protégé of Li Lin-fu, taken part in the court intrigues of Ch'ang-an and successfully wormed himself into the confidence of Hsüan-tsung. Moreover, playing the buffoon, he had become the favourite of the redoubtable Yang Kuei-fei, the all-powerful concubine with whom the emperor was absolutely besotted. Nonetheless, after her cousin Yang Kuo-chung assumed dictatorial powers upon Li Lin-fu's death, An Lu-shan felt his position threatened and masterfully laid his plan for gaining power, while successfully retaining the emperor's confidence. In 755 all was ready, and An Lu-shan marched from Peking at the head of a 150,000-strong army, including a large force of nomad cavalry. His troops met with almost no resistance and, having easily taken Loyang, he proclaimed himself emperor of a new dynasty, Yen, while his chief general, Shih Ssu-ming, also a Turk, advanced on Ch'ang-an. In face of this threat, Hsüan-tsung fled towards Szechuan but on the way his escorting troops revolted, killed Yang Kuo-chung and demanded the death of Yang Kuei-fei. The emperor consented to have her strangled, and thus was able to continue his journey. This dramatic episode has become famous, particularly due to Po Chü-i's best-known poem, 'The Everlasting Remorse'.

In view of his flight, Hsüan-tsung's heir apparent assumed the throne (Su-tsung, 756–62), and the T'ang forces led by the talented and resourceful Kuo Tzu-i (697–781), aided by a large and invaluable Uighur army, began a counteroffensive against An Lu-shan, already in control of Ch'ang-an as well. The war dragged on for years, ending in a partial victory for the T'ang in 763. Its outcome was to a certain degree determined by discord in the rebel camp, which cost both An Lu-shan and Shih Ssu-ming their lives. This made it possible for the T'ang to conclude a peace with the remaining rebel commanders, which left the latter in charge of their forces and in control of a large part of North and Northeast China. The victory was doubly hollow, for the rebellion had not only revealed the dynasty's weakness but also had dealt it a blow from which it was never able to recover fully. The devastation caused by eight years of warfare was immense, but it is impossible to assume, as some authors do, that since the 754 census showed a population of 52.8 million and the one in 766 only 16.9 million, then 36 million had lost their lives. What these figures do show was the loss of the government's effective control over a major part of the country; the provincial authorities did not submit the proper reports, nor pay in the revenue which was due.

After the conclusion of the An Lu-shan rebellion, the T'ang government never succeeded in re-establishing full control over the empire; at least 25 to 30 per cent of the country remained under the rule of the provincial military governors, who, in some cases, converted their posts into hereditary ones. Attempts to curb their power were countered by a new successful rebellion in the northeast in the years 781–2. Only during the reign of Hsien-tsung (805–20), the sole able ruler in the entire Late T'ang period, did the government manage to whittle down the number of completely independent provinces.

The Walled Kingdom

The political status of the T'ang monarchy underwent a steady process of deterioration, which was especially sharply illustrated by the unprecedented rise in power of the eunuchs. Although they had already gained considerable influence during Hsüan-tsung's reign, it was only towards the end of the eighth century that the eunuchs, numbering around 4000, became the strongest faction in the central government, having acquired ever greater control over the armed forces. They were also, once again, in charge of an effective secret police, spying on their potential enemies in the bureaucracy. Henceforth, they became more and more the real masters of the country. Hsien-tsung was the first, though not the last, ruler to be killed by the eunuchs, and eight out of the nine emperors to mount the throne later were handpicked by the eunuchs. These rulers were also a cretinously credulous lot; at least four of them died from imbibing elixirs of immortality (usually mercury) prepared by Taoist alchemists. While conflict between the eunuchs, often divided into rival groups, and cliques of officials was constant, there is no doubt that, after the failure of an attempt in 835 to exterminate them, their position remained practically unassailable until the end of the dynasty, and even stronger than it had been during the Eastern Han. A penetrating analysis of the phenomenon of eunuch power within the framework of the Chinese autocratic monarchy remains to be written.

The loss of Central Asia in the 750s was followed by a series of fierce Tibetan attacks on the northwestern lands of the T'ang. In 763, after conquering most of Kansu, the Tibetans were able to penetrate into Shensi and take Ch'ang-an itself. It was only the aid of the Uighurs, who remained the main power on the steppes up to 840, which made it possible to beat back the Tibetans effectively, but the generally weakened position of the T'ang government precluded any attempt to restore its rule in the Western Regions.

A number of significant changes took place in the government's economic policy in the wake of the An Lu-shan rebellion, which, of course, had brought the T'ang finances to the brink of bankruptcy. The most important of the new measures adopted was the introduction in 780 of an entirely new system of taxation, the Double Tax (collected in spring and autumn), which involved considerable simplification and was, theoretically at least, to be applied to all landowners, large and small. Hence it constituted for a while a certain lessening of the burdens on the peasants, but the effects of this wore off quickly, especially as the great landowning families reverted to their habitual evasion of taxes, always rendered easier by their effective control of the bureaucracy on the central and local level. Thus, after 763, while the government's financial situation improved temporarily and the economy, as a whole, kept progressing throughout the ninth century, the further growth in the size and number of the great estates gathered momentum, thus creating the conditions for a new exacerbation of the social crisis, for a new peasant rebellion destined to bring the T'ang dynasty crashing down.

It seems quite clear that the most famous persecution of the Buddhist church, which was carried out during the reign of Wu-tsung (841–6), was motivated primarily by financial considerations. The immense wealth of the Buddhist establishment appeared irresistible, especially at a time when the government's financial situation left much to be desired. The attack on the Buddhists was preceded by the total extirpation in 843 of the Manichaean church, left deprived of Uighur protection. In 845 an imperial edict called for the destruction of 4600 temples and monasteries, 40,000 smaller shrines, the secularization of 260,000 monks and nuns, and the transfer to the state of 150,000 temple slaves. But the crucial stipulation was the confiscation of the truly vast amount of land owned by the Buddhist establishment. While the edict was repealed two years later by Wu-tsung's successor, and Buddhism largely recovered from these blows, it was never quite able to regain its earlier impressive position. The fate of two other creeds, affected by persecution at the same time, was different. No trace was left of Nestorianism and Zoroastrianism.

The first harbingers of an impending catastrophe also appeared in the 850s. In 859 a peasant uprising, led by Ch'iu Fu, took place in Chekiang; over 30,000 peasants participated in the rising which was suppressed with much difficulty. The reliability itself of the government's armed forces began to seem questionable, especially in view of the revolt in 868 of troops stationed in Kweichow. Led by P'ang Hsün these soldiers marched back to their native Kiangsu, where they gained much support from the local population; after a year's bitter struggle they were finally defeated by the use of nomad auxiliaries.

The floodgates of mass discontent, aroused by a worsening economic situation, verging in places on famine, the rapacity of the bureaucracy, the oppression of the government and ruthless exploitation by the landlords, burst in 874, when one of the greatest peasant rebellions in Chinese history began. Its two principal leaders were Wang Hsien-chih and Huang Ch'ao. Both came from merchant families, and the latter, having failed to pass the examinations, had been unsuccessful in his efforts to become an official. Starting in southern Hopei the insurrection spread, with many local units taking up the struggle against the authorities. The T'ang government, nominally headed by an imbecilic emperor, and, in fact, under total eunuch control, proved utterly incapable of coping with the situation, especially in view of the fact that its generals were completely unwilling to fight for its preservation, and quite ready to support a new dynasty if it were to arise.

Against this background, the insurgents, in spite of some defeats in one of which Wang Hsien-chih was killed, were able to continue their campaign. Under the command of Huang Ch'ao, now their undisputed leader, they marched into Fukien in 878, and then still further west, ultimately reaching Canton. The city refused to surrender, and its capture in 879 was followed by a massacre of the population including, according to Arab sources, a prosperous 120,000-strong community of foreign merchants – Moslems, Zoroastrians, Christians and Jews. It might well be that actions of this kind have caused the *Cambridge History of China* to commit the seeming inconsistency of referring to Huang Ch'ao's followers as 'bandits' – the description employed in orthodox Chinese historical writing – while simultaneously recognizing the movement as a popular rebellion of immense proportions. The victory in Kwangtung soon proved pyrrhic, inasmuch as malaria decimated Huang Ch'ao's army. He led the remnants to the Yangtse Valley and, having crossed the river, was heavily defeated. However, the T'ang generals let him escape and flee southwards. Huang Ch'ao was soon able to gather new forces, recross the Great River, and in 880 capture Loyang without meeting any resistance. The strategic T'ungkuan Pass was also not defended by a starving T'ang force, and Huang Ch'ao's army, its ranks swollen to several hundred thousands by T'ang defectors, made an impressive entry into Ch'ang-an, the troops dressed in brocade, while their leader rode in a golden carriage. A massacre of all the higher officials and members of the imperial family who had not fled the capital together with the emperor soon followed. Huang Ch'ao now proclaimed himself emperor of a new dynasty – the Ch'i.

The success of the rebellion proved, however, to be completely illusory. Although Huang Ch'ao's army had traversed so much of the country, they failed to establish a stable government in any of the areas they had occupied. The same was to hold true after the capture of Ch'ang-an, and the insurgents were soon isolated in the capital, cut off from food supplies, and reduced to desperate straits. Nevertheless, they managed to hold their position for two years in face of incessant attacks by their enemy. It was not, however, the T'ang army which was to achieve a victory in the struggle against Huang Ch'ao, but the Sha-t'o, reputedly the bravest of the brave of the Turkish tribes, called in to aid the faltering T'ang government. Their talented commander, Li K'o-yung, known as the 'One-Eyed Dragon', assembled a 40,000-strong cavalry force of his tribesmen; dressed all in black, and known as Li's Black Crows, they were to become a terror to all Chinese. Li's army was able to drive out Huang Ch'ao, aided in this by defections in the latter's ranks, including that of Chu Wen, one of his chief generals. In 884, after his still sizable army was defeated in Honan, Huang Ch'ao fled with a thousand men to his native Shantung to meet his death there, probably by his own hand. The great rebellion was over; the T'ang emperor returned to desolated and deserted Ch'ang-an, 'where grass grew on the streets and hares and foxes gambolled'. Although it was still to linger on borrowed time for two more decades, the T'ang dynasty had, in reality, received its deathblow. All power now fell into the hands of the provincial warlords, among whom the main contenders were Li K'o-yung and Chu Wen, the future founder of the Later Liang.

T'ang Literature and Art

At no time in the past had culture flourished in China as extensively as it did in the T'ang era, especially during the reign of Hsüan-tsung, justly renowned for his role as a munificent patron of the arts. While this development affected all fields, it was particularly striking in literature and painting.

Poetry constituted the most outstanding achievement of these three centuries, which are unanimously regarded as the Golden Age. The output was certainly prodigious; the corpus of T'ang poetry published in 1707 contains 48,900 poems from the brush of 2600 authors. The intricacies of Chinese poetry are a fascinating subject; it seems advisable to refer the reader to the many specialized studies, of which J. T. Liu's *The Art of Chinese Poetry* is perhaps the most illuminating. Largely due to the difficulties involved, only a minor part of these works has been translated into European languages, but some of the renditions, Waley's in particular, are admirable.

Chinese authors unfailingly cast two writers – Li Po and Tu Fu – in the role of the foremost T'ang poets. Li Po (Li T'ai-po, 701–62), a poetic genius, was noted for his lyricism, the richness of his language and versatility of form and style. An unconventional individual, with strong Taoist leanings, Li Po found it impossible to make a comfortable niche for himself in Hsüan-tsung's court to which, due to his great reputation, he had been invited. His love of wine gave rise to the legend that he met his end by drowning, having wished to embrace the moon's reflection in the water. Tu Fu (712–70) was as talented as his close friend Li Po, but his poetry is considered more sombre and profound, displaying a far greater awareness of the troubled times he lived in, and the suffering to which they gave rise. This may have been caused by the distress with which he and his family were afflicted, particularly during the An Lu-shan rebellion. While acknowledging the eminence of Li Po and Tu Fu, some Western authorities, such as Waley, are inclined to regard another famous poet of the same period, Wang Wei (701–61), just as highly. A brilliant man, equally gifted as a poet, painter, calligrapher and musician, Wang Wei epitomized the ideal which so many future generations of scholar-officials strove to attain.

The most eminent poet of the Middle T'ang, Po Chü-i (772–846), led a much more conventional existence than either Li Po or Tu Fu, having pursued a relatively successful career in the imperial bureaucracy, which led him ultimately to very high posts. While some of his earlier poems can be considered as satirical, in his later works he struck a very personal note and, when read together, his verses make up a touching autobiography. Po Chü-i was famed for the simplicity of his language which was close to the colloquial and hence quite comprehensible to his contemporaries.

Mention should be made of at least two more figures famous in T'ang literature. Han Yü (769–824), a fine poet, was even more renowned for his essays and his efforts to reform literary style by advocating a return to the simplicity and conciseness of the Western Han era. He was also a militantly orthodox Confucianist, later considered to be a precursor of Neo-Confucianism, and a fearless opponent of Buddhism at the height of its power. His objections to Buddhism were based primarily on its foreign origins and its superstitious nature. His best-known work is surely his essay written in 819, condemning a ceremony of worship of a Buddhist relic in which the emperor himself participated. His audacity was punished by exile to malaria-ridden Kwangtung. Liu Tsung-yüan (773–819) was associated with Han Yü in the endeavours to develop a prose style based on the Han model, and equally known as a fine essayist. He was the author of the satirical parable 'The Snake Catchers', portraying the oppression of the peasants by the tax collectors. For his connection with the unsuccessful 805 reform movement, directed primarily against the eunuch ascendancy, Liu Tsung-yüan spent his remaining years in exile.

The great influence exerted by Buddhism on Chinese culture throughout most of the T'ang is illustrated in the field of literature perhaps most aptly by the activities of Hsüan-tsang (602–64), the most famous pilgrim of its early period. Having made his way to India in 629 by way of Central Asia, Hsüan-tsang spent sixteen years studying and collecting Buddhist scriptures. After his return, a much celebrated event, he spent his remaining twenty years supervising, at the head of a large team, the translation of over 1300 works into Chinese. But his place in Chinese literature is due more to the famous account of his adventures, 'The Records of Travels in the Western Countries', a work universally known, due also to the novels and plays based on it.

It is obviously not fortuitous that the origins of printing, perhaps the greatest of all the many Chinese inventions, should reach back to the Early T'ang, although large-scale printing of books was to wait for the Sung era. Block printing, the form adopted, was derived clearly from the practice of taking rubbings, and presented certain distinct advantages in view of the great multitude and variety of Chinese characters. The use of movable type still preceded the Gutenberg Bible by at least five centuries.

During the T'ang era Chinese historiography acquired an organizational form of fundamental significance for its future in the establishment of the Historical Office. Its task was to undertake to record the history of the five preceding dynasties and to gather materials for the future writing of the history of the reigning house. Thus, historical writing henceforth became primarily a governmental function, and this clearly affected the nature of the work to be produced in the future. In line with the general tenor of Confucian philosophy, the past was to be studied not only for its own sake, but also for didactic purposes, to serve as a mirror for the present which would aid, above all, in the achievement of a well-ordered government. Hence, emphasis was placed almost entirely on political history, on the activities of the rulers and the political measures they implemented. Evaluation in this domain tended to follow stereotyped formulas, especially when castigating undesirable phenomena. Thus, the dynastic histories were, in Bálazs's apt phrase, 'written primarily by bureaucrats for bureaucrats'. Little attention was paid to economic problems or social issues, while the lives and conditions of the governed were ignored almost totally. Since the official historiography was to record the doings of the rulers, it was logical that the periodization employed would follow the pattern set by Pan Ku, and segment history according to reigning dynasties. Thus, rather arbitrary and superficial criteria were applied. Nonetheless, whatever its drawbacks, official historiography was to produce a most impressive and monumental series of 24 dynastic histories; the 1747 edition is contained in 219 large volumes. Hence, an authoritative historical record was created, spanning almost two thousand years and unsurpassed by that of any other nation.

The work of the official historians, according to the pattern established during the T'ang, included the keeping of a daily diary relating to the activities of the emperor. This material was used together with reports from the ministries to compose the Daily Records. The latter constituted the basis for compiling the Veritable

Records of each reign, actually a current history. They were, in turn, the main source employed by the subsequent dynasty for writing the history of its predecessor. Hence, official documentation provided the basic material for the dynastic history, arranged in the composite form established by Ssu-ma Ch'ien and Pan Ku. It is difficult to determine the degree of objectivity of these works, but one can assume that it was affected by the generally conservative views of the compilers and the almost inevitable influence exerted by the government itself. The limitations of official historiography were criticized sharply already during the T'ang by Liu Chih-chi (662–721), a talented and independently minded historian. In his *Shih-t'ung* ('Generalities on History'), a pioneer work of historical criticism on a world scale, Liu dealt not only with technical problems and classifications, but also with the most fundamental issue facing a historian, the question of 'honest' writing.

Historical writing was never restricted during any period to dynastic histories. In the T'ang, institutional political history was inaugurated by Tu Yu (735–812) in his *T'ung-tien* ('Comprehensive Statutes'). In this encyclopedia Tu Yu, disregarding the chronological sequence of dynastic history, arranged his material according to a number of basic subjects, thus setting a different pattern for similar works in the future.

It is generally held that Buddhist art, and sculpture in particular, was at its best in the T'ang period. Unfortunately, very few specimens of Buddhist sculpture have survived, with the exception of some statues in Lung-men. The losses sustained during persecution in 845 were severe, probably equalled only by the ravages which so many Buddhist temples were subjected to during the 'cultural revolution' of 1966–76. From the tenth century on, Buddhist sculpture lost most of its originality and vigour and became increasingly stereotyped. There are also only a few extant examples of secular sculpture; the best known are the fine bas-reliefs of his favourite charger on T'ai-tsung's tomb. Paradoxically, it is the funeral pottery figures, intended to please not the living but the dead, which constitute the main form of surviving T'ang sculpture. The marvellously animated and colourful figures, covering a great range of subjects from the famous horses and their grooms to the graceful dancers, unintentionally provide a splendidly vivid glimpse of life in the T'ang age.

There is little doubt that during the T'ang architecture flourished as never before. Not only were the emperors extravagantly lavish in beautifying their capitals, but the Buddhist establishment, at the height of its power, also devoted much of its colossal wealth to the building of innumerable temples and shrines. But here too, as in the case of sculpture, due to the perishability of the material used, and the devastations of war and persecutions, almost nothing has survived with the exception of one small temple in northern Shansi. In Japan, on the other hand, there are 22 extant structures built during the epoch reflecting direct T'ang influence. It is from these, and from Chinese paintings, that one can seek to get an inkling of this lost splendour.

The T'ang era was decisive for painting, the greatest Chinese art, since it saw the establishment of those fundamental principles which were to guide it in the future. It seems quite likely that most of the works produced were devoted to religious subjects, Buddhist ones in particular. However, not a single work of this type from the brush of the renowned T'ang masters has survived; only some murals in Tunhuang, interesting but not great art, date from these centuries.

It can be maintained that Chinese genius in this domain has shown itself mostly in figure painting and especially in landscapes, which might well be considered China's most significant contribution to world art. The T'ang masters had already raised both genres to a very high level and the latter was to be surpassed only by their Sung successors.

The most eminent painters of figures included Yen Li-pen (*fl.* 640–70), the creator of the well-known scroll 'Portraits of the Emperors', as well as Chang Hsüan (*fl.* 713–32) and Chou Fang (*fl.* 780–810), both of whom specialized in portraying lissome court ladies. Han Kan (720–80) was noted for his paintings of horses, a subject pursued with success up to the Yüan. But in the case of the above artists, it seems almost certain that the works attributed to them today are, in fact, all later copies. Only Li Chen's portraits of Buddhist patriarchs, taken to Japan in the ninth century, are unquestionably original.

The vicissitudes of fate have dealt most severely with the work of Wu Tao-tzu (*c.* 700–60), universally considered the greatest painter of the T'ang era. A few originals were supposed to have existed in the eleventh century, but not a single painting has come down to the present. He is said to have been immensely gifted and prolific, with over 300 frescoes in Ch'ang-an and Loyang to his credit. Some idea of what his broad and sweeping style was like might be obtained from the stone engravings reputedly modelled on his paintings. The work of two masters regarded as the initiators of two basic styles in landscape painting, has fared no better. Li Ssu-hsün (651–716) painted on silk, with blue and green being most prominent in his palette, while the picture was rendered with painstaking care in minute detail. Some of the finest works in the long history of Chinese painting were created in this style, but it was also one which could be easily copied or imitated by skilled craftsmen. Wang Wei, already mentioned for his poetry, is credited with originating ink monochrome painting, but he also employed the blue-green style, as shown by the famous hand scroll on which he depicted his estate, Wang Ch'uan. More than likely both these masters did not establish the styles mentioned, but were simply their best-known representatives. The foundations had been laid and the scene prepared for the splendour of the Sung era.

5. The Sung Dynasties and the Northern Invaders

The Five Dynasties and the Ten Kingdoms

The collapse of the T'ang signified that once again China was to undergo an era of anarchy and discord, in which the centralized and unified empire was torn apart, as it had been after the fall of the Eastern Han. Although the consequences were in some respects even more dire, especially as far as the suffering of the people was concerned, this time the period of division, referred to by Chinese historians as the Five Dynasties and the Ten Kingdoms, was to be of much shorter duration, lasting less than two generations. It seems probable that the principal reason for this rested in a general recognition of the obvious advantages of unity, as experienced during the heyday of the T'ang.

The term 'Five Dynasties' is a misleading fiction devised by later Chinese historians for the purpose of presenting a supposed continuity of imperial rule. In fact, the area ruled by them was restricted to a part of North and Central China, while the remainder of the country was divided into a number of various independent states, referred to as the Ten Kingdoms. Politically, the Five Dynasties were in effect military dictatorships, a continuation on only a slightly larger scale of the evil practice of rule by military governors. Instability was their main characteristic, and none of them had the capability of consolidating their power. During the fifty-four years of their existence, there were thirteen emperors from eight different families, the majority of Sha-t'o origin. Warfare was almost endemic throughout this period, the economy ruined as a result, with the northwest suffering further irreparable damage.

The first of the Five Dynasties, the Later Liang, was established in 904 by Chu Wen, one of the most treacherous, ruthless and cruel figures in Chinese history, responsible for murdering the last T'ang

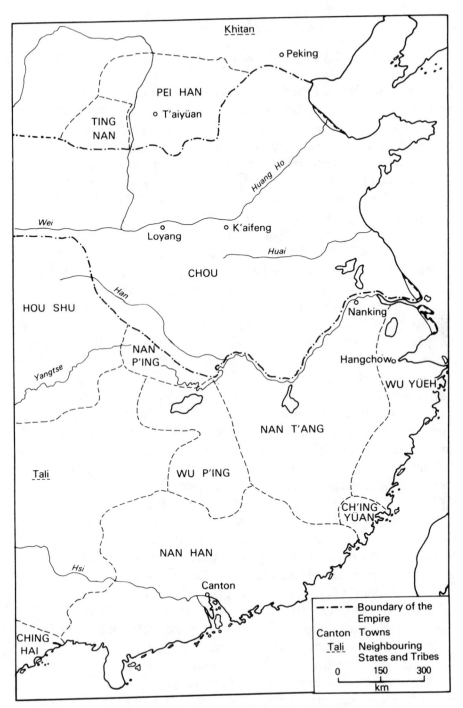

12. The Five Dynasties and Ten Kingdoms, c. 955

ruler and exterminating most of the Li imperial family. The main enemy of the Liang was the Sha-t'o state of Chin (Shansi) ruled by Li K'o-yung's son. In 923 the Chin army easily achieved victory over its rival, thus giving rise to the next dynasty, the Later T'ang (923–36). The Sha-t'o were, however, numerically insignificant, and under their rule the Chinese great landowning families regained most of their previous power, especially their control of local government. A rebellion by one of its main generals, Shih Ching-t'ang, also a Sha-t'o, put an end to the Later T'ang. His dynasty, the Later Chin (936–47), was noted for being the first to bow to the pressure of the Khitan, having ceded a large area in North China to them in exchange for military aid received. The Khitan were said to be descendants of the proto-Mongol Hsien-pi and resided originally in western Liaoning and eastern Inner Mongolia. They had, as noted, already appeared as a threat to China in the eighth century. By the beginning of the tenth century the Khitan tribes had formed a powerful confederation, which was subsequently transformed by Apaochi, one of the tribal chieftains, into a strong nomadic monarchy. In 916 he proclaimed himself emperor of the Khitan, seeking to establish a state on the Chinese model. Having increased the area under their control by expanding southwards, the Khitan adopted in 936 the name of Liao for their empire, and their intentions to undertake further conquests became evident. Although they had been instrumental in aiding the establishment of the Later Chin dynasty, their relations with its second emperor worsened, thus providing a pretext for the beginning of hostilities in 944, followed two years later by a full-scale invasion. The military superiority of the Khitan, due primarily to their excellent cavalry, proved decisive. Their forces swooped down to capture the Chin capital, K'aifeng, and took the emperor prisoner. It was only the determined resistance of the Chinese population which forced the Khitan to forsake their plans for ruling the newly conquered territory and to retreat to the north. Their behaviour followed the habitual mode of the northern nomads; pillage and massacres reduced an immense area around K'aifeng to a desert.

The fourth dynasty, the Later Han (947–50), arose largely against the background of resistance to the Khitan. It proved to be the shortest of these ephemeral regimes, and its second ruler fell victim to a coup initiated by his own army, whose commander, Kuo Wei, a Chinese, now became the emperor of the Later Chou (950–60). This was the only one of the Five Dynasties which sought to deal with the problems of the ravaged country, by lowering taxes and promoting agricultural development. Its rulers also prepared their armed forces for an onslaught against the Khitan, with the aim of recovering the lands lost in the north.

In contrast with the dire conditions prevailing in the 'Empire' of the Five Dynasties, the area constituting the Ten Kingdoms was comparatively peaceful and prosperous. Thus, for example, in Southern T'ang, which covered present Anhwei, Kiangsu and Kiangsi, much progress was achieved in expanding agricultural production by means of extending the irrigation system and cultivating wasteland. On the whole, the governments of the Ten Kingdoms were also much less rapacious and oppressive than the military regimes of the north.

The Establishment of the Sung Dynasty

Another coup by the military put an end to the Later Chou dynasty, and, in a fashion reminiscent of the Roman Empire, the commander of the Imperial Guard, Chao K'uang-yin, was proclaimed the new emperor by the plotters. However, this time the choice had fallen on a remarkably astute individual, for Chao realized that if his new dynasty, the Sung, was to attain stability, then the political role of the army had to be swiftly and effectively terminated. In a renowned and oft-recounted manoeuvre, Chao, having summoned his top generals to a banquet, succeeded in persuading them to relinquish their posts in return for generous rewards. Subsequently, the army was thoroughly reorganized and subjected to strict control by the central government, becoming also in the process primarily a mercenary force. Periodic and compulsory rotation of commanders was introduced, while the post of military governor was abolished. The greatly expanded Imperial Guard, stationed mostly in or near the capital, became the most important component of the armed forces. By means of these measures the political power which the military had exercised for two centuries with such disastrous consequences was

13. Northern Sung, *c.* 1100

completely broken, and authority placed firmly in the hands of the central government and the emperor himself.

Chao K'uang-yin, known by his posthumous name as T'ai-tsu (960–76), demonstrated his political acumen also by the magnanimity he showed not only to the family and followers of the deposed Later Chou dynasty, but which he applied as well when undertaking the conquest of the southern kingdoms. This process of reunification was accomplished without any considerable difficulty and entailed relatively little use of force. However, neither T'ai-tsu nor his brother who succeeded him, T'ai-tsung (976–97), were able to prevail against the Khitan and bring about the restoration of the lands lost in the north. Some Chinese historians maintain that the Sung had waited too long to wage their campaigns against the Liao – the two main ones took place in 979 and 986 – having followed the supposedly faulty strategy of concentrating first on reunifying the south.

The rebuilding of an effective, centralized administration resulted also in the restoration of the examination system which reached its apogee under the Sung, becoming the principal source of recruitment for the government bureaucracy. In view of the clear determination of the first Sung emperors to stress the civilian nature of their administration, the role of the bureaucracy became particularly significant, and it helped to uphold and consolidate the dominance of the civilian element in political life, which was so characteristic of the Sung era. In time, however, the Sung bureaucracy became over-expanded, inefficient and exceedingly costly. As before, the overwhelming majority of those who passed all the three-level examinations, and thus assumed the top government posts, came from wealthy landlord families. But during the three centuries of the two Sung dynasties the composition of the ruling class itself underwent significant changes, with a decrease in the importance of the aristocracy, as compared with the T'ang era, and the emergence of a wide and differentiated stratum of landowning families, referred to usually, for want of a better term, as the Chinese gentry. It was precisely the ability of the gentry to provide the bulk of those destined to become government officials which characterized its political importance.

The successes obtained by the two first and ablest Sung emperors in reunifying the country and consolidating a viable administration also affected the nature of the government. In some respects, it was even more an absolute monarchy than its T'ang and Han predecessors, and thus the individual role of the emperor assumed still greater importance. While opinions differ greatly regarding those rulers who came after T'ai-tsu and T'ai-tsung, it would be fair to consider the majority of them as probably the most enlightened and humane sovereigns who presided over what is almost universally regarded as an era unsurpassed for the brilliance of its cultural and intellectual development.

The Sung empire differed greatly in one vital respect from the T'ang and the Han. It proved unable to engage in a successful policy of external aggrandizement and its territory was restricted mostly to ethnically Chinese lands. This state of affairs resulted probably not so much from a disinclination of the Sung rulers to follow their predecessors' footsteps, but from the largely fortuitous circumstance that their empire was surrounded on two sides by a number of strong and relatively well-organized states. Hence, in spite of numerous efforts, the Sung never succeeded in breaking through this encircling iron ring.

In the first century of Sung rule the Liao empire undoubtedly constituted its most challenging enemy. The Khitan had, in turn, taken their place as the masters of the steppes, and their power extended from the P'ohai Gulf to the T'ien Shan. But in their own state the Khitan themselves were a minority, outnumbered by the Chinese in the northern areas they had annexed. This territory was administered in the Chinese fashion, while in the non-Chinese parts of their empire the Liao sought to preserve their previous nomad governmental structure. Nonetheless, sinification of the Khitan made considerable progress, although they had invented two ways of writing their own language (one derived from the Uighur, the other from the Chinese). The growth of Chinese cultural influence did not signify, however, that the Khitan had abandoned their aggressive intentions towards their southern neighbours. A Khitan invasion of the Sung empire was terminated in 1004 by a peace treaty which, while leaving the frontiers unchanged, provided for the payment by the Sung of an annual tribute of 100,000 ounces of silver and 200,000 bolts of silk. The treaty of 1004, considered by most modern Chinese historians as humiliating and defeatist, did assure almost a century of peace between the two empires. Considering that the cost of the tribute was less than 2 per cent of the government's annual revenue, some of the Sung rulers and officials might well have regarded this Danegeld as both bearable and worth the peace it bought and brought.

The Khitan were not, however, the sole enemy of the Sung. In the northwest the pastoral Tangut tribes of Tibetan origin had grown in strength to the point of being able to organize their own state, the Hsia, by the end of the tenth century. Called Hsi (Western) Hsia by the Chinese, it embraced most of Kansu and northern Shensi, effectively cutting off the Sung from access to Central Asia. A large part of its population was Chinese and its development was much affected by Chinese culture. While the Tanguts had also devised a complex script for their language, based on the Chinese by way of the Khitan, in their case as well sinification advanced constantly, since both the administration of the state and the system of education were based on Chinese models. The Sung waged a number of large-scale and completely unsuccessful campaigns against the Hsi Hsia in the first half of the eleventh century. They were concluded by a treaty, signed in 1044, according to which the Chinese agreed to the payment of an annual tribute of 72,000 ounces of silver, 153,000 bolts of silk and 30,000 catties of tea. In spite of their own conflicts with the Hsi Hsia, the Liao were also able to utilize the hostilities between them and the Sung to extort from the latter in 1041 an increase in the tribute to 200,000 ounces of silver and 300,000 bolts of silk.

The first century of Sung rule witnessed a considerable upsurge in the country's economic development. Unification and the restoration of peace made possible a marked increase of agricultural production, particularly in the south, stimulated by a very extensive expansion of water conservancy projects and an initial reduction of tax burdens on the peasants. An even more impressive growth of industry and trade took place. Thus, for example, the production of metals rose remarkably; by the eleventh century thirteen times more silver, eight times more copper and fourteen times more iron was produced than at the beginning of the ninth century. The expansion of the crafts and commerce was largely responsible for the rapid growth of the urban population; five of the cities are said to have passed the one million mark, while the number of smaller provincial trade centres also increased greatly. On a national scale, population is estimated to have reached the figure of 90 million in 1083 and 100 million in 1124. Thus its size doubled since the T'ang, although the territory was smaller.

The overall growth of the economy also entailed a reversion to a money economy on an unprecedented scale. This led, in turn, to the introduction of paper money – a Chinese innovation – and its ever greater use due to an increasing shortage of metallic currency. The resources of the government grew proportionately, and by the middle of the eleventh century it had become infinitely wealthier than the T'ang had ever been in their heyday. An ever larger proportion of its revenue was now derived not from agriculture but from taxes on industry and trade. However, its financial stability became affected adversely by the rapidly growing cost of the bureaucracy and the army. The upkeep of the latter became an especially onerous burden; the Sung constantly increased the size of their armed forces, from 378,000 in 975, 912,000 in 1017, to 1,259,000 in 1045. However, the army's effectiveness was not enhanced thereby in the slightest, though by the last date purportedly 80 per cent of the government's revenue was swallowed up by its maintenance.

The progress attained in economic development did not signify an absence of social problems. On the contrary, these were present from the very outset, and their principal form rested in the land question. The Sung had not even attempted to establish a land equalization system, and a rapid growth of landed estates, both state and privately owned, took place, while the number of smallholders constantly decreased. By the end of the tenth century over one-third of the peasants were tenants; by the middle of the eleventh century the figure had risen to well over one-half, reaching perhaps 70 per cent. Exploitation of the tenants was severe; the customary rent ranged from 50 to 70 per cent of the crops. Thus the growing pauperization of the peasants, aggravated by an increase of the tax burden, gave rise once again to a cyclical social crisis, on as grave a scale as that of the Late T'ang period, and fully depicted in the sources, including the writings of the most prominent Sung scholars.

It was against the background of the deepening social crisis and the government's growing financial difficulties that serious political controversies within the ruling class arose in the second half of the eleventh century, culminating in one of the most interesting episodes in Chinese history – the reform movement associated with the name of Wang An-shih (1021–86). Generally speaking, two opposing factions, conservative and reformist, took shape. The former, which had the support of the great majority of higher officials and was led by such eminent scholars as Ssu-ma Kuang, came out firmly against any basic changes in the policies pursued heretofore by the government. The latter, grouped around its only prominent leader, Wang An-shih, took up the cause of reform, already raised earlier, although on a very modest scale, by the noted scholar-official Fan Chung-yen (989–1050). Its declared aim was to deal broadly with the current problems in order to alleviate the social crisis and strengthen the government. The position of the conservatives was by far the stronger; they not only had tradition to fall back on, but were also favoured greatly by the inertia of bureaucratic government, always innately opposed to change. It is also worth bearing in mind that it was they who later wrote the history of these dramatic years with the barely disguised intention of discrediting their opponents.

As so often is the case, the conflict between the two factions over policies became inextricably bound up with a struggle for power. Under the conditions of the Sung absolute monarchy, the gaining of the emperor's confidence and support was a crucial factor. When the twenty-year-old Shen-tsung (1068–86) assumed the throne, Wang An-shih succeeded in persuading him to approve the proposed reform programme, and for the next decade Wang's influence was paramount. His personality and policies have given rise to much controversy throughout the ages. Born in Kiangsi in a small gentry family, Wang became known as an outstandingly upright official, fearless in voicing his views. His sincerity was unquestioned, as was his talent, for he was a brilliant polemicist and a fine poet.

The introduction of the reform programme in 1068 was preceded by the dispatching of teams of inquiry to the provinces. The comprehensive nature of the programme was derived from its basic aim, which was to alleviate the conditions of the peasants, raise agricultural production, and simultaneously improve the government's financial position and strengthen the country's defences. The main economic reforms included: (a) the granting of government loans to peasants at advantageous, low interest rates; (b) changes in the corvée system, enabling the peasants to buy their way out of it; (c) a new registration of all landownership, aimed at uncovering tax evasion by the rich; (d) the establishment of government pawnshops and grain markets; (e) the implementation of equitable taxation on a property basis. A number of other measures were also closely intertwined with the above; the principal one provided for the setting up of a system of collective responsibility in the countryside. This was primarily intended to become the basis for the re-establishment of the militia which would replace the huge, ineffective and costly mercenary army. Changes were also introduced into the examination system, with new, more practical subjects added and the number of government schools increased.

Most of the ideas expressed in the reform programme had been formulated earlier, but no other period, with the possible exception of Wang Mang's reign, had witnessed as serious an attempt of government action. The aim was of course not to transform or replace the extant social and economic order, but to make it more viable. However, since the interests of the great landowning families were affected adversely, although only to a limited degree, the reform measures aroused their fierce opposition. Nonetheless, the reforms remained in force throughout Shen-tsung's reign, but even during the first decade of their implementation, when Wang An-shih retained his post as vice-chancellor, their success was partial at best. The main reason for this rested in the fact that most of the bureaucrats were unwilling to carry out the 'New Laws' and welcomed their total abolition in 1086. While a coterie of officials, formerly associated with the reform movement, did gain power again in 1094, the measures they introduced had already very little in common in their spirit and intention with those of Wang An-shih. The social crisis grew still more serious and, for the first time in the dynasty's history, peasant unrest took the shape of uprisings on a considerable scale. A revolt in Chekiang, led by Fang La and probably influenced by a religious sect with Manichaean affiliations, spread to much of the province, and was finally put down in 1121 with customary brutality. Thus the Sung monarchy proved itself unable to effectuate the reforms which might have led to a basic strengthening of its position, an indispensable precondition for dealing with a new threat of nomad invasion.

Southern Sung

The forests of northern and eastern Manchuria were the home for many centuries of the semi-nomadic Tungus tribes, among whom the Jurchen were the most prominent. During its strongest period the Liao empire had extended its control over the lands of the Jurchen, but at the beginning of the eleventh century the Jurchen tribal confederation increased in might and prepared to challenge its Khitan overlords. In 1114, Akuta, the Jurchen leader, declared the independence of his people, and in the next year proclaimed himself emperor of the Chin (often written Kin – the Chinese meaning is gold). The Chin proceeded almost immediately to wage war on the Liao with great success, and within a decade the state of the Khitan crumbled completely under their attacks. A small group of the Khitan did manage to escape the catastrophe of their dynasty. Led by Yeh-lü Ta-shih, an imperial prince, they made their way to East Turkestan, and with the aid of the Uighurs established a new state, Western Liao. The influence of Nestorianism was particularly strong among its ruling class, and Western Liao became a thriving and prosperous state, a 'thorn in the side of Moslems' in Central Asia, until, after almost a century, it fell victim to the Mongol onslaught.

The Sung rulers were not in the slightest perturbed by the rise of the Jurchen, but rather relished the discomfort of the Khitan, their enemies of long standing. Moreover, harking back to the hoary policy of using 'barbarians' to fight 'barbarians', they proposed to the Chin the conclusion of an alliance against the Liao. As a result the Sung armies closed in for the kill on the Liao state but proved as incapable as usual, and the cooperation of Chin and Sung only gave rise to much discord. The wealth of the Middle Kingdom proved irresistible to the Jurchen as well, and they lost little time in attacking the Sung. The first great invasion was launched in 1126, and the Chin cavalry swept down to besiege K'aifeng. To save their capital the Sung agreed to pay the colossal ransom demanded – 5 million ounces of gold, 50 million ounces of silver and 1 million bolts of silk. After receiving half of this immense booty, the Jurchen did retreat, pillaging the entire countryside, only to resume the attack a few months later. This time, they succeeded in capturing K'aifeng.

14. Southern Sung, *c.* 1180

There was little unanimity among the Sung ruling class as to the policy to be followed now towards the Chin. A considerable number of high officials favoured buying off the new enemy in the same fashion as had been done with the Khitan. It would seem that only a minority advocated an active defence. Hence, no consistent line of conduct was ever evolved during this crucial period.

Four months after their capture of K'aifeng the Jurchen retreated again, taking with them two captive Sung emperors – Hui-tsung (1101–25) and his son, Ch'in-tsung (1126–7) – over three thousand courtiers and most of the imperial treasure. A younger son of Hui-tsung had escaped the debacle, and it was he who, after many misadventures, was to re-establish the Sung dynasty as Kao-tsung (1127–62). In 1135, its capital was ultimately located in Lin-an (Hangchow), and the division of the Sung era into two dynasties – Northern and Southern – is derived from these events.

The attacks of the Jurchen continued almost incessantly up to 1141. However, the difficulties which the terrain of the Yangtse Valley presented to their cavalry, and the growing resistance of the rural population, especially in the areas between the Yellow River and the Yangtse, resulted finally in the establishment of the border between the two states on the Huai River, thus leaving an immense territory and tens of millions of Chinese under the iron heel of the Jurchen invaders. It was also largely brought about by the conciliatory policies of the Sung government. Ch'in Kuei, the chancellor since 1138, was the main representative of this tendency, which was probably supported by many of the great landowning families whose estates were located not in the north but in the Yangtse Valley. It was he who was responsible for cancelling a successful offensive of the Sung army, and for bringing about the imprisonment and murder of Yüeh Fei (1104–42), a talented general and leading proponent of an active policy of resistance. Hence, Ch'in Kuei has been universally reviled as a traitor, while Yüeh Fei extolled as a great national hero for over eight centuries, with the exception of that brief period of total intellectual aberration – the 'cultural revolution' of 1966–76.

In 1141 a peace treaty was concluded by the two empires, and the Sung declared themselves vassals of the Chin, agreeing also to the payment of an annual tribute of 250,000 ounces of silver and 250,000 bolts of silk. The border on the Huai was confirmed and ran further directly westward, following the Wei in Shensi. Most modern Chinese historians consider this treaty to be an unjustified act of capitulation. It did, however, largely determine future Chin–Sung relations, in spite of some further hostilities, for the subsequent seventy years.

For the Chinese population of the occupied areas of North China, the rule of the Jurchen was to prove even more unsupportable than that of the Khitan. Much land was confiscated by the Chin government and distributed to Jurchen colonists, settled throughout the countryside for the purpose of controlling the Chinese. In this fashion the majority of the Jurchen became great landowners, and the sharp conflicts between them and their Chinese peasant tenants assumed both a class and a national character. It has been maintained that the Chinese inhabitants of the Chin empire welcomed its annihilation by the Mongols, and utilized it to settle their score with the Jurchen colonists, many of whom were massacred at this time.

Even more ignorant of the nature and needs of an agricultural economy than the Khitan, the Jurchen failed to keep the irrigation system in proper repair with dire consequences for agricultural development. Their taxation of the peasants was still more burdensome than under the Liao, while simultaneously they also forcibly recruited large numbers of them for their armed forces. Just as the Liao had done, the Chin also employed Chinese administrative methods for the lands inhabited primarily by the Chinese, but it would seem that, while employing Chinese officials, they did not succeed in obtaining the same degree of collaboration of the landlord families. Nonetheless, the Jurchen were also affected by sinification, although they made even more strenuous attempts to preserve their national identity. They devised two scripts for their language, one based on the Chinese, one on the Khitan. Edicts issued with the intention of hindering sinification did not prove particularly effective and, in this case as well, the fact that the conquering nomad people were but a small minority proved to be crucial.

The loss of territory, which made the Southern Sung empire only two-thirds as large as its predecessor, did not have a negative effect on economic development. In reality, the progress attained during this dynasty was unprecedented and unsurpassed. Significant advances were made in agriculture, the introduction of a new strain of Vietnamese rice made double cropping possible. Tea plantations increased greatly, as did the growing of cotton. The government devoted considerable resources to the maintenance and expansion of the irrigation system. The resulting growth of agricultural production was sufficient to meet the enhanced demand derived both from the population increase and the influx of refugees from North China. The social basis of agriculture remained unchanged; the great estates continued to hold the dominant position and, according to some sources, embraced five-sixths of the land. Thus the problems of the social crisis in the countryside remained unresolved.

The most striking aspect of the Southern Sung economy was the upsurge in foreign and domestic trade. Its scope was so remarkable that some authors, Reischauer for example, regard it as a 'commercial revolution'. Foreign trade increased on an immense scale, and a great part of it was now managed by Chinese merchants, especially the commerce with Korea and Japan. In Southeast Asia the Chinese began to compete successfully with the Arabs and Persians. This growth of maritime commerce was possibly caused also by the fact that the Sung remained cut off from the traditional trade routes leading through Central Asia. As a concomitant, the Chinese merchant marine increased markedly and the importance of the coastal provinces grew. The overall growth of trade also resulted in an increase of government revenue from commercial taxes to the point where, for the first time in history, they constituted a greater source than the land tax.

The expansion of trade was of course a reflection also of the growth of handicraft production; this was particularly marked in the field of porcelain which became the leading commodity in Chinese exports. The further growth of urban centres went on apace; this was especially true of picturesque Lin-an, with its population of over one million, which was ecstatically described by Marco Polo as 'the finest and noblest city in the world'.

The advances made in the Sung economy were sizable enough to assume that a further development in the direction of a capitalist economy should have been possible, since sufficient elements for such a process were already present. However, in Chinese conditions, urban air did not make men free, for the relatively powerful, absolute and centralized monarchy kept the cities and their inhabitants under strict bureaucratic control. The tradition of discriminating against the merchants, dating back to the Han, remained in full force, as it corresponded fully to the interests of the ruling great landowning families. The latter were the prime beneficiaries of the upsurge of the Southern Sung economy; the upper stratum of the gentry became to an ever greater degree absentee landlords, living lavishly in the cities, and adding to its wealth by all types of speculation. Hence wealthy merchants and owners of manufactures became primarily interested in securing gentry status, and a considerable part of their capital was earmarked for the purchase of land and not reinvested in trade or the crafts. One may also assume that since economic development had reached such a high level, quite capable of satisfying all the needs of the ruling class, there was no pressing stimulus for searching for new sources of wealth. Simultaneously, the ever present availability of unlimited cheap labour rendered the seeking of improved, more modern methods of manufacture seemingly unnecessary.

The splendours of the Sung era, regarded by many as the apogee of traditional Chinese civilization, gave rise also to a number of negative traits, of which perhaps the most outstanding was the smug sense of complacency and superiority which actually led ultimately to stagnation. Many features of the Sung period were to remain dominant during the subsequent seven centuries, but as a part of an ever more moribund society.

The Mongol Menace

While the Southern Sung were basking in their prosperity, a new threat to the very existence of the Middle Kingdom was gathering force in the steppes to the north of the Gobi, which was to prove infinitely more calamitous than all the previous nomad incursions. Fitzgerald has called the Mongol conquest of China an unmitigated curse, but this very accurate assessment should be applied also to all the countries and peoples which became victims of invasion by the Mongols. In all cases, the effects were truly disastrous, with retrogression resulting, and an indelible stamp impressed on their future development in all respects.

The northern and northeastern parts of the present Mongolian People's Republic were the original home of the tribes destined to bear the name of Mongols. They were pure nomads, with an economy consisting only of livestock breeding, supplemented by hunting. The first mention of their new tribal federation under the name of Mongols is dated 1147, but their emergence as a truly formidable force occurred at the beginning of the thirteenth century. It is always linked with the rise to supreme power of Chingghis Khan (1162–1228). Born as Temujin, the son of a tribal chieftain, he succeeded, as a result of incessant warfare, in subjecting all the Mongol tribes to his rule. The culminating stage of this process came in 1206, when he was proclaimed the supreme leader of the Mongols – Chingghis Khan. For the rest of his life he continued to wage war against all his neighbours, spreading devastation and death over an immense part of Asia.

The success of the Mongols was not due to any particular originality in their mode of warfare, which actually represented simply a further stage in the centuries-long process of development of nomad military technique. The organization of their armed forces on the decimal system and the maintenance of an elite bodyguard followed the pattern of the Khitan. Their tactics were practically identical with those of the Khitan and Jurchen, and for that matter, the Hsiung-nu. In one respect, however, the Mongols could almost claim to be innovators. They raised the practice of mass terror to the level of genocide, and massacred all those who dared to oppose them.

Much elaborate speculation has been devoted to examining the cause of Mongol aggression; overpopulation and economic instability are some of the factors usually put forth. It would seem, however, that the issue is really somewhat simpler; the nomads could never resist the urge to plunder neighbouring agricultural areas, especially when their military superiority made their incursions feasible. They were often able to achieve their aims in spite of their numerical inferiority. In the case of the Mongols as well, the disproportion between their population, estimated at between one and two million maximum, and that of the countries they conquered was striking. It is true, of course, that during their most famous campaigns in Europe, West Asia and China, the Mongol army was greatly enlarged by the incorporation of many other tribes, especially those of Turkish origin. The Mongols were also quick to acquire new military techniques from their vanquished foes, especially the art of siege warfare, previously unknown to them, and made much use of foreign specialists in this field.

The first state located within the present boundaries of China to be attacked by the Mongols was Hsi Hsia. It was subjected to two ruinous invasions in 1208 and 1209, but then the Mongols directed their forces primarily against a richer, and hence more attractive, target – the Chin empire. The campaign against the Jurchen lasted from 1211 to 1215; during it the Mongols took one of the Chin capitals, Yenching (Peking), massacring most of its inhabitants, and succeeded in extending their rule down to the Yellow River.

The conquest of Western Liao brought the Mongols into conflict with a number of flourishing Moslem states in Central Asia and diverted their attention from China and the Hsia for almost a decade. Their victories in these campaigns, which resulted in a fierce destruction of these countries, from which they were unable to recover for many centuries, strengthened the Mongols still more and reinforced their resolve to continue their aggression in all directions.

Chingghis Khan waged his last campaign in China once more against the Hsia, whose will to resist had been unbroken by their previous defeats and who had revolted against Mongol rule in 1224. The Mongol policy of genocide was now implemented fully. Western Hsia was totally destroyed; some authors maintain that 98 per cent of its population was exterminated. Chingghis Khan died during the war against the Hsia, but to assure the succession to his designated heir, Ogodei, his death was kept a secret. As his funeral cortège made its long way back to Karakorum, all those who had the misfortune of encountering it were killed.

Some authors see fit to sing the praises of the supreme leader of the Mongols and his supposed achievements. But Chingghis' own description of what constitutes happiness provides the best illustration of his personality. 'Happiness lies in conquering one's enemies, in driving them in front of oneself, in taking their property, in savouring their despair, in outraging their wives and daughters.'

The task of completing the conquest of the remnants of the Chin empire was undertaken by Ogodei, in accord with Chingghis' last wishes. The siege of the remaining Chin capital, K'aifeng, was the main dramatic event of this war. The city, whose immense population, swollen still more by refugees, suffered dreadfully from famine, was finally forced to surrender in 1233. The order was given to massacre all the remaining inhabitants, in accord with Chingghis Khan's rule that any city which had shown the slightest sign of resistance should be totally wiped out. At the last moment Ogodei was persuaded to rescind the order by his advisor, Yeh-lü Ch'u-ts'ai. A completely sinified Khitan prince, Yeh-lü, captured at the fall of Yenching, had become an advisor to Chingghis, and it was largely his influence which had prevented the Mongols from exterminating the Chinese population of the north and turning the countryside into pasture land. He had successfully appealed to the greed of the Mongol ruler by pointing out the material advantages which could accrue from exploiting the land and people in the customary Chinese fashion. After the fall of K'aifeng, he was able to make use of the same argumentation to save millions of human lives once again. Assuredly, the activities of Yeh-lü Ch'u-ts'ai deserve more attention than those of the barbarous Mongol rulers he was obliged to serve.

The Sung had learned nothing from the disastrous results of their alliance with the Jurchen against the Khitan. They now proceeded to follow the same fatal policy and concluded a pact with the Mongols aimed against the Chin, with the illusory aim of recovering thereby the territory previously lost to the latter. Thus, in 1232, Sung armed forces joined the Mongols in the last brief campaign against the Jurchen, which ended the following year with the complete elimination of the Chin state. But when the Sung tried to take over K'aifeng and Loyang they were quickly expelled from these cities by the Mongols, who were shortly to prove to be much more dangerous foes than the vanquished Chin, for they soon showed that they would seek to conquer all of China, whose great wealth they found irresistible. However, the accomplishment of this aim was not as easy as the Mongols had assumed, and forty-five years were to pass from the fall of the Chin to the final collapse of the Sung empire. While the simultaneous waging of great campaigns in Europe and West Asia contributed partially to delaying the conquest of China, the main reason lay in the skilful and often effective resistance of the Chinese.

The Mongols lost no time in attacking the Sung; their first large-scale invasion took place in 1235, when five Mongol armies penetrated the Sung lands from three directions. However, no ultimate decision was gained and almost all the territory overrun was recovered by the Chinese. The next attack was delayed until 1251, partially due to discord among the Mongol rulers, and coincided with the enthronement of Mangu as the Great Khan. The aim was to surround the Sung empire and, with this in mind, Kubilai, Mangu's younger brother, conquered Tibet and the state of Tali (Yünnan) in 1253, and then gained a strong position in Szechuan. In 1257 fierce warfare began to be waged simultaneously in Szechuan and the Yangtse Valley, but the death of Mangu during this campaign in 1259 put an end to further offensive action, for it gave rise to a struggle for the succession between Kubilai and another brother. This internecine struggle absorbed the Mongols for the next five years. Having emerged the victor, Kubilai transferred his capital in 1264 from Karakorum to Yenching, which he rebuilt on a grandiose scale; it was to be known as the fabled Cambaluc (Khanbaligh – the city of the Khan). In 1271, as a clear sign of his intention to vanquish the Sung, he proclaimed himself emperor of a new dynasty, the Yüan.

The last immense campaign of the Mongols had, in fact, begun still earlier, in 1268, but the heroic five-year-long defence of the twin cities of Hsiangyang and Fanch'eng, on the opposite sides of the Han River, frustrated their plans. Only after the final fall of these cities were the Mongols able to continue their advance eastwards, down the Yangtse Valley. All resistance encountered was crushed with customary ruthlessness, while the successes of the Mongols were also facilitated by the vacillation of the Sung, for a significant part of the Chinese ruling class had no desire to continue to defend their country. Hence in 1276, when the Mongol army, now aided by a number of Chinese generals, attacked Lin-an, it encountered almost no resistance and captured the capital easily, taking the Sung emperor prisoner. Now almost all the great landowning families were willing to submit to the conquerors, for the sake of preserving their fortunes. The Mongols responded to this by leaving their property intact, and the landowners of the former Sung realm became the willing collaborators of the Yüan dynasty.

However, some loyal officials escaped to the south, taking with them two very young brothers of the captured emperor. One of these was proclaimed emperor in Foochow; after his death a year later, the other prince succeeded him in Kwangtung. But the Mongol forces, largely composed of former Sung units, closed in on the loyalists, who were completely defeated in a large naval battle in 1279. An official took the last Sung emperor in his arms and jumped into the sea. All resistance came to an end. The Sung dynasty was no more. For the first time in her history, but unfortunately not the last, all of China found herself under foreign rule.

Sung Culture

The relatively short period between the fall of the T'ang and the founding of the Sung had little negative effect on the continuity of development, and the reunification of the country once more created conditions for the further flourishing of culture, notwithstanding the incursions of the Khitan and Jurchen. The level achieved by the Sung was very high in practically all domains, and the contrast with that of contemporary Europe is especially striking.

It is generally agreed that the Sung period is noted above all for its painting which precisely in this era reached unsurpassable perfection. The supremacy of painting among the arts of China rests primarily on its achievements during these centuries. Although it continued to develop along the lines established in the T'ang period, Sung painting demonstrated its own specific traits, while two genres – landscapes and bird and flower – now reached their full maturity. By the time of the Sung, all the characteristic features of Chinese painting were present, derived largely from the materials used – the brush, Chinese ink, water colours, silk and paper. These made the employment of a perfect technique imperative, since corrections were intrinsically impossible. Models were seldom used, while the aim was to grasp the essence of the subject, portrayed by presenting its salient traits. The concept of perspective used by the Chinese artists differed from that of European painting in that there is no fixed vanishing point. A particularly striking effect is the element of mobility introduced in the hand scroll versions of landscape, where the panorama unfolds section by section, thus enabling the spectator to attain progress in time.

As mentioned earlier, the Chinese regard painting and calligraphy as twin arts, primarily due to the identity of materials and technique. The combining of these two art forms in a single work dates from the Sung, and their closeness is particularly evident in one of the most subtle and abstract genres, the painting of bamboos.

In their choice of motifs, especially in landscapes, Chinese painters show an inclination to repetitiousness, which is probably derived from the use of memory images and from the long-established practice of copying old masters. According to the Chinese concept of originality, painting in the manner of an old master was never regarded as plagiarism. In time, however, this practice did have negative and stultifying results, but the Sung era was still one of considerable creativeness.

There is little doubt that the landscape was the greatest achievement of Sung painting and that the works in this genre are unique in world art, unrivalled in their subtlety and beauty. The landscape was transformed by the Sung painters into a purely secular art form, inspired by an attitude to nature which in itself was the product of many centuries of culture. At least a few of the hundreds of masters of Sung landscape painting should be mentioned. The earliest in the Northern Sung period were Li Ch'eng (*fl.* 940–67), Kuan T'ung (*c.* 950), Fan K'uan (*fl.* 990–1030) and Tung Yüan (*fl.* 947–70). It is quite possible that the works attributed to them are later copies, but they do demonstrate their style. Two names figure most prominently in the last period of the Northern Sung – Kuo Hsi (*c.* 1020–90), whose hand scrolls are renowned, and Mi Fu (1051–1107), greatly gifted also as a writer, poet and calligrapher. Of the many artists continuing the T'ang tradition of figure painting, probably the most famous was Li Lung-mien (1049–1106), considered by some as the last truly great representative of this genre.

The Sung artists converted the painting of birds and flowers into an exquisitely delicate form, capable of almost as much expressiveness as the landscape. A major practitioner of this genre was the emperor Hui-tsung, also noted as a generous patron of the arts. The Imperial Academy of Painting organized by him attracted a large number of the period's most eminent artists. He was also an ardent collector of antiquities, for the Sung period witnessed a remarkable upsurge of interest in the past. The study and collecting of ancient bronzes and inscriptions were initiated at this time, and many interesting catalogues, finely illustrated, were compiled and published.

The fall of K'aifeng in 1127 had disastrous consequences for the history of Chinese art. The splendid imperial collection of around 6400 paintings was seized by the Jurchen and probably all of it destroyed. However, after the re-establishment of the Sung court in Lin-an, artistic activity was also resumed, and there are no outstanding differences between the works produced in the two Sung periods, inasmuch as full continuity was maintained. Many painters devoted themselves to a further development of the landscape. Ma Yüan (*c.* 1190–1224) is especially well known, since many of his brilliant works, in which he succeeds in giving an impression of limitless space, have survived. Equally famous is Hsia Kuei (*fl.* 1180–1230), noted for his lengthy hand scrolls, including the fabulous portrayal of the Yangtse.

The most interesting work perhaps of the Southern Sung period, which differed radically from academic painting, was that of those individuals whose primary source of inspiration was Ch'an Buddhism. Executed mostly in monochrome ink, the paintings of Liang K'ai (*c.* 1200) and Mu Ch'i (1181–1239) are remarkable for the terse economy of their brushwork and vivid simplicity which nonetheless conveys everything the artists desired.

Some historians of Chinese art have put forward the view that great painting ended with the Sung era. One can hardly accept this, for not only the Yüan but also the Ming and even the Ch'ing period saw some very fine work produced. But it is true that none of this work ever surpassed the Sung or, in most cases, even came close to its almost unbelievable perfection.

The Sung era was noted not only for its art but also for its many outstanding intellectual achievements, arising from the general expansion of education and literacy, to which the further development and large-scale use of printing also contributed. From a historian's point of view, the most impressive monuments of Sung scholarship are to be found in the domain of historical writing, and of these the indubitably greatest work is Ssu-ma Kuang's immense *Tzu-chih t'ung-chien* ('The Comprehensive Mirror to Aid in Governing'). A prominent leader of the conservative opposition to

Wang An-shih's reforms, Ssu-ma Kuang (1019–96) is regarded, with full justification, as one of China's most eminent historians, and his work as one of the greatest achievements of Chinese historiography. It is not a dynastic history but a chronological exposition, in the form of annals, of the period 403 BC to AD 959, i.e., from where the narrative of the *Tso Chuan* ends to the establishment of the Sung dynasty. With his three colleagues, Ssu-ma Kuang, enjoying the benefits of a sinecure post when removed from office – for Sung politics were truly civilized – prepared a detailed chronology and then a preliminary draft, considerably longer than the finished product edited by him. This, nonetheless, is still a ponderous work indeed, for the 1958 Peking edition is in ten volumes, over 9800 pages altogether. Ssu-ma Kuang demonstrated a highly critical approach to his sources, noting at length the divergences existing therein. The work is remarkable for its comprehensiveness, and constitutes an indispensable reference for all research on the period. Twitchett has stressed its invaluable nature and high degree of reliability in respect to the T'ang period.

As befitting an age of intellectual maturity, the Sung produced many able writers, and a number of them were noted for their versatile talents. Among the three most famous was Ou-yang Hsiu (1007–72), the author of the 'New T'ang History', who was also a poet and an influential essayist, as well as a high official and one of the leaders of the opposition to Wang An-shih. Wang himself was a fine poet, while his prose was renowned for its lucidity and succinctness. Probably the greatest of the three was Su Shih (Su Tung-p'o, 1036–1101) who, while serving the government as an official, was not only a superb essayist, but also a poet, painter and calligrapher.

Some authors maintain that the work done in the domain of philosophical thought should be considered as one of the most important parts of the Sung heritage. It is true that in the history of Chinese philosophy the place of the Sung philosophers is second only to those of the Classical Period and, furthermore, the system they evolved – Neo-Confucianism – had a profound influence on Chinese thought up to the end of the nineteenth century. Sung philosophy can be regarded as a reaction, based on Chinese sources, against the centuries of domination of Buddhist thought, as an attempt to modify and expand Confucian ideology in a manner which would make it fully viable and apposite to current needs, while simultaneously capable of dealing with the metaphysical problems raised by Buddhism, which had been largely ignored both in the Classical and the Han periods. This task was solved by constructing a cosmology which could compete with the Buddhist, but some modern Chinese authorities believe that this was accomplished primarily by plagiarizing Buddhism. In reality, the Sung philosophers had been under a strong and persuasive influence of Buddhist thought, which clearly affected their work. The ultimate product of their thought, Neo-Confucianism, can be considered as a synthesis of Confucianism, Buddhism and Taoism, in which the first element, and especially its agnosticism, was dominant.

The principal Sung philosophers produced their work in the eleventh century. They included Chou Tun-i (1017–73), Shao Yung (1011–77), the brothers Ch'eng Hao (1031–85) and Ch'eng I (1037–1107) and the latters' uncle, Chang Tsai (1020–77). However, the most eminent representative of Neo-Confucianism was active in the subsequent century. Chu Hsi (1130–1200) established himself as the most important commentator of the Confucian Classics since the Han, and his interpretation was later to be regarded as the standard one. Moreover, in his voluminous writings, he systematized the views of his predecessors into a complex metaphysical cosmology, based on an objective idealist concept of the world. Chu Hsi also did not ignore the concern of Confucianism with social problems, but presented them in a fashion which stressed its paternalistic and conservative aspects. Although at first the views of Chu Hsi and his followers, known in Chinese as the School of Tao, were considered overly innovative, they were soon to become recognized as the only valid and orthodox interpretation of the Confucian heritage. Ultimately, Neo-Confucianism took on the shape of dry-as-dust scholasticism, with a thoroughly stultifying effect on further intellectual development. In this way it contributed to the rigid cultural petrification which was to have such fatal effects on China's future, especially when the intrusion of the West became marked.

6. Mongol Rule and Ming Restoration

The Yüan Dynasty

The collapse of the Sung in 1279 now made possible the extension of Mongol rule to the entire country. In this process the Yüan dynasty showed itself to be one of the most oppressive regimes ever to be inflicted upon the unfortunate inhabitants of the Middle Kingdom. Of necessity, the Mongols employed Chinese forms of administration to exploit the agricultural economy, but they simultaneously pursued a distinct policy of national discrimination against the Chinese. The entire population was divided into four groups. The first of these comprised the Mongols as the ruling military elite; most of the top government posts were reserved for them, while Mongol garrisons were located in the principal strategic centres. The second group was made up of the Mongols' allies, primarily the Turkish tribes of Central Asia; its position was almost equal to that of the Mongols. The aid offered by these peoples, especially the Uighurs, was invaluable, inasmuch as they were infinitely more civilized than the Mongols. The third included the inhabitants of North China, Chinese as well as Khitan and Jurchen. It was not discriminated against quite so blatantly as the last group, the Chinese of the south, who were completely set aside from the government and forbidden to possess arms. Thus, for the first time under circumstances of nomad rule, a large part of the Chinese gentry was deprived of its customary hold on the administration, although its economic position was left largely undisturbed. Probably the most important reason why the Mongols were able to dispense with the gentry's service rested in the great size of their empire; they were able to bring in the needed administrators from other parts of their realm.

The social and economic effects of Mongol rule were almost entirely negative and, in some respects, well-nigh disastrous.

138

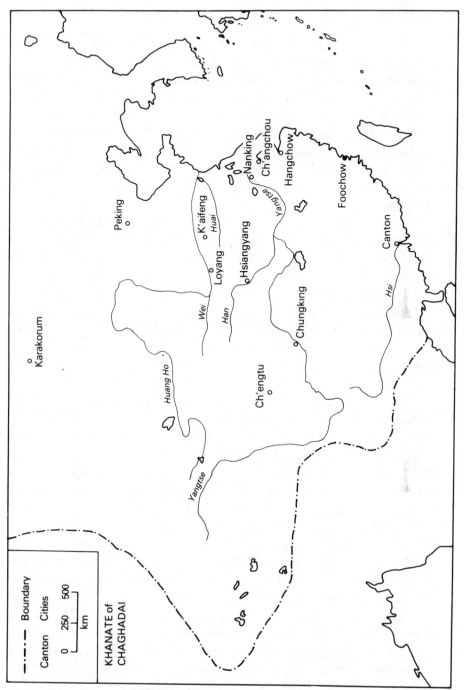

15. Mongol Rule. Kubilai's Empire

Initially, the Mongols had confiscated much land in North China, distributing it to members of the Mongol aristocracy and also to the Buddhist establishment for, while originally shamanists, the Mongols had become converted relatively quickly to the most debased form of Buddhism – Tibetan Lamaism. This policy, and the heavy taxation introduced, brought about the further impoverishment of the peasants as well as the growth of large estates. The position of the artisans, many of whom were forced to work for the government on unfavourable terms, was almost as disadvantageous as that of the peasants. The Yüan rulers also failed to maintain properly the water conservancy system in North China, thus causing further damage to the economy. This, in turn, was reflected in the sharp decline of the population; some historians believe that the Mongol conquest of North China had itself cost the lives of at least five million people.

It is true that the *pax mongolica* prevailing over an immense area facilitated the marked increase of foreign trade. However, this was almost entirely in foreign hands, mostly those of Moslem merchants from Central Asia, and the profits did not accrue to China. In fact, a drain of metallic currency took place, while the Yüan government's unrestricted use of paper currency also helped to bring about inflation. Simultaneously, the Mongol administration was riddled with corruption on a stupendous scale.

The conquest of China did not put an end to Mongol expansion, since even now their greed for plunder and power remained unsatiated. They utilized the Middle Kingdom as a base and principal source of manpower and means to wage war on almost all the neighbouring countries. However, the attempts to subdue Southeast Asia ultimately failed, primarily due to two factors – the staunch resistance of the local population, especially the Vietnamese, who conducted an extremely skilful and successful guerrilla campaign against the invaders, and the unfavourable climatic conditions. The expeditions against Japan also ended in complete disaster. The first one, launched in 1274, involving the use of a large Chinese and Korean fleet and over 20,000 Mongol, Chinese and Korean troops, was successfully beaten back by the Japanese. A much larger force was dispatched in 1281. The great armada of Chinese and Korean ships carried 100,000 Chinese troops from South China and 40,000 Mongol, North Chinese and Korean soldiers. Again, brave Japanese resistance, aided by a timely typhoon – the 'Kamikaze', the Divine Wind – which destroyed most of the fleet, brought Kubilai's megalomaniac plans to naught.

During the existence of a unified Mongol empire, contacts between China and other parts of the Eurasian landmass increased significantly. Numerous merchants and missionaries left their accounts of travels in the Middle Kingdom, of which the best known is undoubtedly that of Marco Polo. Although it contains some inaccuracies as well as astounding omissions, the Venetian merchant's narrative was the best and most extensive source of knowledge about China before the arrival of the Jesuits in the seventeenth century. One can assume that the Chinese also gained more information regarding other parts of the world, and of West Asia in particular, during this period. Nonetheless, this had remarkably little effect on the future development of China, inasmuch as the nationalist reaction, which took place after the downfall of Mongol rule, led to a sweeping away of most things foreign. At the same time, the feeling of superiority, which had been so characteristic of the Sung period, when it could be considered at least partially justified due to the high level of Chinese civilization, was only stimulated still further by the bitter experience of barbarous Mongol rule.

Fortunately for the Chinese, the domination of the Mongols lasted less than a century. After the death of Kubilai in 1294, not a single occupant of the Yüan throne deserves separate mention. The incapacity of these rulers was matched by that of the Mongol aristocracy, with its astounding propensity for vicious struggles for power, which brought about the collapse of the unity of the Mongol realm. In China itself, the Mongols lost much of their vaunted military prowess within a single generation. Nevertheless, largely due to the acquiescence of the Chinese landowners, they were still able to preserve their domination, and their nature as a culturally distinct ruling caste. This ability to withstand the effects of sinification to a much greater degree than the Khitan or Jurchen might well have ultimately contributed to their downfall.

The concept of the decisive historical role of the masses, stressed so often by Chinese Marxist historians, although not always entirely convincingly, was, in fact, fully demonstrated in the struggle to rid China of the Mongol yoke. While the Chinese gentry, in spite of being deprived of any meaningful participation in the administration, continued to collaborate with the Yüan dynasty, it was the peasantry which, as the object of double oppression – by the Chinese landowners and the Mongol authorities – became the principal force in opposing Mongol rule. The continuously deepening agrarian crisis, as well as the generally aggravated economic conditions, gave rise to a series of peasant disturbances. The first risings took place in the 1320s, and were put down primarily by armed units organized by the Chinese landowners, who helped in this fashion to preserve the domination of the Mongols for several more decades.

A vital role in the development of this peasant movement was played by the secret societies, among whom the White Lotus was the most important. Basically an unorthodox Buddhist sect with messianic overtones in its worship of Maitreya, the future last Buddha, the White Lotus began its agitation against Mongol rule at the beginning of the fourteenth century, and its activity was quickly proscribed by the Yüan government. In 1351, when the authorities impressed a great number of peasants and soldiers for repairing the broken dykes on the Yellow River, the White Lotus successfully utilized this occasion for organizing an armed revolt, which took the name of Red Turbans. Within a short time, the rebellion spread from Honan to Hopei, Shantung and Anhwei. In 1355, the Red Turban leaders, mostly peasants, as were practically all their followers, planned a restoration of the Sung dynasty, placing a supposed descendant of Hui-tsung on the throne. However, the movement was at least as much social as national in character, with the Red Turbans fighting against the Chinese gentry just as much as against the Mongols. Although the Red Turban armies were able to conduct a number of successful campaigns in North China in the years 1357–9, the rebellion demonstrated the basic weakness of other great peasant revolts in that it failed to consolidate its political hold on the territories that had been overrun. Moreover, a struggle for power between its leaders came to the fore at an early stage, thus weakening the movement still further. As a result, the Yüan were able, with the aid of the Chinese gentry, to achieve by 1363 the complete defeat of all the insurgent armies in North China.

In the Yangtse Valley, a peasant leader of a different mould rose to prominence, destined to bring about the overthrow of Mongol rule.

Chu Yüan-chang (1328–98), often compared to Liu Pang, came from a family of poor tenants. When he was seventeen, his entire family fell victim to famine and the plague, and the orphan Chu became a Buddhist monk in order to survive. It is quite probable that he was a member of the White Lotus, although he later denied this adamantly, and not surprisingly, since after becoming emperor he had proscribed the sect. Having joined, in 1353, a local unit of the Red Turbans, Chu, due to his skill and bravery, quickly assumed a leading position. Shortly thereafter, some members of the gentry joined his forces, and their influence proved to be decisive, since they advised him to cease struggling against the Chinese landowners, to attract support from all strata, and to concentrate on overcoming the Mongols, with the imperial throne for himself as the ultimate goal. Chu Yüan-chang adhered to these policies unhesitatingly, and this not only differentiated him from other Red Turban leaders, but also improved his position markedly. Initially, Chu's prime concern was to strengthen his armed forces and, after taking Nanking in 1356, he came into control of a large part of the country's richest economic area – the lower Yangtse Valley. Soon, many of the gentry, who looked on Chu's policies with favour and regarded the Yüan as a lost cause, joined him along with their own armed forces. Chu established an efficient administration, and his army's discipline contrasted distinctly with the bandit-like behaviour of some of the Red Turban forces. In the years 1363–7 he struggled successfully against other rivals, and was able to extend his rule to most of the Yangtse Valley, and later to South China as well.

In 1367 Chu Yüan-chang launched his final campaign against the Mongols, sending his best general, Hsü Ta, with a quarter-million-strong army, northwards. The Mongols, who had been, as usual, busy fighting among themselves, offered almost no resistance. In 1368 Hsü Ta took Peking easily, while the last Yüan emperor and his court fled to the Gobi. The remaining Mongol garrisons were also all shortly defeated. In the same year, Chu Yüan-chang proclaimed himself the first emperor of the Ming ('Brilliant') dynasty.

Chinese Culture During the Yüan Period

'The Mongols were merely policemen.' With this succinct phrase Waley answered the question regarding the influence on Chinese culture of nearly a century of Mongol rule. In reality, it developed almost completely unaffected by the foreign domination on the basis of its previous achievements, preserving continuity with the Sung era. The Yüan period is considered to be especially noteworthy for the flourishing of drama. While performances had been held in the preceding ages, it is only from the fourteenth century onwards that both librettos and the names of the authors are known. It should be borne in mind that Chinese drama is a mixed form, embracing also music, singing and acrobatics, and therefore usually referred to, more accurately, as Chinese opera. The range of subject matter is very wide, but most of it deals with themes from Chinese history. Two of the most prominent authors were Kuan Han-cheng (*c.* 1234–1300), a prolific writer much admired by the Chinese, and Wang Shih-fu (*fl.* 1290–1310), known particularly for his famous love story, 'The Western Chamber'.

Continuity with the past was demonstrated with perhaps the greatest clarity in painting which, in the Yüan period, lost little of its creativeness, while at the same time it drew still closer to calligraphy. One of the most eminent artists, versatile in the classical tradition, was Chao Meng-fu (1254–1322), probably best known for his splendid portrayal of horses. He was also reputed to be the greatest calligrapher. It was, however, the Five Masters of landscape painting who constituted the glory of Yüan art. Among them was Kao K'o-kung (1248–1310), noted for his impressionistic style, and Wu Chen (1280–1354), a Taoist recluse, whose rendition of solitary pines was famous. Wang Meng (1310–54) and Huang Kung-wang (1269–1354), the former known for his archaizing trend, and the latter for paintings resembling 'essays in constructional design', exerted considerable influence on this genre's further development. But undoubtedly the most remarkable of this group was Ni Tsan (1301–74), later considered as the model of an amateur painter, working solely for his

144

own satisfaction. In his work Ni Tsan advanced the tendency towards simplicity, inherent in Chinese painting, to its final limits. His style, as fine as a spider web, is unmistakable, and it was said that he treasured ink like gold, so sparing was he in its use.

The example of Yüan drama and painting shows that Chinese culture, as a whole, was still capable of much creativeness; the removal of Mongol domination and the restoration of Chinese rule could, therefore, establish conditions for its further flourishing, although signs were already present that this future development might become affected adversely by an over-rigid adherence to the traditions of the past.

The Ming Restoration

It was the peasant insurrection which had been instrumental in creating a new Chinese Empire. It was greater in size than the Northern Sung, for it included new areas in the southwest – Yünnan and Kweichow – and in the northeast – Liaotung. However, there was no attempt, in contrast with the Han and T'ang, to extend Chinese rule to Central Asia.

The restoration of the Chinese state by the Ming implied a return to the Chinese past, with the T'ang regarded as the worthiest model to emulate. This reversion to Chinese sources, not untinged by a nationalist reaction to Mongol rule, was still, nonetheless, capable of some innovation and originality. The shaping of the Ming monarchy was undoubtedly influenced to a marked degree by the policies pursued by its founder, Chu Yüan-chang, who remained on the throne for its first three decades. He is customarily referred to, as are all Ming and Ch'ing emperors, not by his posthumous name, but by his reign title – Hung-wu. It is clear that Chu was an able and intelligent man, who devoted himself unsparingly to his tasks as ruler. It is also equally obvious that in time Hung-wu became a more and more ruthless despotic autocrat. He turned completely paranoiac, suspecting plots everywhere. This served as a pretext for the launching of a violent campaign of terror against his own officials, which resulted in the death of many thousands, including some of

16. The Ming Empire, *c.* 1600

Hung-wu's closest followers, whose aid had placed him on the throne. Thus, the vitriolic attack in 1965 on Wu Han, the gifted historian and greatest specialist on Chu Yüan-chang, which actually inaugurated the 'cultural revolution' of 1966–76, must have given much food for thought to the Chinese intellectuals, historically minded by tradition.

Hung-wu also followed the customary pattern of easing social tensions by improving the position of the peasants. Much resettlement was undertaken, fallow land brought under cultivation, and the neglects of the Yüan period as regards the water conservancy system extensively remedied. The result was a considerable increase in agricultural production which, in turn, gave rise to a marked population growth. The situation of the artisans was also improved; the restrictions of the Yüan period removed, and the process of replacing compulsory work for the government by taxation initiated. However, towards the merchants, the Ming government pursued the traditional policies of discrimination.

Hung-wu continued to use Nanking as his capital, and enlarged the city greatly, engirdling it with immense walls, twenty miles in length. This was typical of the Ming, whose place in Chinese history is precisely that of builders on an impressive scale, and much of surviving traditional Chinese architecture dates from their era.

The Ming empire was divided into fifteen provinces, all corresponding, with minor differences, to the present ones; Hunan and Hupei, however, constituted one province – Nanking – while Hopei, then called Chingshih, was larger. The organization of the Ming government followed basically the six ministries pattern evolved by the T'ang. Three separate elements, a civil and military organization, and the censorate with its supervisory role, were maintained. However, all effective political power was to a still greater degree than earlier centralized in the hands of the emperor, especially after the abolition of the office of chancellor in 1380. It seems unquestionable that Mongol despotic rule influenced its successor in this respect, and this was one more negative aspect of the legacy. In this case, as shown by the example of Muscovy, the experience of China was not unique.

In his striving for a strong absolutist monarchy Hung-wu did initiate one policy which was contrary to this purpose. In his old age he began to rely solely on his own family, and created appanages for his many sons and grandsons. The consequences were perhaps not as far-reaching as in the case of the Western Han, but this factor did contribute to the struggle for power after his death. Having attempted for a while to recruit officials on the basis of recommendations, Hung-wu restored the examination system in 1382, which was to persist almost to the end of the empire in the twentieth century. By the Ming period the preparations necessary for taking the examinations became more and more costly, and thus the entry into the bureaucracy was restricted almost exclusively to the wealthy. The subject matter was more than ever confined to the Classics, with the Chu Hsi interpretation regarded as the only valid and acceptable one. Ultimately, the examination system became an ever greater obstacle to the development of any intellectual initiative or creativeness, while the famous 'eight-legged' prescribed form of literary essay put paid to any originality.

The problem of the Mongols remained a most significant one during Hung-wu's reign. The final expulsion of the Mongol garrisons was completed by 1382, and followed by expeditions into Mongolia itself, aimed at shattering the Mongol military power once and for all. However, the successes obtained were only partial at best, while the campaigns were very costly and necessitated the setting up of military colonies in North China, as well as the stationing of large armies there. Simultaneously, the Ming faced a new danger in the east, in the form of Japanese piracy, which was to remain troublesome for the next two centuries and had to be countered by building up the defence system of the southeastern coastal provinces. Nevertheless, trade relations between China and Japan developed markedly in the fifteenth and sixteenth centuries, and eleven large Japanese trade missions are recorded arriving in China during the years 1433–1549.

The restored Chinese monarchy logically resumed a vision of itself as the Middle Kingdom – the only true centre of civilization – and this formed the basis of its policy and relations with all its neighbours. Hence, the relations could only be those of superior and inferior, of suzerain and vassal, although in many cases the suzerainty was quite superficial and actually meaningless. The tribute system thus became the principal form of foreign relations, often masking what were simply extensive trade links.

Even the most autocratic ruler cannot safeguard his plans for the succession from going astray. Such was the case of Hung-wu. His choice, his sixteen-year-old grandson Hui-ti (1399–1402), did ascend the throne, but he soon became enmeshed in an acrimonious conflict with his uncles. The most powerful of them, the Prince of Yen, in control of the armed forces of North China, challenged his nephew's right to the throne. A sanguinary and ruinous civil war broke out, bringing ruin to much of North and Central China, which ended in 1402 with the capture of Nanking by the Yen army. In the mêlée, Hui-ti disappeared, and tradition has it that he actually survived to live out his days as an itinerant Buddhist monk. Whatever his fate, the Prince of Yen proclaimed himself emperor (Yung-lo, 1403–24), and commenced his reign with a large-scale massacre of those who had loyally served his nephew. Yung-lo is known as the second and last 'strong ruler' of the Ming, and the absolutist character of the monarchy was perceptibly strengthened during his reign. He was perhaps best known for his decision to transfer the capital to Peking, which he rebuilt on a monumental scale. The basic outlines of the Imperial City at present correspond to his reconstruction. If one views it from the top of Prospect Hill, noting the wonderful symmetry of the palaces, with their yellow-gold tiles shimmering in the sun, it is one of the most beautiful and impressive sights in the world. One might even tend to forget the human costs, the immense amount of arduous toil by tens of thousands of labourers, forced to create this splendour for the sole use of their despotic masters.

One of the fundamental reasons for Yung-lo's decision to shift the capital to Peking was the city's suitability to serve as the base for further military operations against the Mongols. Although the Mongols had now lost the unity which had made their predatory conquests possible, they remained a threat to North China. Yung-lo himself led five large expeditions against them in the period 1410–24, and while the danger of a new Mongol invasion was partially averted, the Mongol problem was still to prove troublesome for the next hundred years. The Mongols raided North China almost constantly, but simultaneously they sent annual trade missions, exchanging horses and furs for Chinese goods, mainly tea and silk.

The Yung-lo period also witnessed an unusually active expansion of maritime enterprise. During the years 1405–33, seven great government-sponsored expeditions were launched, under the command of Cheng Ho, a Moslem eunuch. Their routes extended far beyond Southeast Asia, reaching the Persian Gulf and the east coast of Africa. It is possible that the wish to demonstrate the power of the new dynasty and the desire to expand trade were among the main motives. They did succeed, at least partially, in achieving these aims, as well as revealing the high level of Chinese navigation and shipbuilding. But in 1433 a sudden end was put to this endeavour, primarily due to its costliness, and thus this promising start, which could have led to the development of China into a maritime power, was largely wasted. The significance of these decisions was truly far-reaching, since they took place at the time when the Europeans were about to start their era of great maritime expansion, and when a century later they were to reach the shores of China, the Chinese were no longer in a position to compete with them for the mastery of the seas, with fatal consequences for their own future. It would seem reasonable to assume that the selection of such a course resulted largely not so much from immediate political considerations, but from the self-sufficient nature of the Chinese economy, still dominated by agriculture, in which foreign trade played a marginal role.

The accomplishments of the Ming monarchy, especially its restoration of Chinese rule, were considerable, but the absolutist system it favoured bore within itself the seeds of decay, as could be noted already during the first century of the dynasty's existence. One of the signs of this process was the marked growth in the intensity of the struggle for power at the top levels of the government, and in this the recurrent rise of the eunuchs was perhaps the most significant factor. In spite of Hung-wu's injunction against granting them any political standing, the eunuchs had already become an important political force during the Yung-lo period, serving once more as a tool of the ruler against other cliques of officials. By the middle of the fifteenth century, they were well on their way to transforming themselves from servants to real masters of the empire, having skilfully taken advantage of their position at the centre of power. The principal aim of the eunuchs was uncomplicated – the acquisition of wealth and power – and being usually totally corrupt, they used the latter for selling offices to the highest bidder. They were often in complete control of the emperors, ridding themselves of inconvenient ones in the fashion of their T'ang predecessors. The number of eunuchs grew constantly; in the middle of the Ming era they were said to number 10,000, while by its end they had increased to around 100,000. Most significantly perhaps, they functioned also as a secret police force, and were thus able to achieve effective control of a number of central government departments, including the armed forces. The baneful and all-pervasive influence of the eunuchs was indisputably an unmitigated disaster for the Ming monarchy.

The rise to power of Wang Chen was one of the earliest examples of the consequences of eunuch domination. As the real ruler during the first part of Ying-tsung's reign, he brought the empire to the brink of complete catastrophe. Under the leadership of the able Esen, the Mongols were again on the warpath, and in 1449 their forces streamed into North China. Wang Chen led the imperial army against them, but his total military incapacity made it possible for the Mongols to surround the entire Chinese host close to Peking, and then annihilate it completely. Wang Chen himself was killed, and the emperor taken prisoner. Only a determined defence of Peking, well led by the talented general Yü Chien, prevented the capture of the capital. Since a brother of his had been placed on the throne, the Mongols returned Ying-tsung to the Chinese. Subsequently, in 1457, he was restored to power by a coup, and immediately proceeded to exterminate his brother's supporters, including Yü Chien.

The almost incredible degree of corruption and greed of the eunuchs is well illustrated by the case of Liu Chin. When he was finally disgraced in 1510, his fortune was assessed at over 251 million ounces of silver, without counting an immense hoard of jewellery and other riches. But, in fairness, it should be stated that the eunuchs were not alone in this mad pursuit of wealth, or in nepotically furthering the interests of their relatives. Other segments of the ruling class were not far behind in this respect, in particular, the members of the very numerous imperial clans, many of whom acquired landed estates of vast proportions, thus deepening the social crisis which was ultimately to bring down the dynasty.

The unedifying aspect of much of its political history should not cause one to disregard the significant economic development of the Ming era, particularly in agriculture. Irrigation methods were improved, new crops, such as Indian corn, the sweet potato and

151

peanuts introduced, while crop rotation was used more frequently. As a result, agricultural production increased and, in consequence, the population grew as well, reaching the figure of at least 100 million by the beginning of the seventeenth century. The Yangtse Valley became still more clearly the country's main economic centre, and it was here that the process of urbanization was most advanced. Nanking itself had a population of over one million, while new centres of industrial activity, such as Soochow for silk textiles and Sungkiang for cotton goods, also grew in size. The famous porcelain-manufacturing centre in Kiangsi, Chingtechen, expanded considerably, since production there, both for export and the domestic market, had increased greatly. While some Chinese historians place the existence of 'sprouts' of capitalism in the Sung period, their presence in the Ming seems even more obvious and undeniable. But the factors militating against an unhampered development in this direction – the policies pursued by a relatively strong absolutist monarchy and the great landlord families who continued to man the ranks of the imperial bureaucracy – were perhaps even weightier in the Ming era. This was particularly so in the case of the countryside, where the domination of the gentry was stronger than ever before. In aiding the central administration to govern at the county level, the gentry also supervised public works, educational facilities and organized the rural militia, and were thus in almost total control of local affairs. Their prime concern was to make certain that most of the tax and labour burdens would be shunted off on to the peasants, and they succeeded in accomplishing this unfailingly, contributing thereby to the exacerbation of the social crisis.

In the sixteenth century the Ming empire continued to be troubled both by the Mongols and the Japanese. The former kept up their inveterate custom of engaging simultaneously in trade and raiding across the border, even up to Peking itself. The Chinese rebuilt the Great Wall on an extensive scale, but it was never more than a hindrance which could be overcome by a truly determined incursion. The damage inflicted by the Japanese pirates was probably greater, especially when they began to attack not only Fukien and Chekiang, but also penetrated into the Yangtse Valley, looting and burning. In reality, a large part of the pirates were not Japanese but Chinese collaborating with them. The authorities finally undertook the policy of organizing strong military forces in the coastal provinces, which were able to reduce this menace to manageable proportions.

However, this same period saw the emergence of a much more ominous and significant factor. This was the coming of the Europeans to China, which was ultimately to affect its fate to a much greater degree than any previous foreign invasion. While formerly Chinese policy towards foreign merchants, as shown by the T'ang treatment of the Arabs and Persians, had been fairly liberal, this could not, of necessity, be applied to the Europeans for, from the outset, their violent and arrogant behaviour and their inclination towards rapine and plunder, caused them to be regarded as foreign devils, as menacing as the Japanese pirates.

The Portuguese were the first to reach Canton in 1516, and their attempts to establish themselves failed completely. However, somewhat later, they succeeded in setting up factories in Ningpo (Chekiang) and Ch'üanchou (Fukien), but their brutality and depredations led the Chinese to eliminate these colonies relatively quickly. The Portuguese were finally able to gain a foothold near Canton, when they were permitted to settle in Macao in 1557, which became a centre of their trade with China and all of East Asia. The record of other Europeans was as sorry as that of the Portuguese. Their great rivals, the Dutch, established themselves temporarily in Taiwan in 1624, holding on to their positions there until they were driven out in 1661 by the anti-Manchu leader, Koxinga. The English showed up for the first time in 1637, when three ships arrived in Canton; conflict with the Chinese put paid to the attempt to open up trade contacts. It is not particularly surprising that, in view of these experiences with the European merchant-pirates, the Chinese authorities were quick to embark on a policy of restricting trade and relations with them to a minimum, thus making their penetration of China impossible for the time being.

In this period East Asia also became an area to which extensive missionary efforts, primarily conducted by Roman Catholics, were devoted. In the sixteenth and seventeenth centuries the Jesuits were clearly the most active among the Christian missions. In China, their endeavours were initiated by the Italian, Matteo Ricci (1557–1610), one of the ablest members of an order which was never short of talents. After arriving in China in 1583 and joining the Jesuit mission in Macao, Ricci, a gifted linguist, accomplished the prodigious task of mastering Chinese perfectly. He finally managed to reach Peking in 1601, remaining there until his death. Ricci fully shared, and, more than likely, helped to formulate the Jesuit view that proselytizing efforts should be concentrated on the ruling class rather than on the people, since, if they were to bear fruit, the whole country could then be converted. He also advocated a policy of far-reaching compromise with Chinese habits and customs. Thus, for example, ancestor worship was to be viewed not as a religious ceremony, but as a permissible civic observance. Due to his training in European science, Ricci was able to impress the emperor and some of the scholar-officials with his knowledge of astronomy, mathematics and geography, and gain some converts in this milieu. He was sanguine as to the prospects for his creed, and on his deathbed proclaimed to his associates: 'I leave before you an open door.' The door was, in fact, to remain largely closed, partially due to the policies of the Chinese authorities, but even more as the result of the aggressive activities directed against China by the nominally Christian European powers.

The Crisis of Ming Rule and the Rise of the Manchus

The long reign of the inept Wan-li (1573–1629) saw the further deterioration of the Ming monarchy, whose position was to be worsened still further by Japanese aggression against its vassal, Korea. The invasion of Korea in 1592 was undertaken by Toyotomi Hideyoshi, the military dictator of Japan, who now embarked on a policy of external expansion, the ultimate aim of which was the conquest of China. The Koreans, having refused to join him as allies or to give free passage to his troops, thus became the first victims. A powerful Japanese army quickly conquered most of the country, including Seoul, the capital, and advanced towards the Yalu River, which formed the Sino-Korean boundary. It was only now that the Ming government finally responded to the desperate appeals for aid from the Korean king, and Chinese forces slowly entered Korea. After meeting initially with a number of defeats, the Chinese did succeed ultimately in driving the Japanese out of most of the territory they had overrun. However, in 1597, Hideyoshi renewed his invasion of Korea, and once again the Chinese were compelled to come to the rescue of the Hermit Kingdom. The second invasion met a similar fate to that of the first, and the death in 1598 of the megalomaniac Japanese warlord put an end to this adventure which, nonetheless, his countrymen were only too eager to resume in the nineteenth and twentieth centuries. The results of this conflict were truly disastrous for Korea, devastated almost completely by the depredations of the Japanese, and almost equally adverse for the Ming government, since the two campaigns had been very costly and had strained its weak finances to the utmost.

At the Ming court itself the customary intrigues spread still more, while the power of the eunuchs grew mightily. Wan-li's successor was poisoned by them, and the next emperor, his imbecilic son, meekly allowed Wei Chung-hsien, perhaps the most notorious of all the Ming eunuchs, to become, in reality, the true ruler. The corruption and terror of Wei's regime reached such proportions that even the pliant Ming bureaucrats could not stand it any longer. A large group of scholar-officials, known as the Tung-lin (the name of an academy), sought to put an end to eunuch domination. However, Wei Chung-hsien and his henchmen responded to this in 1625 by an extensive and brutal persecution of their opponents in which many Tung-lin members lost their lives. While the accession of the last Ming emperor, Ch'ung-cheng (1627–44), did entail the downfall of Wei Chung-hsien, the position of the Ming monarchy had reached its nadir. The government was bankrupt and its revenues completely insufficient to meet its needs, especially in view of the rapidly growing costs of the struggle against the Manchus. However, the principal source of the crisis of the Ming rested in the profound discontent of the Chinese peasants, driven to open revolt by the unrestrained oppression and exploitation from which they suffered during the last decades of Ming rule. The scene was set for the outbreak of one of the most dramatic of the great peasant rebellions which characterize the history of Chinese feudalism, and were always the ultimate protest against insufferable misery and degradation.

A horrifying famine in northern Shensi in 1626 provided the spark for the great rebellion whose scale deserves to be compared, above all, with the Taiping Movement of the nineteenth century. It bore also all the usual traits of a Chinese peasant insurrection, being largely spontaneous, hazy in its aims, and prone to inner strife. Its development was also characteristically uneven; the peasant army succeeded in overrunning vast areas, only to be smashed almost completely and then, shortly thereafter, to reappear once more with full force. Ultimately, a considerable degree of coordination of the insurgent forces was obtained from 1640 on, and this was largely connected with the rise of the Shensi-born peasant, Li Tzu-ch'eng (1606–45), to the position of the rebellion's strongest leader. The last years of the insurrection became inextricably bound up with the growing danger which China faced once again from its northern neighbours, this time the Manchus.

Inhabiting the central, north and northeastern parts of Manchuria the tribes to be known later as the Manchus, were in reality the Tungusic Jurchen, the descendants of those who had created the Chin empire in North China. Primarily hunters and fishermen, the Jurchen also engaged in agriculture and animal husbandry, being skilled horsemen and archers as well. Politically, they were vassals of the Ming empire from its early days, remaining as such until the end of the sixteenth century. The disunited and usually hostile Jurchen tribes were forged into a powerful force largely due to the activities of Nurhachi (1559–1626), a tribal chieftain of the Aisin Gioro clan. The unification of the Jurchen was a complicated, thirty-year-long process of almost constant strife, which met with the relentless opposition of the Chinese authorities. Nurhachi's introduction of the Banner system facilitated the task of building the future Manchu state. While their primary role was military, the Banners were also utilized for administrative purposes as a supra-tribal institution. Originally, four Banners were established, later the number was increased to eight; each was distinguished by a flag of a different colour. After the expansion of the Manchu realm, eight Mongol and eight Chinese Banners were additionally set up.

The adoption of the Banner system has been regarded by some authors as a very significant reflection of the transformation of Jurchen society. However, the creation, even before the conquest of China proper, of the Manchu monarchic government, as a faithful copy of the Chinese model, was undoubtedly of still greater importance. It was closely bound up with the successful invasion and piecemeal overrunning of Liaotung which, for at least two millennia, had formed a part of the Chinese cultural area. Its sizable population was predominantly Chinese, and numerous members of the Chinese gentry of Liaotung were to collaborate in the organization of the new Manchu state to which already in 1616 Nurhachi had given the name of Late Chin. In this way the Manchus, in contrast with the earlier northern nomad invaders, had built an effective state organization before accomplishing a conquest of China, and this may well have been one of the decisive factors which accounted for the unusual length of their rule.

After achieving their control of Liaotung, the Manchus continued their attacks on Chinese positions west of the Liao River. While they met with some difficulties in these encounters, the progressing disintegration of the Ming government under the blows of the peasant rebellion made their further advance possible. Nurhachi died in 1626 during this campaign. He was succeeded by his eighth son, Abahai (1592–1643), a gifted general. It was Abahai who introduced the use of the term 'Manchu' for his people, and in 1636 proclaimed the establishment of the Ch'ing ('Pure') dynasty replacing the Late Chin, and thereby expressing clearly its intention to become the ruling house of China. Abahai was eminently successful in expanding the area and the power of the Manchu state. Korea was reduced to vassal status, the entire Amur region brought under control and, perhaps most important of all, the tribes of Inner Mongolia became the subjects of the Ch'ing, thus enabling the Manchus to cross the Great Wall almost at will and launch expeditions into North China, inflicting immeasurable sufferings on its people. Thus, by the time of Abahai's death (he was succeeded by his six-year-old son Fu-lin, while his brother Dorgon assumed the regency), the Manchus were poised on the northern border, ready to strike the Chinese Empire a mortal blow.

In the meantime, the peasant rebellion was pursuing a shifting course. After suffering a serious defeat in 1640, Li Tzu-ch'eng managed to regroup his forces and renew the struggle, calling for the overthrow of the Ming dynasty, and promising the peasants land equalization. By 1641 he was able to conquer much of Honan and capture Loyang. Another rebel leader, Chang Hsien-chung (1606–

46), to whom innumerable massacres are ascribed by gentry chroniclers, succeeded simultaneously in becoming the master of Szechuan. However, there was no cooperation between these two leaders, since they regarded each other as rivals for the imperial throne.

In the first month of 1644, Li Tzu-ch'eng embarked on his final campaign against the Ming, proclaiming the establishment of a new dynasty, the Shun. His immense army marched from Shensi towards Peking, encountering practically no resistance. The capital fell without a struggle and the last Ming emperor, abandoned by most of his officials, hanged himself on Prospect Hill. The Ming dynasty had collapsed completely, but there were still large government armies in many parts of the country. The most important of these was the force stationed in Shanhaikuan, the key fortress located on the coast where the Great Wall reaches the sea. This army, whose task was to defend the frontiers against the Manchus, was under the command of Wu San-kuei (1612–78). Coming from a Liaotung landlord family, Wu was well aware of the Manchus' willingness to draw high Chinese officials to their side, and of the true nature of their plans regarding China. Li Tzu-ch'eng's attempts to persuade Wu to struggle together with the insurgents against the Manchus failed completely, probably primarily because of Wu's unwillingness to ally himself with an army of peasant rebels. Hence, when Li marched with a large army against Wu, the latter scurried to submit to the Manchus and to request their aid. The Manchus lost no time in availing themselves of such a superb opportunity and, during the crucial instant of the struggle between the armies of Li and Wu, the waiting Manchu cavalry joined the mêlée to inflict a crushing defeat on the peasant insurgents.

Li Tzu-ch'eng fled back to Peking with the remnants of his army and then sought refuge in his native Shensi. Shortly thereafter, the Manchus entered the capital and proclaimed their ruler, Fu-lin, as the emperor of China. Posing also as the avengers of the Ming, the Manchus expressed their intention to suppress the peasant insurrection. The great majority of the Chinese gentry responded favourably to this appeal to their class prejudices and interests, and hastened to recognize the Ch'ing as the new rulers of China. Almost all the Ming officials and generals were quick to surrender and, in the apt phrase of a modern Chinese historian, 'to lick the boots of their new masters'. They then rendered the Manchus invaluable aid in organizing new armed forces for the purpose of eliminating the still numerous peasant armies. There is little doubt that, in view of the relative numerical weakness of the invaders, it was the collaboration of the Chinese landlord gentry which made the Manchu conquest feasible.

Ming Culture

Cultural development in the Ming era also reflected the general tendency of reverting to Chinese sources, with the aim of reviving native intellectual and artistic traditions. A conscious attempt was made to hark back to the T'ang, but, as Waley has put it, the verve and grandeur of the latter were never truly recaptured. Nonetheless, there were many noteworthy achievements in the close to three centuries of Ming rule.

In philosophy, the work of Wang Yang-ming (1472–1529) was undoubtedly the most outstanding. Wang represented a distinct trend of thought, opposed to the ever more moribund official Neo-Confucianism of the Chu Hsi school. In his highly speculative philosophy, which Chinese Marxist historians classify as subjective idealism, Wang devoted much attention to problems regarding human nature, stressing, probably under the influence of Buddhist ideas, the importance of meditation and intuitive knowledge. His views gained considerable support and some authors maintain that during the last century of the Ming era their influence was greater than that of the orthodox Chu Hsi philosophy.

As a concomitant of the tendency to recreate the past, the Ming period was noted for its gigantic encyclopedias. The most famous was the *Yung-lo ta-tien*, compiled on the orders of the emperor in the years 1403–8. 2180 scholars were engaged in this task, and the finished product consisted of 11,095 volumes dealing with every aspect of knowledge. Unfortunately, since it was too expensive to print it, only three sets of this valuable work were produced, and its fate was to be as sad as that of so many other Chinese cultural monuments. Two of the sets were lost during the Manchu conquest, and the remaining one

159

was destroyed, almost in its entirety, when the Hanlin Academy which housed it was burned down in 1900 during the siege of the legations. Only slightly over 800 volumes are known to have survived.

It is customary to refer to the Ming as the age which saw the flourishing of a new literary genre, the novel, an event considered by many authors as the most telling development in Chinese literature during the last 600 years. The most significant feature of the novel rested in its employment of the vernacular; hence, its accessibility and popularity with an ever more literate public. However, for this very reason, the scholar-officials denigrated this genre as frivolous, and thus the authors preferred, in most cases, to remain anonymous. The Ming novel is characterized by its realism and critical approach to social problems, and these traits appear in most of the great works for which the era was famous.

Historical themes, which had earlier figured in Chinese drama, continued to be of prime importance. This was the case with the *Shui-hu chuan* (known in English as 'The Water Margin' or 'All Men are Brothers'), the picaresque epic portraying the largely authentic struggle of a famous group of outlaws during the Northern Sung period. The vivid, dramatic narrative was replete with revolutionary overtones, since the abuses against which these rebels fought were equally, or perhaps even more, present during the Ming. Historical events also constituted the subject matter of perhaps the best-known work in Chinese literature, the *San-kuo chih yen-i* ('The Romance of the Three Kingdoms'), a sprawling account of one of China's most strife-ridden eras. The heroes and villains of this work became familiar to practically all Chinese, literate or otherwise, since innumerable plays were to be based on it. While dealing with the adventures of a historical personage, a famous Buddhist pilgrim, the *Hsi-yu chi* ('Pilgrimage to the West' or 'Monkey') is more akin to a legendary fable, with much of the fantastic and supernatural. Its main hero is not the pilgrim, but one of his companions, the monkey Sun Wu-kung. Brilliantly portrayed, the monkey is actually only too human and one of the best-loved characters in Chinese fiction, while the novel is renowned for its wit and imaginativeness. The last of the four most famous Ming novels, *Chin P'ing Mei* (usually called 'The Golden Lotus'), does not deal with an historical subject but concerns itself with a richly circumstantial description of the life of its main character, a rake-like, rich apothecary. Its portrayal of women was innovatory in its high degree of realism, while its unrestrained eroticism may draw attention away from its value as a social document for, while pretending to take place during the Northern Sung, it actually presents a devastating picture of Late Ming society.

There is no easily perceptible transition in painting between the Yüan and the Ming, since the traditions established in the Sung were faithfully, perhaps even too much so, continued. During the Ming, appreciation of the works of past ages reached still greater heights, art criticism flourished and magnificent collections were formed. It is probably true that creativeness and originality slackened, since the traditions accumulated for over a millennium did weigh heavily on the brushes of the Ming painters. Nonetheless, there were many outstanding masters among the more than one thousand known painters of this era whose production was prolific. Some authors consider Shen Chou (1427–1509), who employed a great variety of styles, as perhaps the most eminent artist of this era. He was also regarded as a leading light of a trend which was to gain predominance – the 'wen jen hua' – the painting of the scholars. This tendency was also ably represented by Wen Chen-ming (1470–1567?), noted for his versatility and his unmistakable, marvellously pellucid calligraphy. Two other greatly famous Ming painters cannot be easily pigeonholed as followers of any school or trend. The unconventional T'ang Yin (1470–1523) was both a superb landscapist and an original painter of figures, birds and flowers, whose works tended basically to realism. Ch'iu Ying (1522–60) produced large quantities of finely detailed and splendidly coloured scrolls, mostly on classical historical subjects, and is considered to be the last great master in the 'blue and green' tradition. However, the forgery of paintings had by this time become almost a major industry, and genuine originals, both in his case and that of T'ang Yin, are truly rare.

The painters mentioned above are referred to as the Four Great Masters of the Ming, whose work still shows commendable vitality. The triumph, however, of the 'wen jen hua' school, whose views were epitomized by its leading theorist, Tung Ch'i-ch'ang (1555–1636), led to a highly formalistic approach to painting. Much attention was devoted to the study of technique, and to the compilation of manuals containing minute descriptions of the proper methods of rendering given objects. This mania for classification was extended also to the history of Chinese painting, and a completely spurious division of painters into a Northern and Southern school was undertaken by Tung and his associates, which is still, at times, repeated uncritically by Western historians of Chinese art. It is rather doubtful whether any truly great pictures were produced by Tung and the school of scholars' painting.

The Ming age is also deservedly famous for its ceramics. The well-known imperial potteries in Chingtechen (Kiangsi) were founded in 1369, and quickly became a major centre producing a beautiful translucent white ware. Almost from the outset it was painted in various colours, with the blue on white as the most renowned. While some authors regard Sung porcelain as unsurpassable, others are inclined to the belief that the apogee of the potter's art was reached by the Ming. The practice of placing reign marks on the ware was introduced at the beginning of this period. It would be naive, however, to believe that the presence of such a mark can vouch for the authenticity of a given piece of porcelain. As in the case of painting, the remarkable skill of the Chinese craftsmen has been responsible for the production, especially in the nineteenth century, of immense quantities of excellently executed copies.

As mentioned earlier, the Ming also have their place in history as great builders, and hence many works on Chinese art deal with architecture in connection with this period, particularly due to the fact that most of the extant edifices constructed in the traditional style date from these centuries. However, Ming architecture displayed little originality, since the aim was, once again, to reproduce the glories of the past, and hence the style of the Imperial City in Peking reflects that of Ch'ang-an and the Southern Sung. It is possible that the monumentalism so typical of it was partially an innovation, but the profuse ornamentation, as in the roof decorations, the marble staircases and balustrades, can be shown on the basis of T'ang and Sung painting to be quite traditional. This was in line with the generally conservative nature of Chinese architecture, as evinced not only by its style, but also by the materials employed and the methods of construction. Nevertheless, in spite of its archaizing tendencies, Ming architecture was at least impressive in the ambitiousness of its scope and occasionally showed, especially in its early years, some glimmer of originality, which is certainly more than could possibly be said of the decadent work of its Ch'ing successors.

7. China Under Manchu Rule

The Foundation of the Ch'ing Empire

Although the Manchus entered Peking unopposed in 1644, almost five decades were to pass before the rule of the Ch'ing dynasty was to be fully stabilized and to encompass the entire country. On the advice of their Chinese collaborators, the Ch'ing preserved the Ming system of administration with almost no alterations. However, the Manchus placed themselves in the privileged position of a ruling master race, and made a successful effort to preserve their distinct identity. The Banner system served as the principal mode of military control of the conquered country, with garrisons of Bannermen stationed in the main strategic centres. For the purpose of assuring adequate control of the administration, the Ch'ing pursued a policy of dividing the principal posts between the Manchus and Chinese. Some authors regard this arrangement as a form of diarchy, but although the Chinese scholar-officials did participate in ruling the country, the partnership was never an equal one, for the dominance of the Manchus was transparently obvious. The collaboration of the Chinese gentry had been achieved largely by leaving their economic status unchanged.

The Manchus lost little time in seeking to extend their rule over all of China. In 1644 most of the country was still under the control of the peasant insurgents or of Ming officials. The Ch'ing were soon able, with the aid of Chinese forces led by their collaborators such as Wu San-kuei, to defeat the remnant army of Li Tzu-ch'eng, gain mastery of North China, and ready themselves to attack the centres of Chinese resistance in Central and South China. After the fall of Peking members of the Ming imperial family and their followers set up a government purporting to be a continuation of the dynasty, with its capital in Nanking. However, defeat had done little to improve the nature of the Ming government, and all its previous negative traits remained apparent. Nonetheless, resistance to the Manchus in some parts of China persisted until 1662, and this period is referred to in Chinese historiography as the Southern Ming. The Nanking regime itself collapsed within a year, but some of its followers, such as Shih K'o-fa, did try to oppose the Manchus staunchly. As the commander of populous and wealthy Yangchow, Shih refused to surrender the city, which was then stormed and taken. For ten days the Manchus systematically massacred most of its inhabitants; Shih himself was executed for refusing to follow the great majority of his Ming colleagues and serve the Ch'ing.

Some of the refugee Ming princes headed ephemeral governments in South China but the Manchus, or rather the armies of their Chinese collaborators, had no difficulty in putting an end to them quickly. Nonetheless, prolonged resistance did persist in the southwest, where the forces of the last Ming ruler were composed largely of the remnants of the peasant armies of Chang Hsien-chung, who waged effective guerrilla warfare. However, inner dissensions hastened the collapse of this movement, and the Ming prince was forced in 1659 to take refuge in Burma. Three years later, the Burmese were induced to hand him over to Wu San-kuei, who promptly had him strangled.

The southeastern littoral also witnessed considerable resistance to the Ch'ing, connected with the activities of Cheng Ch'eng-kung (1623–66), the famous Koxinga of European literature. From his base in Amoy, Cheng and his large fleet kept harassing the Ch'ing successfully, extending the area under his control in the coastal provinces. The Manchu authorities responded to this threat by a forcible evacuation of the population of the coastal areas in order to deprive Koxinga of his support. Ultimately, in 1661, he established himself in Taiwan, having successfully driven out the Dutch from their factories on the island. Taiwan remained under the rule of the Cheng family up until 1683, when the Ch'ing fleet under a Chinese admiral conquered the last bit of free Chinese territory.

The Manchu conquest of Central and South China was accomplished primarily by the forces of the Chinese collaborators of the Ch'ing, and the government of these areas rested, as a result, largely in their hands. The most powerful was Wu San-kuei, whose control extended to practically the entire southwest. In 1673, the

Ch'ing government decided to put an end to this state of affairs by calling on these satraps to disband their armed forces. The result was a revolt against the Manchus, covering an immense area from Fukien to Yünnan; headed by Wu San-kuei it is known as the Rebellion of the Three Feudatories. It posed an extremely serious threat to Ch'ing rule, which was still far from being stabilized, even in the north of the country. However, Wu, who now proclaimed himself emperor of a new dynasty, failed to launch a quick and decisive attack on Peking. The Manchus were able to rally their armies for countering their many opponents, to take advantage of the dissensions within the Chinese camp, and to isolate the forces of Wu San-kuei. Nonetheless, to defeat the latter proved to be an arduous task, and it was only in 1681 that the Manchus extinguished the revolt by completing the conquest of Yünnan, where they exterminated the entire Wu family.

The decision to suppress the independent rulers of South China was to a large degree that of the emperor, K'ang-hsi, who at the age of eight had succeeded his father Fu-lin in 1661. During the above rebellion K'ang-hsi, having dispensed with his regents, first demonstrated his considerable talents, and the very length of his reign, which lasted until 1727, was a factor contributing to the stabilization of Manchu rule. There is little doubt that in this process of consolidation K'ang-hsi's own role, for there is no denying his intelligence and ability, was of significance. A prominent feature of his reign was the systematically pursued policy of seeking to gain the wholehearted support of the Chinese gentry by various means, among which the patronage of Chinese culture, assumed by K'ang-hsi himself, was especially important. Considerable success was obtained in this respect, since, with the honourable exception of some individuals from the generation still brought up under the Ming, the Chinese scholar-officials quickly transformed themselves into faithful servitors of the Ch'ing.

The successful political consolidation of Ch'ing rule and the maintenance of internal peace – a *pax manchurica* which lasted to the end of the eighteenth century – helped to eliminate the ravages caused by the conquest, and to bring about further economic growth, in particular a rise in agricultural production. This was accompanied by a steady growth of population, which was to take on spectacular proportions in the second half of the eighteenth century. There was, however, no fundamental change in the social relations of production, particularly in the countryside.

A large part of the energies of the Ch'ing was devoted to an expansion of their empire. This was particularly true of the Manchu aim to subject all of Mongolia to their rule. The task was facilitated by the continuing dissension among the Mongols themselves, and especially by the activities of Galdan (1644–97), an Eleuth (Western Mongol) leader, whose ambition was to follow in the footsteps of Chingghis Khan. In 1688 Galdan sought to achieve his goal by undertaking the conquest of the Eastern Mongols in Outer Mongolia. The latter appealed to the Ch'ing for aid, which the Manchus were only too eager to grant. By 1696, a powerful Manchu army, led by K'ang-hsi himself, crushed Galdan's forces completely, leading to the inclusion of Outer Mongolia in the Ch'ing empire. The struggle with the Eleuths was to continue, however, for another sixty years. It was also intertwined with a rivalry between them and the Manchus for the control of Tibet. In 1720 the Ch'ing succeeded in eliminating the influence of the Eleuths in Lhasa and established their suzerainty over Tibet which was to last to the end of the dynasty.

In the course of strengthening their empire the Ch'ing were to come relatively quickly into conflict with the only European power to approach China not from the sea but from the land. The Russians, in extending their mastery over Siberia, came into contact with territory claimed by the Manchus as their own already in the 1650s. After initial defeats, the Russians built a fort in 1669 in Albazin on the Amur, which immediately became a bone of contention between them and the Ch'ing. It was destroyed by the Manchus in 1685, only to be rebuilt by the Russians shortly thereafter and then besieged by the Ch'ing. Ultimately, negotiations between the contesting sides were initiated, terminating in the signing on 7 September 1689 of the Treaty of Nerchinsk, the first ever to be signed with a European state. The boundary between the two empires was fixed on the Gorbitsa and Argun rivers, and thus the lands to the north of the Amur were recognized as Ch'ing territory, a state of affairs which was to remain unaltered until 1860. Questions relating to the borders between Russian and Mongolia and Sino-Russian trade were regulated somewhat later by the Treaty of Kiakhta, signed in 1727. The Russo-Mongolian boundary established at this time coincides almost entirely with the present border between the Soviet Union and the Mongolian People's Republic. Permission was granted for the entry into Peking every three years of a Russian trade mission; the site was later transferred to Kiakhta.

The last years of K'ang-hsi's life were much embittered by the acrimonious strife for the succession among his many sons. His fourth son, known to posterity as Yung-cheng (1723–36), emerged the victor under rather dubious circumstances. His reign was marked by a further increase of despotism, to which a number of his brothers also fell victim. An all-pervasive system of secret surveillance was established, directed primarily towards the imperial bureaucracy. However, this did contribute to a certain degree to checking the further spread of corruption, the endemic disease of the Chinese monarchic government. Among the innovations introduced by Yung-cheng was the establishment of a Grand Council, a small body composed of the highest officials, which was destined later on to become the most important institution in the government. To avoid the calamities which beset his father, Yung-cheng named his successor in a secret will. His choice fell on his fourth son, destined for the longest reign in Chinese history – Ch'ien-lung (1736–96).

The Heyday of the Ch'ing Empire

Many historians tend to describe the reign of Ch'ien-lung as that of a great emperor, equal in its splendour to that of his grandfather K'ang-hsi. It would seem that, in view of the oppressive nature of the Ch'ing government, this enthusiasm for these absolute monarchs is hardly warranted. While further territorial expansion was achieved, the process of corruption and decay progressed steadily during Ch'ien-lung's years on the throne. This was particularly true of the last decade, which saw the dominance in the government of Ho-shen, the emperor's favourite courtier. Ho-shen's power was practically unlimited and his greed even more boundless, perhaps exceeding even that of the notorious eunuchs during the Ming. A high proportion of the government's revenue found its way into his coffers, and his example must have done much to demoralize still further the entire governmental establishment.

Ch'ien-lung, imitating his grandfather, was also prone to present himself as a munificent Maecenas of Chinese culture, but as will be seen later this patronage was simultaneously connected with a malevolent literary inquisition. He did amass an immense quantity of art, especially over 10,000 paintings, which later formed a major part of the famous and ill-fated Peking Palace Museum collection. His huge seal is affixed on many of the surviving works and strikes Europeans as a crude disfigurement.

When in 1796 the six decades of his reign had come to an end, Ch'ien-lung, not wishing to be emperor longer than K'ang-hsi, officially retired in favour of his son, Chia-ch'ing. This was of course pure fiction inasmuch as he continued to exercise supreme power until his death three years later.

By the end of the Ch'ien-lung period the seeming stability of the Ch'ing monarchy was to be shaken by the renewed activities of secret societies and popular revolts, which revealed the existence of a grave social and economic crisis. One of its main contributing factors was the unusually rapid growth of population, which quickly exceeded the country's economic potential, particularly in agriculture. The population rose from the figure of perhaps 100 million in the 1650s (estimates vary from 60 to 100 million) to 142 million in 1741, 243 million in 1778, and possibly 300 million by 1800. It was to increase by another 100 million by 1840. The data for the amount of land under cultivation vary considerably and are not particularly reliable, but whichever set of figures one follows it is clear that the growth of population was much more rapid than the increase of cultivated land or of agricultural production. This situation was further aggravated by the continuing process of concentration of landownership.

Among the numerous secret societies hostile to Ch'ing rule the White Lotus sect, famous for its role in expelling the Mongols, was the first to organize, in response to persecution by the authorities, an armed revolt against the Manchus. It had all the basic earmarks of a peasant rebellion and spread quickly to large areas in Hupei, Honan, Shensi and Szechuan. At the outset, the Ch'ing proved quite incapable of dealing with the insurrection, which incidentally revealed that, due to their parasitic mode of life, the Manchu Banners had lost most of their vaunted military prowess. Nine years of warfare, 1795–1804, proved to be necessary for the suppression of the rebellion, largely with the aid of newly recruited Chinese militia units. As usual, ruthless methods of pacification were employed and countless thousands of peasants were massacred.

Ch'ien-lung was prone to boast of the great military victories achieved during his reign. Of the ten campaigns he referred to, some were, in fact, quite insignificant. The most important was the renewal in 1755 of the war against the Eleuths which did end, after two years of hard fighting, in a complete victory and the almost total annihilation of the Eleuths. This success made it possible to extend Ch'ing rule to the entire Ili area, the northwestern part of present Sinkiang. It also facilitated a conquest in 1758 of the Uighur-inhabited areas in East Turkestan, thus bringing the borders of the Ch'ing empire to the Pamirs.

The Manchus also waged two prolonged campaigns against the Chin-ch'uan tribesmen in western Szechuan, who refused to acknowledge Ch'ing rule. The second one ended in 1775; three years of stubborn fighting resulted in the submission of the tribes after the stone towers in their remote mountain villages had finally been smashed by the use of European artillery. This war was particularly costly, largely due to the peculation of the Manchu generals, already very much in evidence in all the other current Ch'ing military operations.

Probably the only campaign which could have deservedly been considered a military feat was waged against the Gurkhas of Nepal, whose incursions into Tibet goaded the Ch'ing into a counteroffensive. The Manchus drove the Gurkhas back across the Himalayas, gaining their final victory close to Khatmandu. In this fashion the Ch'ing control over Tibet was strengthened still further. Military activities were also conducted by the Manchus in Burma and Vietnam, and both countries agreed to recognize the suzerainty of the Ch'ing empire.

Nonetheless, territorial expansion notwithstanding, the principal result of the policies pursued by the Manchu monarchy in the eighteenth century was to intensify the ossification of Chinese society, and to slow down the dynamism of its development, especially as compared with the Sung era, thus ultimately reducing drastically its chances to deal successfully with the challenge it was soon to face in the shape of Western penetration and aggression in East Asia in the coming century. Paradoxically, it was precisely this increasingly moribund society which was considered by many of Europe's greatest eighteenth-century thinkers as the model of an enlightened and benevolent monarchy. These views were derived primarily from the copious works of the Jesuits who, for almost two centuries, were the principal transmitters of things Chinese to Europe. The despotism of the Ch'ing did not disturb or dismay the Pope's militant soldiers in the slightest, and they continued to cherish the hope that their flexible policies would ultimately bring about the conversion of the Manchu empire. But, ironically, their work proved to have much more effect on European thought than on the future of China. In fairness, nevertheless, it must be stated that the Jesuits numbered in their ranks many outstanding scholars, deeply steeped in Chinese traditional culture. The works of Couplet and du Halde constituted the main sources of concepts and data relating to China to be reflected in the writings of Leibniz and Voltaire, while de Mailla's translation of Chu Hsi's abridgement of 'The Comprehensive Mirror' was utilized by Gibbon. An impressive amount of material was made available in two other famous collections of Jesuit writings, the 'Lettres édifiantes et curieuses' and the 'Mémoires concernant l'histoire . . . des chinois'. But the fundamental goal of the Jesuits – the conversion of China to Christianity – proved to be unattainable. Many factors contributed to such an outcome; a shift from tolerance to persecution in the policies of the Ch'ing, acrimonious rivalry among the Catholic missionaries and, perhaps most significantly, the growing disrepute brought upon the Christian faith by the activities of its purported believers, the European colonizers of East Asia.

Culture in the Early and Middle Ch'ing

In achieving the political consolidation of their empire, the Ch'ing rulers paid much attention, as mentioned, to gaining the acquiescence of the Chinese scholar-officials to their rule. The considerable success they achieved was largely due to the very nature of the Confucian cultural tradition, whose most orthodox forms they supported and encouraged. However, while the great majority of the Chinese gentry quickly became loyal servitors of the Ch'ing, a few outstanding scholars, such as Huang Tsung-hsi, Ku Yen-wu and Wang Fu-chih, retained their intellectual independence and, although remaining within the bounds of this tradition, made significant contributions to the further development of Chinese thought. In all cases, the influence of their work was to become much greater during the final crisis of Ch'ing rule in the nineteenth century than in their own lifetime.

Huang Tsung-hsi (1610–95), an eminent scholar, well-versed in all fields of classical culture, was particularly renowned as a historian. Coming from a family prominent in the Tung-lin reform movement, Huang himself took part initially in the Southern Ming resistance to the Manchu conquest. Convinced finally of its futility, he retired to devote himself to learning, becoming the most outstanding specialist on Ming history. Among his many works the most significant perhaps is 'A Plan for a Prince'. In it Huang, analysing the causes of the downfall of the Ming, trenchantly criticized many aspects of the absolute monarchy, and some of these views were to be adopted by the leaders of the reform movement at the end of the nineteenth century. Huang was also the author of a lengthy history of Ming philosophy, regarded as the first great work devoted to Chinese intellectual thought, in which he emphasized the negative effects of Neo-Confucianism.

Ku Yen-wu (1613–82) had also participated in a resistance to the Manchus, refusing to collaborate with them during his entire life. Delving into the causes of the collapse of the Ming dynasty, Ku concluded that the debilitating effects of Neo-Confucianism, both the orthodox Chu Hsi school and even more the views of Wang Yang-ming, had been primarily responsible for this catastrophe. According to Ku, a proper renovation of classical scholarship, combined with an appreciation of practical activity, was indispensable. Devoting himself to such a task, he became an outstanding scholar, noted for his works on historical phonetics, historical geography and epigraphy. Ku's approach was to form the basis for the Han School of Learning, which applied more objective and precise methods of research to historical writing.

Wang Fu-chih (1619–92) had also opposed the Manchus,

adamantly rejecting the legitimacy of the Ch'ing government. Living in retirement on his estate, he devoted almost his entire life exclusively to scholarship. A talented philosopher, Wang continued the sceptical trend present in Confucianism. His most famous works, however, dealt with historical problems, and in them he expressed his critical appraisal of the autocratic and bureaucratic nature of the Chinese monarchy. Wang also evolved an unconventional approach to historical evolution, which he perceived as a process of development by stages. His strong anti-barbarian, and hence anti-Manchu views, were most likely the reason why the majority of his works were to be published only two centuries later, when they were to be admired by the advocates of the reform movement.

The achievements of the above scholars, and others who followed similar paths in the seventeenth and eighteenth centuries, such as Yen Yüan (1635–1704), an iconoclastic critic of Neo-Confucianism, or Tai Chen (1724–77), probably the ablest philosopher of the Ch'ing era and the most skilful opponent of the Sung school, assured them an eminent place in the history of Chinese thought. Nevertheless, due primarily to the consistent and constant support of the Ch'ing government, Neo-Confucianism retained its dominant position as the obligatory and solely acceptable orthodox ideology up to the end of the nineteenth century.

The patronage of Chinese culture, as implemented by K'ang-hsi and Ch'ien-lung, had, as noted, the clear political aim of assuring the adherence and submissiveness of the Chinese scholar-officials and of promoting an ideological conformity conducive to the stability of Ch'ing rule. Simultaneously, the Manchu emperors sought to prove their capacity for appreciating the culture of the country their ancestors had subdued. In all these respects, the success obtained was far-reaching.

The K'ang-hsi era witnessed the production of many famous works, in the preparation of which numerous Chinese scholars were employed. In line with the accepted tradition, the history of the preceding dynasty was compiled in the fashion of the previous Standard Histories. The renowned and voluminous K'ang-hsi dictionary appeared in 1716. But undoubtedly the greatest scholarly work was the *Ku-chin t'u-shu chi-ch'eng* ('Synthesis of Books and Illustrations of Ancient and Modern Times'), a gigantic compendium, composed primarily of extracts, contained in 10,000 chapters (100 million characters). An edition printed in 1888 comprises 1700 volumes. During the Ch'ien-lung period an even more grandiose project resulted in the production of the Imperial Manuscript Library, *Ssu-k'u ch'üan-shu* ('Complete Library in Four Branches'), incorporating either summaries or the entire texts of thousands of ancient works. Due to its immense size (36,000 volumes) the Manuscript Library was never printed, but seven handwritten sets were made, of which four are believed still to be in existence. However, and this was characteristic of the Ch'ing, the compilation of this work was also utilized for the destruction of thousands of works which the Ch'ing authorities found objectionable, while in many others all the references to the Manchus or earlier nomads deemed to be pejorative were expunged, as were concepts regarded as unorthodox. But this literary inquisition did not limit itself to the written word, for a number of authors were executed and their families persecuted, thus revealing the Ch'ing patronage of culture in its true light.

The Early and Middle Ch'ing are probably the last occasion when it is justified to devote at least a few lines to Chinese painting. There was no noticeable break of continuity with the Ming, but the previous tendency to eclecticism and the lack of originality grew stronger. Still, there were quite a few outstanding talents among the thousands of scholar-officials who practised this art. Wang Shih-min (1592–1680), a pupil of Tung Ch'ing-ch'ang, devoted himself to a thorough study of the Yüan masters, amassing a large collection of their works. His own paintings were noted for their technical proficiency. Wang Chien (1598–1677), a close friend of Wang Shih-min, who also came from a prosperous gentry family, followed much the same tendencies. Both of them are regarded as first-rate landscapists. Wang Hui (1632–1717), a pupil of Wang Shih-min, immersed himself in copying the style of the Yüan, Sung and T'ang eras, becoming, in the words of one author, 'the epitome of an eclectic artist'. Wang Yüan-ch'i (1642–1715), Wang Shih-min's grandson, became K'ang-hsi's court painter and one of the compilers of an immense compendium on painting and calligraphy. Wu Li (1632–1718) who, interestingly enough, became a Jesuit missionary, has some very fine landscapes to his credit, while Yün Shou-p'ing (1633–90) is regarded as the last truly great painter of flowers. The artists mentioned above are generally referred to as the Six Great Masters of the Ch'ing.

A completely different tradition, much closer to that of the Ch'an Buddhist painters than to the 'wen jen hua' represented by the Six Masters, was followed by perhaps the most talented, and certainly the most remarkable two painters of the Ch'ing period, both of them Buddhist monks. Chu Ta (Pa-ta shan-jen, 1626–1710), purportedly a Ming prince who retired to a monastery, chose birds and flowers as his favourite subject. But his ominous, weird but highly expressive birds, done in monochrome ink, have nothing in common with the glossy pedantic realism of Hui-tsung. Tao-chi (Shih-t'ao, 1630–1707) is regarded by some art historians as probably the greatest Ch'ing painter, whose markedly impressionistic style resembled that of some of the Northern Sung masters. These men, with their strong individualistic bent, were an exception, while painting, as a whole, also became affected by the moribund sterility, characteristic of Ch'ing rule, which with its penchant for everything conservative, almost succeeded in reducing to nothingness the greatest of the Chinese art forms. Since it will be impossible to find space for Chinese art in the twentieth century, a short postscript here might be appropriate. Traditional Chinese painting did find able practitioners, such as the renowned Ch'i Pai-shih (1863–1957). At present, after the ravages of the 'cultural revolution', during which almost everything connected with the country's heritage, including this art, was proscribed, the new works produced show much promise and demonstrate that the traditional technique of Chinese painting can undoubtedly be endowed with new vitality, and the immense treasure house of its glorious past used as a fruitful source of inspiration.

It goes almost without saying that the Manchu conquest did not cause the splendidly skilled and highly talented Chinese craftsmen to suddenly lose all their capabilities. Nonetheless, the Ch'ing era can be generally considered as almost devoid of any inventiveness and addicted to obnoxiously tasteless archaism in all domains. One can maintain that in ceramics, the youngest of the Chinese arts, these tendencies were not as apparent, at least during the first century of Manchu rule when further significant progress was still being made in this field. The famous works in Chingtechen were expanded still further, and an even higher level of technical proficiency attained.

This was particularly true of the production of enamel ware during the K'ang-hsi period. Some new monochrome glazes, such as the marvellous 'sang de boeuf', were also introduced. The export of increasingly large quantities of Chinese ware to Europe from the beginning of the eighteenth century onwards accounts for the profusion of Chinese porcelain in European museums and collections, causing it also to be assuredly the best known of all Chinese art forms, to which much valuable research and study has been devoted. However, it probably also brought about a lowering of the quality of the ware produced, and thus by the nineteenth century there was practically no trace left of originality, or much taste for that matter, but only ingenious imitations.

The general desiccation of Chinese culture under the Ch'ing did not fail to affect literature as well. But, as in the case of other domains, there were exceptions to the rule, and two of them are especially noteworthy. *Ju-lin wai-shih* ('The Scholars'), the work of Wu Ching-tzu (1701–54), an impecunious scholar and writer, is a splendid satirical novel, whose loosely connected episodes are devoted largely to an unmasking of the hypocrisy and cringing conformism of the scholar-officials, and to a relentless criticism of contemporary institutions, especially the examination system. The same century also saw the appearance of what is considered by many as the greatest Chinese novel, *Hung-lou meng* ('The Dream of the Red Chamber', or 'A Dream of Red Mansions'), written by Ts'ao Chan (1715–63), although it is maintained that the last 40 of the 120 chapters were added by another author after Ts'ao's death. The work is considered largely autobiographical and relates, in infinite detail and much subtlety, the history of Ts'ao's own very wealthy family, whose fortune was derived from its faithful service to the Manchu imperial house during the K'ang-hsi era. The decay and descent of this family into ruin constitutes the book's basic theme. But, at the same time, it narrates the tragic love story of its two principal characters. A large gallery of other members of the household is portrayed with vivid skill as well. The interpretation of the novel's fundamental significance has given rise to innumerable controversies, especially during the past fifty years. Some of them were conducted on a proper intellectual level, while others, during the 'cultural revolution', served only as a political weapon for denigrating supposed ideological opponents.

China in the First Decades of the Nineteenth Century

The steady process of decline of the Ch'ing government became still more apparent during the reign of Chia-ch'ing (1796–1820). Although the White Lotus rebellion had been crushed, further popular discontent manifested itself in new disturbances of which the most important was an armed insurrection organized by the T'ien Li (Heavenly Reason) secret society. While the plans of the rebels to capture Peking itself were frustrated, the rising nevertheless embraced a large part of Shantung, Hopei and Honan, and was put down only with difficulty and the usual brutality. During the thirty years' rule of the subsequent Manchu emperor, Tao-kuang (1821–51), the position of the Ch'ing monarchy was to be weakened still further, since all the factors contributing to the social crisis became exacerbated. Moreover, a new element of crucial significance now appeared on the scene – the enhanced, aggressive penetration of East Asia by the Western powers.

Trade relations between China and the West had increased considerably from the middle of the eighteenth century, and it is indisputable that the initiative in this development rested solely with the latter. In view of the economic self-sufficiency of its immense empire, the Ch'ing government had no particular interest in favouring a further growth in foreign trade, which it regarded as of marginal importance. The Western powers, however, and Great Britain in particular, strove not only to increase their import of Chinese goods, primarily tea, silk and porcelain, but were especially anxious to gain access to the Chinese market for the export of their own manufactured products. The attainment of such a goal was frustrated by the policies of the Manchu government, aimed at maintaining the isolation of China and limiting the scope of foreign trade. Since 1757 the Ch'ing authorities restricted trade exclusively to Canton, placing it in the hands of a small guild of merchants, the Cohong, which, in effect, became a government-supervised monopoly. The vexations and tribulations of doing business in Canton with the Cohong and the greedy, bribe-seeking Chinese officials, narrated prolifically in contemporary accounts, only served to stimulate the desire of the foreign merchants to remove these hindrances. These aims were also fully shared by the British government, which sought to create more favourable conditions for the further development of trade with China by establishing direct contact with the Ch'ing monarchy. However, two British ventures, the expediting in 1793 of a mission to Peking, headed by Lord Macartney, and of a subsequent one in 1861, led by Lord Amherst, ended in total failure, since the Manchu rulers saw no reason to change their basic policy of isolation.

The bulk of the China trade rested in British hands, with the East India Company playing the principal role, until its demise in 1834, and developing the famous triangle – English textiles to India, Indian cotton to China, Chinese tea, silk and porcelain to England. But the triangle had one serious drawback, the value of the goods sold to China was considerably lower than the cost of the imports from China, hence necessitating supplementary payment in silver. Thus the problem of eliminating this imbalance, especially if the trade relations were to grow as the British desired, became an urgent issue. The lack of demand for European products, in view of the above-mentioned self-sufficiency of the Chinese economy, continued to present a seemingly insuperable obstacle. Nonetheless, the British did manage to solve the problem most ingeniously by stumbling on a product with the aid of which they could force their way into the Chinese market – opium.

The custom of smoking opium, probably introduced by the Dutch in the seventeenth century, began to spread in the next century. By the first years of the nineteenth century it had become a plague, since the usage of this horrible drug reached out from the urban centres to cover a large part of the entire country. By 1840 the number of addicts was counted in the millions. A convincing sociological study of this phenomenon still remains to be written. Some authors regard it as a specific reflection of the decay of Chinese society under Manchu rule. Practically all the opium consumed was imported since, surprisingly enough, large-scale growing of the opium poppy was started in China much later and the foreign narcotic was always considered superior. The data on import give a clear picture of the growth of this traffic. In the 1760s, an annual average of 1000 chests (133 lb each) was brought into China, to increase by the 1820s to close to 10,000 chests and reach 40,000 in 1838–9. The profits gained from this 'most infamous and atrocious trade' (Gladstone), the lion's share of which accrued to the British, were huge, exceeding by 1836 the value of the tea and silk imported from China. The gains were, in fact, even more substantial, since almost all the opium was produced in India, and the margin between its price there and that charged in Canton was very considerable, to the benefit of the British merchants handling it. Taxes on the opium trade made up one-seventh of the revenue of the British government in India, while the tax on tea, now paid for by the sale of opium, provided one-tenth of the total revenue of the United Kingdom government.

The Ch'ing government failed to face up to the problems of the opium trade, but it did ban it at an early stage, and hence it assumed the character of a completely illegal contraband traffic. The drug was smuggled into China by the foreign merchants with the connivance of appropriately bribed Ch'ing officials, while the authorities proved entirely incapable of enforcing the prohibition. However, the sharp alteration in the balance of payments, caused by the growth of the opium trade, resulted in a sizable drain of silver from China, with very serious consequences for the country's economic position. This impelled the Ch'ing government to re-examine its policy; the decision to grapple finally with this evil led it to its first confrontation with the West, which was to reveal the utter incapacity of the Manchus to defend effectively the country they ruled by right of conquest.

8. The Opium Wars and the Taiping Revolution

The First Opium War

In the 1830s the British attempted once again to alter the conditions of the China trade to their satisfaction, but the mission headed in 1834 by Lord Napier, which never got further than Canton, ended in a farcical failure. The majority of the British merchants were inclined ever more to advocate a policy of employing force in order to achieve the desired goal of 'opening up' China, and these views were shared enthusiastically by the new Superintendent of Trade in Canton, Charles Elliot. Simultaneously, the Ch'ing government continued the review of its policies towards the opium problem; the great debate, involving almost all its highest officials, ended in 1838 with the victory of the group favouring the complete suppression of the opium trade and the eradication of its usage. Its main representative was Lin Tse-hsü (1785–1850), a prominent official, noted for his probity, justice and humaneness, and it was his eloquent advocacy of this cause that finally persuaded the inept and vacillating Tao-kuang to adopt an anti-opium policy. Lin himself was appointed Imperial Commissioner, with orders to proceed to Canton and undertake the appropriate measures to liquidate the opium traffic. Fundamentally, it was Lin's attempt to carry out his mission which constituted the immediate cause of the First Opium War.

After his arrival in Canton in March 1839, Lin Tse-hsü, tackling the issue at its primary source, ordered the foreign merchants, overwhelmingly British, to surrender the immense stock of opium held by them. When his appeal remained unanswered, Lin caused the foreign factories to be blockaded and all the Chinese servants employed there recalled. Thus the 350-strong merchant colony was reduced to the terrible privation of having to cook and keep house themselves. This 'inhuman and barbaric' treatment proved sufficient to effect a surrender of opium involved and to obtain a pledge from the merchants, soon to be broken by almost all of them, that they would never again engage in this commerce. Elliot himself confirmed the agreement; over 20,000 chests of opium were handed over and, subsequently, on Lin's orders, destroyed in public. Lin quickly lifted the restrictions imposed on the merchants but the latter, at Elliot's instigation, left Canton, immediately went back on their pledges and started smuggling new supplies of their prize product in other localities on the seacoast. In fact, Elliot awaited the arrival of military forces and had agreed to surrender the opium primarily to create a *casus belli*.

In July, the murder of a local villager by drunken British sailors led to a further exacerbation of the situation. The British refused Lin's demand that those responsible be handed over, having in the meantime quickly set them free after a parody of a trial. Lin countered this action with a complete boycott of the British ships. Ultimately, the arrival of the awaited British naval and land forces decided the issue. On 3 November, two British men-of-war attacked a fleet of Chinese war junks in the Pearl River estuary. The First Opium War was on.

The outbreak of the conflict with China gave rise to much controversy in England itself, since there was considerable opposition to this unsavoury enterprise. Gladstone's opinion was particularly pertinent: 'A war more unjust in its origin, a war more calculated to cover this country with permanent disgrace, I do not know and have not read of. The British flag is hoisted to protect an infamous traffic.' Nonetheless, the Melbourne government, having scraped through a debate in the House of Commons in April 1840 on the China issue with a bare majority, proceeded further with the military operations, without bothering to declare war.

After the arrival in June 1840 of further reinforcements from India, the British, having blockaded Canton, dispatched their fleet to the north, ultimately reaching Taku, the port of Tientsin, on 10 August, where they were able to present their demands to the Ch'ing government. These included compensation for the confiscated opium, an indemnity to cover the cost of the war, the removal of barriers on future trade, the establishment of relations on an 'equal' footing, and the granting of an island base. The Manchu court, thoroughly frightened by this advance to a point so relatively close to Peking and anxious to bring about the retreat of the British from North China, agreed to begin negotiations. An influential imperial clansman, the utterly corrupt and fantastically wealthy Ch'i-shan, was appointed negotiator, and was soon to replace Lin Tse-hsü as the Imperial Commissioner in Canton, where the talks began in September.

The opening of negotiations and Ch'i-shan's appointment actually signified a victory of the court faction which had been in favour of retaining a status quo in respect of the opium problem, and was now willing to capitulate to the British demands. Composed mostly of Manchu aristocrats, this group was concerned primarily with preserving the power of the Ch'ing regime, subordinating everything to this aim. One of this faction's first moves was to bring about the disgrace of Lin Tse-hsü, who was promptly saddled with the responsibility for the Ch'ing failure to face up to British aggression, removed from office and later exiled to Ili. It is worth noting that Lin was one of the first individuals to become aware of the abysmal ignorance of the Chinese as regards the rest of the world, and to realize that, in view of the technical superiority of the West, this constituted a factor militating against the chances of defending China effectively. This was especially apparent in the military domain, for the arms of the Ch'ing forces, basically unchanged since the seventeenth century, could not possibly match those of the British. Lin therefore initiated the translation of a number of works on European geography and science, but this pioneering endeavour found little support or understanding, for the arrogance of the Manchu aristocrats and the cultural superiority complex of the Chinese scholar-officials were barely perturbed by the critical outcome of the First Opium War.

The negotiations in Canton having failed to produce concrete results, the British launched an attack on Chinese positions near the city, thereby forcing Ch'i-shan to sign the Ch'uan-pi Convention on 20 January 1841. It provided for the cession of Hong Kong, the payment of an indemnity of six million yuan (Chinese dollars), the recognition of 'equality' in official Sino-British negotiations, and a full resumption of trade. However, when Tao-kuang finally discovered what the terms really were, the treaty was quickly repudiated, and Ch'i-shan recalled in disgrace to lose his entire, immense fortune. The emperor ordered an offensive against the British which ended in a fiasco; by the end of May all the defences of Canton had been lost and a truce reached, with the Ch'ing authorities agreeing to pay a six-million-dollar ransom in order to save the city.

The last stage of hostilities, lasting exactly a year, began in August 1841. Since resistance in the Canton area had been effectively crushed, the British dispatched a new expedition to East and Central China which succeeded in capturing first Amoy, and later a large part of eastern Chekiang, including Ningpo. The attempts of the Manchus to launch a counteroffensive failed dismally, and the arrival of further reinforcements from India in the spring of 1842 enabled the British to begin a new campaign in the Yangtse estuary. In some cases resistance was very strong, with the Chinese and Manchu garrisons fighting to the last man, but the superiority of British arms was overpowering. The British fleet and army began its slow ascent of the Yangtse, China's jugular vein, capturing the important strategic city of Chinkiang, where the Grand Canal crosses the Great River, on 21 July. The men-of-war then crept ahead towards Nanking, with the opium ships trailing immediately behind; by 10 August their guns were trained on the great southern metropolis.

The threat to Nanking was sufficient to extinguish the last spark of a will to resist in Peking. The Ch'ing government, apprehensive of the political consequences of further disasters, quickly empowered a new Imperial Commissioner, the imperial clansman Ch'i-ying, to open peace negotiations. The talks, held from 24 to 26 August under the shadow of British naval guns, hardly deserve to be called negotiations, since the terms were dictated by the British. After a properly pious introductory phrase regarding future 'Peace and Friendship' between the two countries, the text of the accord dealt with more mundane issues. Its main provisions stipulated, *inter alia*, the payment by China of $21 million ($6 million compensation for the confiscated opium, $12 million war costs indemnity, $3 million to cover Cohong debts), the opening of five ports (Canton, Amoy, Foochow, Ningpo and Shanghai) to British trade and residence, the cession of Hong Kong and the establishment of a customs tariff. The last point was later interpreted to signify that any changes of the tariff rate required British assent. In effect, this entailed the loss by China of tariff autonomy for almost a century, and constituted a grievous blow to future attempts at economic modernization. Charac-teristically, there was no mention in the treaty of the principal direct cause of the war – the opium question. Chinese requests that the British should seek to limit the drug's production and export were dismissed with the casual remark that if the British were not to sell it, others would. The opium trade, with Hong Kong as its main base, flourished splendidly in the decades following the Nanking Treaty.

The terms extorted in Nanking were supplemented a year later by the Treaty of the Bogue (Humenchai). Apart from setting the tariff rate at a low 5 per cent, the treaty also called for the future application of the 'most-favourite-nation' principle, fittingly described by Dennett as 'a device by which every nation thereafter could secure for itself any privilege which had been extorted by some other power from China by force, or tricked from her by fraud, without having to assume the moral responsibility for the method by which the concession had been obtained'.

The significance of the Nanking Treaty, the first of the unequal treaties to be imposed on China, was truly far-reaching, since it ushered in a century of degradation and ignominious humiliation, bitterly resented by the Chinese to the present. The opening up of China, which ultimately resulted in the transformation of the country into a semi-colony, also led to consequences more extensive than those of any other previous incursion. All of the earlier invaders had been either assimilated or finally expelled; in the nineteenth and early twentieth century these processes could not be repeated, and hence the task of re-establishing China's full independence and rightful position in the modern world posed completely new problems. The search for the correct solutions and the proper ways to implement them occupied the best minds of the country for over a century, and constitutes a fundamental component of modern Chinese intellectual and political history.

The initiative lay with Britain, but other Western countries were just as anxious to participate and avail themselves of the new opportunities. The Americans were first in the queue; their trade with China had already reached fairly respectable dimensions, although it could not be compared with that of the British. In order to avoid paying for Chinese goods with silver, almost all the American merchants also engaged in the opium traffic, but their share of it was only 3 per cent. Having remained neutral during the First Opium War, and reaped handsome profits during the suspension of Anglo-Chinese trade, the Americans lost no time in turning to their own account the successes of the British, while expressing much pious indignation regarding the actions of the latter. A special mission, headed by Caleb Cushing, a Massachusetts politician, was dispatched to China in July 1843; its supposed aim was 'to save the Chinese from the condition of being an exclusive monopoly in the hands of England'. This noble motivation was also reflected in a letter from President Tyler to the Emperor of China, couched in the language customarily employed by the Great White Father in addressing American Indian chiefs. After his arrival in Macao towards the end of February 1944, Cushing managed to obtain the desired treaty, which was signed on 3 July in Wanghsia (Wanghia). The most-favourite-nation clause which it contained made it possible for the Americans to obtain all the concessions granted by the Nanking Treaty. In addition, the Wanghsia Treaty established consular jurisdiction over American citizens in China, a provision which was to serve as the basis for the principle of extraterritoriality, a crucial factor in future foreign penetration. It also stipulated a review of its terms after twelve years; this was to be used later by England and France to impose a new treaty on China.

France also followed in the footsteps of Britain and the United States, although its economic interests in East Asia were as yet almost non-existent. The Sino-French treaty was signed in Whampoa on 24 October 1844; it was based practically in its entirety on the Sino-American accord. One additional provision was to prove to be of much importance. The French obtained the permission to erect Catholic churches in the treaty ports, which they later interpreted unilaterally as the right to act as the protectors of Catholic missions in the entire country, while simultaneously exerting pressure on the Ch'ing authorities to extend toleration towards missionary activity. The latter, unaware of the future implications of the privileges they agreed to, hoped that the treaties with France and the United States might make possible the application of the hoary policy of setting the foreign barbarians against each other.

The Taiping Revolution

The general crisis of Ch'ing rule and the first phase of Western encroachment and penetration of China gave rise to the greatest of all the many peasant rebellions in Chinese history, the Taiping movement. The most significant aspect of the crisis was social, resting primarily in the marked deterioration of the position of the peasantry, further accentuated by the continuing growth of population and the economic consequences of the Manchu government's defeat in the First Opium War. Politically, the general debility of the Ch'ing regime, with its endemic corruption, had also become more conspicuous, while the exposure of the worthlessness of its armed forces undermined its prestige. Thus, in the period 1841–50, unrest became widespread, especially in the southern provinces, where the secret societies, among whom the Triad with its slogan of abolishing the Ch'ing and restoring the Ming was the most prominent, became very active.

The Taiping movement differed in some important respects from its predecessors in that it possessed to a greater degree a distinct ideology and sought, while overturning the existing feudal order, to replace it, at least theoretically, with a new form of society. For this reason it deserves to be classified as a revolution, in spite of its numerous limitations, negative features and finally disastrous outcome. Although it drew to its side a great multitude of followers, it was primarily the product of the activity of a few individuals. The most important of these was Hung Hsiu-ch'üan (1814–64), the originator of the Taiping ideology. Born not far from Canton in a poor peasant family of Hakka origin (the Hakkas were descendants of later immigrants to the southern provinces, distinguished by their dialect and usually inferior social position), Hung failed in his attempts to pass the examinations and thus to ascend the ladder of success, open in theory to a talented peasant son. He remained a humble village schoolteacher and the frustrations he had suffered may well have been the cause of his illness and visionary hallucinations. In 1843, influenced by Christian missionary tracts, he transmuted his visions

186

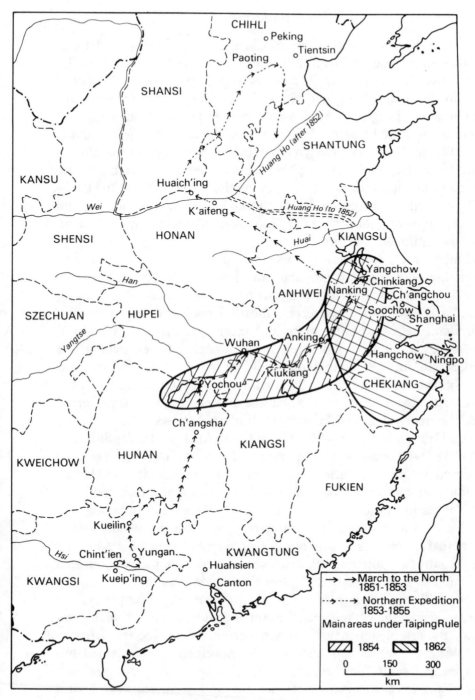

17. T'ai-p'ing T'ien-kuo

into a creed, in which elements of Christianity and concepts derived from Chinese classical tradition were inextricably intermingled. Its fundamental purport was the mission to create a Heavenly Kingdom in China, in which all men would be brothers. The revolutionary potential of Hung's doctrine is apparent, especially if one adds that he also postulated terminating the rule of the demons, the Manchus. Visualizing himself as the younger brother of Jesus in his altered version of the Trinity, Hung Hsiu-ch'üan began to preach his new religion, gaining some converts, among them Feng Yün-shan (1822–52), his fellow villager and schoolteacher, destined to become the principal propagator of the faith, and to organize its followers into the God Worshippers' Society.

Due to their iconoclastic activities Hung and Feng were shortly forced to take refuge in neighbouring Kwangsi. There, in the years 1847–9, the sect grew in strength, for Feng succeeded in gaining hundreds of new converts, mostly poor Hakka peasants, simultaneously assuming more and more the nature of a political movement. The God Worshippers also organized their own armed forces, an understandable undertaking in view of the turbulent conditions of Kwangsi and the hostility which their activity aroused among the local gentry and the Ch'ing authorities. This same period saw the emergence of additional new leaders of the sect; they included Yang Hsiu-ch'ing (1817–56), Hsiao Ch'ao-kuei (d. 1852), Shih Ta-k'ai (1831–62) and Wei Ch'ang-hui (d. 1859). The first two also claimed to be visionaries, but while the authenticity of Hung's hallucinations seems to be undoubted, it is rather clear that the claims of Yang and Hsiao were spurious trickery, aimed at obtaining the support of the credulous new converts. These six men constituted the principal historic leadership of the Taiping movement which, in spite of the latter's egalitarian tendencies, assumed from the very outset a position far superior to that of the ordinary members.

In 1849 the Taiping leaders began to formulate their plans for a revolt against the Ch'ing with the aim of achieving their fundamental goal, the establishment of a new government and society. Broadly speaking, the subsequent history of the movement can be divided into two basic periods. The first embraces the years 1850–6, during which the Taiping government was set up and numerous successful campaigns against the Manchus were waged, the second, covering the period 1856–64, witnessed the decay and ultimate downfall of the Taiping state.

After numerous local struggles with the Ch'ing authorities, which began in July 1850, the Taiping leaders, having gathered all their followers, numbering at most twenty to thirty thousand people, perhaps five thousand of whom could serve as soldiers, openly proclaimed the establishment of their new state, the T'ai-p'ing T'ien-kuo – the Heavenly Kingdom of Great Peace. The name itself revealed the eclectic amalgam of Christian and traditional Chinese concepts, in which the potentially revolutionary elements of a fundamentalist Christianity were blended with the ancient and ever present utopian trend of Chinese classical thought, as expressed in particular by the idea of 'Ta T'ung' (the 'Great Togetherness'), that splendid vision of Paradise Lost. The avowed aim was the creation, in line with these views, of a new egalitarian society, the age-old dream of the Chinese peasants. The achievement of this goal necessitated the overthrow of the Ch'ing and, as the movement grew, this anti-Manchu aspect, with its nationalist overtones, became ever more prominent. The Taipings, fervently convinced of the unique validity of their creed, also became automatically the opponents of Confucianism and hence of its main advocates – the scholar-officials. The enmity of the Taipings towards the gentry also had two additional important aspects; they despised them for being loyal servitors of the Ch'ing and, as mostly poor peasants, hated them as landlords.

The egalitarianism of the Taiping movement was also shown in the setting up of a common treasury, in which all the possessions of its followers and captured supplies were pooled for later distribution. Its armed forces, organized on traditional lines as a disciplined unit and inspired by well-nigh fanatic religious fervour, soon proved to be formidable. Five of the principal leaders shared the command of the Taiping army with each receiving a royal title, while Hung Hsiu-ch'üan himself assumed the supreme title of the Heavenly King. However, already at this early stage, signs of rivalry among them became apparent, with Yang Hsiu-ch'ing appropriating a dominant position, while Hung was slowly relegated to the role of the sect's founding father.

From September 1851 on, the Taipings were engaged in hostilities with the Ch'ing forces. Having let themselves become bottled up in the town of Yungan, they broke through the besieging troops in April 1852, and sought to capture the provincial capital, Kweilin. Although they stormed its walls with indomitable courage, the attempts failed, largely due to the inferiority of their weapons, since they possessed few firearms and no artillery. Giving up the siege of Kweilin the Taipings resolved to march into Hunan, thus beginning the transformation of their revolt from a local, provincial affair into a general, almost national, rebellion. The campaign in Hunan cost the life of Feng Yün-shan, probably the ablest and certainly the most unassuming of the Taiping leaders. Joined by many thousands of new followers, the Taipings rushed through the rich province like a mountain torrent. In the autumn of 1852 they attempted to take Ch'angsha, and failed, as in Kweilin, losing also another of the initial leaders, Hsiao Ch'ao-kuei. Abandoning the provincial capital and marching northwards they did succeed in capturing Yochow, where they were fortunate to find an immense store of weapons and ammunition. With fresh arms and countless thousands of new recruits, the Taipings swept into Hupei, capturing its capital, Wuchang, in January 1853. Relinquishing the city, a typical trait of a peasant rebellion, already an immense host in the hundreds of thousands, the Taipings swarmed down the Yangtse by water and land. The Ch'ing troops fled in panic in face of this invincible avalanche. In February, two key cities on the Great River, Kiukiang and Anking, fell into their hands, and by 8 March the Taiping army verged on Nanking, capturing it after a stubborn struggle with its Manchu garrison. Keeping up their fantastic pace, the Taipings drove further down the river to take both Chinkiang and Yangchow.

The Taiping leaders resolved to make Nanking their capital, and this decision proved to be a fateful one, for it marked both the loss of momentum of their offensive operations and the beginning of a slow process of the movement's deterioration. Nanking became the Capua of the Taipings, since here the demoralization of the leadership made steady progress, affecting especially both Hung and Yang, who became absorbed in the construction of splendid palaces to house their ever more sizable harems. The remaining original followers of the sect, perhaps 10,000 at most, also became a privileged caste in relation to the mass of new members. In their march to the Yangtse the Taipings had traversed an immense span of territory, but, although they had destroyed much of the local government, they failed to consolidate their own hold on most of these areas, which were quickly reconquered by the Ch'ing. The Manchus, while unable to face up to the offensive of the Taipings, followed in their wake and were soon to concentrate two large armies on both banks of the Yangtse, which became a constant threat to Nanking itself. Nonetheless, the Taipings did manage to retain possession of a considerable and rich area on both sides of the Yangtse, and to control the middle reaches of the Great River.

The establishment of the capital in Nanking did not actually signify an abandonment of the basic aim of the Taipings – the overthrow of the Ch'ing government. Two great expeditions, the first with the aim of conquering Peking and North China, the second with the goal of gaining mastery of the Upper Yangtse Valley, were planned and launched. However, for some reason, perhaps overconfidence, the Taiping leaders mismanaged these campaigns woefully. This was particularly true of the Northern Expedition, sent off in May 1853. Only a small force of perhaps 30,000 men was assigned to it, which, with considerable difficulties and great losses, did finally reach the area of Tientsin by the end of October. Unable to advance further, the southerners, exposed to the severity of a North China winter and constant attacks by Ch'ing cavalry, suffered incredibly. The reinforcements sent to join them failed in their mission and were themselves destroyed. After an undaunted defence of over one year, the remnants of the Northern Expedition were utterly annihilated. This disaster was to have serious consequences for the Taiping cause, for its failure gave the Ch'ing government the first opportunity to recover itself.

The Western Expedition, also launched in May 1853, did not meet with such a tragic fate, since the struggle for the mastery of the Upper Yangtse turned into a drawn-out see-saw campaign, lasting three years and revolving largely on the control of Wuhan (i.e., Wuchang, Hanyang and Hankow), repeatedly conquered and lost by the Taipings. It was in the course of this warfare that the Taipings came up against the forces which were to become their most serious antagonists. These were not the once mighty Manchu Banners, but new provincial formations organized by the Chinese gentry, the best

191

known of which was the Hunan Army, led by Tseng Kuo-fan (1811–72). A wealthy Hunanese landlord and high Ch'ing official, Tseng began the organization of his unit already in November 1852, and succeeded in transforming it from a local, gentry-led militia into a powerful army which, although it met with numerous defeats, was to become the principal anti-Taiping force. Staffed and financed by the Hunan gentry and highly paid, the Hunan Army was in effect practically Tseng's private army; the Ch'ing had no choice but to give their grudging acquiescence to its activities.

Some Western authorities have sought to glorify Tseng Kuo-fan as a defender of the Confucian tradition against the crude iconoclasm of the Taipings. While it is true that Taiping Christianity aroused, by its alien origin, the inherent xenophobia of the Chinese gentry and offended their tender Confucian sensibilities, this was not, in all certainty, the principal issue. The Taipings did support, albeit unsystematically and inconsistently, the struggle of the peasants against the landlords, themselves expropriating much of the latter's property. Thus it was in defence of their land rents and wealth, and not of the overthrown tablets in the Confucian shrines, that the Chinese gentry organized its armed forces against the Taipings. It is hard to believe that the fierce anti-Manchuism of the Taipings could not have appealed in some degree to the latent nationalism of the gentry. Had their property been left intact they might well have taken a different course and tried to join the Taipings as the seemingly winning side, notwithstanding the obnoxiousness of their ideology, in the hope that this peasant rebellion could be mastered, as had been the case so many times in the past. However, the Taipings made no attempts, at this stage, to win over this decisive class or to draw them into the new government in Nanking, and thus the gentry, in struggling against the Taipings, became the principal force responsible for propping up the tottering regime of the alien Manchus.

In spite of the failure to conquer North China and the setbacks in the struggle for the Upper Yangtse, the Taipings still held a strong position, while the possibility of gaining further victories, if offensive operations were to be conducted properly, was certainly not excluded. But the future prospects of the Taiping movement were almost totally destroyed by dissension within its own ranks, which culminated in the tragic events of the autumn of 1856. Since the arrival in Nanking, Yang Hsiu-ch'ing's power had grown immeasurably, and his despotic rule and arrogant behaviour had greatly antagonized the remaining original leaders. A plot was hatched against him, and, in September, Yang and thousands of his followers were massacred by the soldiers of Wei Ch'ang-hui, acting most probably on the orders of the Heavenly King. Wei's rule soon proved to be even more oppressive; the Taipings' best general, Shih Ta-k'ai, fled Nanking and in reprisal his entire family and many followers were killed by Wei's men. Shih returned later with his own powerful army to the capital to find that in the meantime another fearful bloodbath had occurred, since Hung Hsiu-ch'üan had caused Wei and his cohorts to be exterminated. While Shih now was named the commander in chief, he soon became apprehensive of the vicious atmosphere. In June 1857, he left Nanking for good, taking with him his army, the best the Taipings had left. He was to continue his own dramatic and forlorn struggle against the Ch'ing until 1862 when, trapped in Szechuan, he and the remnants of his force were completely wiped out.

The September massacres and Shih Ta-k'ai's departure weakened the Taiping state drastically. The control of the government remained primarily in the hands of the Heavenly King's relatives, especially his two totally inept brothers, for Hung Hsiu-ch'üan now trusted only his own family. His mental balance, never too stable, underwent further deterioration. An interlude, during which his cousin, Hung Jen-kan (1822–64), an early convert who rejoined him in Nanking in 1859, was made head of the government, seemed to offer some promise. Hung Jen-kan, a relatively well-educated Protestant preacher, and the only Taiping leader with some semblance of knowledge of the outside world, sought to reorganize the Taiping government and even to embark on a sensible programme of modernization. However, the growing crisis of the Taiping state frustrated the implementation of his plans and, anyhow, he was soon removed from power by the paranoically suspicious Heavenly King.

The struggle for survival now became the paramount issue, and this factor enhanced the role of the Taiping military leaders, whose position became ever more independent. Among the generals two young and talented individuals, Li Hsiu-ch'eng (1824–64), and

Ch'en Yü-ch'eng (1836–62), came to the forefront. Both were born in poor peasant families in the same Kwangsi village, and had risen from the ranks due to their ability. Li proved to be an outstanding commander of considerable tactical skill, and was granted the title of Chung Wang – the Loyal King. Ch'en, renowned for his personal courage, received the title of Ying Wang – the Brave King. Both were to be the mainstay of the Taiping state during its last tragic phase.

The Decline and Fall of the Taiping Kingdom

Until the spring of 1860 the position of the Taiping state continued to deteriorate, as the forces of Tseng Kuo-fan began to implement their strategic plan of depriving the Taipings of their control of the Yangtse in order to encircle Nanking, which was once more under direct threat of attack. However, the Taipings were still capable of formulating an offensive strategy of their own, which called for a new attempt to regain mastery of the Upper Yangtse by a great pincer operation on both banks of the Great River. The launching of this new Western Expedition was preceded by a masterful diversion; Li Hsiu-ch'eng's troops invaded Chekiang, returned to destroy the Ch'ing army threatening Nanking, and then conquered a large part of Kiangsu, including the important centre of Soochow. Thus, finally, the Taipings gained control of much of these two provinces, the richest and most important in the entire country, making up for their inexplicable failure to advance in this direction earlier. Having secured this significant victory, the Taipings started the Western Expedition in the autumn of 1860. Unfortunately, in spite of initial successes, the coordination between the army of the Chung Wang on the southern bank and that of the Ying Wang on the northern was defective, and the pincers failed to close. The Taiping armies eventually retreated to the east. The Hunan Army followed up this fiasco by capturing Anking in September 1861. Along with Wuhan and Kiukiang, lost by the Taipings earlier, Anking was one of the three vital strategic strongholds on the Yangtse, whose fate could prove decisive for the outcome of military operations. For this reason the fall of Anking is regarded by many authors as the crucial turning point of the entire war, since from this moment on the Taipings were forced to remain solely on the defensive.

In spite of these setbacks the Taiping kingdom was still able to continue its struggle, with the stage of its agony lasting almost two years. The surprising duration of this defence may be explained by the considerable support it still enjoyed from the population, especially in Kiangsu and Chekiang, the great majority of which much preferred the rule of the Taipings, particularly when faced with the prospect of having these areas reconquered by the Ch'ing army, notorious for its plundering and massacring of civilians. The brutality of the Imperial forces was also a calculated policy, for Tseng Kuo-fan clearly stated the aim of exterminating all the Taipings, so as to prevent a future recurrence of the peasant revolt. Hence, the Taipings fought with a courage born also of despair, with death in battle preferable to the terrible fate which awaited them if they were captured or surrendered.

A major goal of the Ch'ing, while tightening the noose on Nanking, was to recover the lands lost in Kiangsu and Chekiang. In these operations two individuals, both destined to become leading collaborators of the Ch'ing regime, rose to prominence. Li Hung-chang (1823–1901) came from a rich gentry family in Anhwei. Having served under Tseng Kuo-fan, he returned to his native province, where he was to establish the Huai Army on the same principles as Tseng's unit. In 1862 he was dispatched to Shanghai, threatened by the Loyal King's army, and as governor of Kiangsu became instrumental in obtaining substantial foreign aid for the struggle against the Taipings. With this and the use of foreign troops, Li succeeded in recovering most of Kiangsu, his campaign culminating in the capture of Soochow in December 1863. Tso Tsung-t'ang (1812–85) came from a gentry family in Hunan, and his initial career was also made as a protégé of Tseng Kuo-fan. In 1861, he was appointed commander of the Ch'ing troops in Chekiang, and later its governor. Relying also heavily on foreign aid, Tseng conducted a long campaign to reconquer Chekiang, brought to an end by the fall of Hangchow in March 1864. Whereas Li Hung-chang went on to become probably the most important single figure in the Ch'ing bureaucracy during the next 35 years, Tso Tsung-t'ang became the leading Ch'ing general, notorious for his incredible ruthlessness.

By the end of 1863, although many Taiping garrisons continued their brave and forlorn defence, Kiangsu and Chekiang had been basically lost. In the face of these disasters, Li Hsiu-ch'eng advocated the abandonment of Nanking, and a return to the south. However, the Heavenly King, still firmly convinced of the divine nature of his mission, rejected the proposal. A sizable part of the Taiping army was bottled up in Nanking, totally encircled from February 1864 on. The besieged capital was now doomed; during the siege, which began in May, Hung Hsiu-ch'üan died, to be succeeded by his fourteen-year-old son, Hung Fu. Finally, on 19 July, the Ch'ing army managed to break through Nanking's strong walls; the Taipings fought to the last man, and an incredible massacre both of the soldiers and of the remaining civilian population ensued.

A few of the leaders, among them the Chung Wang and Hung Jen-kan, managed to escape with the young king. The Loyal King, having given his better horse to his ruler, was the first to be captured. The Ch'ing had the custom of compelling their more important prisoners to write, before execution, an account of their activities. Availing himself of this, Li Hsiu-ch'eng wrote his narrative of the T'ai-p'ing T'ien-kuo – the famous Autobiography of the Chung Wang, still a fundamental source for the history of the Taiping movement. As soon as the writing was finished, Tseng Kuo-fan had him quartered. For his action Li was to be despicably maligned by the super-revolutionaries of the 1966–76 'cultural revolution', who deemed it a betrayal of the cause to which he had devoted his entire life.

The young ruler and Hung Jen-kan were soon taken prisoner also and suffered the same fate as the Loyal King. The still numerous Taiping remnants in the southern provinces, now largely deprived of leadership, continued their hopeless struggle until 1866, when most of their units were wiped out. Those to the north of the Yangtse joined forces with the Nien, the large-scale peasant movement, unconnected with the Taipings, which had been fighting the Ch'ing with varying success in Shantung, Honan and Anhwei since 1853, to keep up the struggle until the final collapse of the Nien in 1868.

The Taiping revolution was thus drowned in a sea of blood. A large part of Central China had been devastated, hundreds of towns lay in ruins, and probably fifteen to twenty million lives had been lost. Such was the price paid for the further maintenance of Manchu rule. Although the mistakes of its leadership were considerable, and its internecine struggle disastrous, the cause of the Taiping movement's defeat rested primarily not in these factors, but in the greater strength of its allied enemies – the Ch'ing regime, the Chinese gentry and the foreign powers. However, the history of these tragic years demonstrates quite clearly that the totally inept Ch'ing government could not possibly have achieved victory without the domestic and foreign aid it received. The rule of the Manchus could well have come to its deserved end in the middle of the nineteenth century had it not been propped up by the Chinese upper class and the European colonizers. Thus, guided exclusively by its own narrow class interests, the Chinese gentry played a crucial role in suppressing the great peasant revolution which it was unable to master by previously applied means, keeping in power an alien ruling caste (once regarded by its own most enlightened representatives as uncouth barbarians), whose conquest of China had been an unmitigated disaster. Moreover, by soliciting and obtaining the aid of the Westerners, the gentry facilitated the further encroachment and subjugation of their own country by the foreign powers, bringing it to a point of ignominious humiliation. The part played by the powers, dealt with later on, was perhaps of almost equal significance. Fashions change. The Middle Kingdom was no more a country to be admired from afar as a model of enlightenment and civilization. Now it was only a potential India, a country to be colonized, a nation and people to be despised and treated as coolies by the representatives of a purportedly superior Western civilization.

In suppressing the Taipings with utter ruthlessness, the Ch'ing sought to destroy all vestiges of the movement's existence; hence it is difficult to reconstruct the exact nature of the policies pursued and implemented by the Taiping kingdom. It is known that, after the establishment of their capital in Nanking, the Taipings promulgated a Land Law which envisaged a complete social and economic reorganization. Its provisions called for a total redistribution of land and the establishment of a hierarchical structure of society, similar to that of the Taiping armed forces. This programme, with its distinct overtones of egalitarian communism, remained more than likely a utopia, since there is no evidence that it was ever put into actual practice. It would seem that the Taiping leaders, absorbed primarily by their military campaigns, paid relatively little attention to a restructuring of society, contenting themselves with setting up an administration on the traditional pattern of the Chinese feudal monarchy. Attempts were made, especially after the conquest of Kiangsu and Chekiang, to obtain the participation of the gentry in the administration, and for this purpose the examination system was employed, although its contents had been appropriately altered in line with the Taiping ideology. There is no evidence to prove that, as some of its admirers maintain, the Taiping government introduced democratic features into its administrative practice. The absolutist monarchic character of the government precluded such a possibility, and there was certainly no provision for popular participation in the administration. Nonetheless, during the first period, the position of the peasants in the areas under Taiping rule had clearly improved; they had either ceased to pay land rent or paid much less, while the taxes required by the Taipings were also considerably lower. Later on, under the pressure of intensified Ch'ing attacks, the Taipings increased their demands on the peasants, thus probably alienating much of the support which they had initially gained.

The high degree of eclecticism of the Taiping ideology, compounded by divergences between aspirations and practice, makes it difficult to ascertain the actual character of the movement. The prominent Marxist historian Fan Wen-lan regards it as a form of subjective peasant socialism. Its peasant, plebeian nature is, of course, obvious; 'utopian' would perhaps be preferable to 'subjective', but the use of the term socialism is questionable. Although the Taiping movement was an effort to envisage at least a new society – which is why it deserves to be called a revolution – its ideological premises were still rooted in peasant egalitarianism and influenced by traditional utopian visions. Simultaneously, the Taiping sinification of Protestant Christianity was so far-reaching as to deprive the final product of almost any semblance to the original creed. This was not to be the last time that such a fate was to meet a doctrine from abroad, since the process of adaptation to specific Chinese circumstances leads most often to a practically total transmogrification. On the other hand, the great significance which Chinese Marxists attach to the Taiping movement does not give rise to any doubts. The problems of leading a peasant revolution endow the history of the T'ai-p'ing T'ien-kuo with great topicality, while the similarities and differences between its development and that of the revolutionary movement in the twentieth century offer a fertile field for study and reflection. The historical place of the Taipings as the greatest social movement of the nineteenth century, and the next to the greatest and next to the last peasant revolution in Chinese history, is transparently clear.

The Foreign Powers and China, 1842–64

The advantages gained by the West, as embodied in the Treaty of Nanking and the subsequent accords, were by no means considered to be sufficient, and hence the principal aim of the foreign powers was not only to effectuate the full implementation of what had been extorted but, even more, to secure the possibilities for a speedier and greater penetration of China. Thus, the initial unequal treaties were but a foot in the door; the task now was to force it wide open.

Due to its position as the largest and strongest colonial power in Asia, with dominant commercial interests in China, Great Britain continued to play a leading role in the new phase of foreign aggression directed against the Middle Kingdom. Special attention was paid by the British to the prospects of exploiting the great potential riches of the Yangtse Valley, while simultaneously they were the most active in implementing the provisions of the Nanking accord. Consulates were quickly set up in all the five Treaty Ports, while Hong Kong soon proved to be a superb base not only for the expansion of trade, but for the launching of military campaigns as well. It was also the British merchants and officials in China who often took the initiative in voicing the necessity for further expansion and a favourable revision and modification of the existing treaty rights.

In the aftermath of the First Opium War Shanghai quickly became the main centre for foreign trade; by 1852 over one-half of all Chinese exports passed directly through it. The scope of exportation, especially of tea and silk, grew markedly, and the problem of paying for these goods continued to be solved by the British merchants with the greatest ease by a steady increase in the sale of opium. This traffic, still formally illicit, was now conducted unabashedly without the slightest hindrance, spreading to the entire littoral. In 1855, over 63,000 chests of the deadly narcotic were dumped on the China market by the traders, undoubtedly all God-fearing churchgoers.

While it had been relegated to second place in foreign trade, Canton continued to be of considerable importance not only economically, but even more politically, since it continued to be the only venue designated by the Ch'ing for the conduct of relations with the foreign powers. The Kwangtung metropolis also became the scene and cause of continued friction with the British, since the latter claimed that the Nanking Treaty had granted them the right to enter the walled city, a point adamantly and justifiably contested by the Ch'ing authorities. Two attempts by the British to resolve the Canton Entry issue by the use of force and pressure ended in a complete failure.

The Ch'ing government had understandably not the slightest desire to expand its relations, political or commercial, with the foreign powers, and clung to the fond hope that the concessions it had been forced to grant would prove sufficient to satisfy the greedy and incomprehensible foreign devils. In particular, it had no intention of altering its policy of isolation, fearing that its abandonment might result in consequences fatal to the continued maintenance of Manchu rule. Hence, the Ch'ing remained totally hostile to the idea of establishing diplomatic relations, and considered that the presence of foreigners in Peking could foreshadow the downfall of the dynasty.

The great initial success of the Taiping movement, culminating in the capture of Nanking and the establishment of the Taiping government, brought into existence an entirely new element in the relations between the foreign powers and China. There now arose the distinct possibility that the Ch'ing dynasty might be swept aside, and hence the foreigners, almost totally lacking any knowledge regarding the Taipings, hastened to establish contact with the potential new masters of the empire. Understandably, the British were the first in line, and the British mission arrived in Nanking in April 1853. Two questions were uppermost in the minds of the foreigners; did the Taipings have a chance of gaining complete victory and, if so, what would be their policy towards the foreign powers? In spite of its oddity, the Christianity of the Taipings gave rise to some hopes that their victory would greatly facilitate 'the opening of China to religious and commercial enterprise'. But God and Mammon aside, the thoroughly confused situation inclined the British to adopt a 'wait-and-see' policy and proclaim their neutrality. The increasing tensions in Europe, culminating in the Crimean War, served simultaneously to distract attention away from China, and made the 'wait-and-see' approach quite appropriate and useful. Neutrality also proved profitable, since British and American merchants did a fine business in selling arms, almost always worthless, to both sides.

The attitude of the Taiping leaders was touchingly naive. Guided by religious fervour, they regarded the foreigners, especially the Protestant British and Americans, as 'Brothers in Christ', ready to offer fraternal aid and sympathy. At the same time, due partially to the Heavenly King's messianic inclinations and their own inherent sinocentricity, the Taipings did almost nothing to further relations with the outside world in order to obtain the expected and desired aid.

The events which took place in Shanghai in the years 1853–5 constituted, in fact, a foretaste of the real intentions and attitudes of the foreign powers. The Taipings had not extended their military operations to Kiangsu and Chekiang, a costly error which they themselves later bitterly regretted, but nonetheless an uprising against the Ch'ing occurred in Shanghai in September 1853. Its participants, originating mostly from Kwangtung and Fukien, members of the Small Swords Society, a Triad offshoot, succeeded completely in occupying the Chinese walled city, while leaving the adjacent foreign settlements untouched. The Ch'ing authorities were totally incapable of dealing with the insurgents, and it was only the significant aid of the powers, especially of France, whose troops took part in the fighting, which enabled the Manchus to recapture the city in February 1855. The Shanghai rising also had other important consequences, for in the resulting confusion the British and Americans took over the administration of the local customs office, thus laying the foundation for future foreign control of the entire Ch'ing maritime customs service. It was this period as well which witnessed the first steps leading to the creation in Shanghai of that curious, cancerous anomaly – the International Settlement and the French Concession – those parts of the city which were to be under the direct rule of its foreign residents, although their population was always overwhelmingly Chinese.

In 1854 the British began their attempt to initiate negotiations with the Ch'ing for the purpose of revising the Anglo-Chinese treaty; the basic aims postulated included the expansion of foreign trade by opening up the interior and the designation of additional ports, freedom for missionary activity in the entire country, and the establishment of legations in Peking. Initial talks in Canton having produced no results, the British, now joined by the Americans, whose policies on the basic question of relations with China were almost identical, tried to hold negotiations in Shanghai and Tientsin, but these also proved to be of no avail. The conclusion drawn was succinctly phrased by the American representative as follows: 'Diplomatic intercourse can only be had with this government at the cannon's mouth.' It was soon to form the basis for the subsequent actions of the foreign powers which led to the Second Opium War (October 1856–October 1860).

The continuing friction between the British and the Ch'ing authorities in the area of Canton served as the background for the outbreak of this new phase of armed aggression by the foreign powers. Numerous incidents, including the droll case of the *Arrow*, a supposedly British ship whose Chinese crew were accused of piracy, were blown up by the British to provide a *casus belli*, in line with Palmerston's avowed theory that 'such half barbarian countries as China . . . needed a dressing down every ten years or so'. A number of military actions were started in October 1856, which brought about the desired results of increasing tension in the Canton area, and thus, by means of these 'miserable proceedings' (Lord Derby), the scene was set for the war. Its first stage was fated to be a drawn-out affair, lasting until March 1858, for the outbreak of the Great Revolt in India in May 1857 diverted the attention of the British. Nonetheless, the British Commissioner, Lord Elgin, reached Canton in July 1857, where he was soon to be joined by the French representative, Baron Gros, for France was eager to participate in the campaign against the Ch'ing. The slaying in Kwangsi of a French missionary, for which the required satisfaction had not been obtained, served as the purported cause for the French action.

After the failure of initial negotiations, in which the demand for entry into Canton and reparations for damages to foreign property figured prominently, the arrival of awaited reinforcements enabled the British and French to launch a direct assault on the city. On 29 December 1857, Canton, having been bombarded for a whole day, was taken, to rest under Anglo-French occupation for almost four years. The basic aims of the Allies still remained to be achieved, and for this purpose the British and French envoys proceeded to Shanghai, where they were joined by representatives of the United States and Russia. Although they remained allegedly neutral, these two powers were anxious to participate in the negotiations and to benefit from the military pressure exerted by Britain and France.

The talks in Shanghai did not produce any results. All four envoys sailed with the Anglo-French fleet to Taku, which was occupied by the Allies on 20 May 1858. The new menace to the capital had the desired effect, and the frightened Ch'ing court agreed to open negotiations which began in June. By appropriate browbeating and the implied threat of supporting the Taipings, the British succeeded in breaking down the resistance of the Manchus to their demands. However, the Ch'ing deemed it preferable, probably with the thought in mind of splitting the four powers, to conclude the negotiations first with the 'neutrals'. The Sino-Russian treaty was signed on 13 June 1858; while dealing mostly with commerce, it also contained the crucial most-favourite-nation clause, and thus all the privileges extorted in the earlier treaties now accrued to Russia. Simultaneously, even more significant negotiations were being held with the Manchus by N. N. Muraviev, the governor of East Siberia. Having carried out an energetic policy of colonizing the Amur River area, still officially a part of the Ch'ing empire, Muraviev now sought a revision of the Nerchinsk accord. The Manchus gave in to his demands and the Treaty of Aigun, signed on 28 May, established new boundaries between the two empires. All the territory north of the Amur was recognized as Russian, while the area between the Ussuri and the Sea of Japan was to belong temporarily to both countries. Hence, the immediate task for the Tsarist representative was to obtain the quick ratification of both treaties.

The treaty with the United States, signed on 18 July, also reaffirmed the most-favourite-nation provision, and thus whatever new privileges the British succeeded in obtaining in their continuing negotiations would automatically benefit the Americans. The

Manchus still balked at accepting two British demands relating to the residence of foreign envoys in Peking and the opening of the interior. Ultimately, the threat to march on the capital broke down their resistance, and the treaty, concluded in Tientsin on 26 June, was imposed, in Elgin's own words, 'with a pistol at the throat'. The French obtained their accord on the following day. On the basis of the Tientsin treaties eleven more ports were opened up to Western trade; when added to the original five, this made almost all of China accessible, especially since the Yangtse, the country's jugular vein, was also opened to foreign shipping. Foreigners obtained freedom of movement in the entire country and missionary activity could be conducted anywhere. An indemnity of 4 million taels each (one tael was equivalent to one ounce of silver, worth Ch $1.38) was to be paid to the British and French for their trouble. Thus the new accords constituted an extremely significant step forward in the penetration and subjugation of China by the West.

Although the four treaties were soon ratified by the weak and dissolute Emperor Hsien-feng (1850–61), the terms were really quite a difficult pill to swallow for the Manchus. The provision for residence of foreign envoys in Peking was especially galling, and the Ch'ing offered to abandon even the low tariff rates, established in supplementary negotiations, if this point were to be omitted. Simultaneously, the Manchus, wishing to prevent a new incursion by the British and French, prepared their forces for the possibility of a renewal of the conflict and strengthened the defences of North China.

The exchange of ratifications remained to be accomplished, and here the demands of the British were unrelentingly provocative. They insisted that the exchange take place in Peking, to which the envoys were to proceed with a large military escort. The Ch'ing government proposed alterations in the route to be taken, and asked for a reduction in the size of the escort; its requests were rejected out of hand, and on 25 June an Anglo-French landing party attacked the Taku forts as the first step in the planned march on Peking. It met with total defeat, for this time, for once at least, the artillery fire of the defenders proved effective. The Westerners were not invincible after all; they beat a fast retreat to Shanghai to await further reinforcements.

Communications being what they were in the middle of the

nineteenth century, it was only by the summer of 1860 that the British and French managed to assemble sufficient forces for a new offensive in North China. In August, the Allies stormed the Taku forts and occupied Tientsin. The Ch'ing were forced to resume negotiations, the venue of which was shifted by the Allies to a locality close to the capital, and here the terms of a new Peking Convention were determined. However, the detention of a group of 39 Allied negotiators by the Ch'ing led to a breakdown of the talks and to further military action in September, in which the Ch'ing troops were heavily defeated. Only the lack of ammunition prevented the Allies from advancing on Peking, now abandoned by Hsien-feng, who had fled to Jehol.

Having received the necessary supplies, the British and French marched on Peking and on 6 October reached the fabulous Yüan Ming Yüan, the Summer Palace of the Manchu emperors. Colossal sums, all ground out from the sweat and toil of the Chinese peasants, had been expended on its construction and on the accumulation of the countless treasures it contained. It took the Allies more than three days to loot the palace systematically, although the British complained sourly that the French had grabbed more than their fair share. Talks regarding the entry of the Allies into the capital were resumed, and the negotiators taken prisoner earlier released. However, due to Manchu barbarity, only 19 of them were still left alive. As an act of reprisal, Elgin ordered the British troops to burn down completely the 200 buildings of the Summer Palace. It is something of a problem to determine whose barbarity was greater. After this, the signing of the new treaty presented no difficulties. Elgin marched through the city with a military escort to the Hall of Rites, where the ceremony was held on 24 October. The French repeated the same scene the next day. The Peking Convention provided *inter alia* for the residence of foreign envoys in the capital, the addition of Tientsin to the list of Treaty Ports, an increase of the indemnities to 8 million taels each, and the cession of a part of Kowloon to Britain.

Simultaneously, with the signing of the Convention, the exchanges of ratifications of the Tientsin Treaty were carried out, and due to the most-favourite-nation clause the privileges of those accords were extended to the Americans and Russians. But the latter had still more irons in the fire, and the Russian envoy utilized the occasion for obtaining a new treaty, signed on 14 November. The Tsarist government now achieved not only the ratification of the Aigun Treaty, but also the cession of the lands between the Ussuri and the Sea of Japan, close to 63,000 square miles. The foundations of Vladivostok ('Rules the East') were laid down in the same year.

The new concessions extorted as a result of the Second Opium War were an important stage in the process of transforming China into a joint semi-colony of the foreign powers. The Ch'ing policy of isolation lay in ruins and the Manchus, now properly chastened, were well on their way to becoming subservient tools to be employed for the extension of foreign control, thus obviating the necessity of the direct rule. These changes, so eminently satisfactory to, and appropriately appreciated by the foreign powers, were also to give rise to a complete shift of the latter's policy towards the Ch'ing government. Almost immediately, Britain and France exchanged the role of enemies of the Manchus for that of their cordial allies and assistants. Actually, even during the course of the war, the Allies had never desired to bring about a collapse of the Ch'ing dynasty. Now that the Manchus had submitted to all the demands of the foreign powers, it was deemed advisable to support them unreservedly against any domestic foes, by all means possible, not excluding direct military intervention. The reason was transparently obvious; the fulfilment of the treaty obligations was to be exacted from the Ch'ing government.

Another vital factor entered into the calculation of the powers. The Taipings still held most of Kiangsu and Chekiang and a good part of the Yangtse Valley, precisely the areas to be opened up under the provisions of the Tientsin Treaty, thus constituting a hindrance to the penetration of this territory. Elgin considered that 'the opening of the river ports is contingent on the suppression of the rebellion', and this view formed the basis for future British policy.

Already in August 1860, on precisely the same day on which British and French soldiers assaulted the Taku forts, troops of these countries were engaged in fighting against the army of the Chung Wang approaching Shanghai, and it was their involvement which prevented Li Hsiu-ch'eng from capturing this vital centre. In January 1862, during Li's second advance on Shanghai, the Anglo-French intervention was on a considerably larger scale; it continued throughout most of that year with the avowed aim of clearing all the territory within a thirty-mile radius around the city. The action of foreign troops was not confined by any means to Kiangsu, for they participated in the operations against the Taipings in Chekiang as well, joining the assault on Ningpo in May 1862.

In addition to the above activities of British and French regular forces, foreign intervention was also present in the inglorious feats of the so-called Ever Victorious Army. Organized in 1860 by an American adventurer and former filibuster, F. T. Ward, this somewhat inaccurately entitled unit, composed of European and Asian riffraff and officered primarily by Americans, served as a Ch'ing auxiliary force in attacking Taiping-held towns. By 1862, when its soldiers were mainly Ch'ing conscripts, this 'army', specializing in rapine and plunder, began to enjoy the full support of the British, who supplied it with all needed arms. In March 1863, after Ward's death and the disappearance of his successor, the British seconded C. G. Gordon to act as its commander, furnishing him with everything he required in the way of artillery, ships and money. Gordon's outfit now served as a spearhead of Li Hung-chang's offensive in Kiangsu, which led to the fall of Soochow in December 1863, and terminated in the capture of Ch'angchou in May 1864. By this time the position of the Taipings was hopeless, and further direct foreign military assistance could be dispensed with during the final assault on Nanking. Thus, the fundamental goal of suppressing the Taiping movement had been achieved and the only potentially serious hindrance to further foreign encroachment had been effectively eliminated.

9. The Problems of Modernization and Further Foreign Aggression

Domestic Development in China, 1864–94

The humiliating defeat suffered in the Second Opium War and the simultaneous downfall of the Taipings significantly altered the status of the Ch'ing monarchy. A noticeable shift in the balance of forces within the ruling class took place, which found its expression in the enhanced position of Chinese officials, particularly those, such as Tseng Kuo-fan, Li Hung-chang and Tso Tsung-t'ang, whose forces had been primarily responsible for achieving victory over the Taipings. Although they still remained loyal to the Ch'ing, their armies, now the strongest and best equipped in the whole country, constituted a prime source of power. The large degree of financial independence possessed by these provincial satraps, in control of the rich areas of the Yangtse Valley and of Chihli, also strengthened them considerably. While they were not yet completely autonomous warlords, their rise inaugurated the process of political and military decentralization, which was to progress steadily until the collapse of the dynasty.

The increase in influence of the Chinese officials, gained at the expense of the Manchu aristocrats, was reflected in appointments to top bureaucratic posts. Thus, in the years 1861–90, 34 out of 44 governors general and 104 out of 117 governors nominated were Chinese, with over half coming from the anti-Taiping gentry-led armies. However, the effect of this phenomenon was undoubtedly weakened by the rivalries between various provincial cliques of Chinese military and civil bureaucrats. The most important contending factions were those connected either with Li Hung-chang's Huai Army or Tseng Kuo-fan's Hunan Army.

An even more envenomed struggle for power also took place within the Manchu aristocracy, which came to a head after the death of

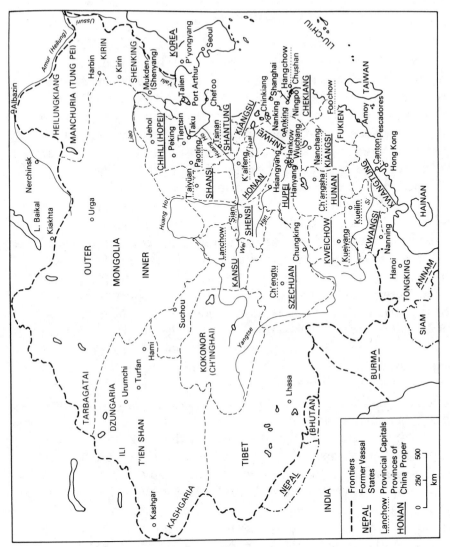

18. The Ch'ing Empire, *c.* 1893

Hsien-feng in 1861. It was largely bound up with the rise of Yehonala (1835–1908), Hsien-feng's concubine, which culminated with her becoming the sole autocratic ruler of the Ch'ing empire almost up to its very end. Wily, shrewd, avid for wealth and power, without a shred of scruples, Yehonala was fortunate enough to give birth in 1856 to Hsien-feng's only son, which raised her rank to that of secondary empress. She participated in the devious plot which in 1861 deprived the regents appointed earlier of their posts and lives, and easily putting aside her cousin, the principal empress, began to rule in the name of her son, T'ung-chih (1862–75). She was to be known from this period on as Tz'u-hsi, one of her numerous honorific titles. Tz'u-hsi was quick to concentrate all power in her hands and proved to be a clever manipulator of the Manchu aristocrats and the Chinese high officials. Politically, she was a diehard reactionary, obstinately opposed to the slightest change of the status quo. Her unrestrained greed led to a marked increase of corruption, for with the help of her eunuchs she established a system of 'squeeze' levied also on the top ranks of Ch'ing officials. T'ung-chih's death could have deprived her of the position she held, but Tz'u-hsi skilfully imposed the selection of her infant nephew as the successor and, as Empress Dowager and regent, she continued to rule undisturbed in the name of the new emperor, the unfortunate Kuang-hsü (1875–1908).

It is not particularly surprising that with such a court and ruler the Ch'ing were barely capable of even dealing with or comprehending the problems which the country now faced. In any case, there was almost complete accord among all the leading groups of the ruling class, the Manchu aristocracy and the Chinese high officials, as to the indispensable necessity and desirability of achieving a complete restoration of the Ch'ing autocratic regime's power and of the Chinese gentry's political and economic position. The policy designed for this purpose constituted the principal content of what is referred to at times as the 'T'ung-chih Restoration'; it was to remain, in reality, dominant until the end of the nineteenth century. Nonetheless, even the problem itself of retaining power by the Ch'ing necessitated drawing conclusions from the dramatic experiences of the preceding decades. The majority of the ruling class remained utterly opposed to innovations in any domain and desired, if it were only possible, the restoration of China's isolation, thus ignoring completely the inevitable consequences of foreign penetration. Only a relatively small group of highly placed, prominent officials, composed mostly of those who had been the leaders in the campaigns against the Taipings, held somewhat divergent views. Convinced by their own experiences of the superiority of Western technology, particularly and above all in the military field, the spokesmen of this group, referred to as the 'Westerners', stressed the need of acquiring modern military technique from the West, primarily for the purpose of strengthening and preserving the existing political system and socioeconomic order. These 'self-strengthening' policies did not, however, envisage a consistent programme of modernization, since they were based on the assumption of leaving the semi-feudal political and economic structure intact. Hence, there was no place in this programme for the introduction of large-scale industrialization, for reforming the government or the antiquated administrative system, and thus removing any of the obstacles blocking the development of capitalism.

The opening up of Japan had been hardly less traumatic than that of China, but the contrast between the conclusions drawn from this experience and the policy pursued is truly striking. The leaders of the Meiji Restoration seemed to have shown much more awareness of the dangers to their country's independence, and it is possible that the existence of a native instead of an alien dynasty was a positive factor. The Japanese were certainly not less inclined to xenophobia, but they were not affected to perhaps as great a degree by the complex of cultural superiority since, after all, their own civilization was so largely a borrowed one. The Chinese scholar-officials, in upholding their moribund culture and opposing any change, were, in fact, also defending their 'rice bowls', since they feared that the introduction of even a modicum of Western Learning would ultimately undermine their very existence.

The 'Westerners' were able nonetheless to effectuate some measures aimed at 'self-strengthening', since some of them held crucial high positions in the Ch'ing administration and were in charge of military operations against various insurgent forces. It was in the areas governed by such men as Li Hung-chang or Tseng Kuo-fan that the first steps were taken to introduce Western manufacturing methods, primarily for the production of arms. The Kiangnan arsenal in Shanghai founded in 1865, and the Mawei shipyards established near Foochow in 1866, were probably the best-known examples of this type of enterprise. In both cases modern Western equipment was installed, foreign engineers employed and language schools founded. Later on, this very modest programme of industrialization was extended to provide some elements of a limited infrastructure with the establishment in 1872 of a shipping company, the opening in 1878 of a modern coal mine in K'aip'ing, and the installation of the first telegraph line in 1881. The first textile mills were also built in the 1880s. The virulent opposition of reactionary Ch'ing officials delayed, however, the construction of railroads; the first short line built by the British in 1876 was promptly bought up by the Ch'ing and immediately destroyed. Only the next decade witnessed the slow beginnings of development of this vital domain.

The circumscribed scope of industrialization, represented by the above ventures, resulted not only from the lack of foresight, but also from the hindrances inherent in the very nature of the Ch'ing regime. The enterprises established in this period remained mostly under bureaucratic control which, in effect, signified that the customary practices of corruption and nepotism were extended to them as well. Li Hung-chang himself acquired a fabulous fortune from the firms under his control. Thus the development of capitalist industry continued to be hampered, since such conditions tended to discourage and limit private investment and participation by the merchants, whose resources were quite considerable. The restriction of modernization to a marginal phenomenon, at the time when the foreign powers had not yet achieved a leading position in the Chinese economy, was to have extremely adverse consequences, since later on their overpowering dominance would render the development of Chinese industrialization infinitely more difficult.

The main attention of the Ch'ing government during the 'T'ung-chih Restoration' was not focused therefore on effectuating a consistent programme of modernization, which could truly safeguard the country's independence, but on consolidating its own position by suppressing the many rebellions still persisting after the downfall of the Taiping kingdom. In the fulfilment of this task the Ch'ing were now to benefit from the benevolent support and aid of the foreign powers, while its execution was entrusted to the very same men whose armies had been instrumental in crushing the great peasant rebellion.

The Nien rebellion in North China constituted the most urgent problem for the Manchus, since it showed no signs of ebbing after the fall of the Taiping state. Reinforced by Taiping remnants, the Nien forces, largely cavalry, continued their raids from their bases in fortified villages and successfully defeated all Ch'ing attacks. Ultimately, the Ch'ing commanders, having blockaded the Nien-held areas, managed to separate the Nien armies from their bases. Divided into two forces, the Nien were finally surrounded and exterminated in 1868.

A revolt of equal significance had been raging in Yünnan since 1855 when the Moslems, a sizable part of the province's population, had risen against Ch'ing oppression. Led by Tu Wen-hsiu (1828–73), the insurgents succeeded in overrunning most of Yünnan and established their own state with Tali as its capital. The Ch'ing proved incapable of dealing with this rebellion for many years until it became weakened by internal dissension. The reconquest of the province ended in 1873 with the fall of Tali, most of whose many inhabitants were treacherously put to the sword. The methods used by the Manchus in 'pacifying' were such that only three out of the eight million population of Yünnan were left at the end of the rebellion. The conduct of the Ch'ing authorities was not any different in relation to the revolt of the Miao, the autochthonous inhabitants of neighbouring Kweichow. The Miao, having been systematically despoiled of their lands, especially in the lowlands, rose against Ch'ing rule once more in 1854, and became masters of almost the entire province. Their desperate rebellion was crushed in the early 1870s with the loss of over one million lives. The remaining Miao were deprived of most of their lands and forced to seek refuge in the highlands.

While the above rebellions in the southwest were serious enough, the great Moslem uprising in the northwest, which started in 1862, presented a still greater threat to the Manchus. Almost all of Kansu and most of northern Shensi were affected by the revolt, and the Ch'ing, still coping with the Nien, were unable to direct sufficient forces against it. In 1869, however, Tso Tsung-t'ang, in command of Hunanese troops, began an offensive in Shensi, employing his practice of wholesale massacres of the civilian population. After the reconquest of Shensi, the military operations were concentrated on the long-drawn-out siege of Chin-chi-pao in Kansu, the stronghold of the revolt's principal leader, Ma Hua-lung. Finally, the use of Krupp guns, especially imported by Tso for this purpose, brought about the city's surrender in October 1870, and a dreary spectacle of a treacherous massacre of the garrison and the cruel execution of Ma and his family was repeated again. Similar atrocities accompanied Tso's final campaign in the northwest, the capture in October 1873 of Suchou, the last Moslem fortress.

Under the influence of rebellion in the northwest, the overwhelmingly Moslem population of Kashgaria and Dzungaria, the lands to the south and north of the T'ien Shan, also rose in 1864 against its Ch'ing rulers. Yakub Beg, the revolt's principal leader, became by 1873 the master of the entire Tarim Basin. His troops also penetrated northwards to take Urumchi, and had it not been for the Russian occupation of the Ili region in 1871, Yakub Beg would have easily conquered all of Dzungaria. The problems of this rebellion were complicated still further for the Ch'ing government by the policies of both Russia and Britain. These powers recognized Yakub Beg's rule and while the Tsarist government, having only recently completed the conquest of West Turkestan, was obviously hoping, as shown by its action in Ili, for an opportunity to extend its gains eastwards, the British toyed with the concept of converting Kashgaria into a buffer state.

As long as the Moslem uprising in the northwest lasted, no attempt to reconquer Kashgaria and Dzungaria could obviously be initiated. Once it was suppressed, the Ch'ing government had to decide whether to undertake this costly and hazardous enterprise. Opinions among the highest officials were sharply divided; Tso Tsung-t'ang, logically enough, came forth as the main advocate of the reconquest, while Li Hung-chang favoured the utilizing of the limited resources available on the development of the coastal provinces. The views of Tso's group prevailed, and in 1875 he embarked on the first stage of the campaign, which quickly led to the occupation of the lands north of the T'ien Shan. Notwithstanding British efforts to save him, Yakub Beg's state rapidly collapsed after his death in 1877, and in the next year the reconquest of Kashgaria was completed. On Tso's proposal both the conquered areas were reorganized in 1884 into a regular province – Sinkiang ('New Dominion').

The conquest of Sinkiang concluded the process of re-establishing full control of the Ch'ing over the entire country and, in effect, these various military campaigns, so immensely costly in human terms, were the principal achievement of the leaders of the 'T'ung-chih Restoration', lauded by some uncritical Western historians as supposed great statesmen.

Political stabilization of Manchu rule was accomplished primarily by rebuilding the traditional governmental structure in the areas affected by revolt. No innovations were introduced, since even the 'Westerners' were in full accord with the premise that all the fundamental political and ideological aspects of the old order should be left intact. Hence, too, their renowned formula to the effect that 'Chinese Learning is the basis; Western Learning is for practical use'. The restoration of the economy was also achieved, not due to the actions of the government but, as so often in the past, to the hard toil of the Chinese peasants. The main concern of the Ch'ing officials in the areas undergoing rehabilitation was to strengthen still further the position of the gentry landlord families. This led, in turn, to the growth of all the features denoting the social crisis in the countryside which thus, in spite of all the bloodletting, was not really alleviated.

Thus the policies of the leaders of the 'T'ung-chih Restoration' demonstrated almost total sterility; for this they were to be castigated in the twentieth century by progressive Chinese historians who held them largely responsible for preserving China's backwardness and her ensuing tragic fate. But, characteristically, these same men were hailed as model statesmen by Chinese reactionaries, and it was not coincidental that Tseng Kuo-fan became Chiang Kai-shek's favourite hero. However, it should be recalled that in the 1860s and 1870s there were some enlightened thinkers in China, who could comprehend the country's problems and advocate a programme of proper modernization. This could certainly apply to Yung Wing (Jung Hung, 1828–1912), the persistent advocate of modern education and industrialization. But the frustrations encountered in his interesting career also show how completely unreceptive China's rulers were to new, fruitful ideas.

The disastrous outcome of the Opium Wars, which had shattered the Manchus' policy of isolation, impelled them to formulate an appropriate, new foreign policy. While its approach towards the West was still largely marked, understandably, by hostility and distrust, the Ch'ing government, having realized that the foreign powers were intent not on overthrowing but on preserving the Manchu dynasty, sought proper methods to arrange its relations with them. Although they harboured no illusions as to the aims of the 'Western barbarians', and considered that their appetites were basically insatiable, the Ch'ing hoped that by applying appropriately conciliatory means the pressure for new privileges could be somewhat lessened. Such an appeasement scheme was followed constantly by Li Hung-chang, whose position as governor-general of Chihli for a quarter of a century (1870–95) made him the most important high official in respect to the formulation and implementation of foreign policy. His residence in Tientsin played the role of a foreign office to an even greater degree than the Tsungli Yamen established in Peking in 1861. During the first decades of its existence the Tsungli Yamen was very much a provisional institution, with its top officials simultaneously holding other posts in the central government. In time, however, a permanent staff of officials was assembled, a certain amount of expertise in international relations acquired, and a foreign language school for the training of future diplomats established.

The fundamental policies of the Tsungli Yamen did not differ from those of Li Hung-chang, and were also partially based on the vain hope that the time-worn formula of 'using barbarians to control barbarians' could be utilized successfully in dealing with the West. At the same time the Ch'ing were not in the least anxious to establish quickly full diplomatic relations with the foreign powers. It was only in 1876 that the process got under way under foreign pressure, with the appointment of Kuo Sung-tao (1818–91) as the first Ch'ing envoy to London. Kuo was soon deeply shocked by the discrepancies between the level of development of China and Europe, and his advocacy of a consistent programme of modernization, along the lines pursued by the Japanese, quickly put an end to his promising career.

The next two decades were to demonstrate that this 'entry of China into the family of nations' – the philistine term employed by some Western historians – was to prove completely futile as far as the country's defence against further foreign aggression was concerned, since it did not form a part of an all-embracing programme of modernization.

The Foreign Powers and China, 1860–94

The basic immediate aims of the Western powers having been attained as a result of the Second Opium War and the destruction of the Taiping state, a stabilization of the situation in China was now deemed necessary in order to make full use of the new privileges extorted by the Tientsin treaties. It was probably with this aim in mind that the foreign powers, among whom Great Britain still held the dominant position, pursued their 'policy of cooperation' which signified, firstly, the consistent propping up, for reasons referred to earlier, of the Ch'ing government, and, secondly, the maintenance of an accord between the powers in respect to their activities in China. While rivalry was of course already present, it was still possible during this period for the Westerners to act together in relative harmony, since the advantages of exerting joint pressure on the Ch'ing to fulfil their obligations were obvious. It was also clear that it would take some time to make effective use of the newly gained rights before proceeding with further and more extensive demands. However, the vision, always rather illusory, of China as an unlimited market for Western manufactured goods, also began to give way to a new concept, only slightly less unrealistic, in which China was to be regarded as an excellent location for the export of capital and an inexhaustible source of invaluable raw materials. It was apparent that for these purposes the rights already held were insufficient, and hence a new round of demands would soon be presented.

During the years when the 'policy of cooperation' was being adhered to, the foreign powers constantly exerted pressure on the Ch'ing to establish full diplomatic relations, in the belief that this would ultimately facilitate the extension of foreign influence. The placing of the Chinese maritime customs service under foreign supervision proved useful also in this respect, especially when its inspector-general, R. Hart, an energetic Ulsterman, assumed as well the function of an advisor on foreign affairs. The first mission was

19. The foreign powers and China (up to 1906)

dispatched abroad in 1867 on his recommendation, and the rather odd idea of employing a former American minister as the head of a subsequent delegation was also the result of Hart's fertile inventiveness. The outcome of both missions was actually negligible, but the Ch'ing did finally establish the diplomatic relations required by the West.

Christian missionaries, both Catholic and Protestant, had been quick to avail themselves of the newly acquired right to spread their faith unhampered in the entire country. But the aggressiveness, arrogant intolerance and barely concealed contempt for Chinese customs and habits displayed by many of them gave rise to innumerable conflicts both with the local inhabitants and the Ch'ing authorities, and their activities were regarded with growing hostility by almost all strata of Chinese society. The gentry, in particular, despised them as propagators of unorthodox and subversive views. As subjects of those foreign powers, whose acts of aggression were fresh in the minds of all Chinese, the missionaries were inevitably tainted by this association, and their insistence on exercising their right to proselytize, acquired so dubiously, only exacerbated the situation still further. Under these circumstances it was not difficult for their many enemies to spread the most far-fetched and preposterous rumours regarding their conduct. In this fashion anti-Christianity became more and more inseparably intertwined with anti-foreignism, and both were to be stimulated by subsequent Western aggression.

It is against this background of innumerable local conflicts in the late 1860s that the Tientsin Incident occurred in June 1870. Vicious rumours regarding the practices of French nuns in an orphanage they supervised created an incredibly tense situation. Sparked off by the irresponsible behaviour of the French consul, a riot broke out which resulted in the murder of 16 foreigners, mostly French, and up to 40 Chinese. The French Cathedral, mission and other buildings were destroyed. The Tientsin affair actually marked the end of the 'policy of cooperation', for all the foreign powers joined in demanding that an exemplary punishment be meted out to those responsible, and that adequate protection for all foreigners be guaranteed by the Ch'ing authorities. Only the outbreak of the Franco-Prussian war prevented the French government from dispatching an expeditionary force, thus giving the Manchus enough time to resolve the problem by paying a suitable indemnity and executing 16 supposed participants in the riot.

The treaties concluded by the Ch'ing government in the years 1842–64 pertained only to the Western powers and did not affect its relations with Japan. After the Meiji Restoration of 1868 Japan had embarked at a forced pace on its programme of modernization, which was soon to convert it into a particularly aggressive and expansionist capitalist power. On the initiative of the Japanese the Treaty of Tientsin was concluded in September 1871, which placed the relations between the two countries on a basis of equality.

However, since the accord did not contain the most-favourite-nation clause, the rights gained by the Japanese were considerably more limited than those obtained by the West. The territorial appetites of Japan were also soon to be revealed; the first instance pertained to the Liu-ch'iu (Ryukyu) Islands which, since the Ming, had been in the anomalous situation of being a vassal of both China and Japan. In 1874, skilfully utilizing a flimsy pretext and taking advantage of the incompetence of the Ch'ing officials, the Japanese put forth their claim to sovereignty over the islands, which they proceeded to bolster by launching an expedition against another goal of their expansion, Taiwan. Ultimately, the conflict was resolved without the use of force with the Ch'ing paying an indemnity to the Japanese who agreed to withdraw from Taiwan. This accord also constituted a passive recognition of the claims of Japan to the Liu-ch'ius, which were annexed in 1881. The unpreparedness of the Ch'ing regime to defend itself, even against the Japanese, was fully revealed by this sorry incident.

At the same time British pressure on the Manchus was resumed in connection with the Margary Affair. The death, while on a mission in the Yünnan-Burma border region, of A. R. Margary, a young British consular official, was utilized by T. Wade, the British minister in Peking, to present a new series of demands. His peculiar methods, which included threatening the Manchus with a breach of diplomatic relations and war, proved to be effective, and the apprehensive Ch'ing government hurriedly agreed to a new accord, the Chefoo Convention, signed by Li Hung-chang on 13 September 1876. Its terms included the opening up of four additional ports and further concessions aimed at facilitating economic penetration of the country's interior.

The Problems of Modernization and Further Foreign Aggression

As mentioned earlier, Russia had utilized the anti-Ch'ing Moslem revolt to occupy the strategically important Ili region in Dzungaria, promising to return the area when and if peace was to be restored. In July 1878, the Ch'ing, having succeeded, probably much to the surprise of the Tsarist government, in suppressing the Moslem insurrection, dispatched an envoy to St Petersburg to negotiate the return of the Ili area. However, the Treaty of Livadia, finally signed on 5 September 1879, stipulated the cession to Russia of a major part of the territory, as well as the payment of 5 million roubles indemnity to cover the costs of occupation. The terms gave rise to a tumultuous controversy in Peking, with some high officials vociferously clamouring for war, and the treaty was repudiated. Subsequently, a more realistic appreciation of the situation, induced by a strong Russian naval demonstration, prevailed, and negotiations were resumed, leading ultimately to the conclusion on 24 February 1881 of the Treaty of St Petersburg, according to which Russia returned almost all of the Ili region in exchange for an increase of the indemnity to 9 million roubles and additional trade facilities in Sinkiang and Mongolia.

Although in the eighteenth century the Manchu government had succeeded in extending its suzerainty over much of Southeast Asia, the expansion of the British and French colonial empires in the nineteenth century in this area soon reduced the claim to nothingness. The Ch'ing had to recognize tacitly the British conquest of Lower Burma in 1862, while the aggressive policy pursued by France in Indochina was to lead to a new confrontation with the West. Having colonized South Vietnam in the 1860s, and converted Central Vietnam into a protectorate by 1874, the French embarked in 1881 on the conquest of North Vietnam. It was this campaign, marking the beginning of the infamous 'pacification of Tongking', which was to bring on the Sino-French war of 1884–5. Among its immediate causes was the involvement on the Vietnamese side of Chinese military units; these were the Black Flags, remnants of the Taiping army, who had taken refuge in the border areas of Vietnam and China. As the initial conflict in North Vietnam grew sharper, the Ch'ing government finally dispatched some of its own troops for the purpose of aiding the Vietnamese. However, in the spring of 1884, the French continued their offensive in Tongking, defeating both the Vietnamese and

Chinese troops, and drove towards the Chinese border. Since the policies of the Manchu government were, as usual, both vacillating and contradictory, such a turn of events was quickly utilized by Li Hung-chang, a consistent advocate of appeasement of the West and an opponent of war with France, for initiating negotiations. The terms, agreed to on 11 May 1884, called for the withdrawal of all Ch'ing troops from Vietnam and the recognition by the Ch'ing of all the treaties which had been imposed by France on that country. But further military operations during the summer, including, in particular, a perfidious attack by the French navy, which resulted in the destruction of the entire Ch'ing southern fleet in Foochow, exacerbated the situation, causing the Ch'ing government to declare war on France, and thus temporarily frustrated Li's attempts to end the conflict.

In the first months of 1885, the French resumed their offensive in North Vietnam, but in March they suffered a sharp and unexpected defeat, which led to the fall of the government in Paris. Secret negotiations had been going on since January, conducted by a representative of the ubiquitous Hart, and after this fiasco the French were also willing to terminate the war. A peace treaty was finally signed on 9 June in Tientsin; apart from giving up two border towns, the Ch'ing now resigned from suzerainty over Vietnam, leaving their former vassal to the tender mercy of the French colonizers. Soon, all of Southeast Asia, with the exception of Siam, came under foreign rule and the entire southwest border of the Ch'ing empire became directly exposed to further penetration. Within ten years the weakness of the Ch'ing regime, already partially revealed in course of the Sino-French war, became completely apparent in the subsequent conflict with Japan.

The Sino-Japanese War, 1894–5

The decade following the conflict with France did not witness any significant change in the internal political situation. Although Tz'u-hsi formally relinquished the regency in 1889, she retained complete control over all important affairs, and it was obvious to all that she, and not Kuang-hsü, was the real ruler of the Ch'ing empire. Simultaneously, the ever present conflict of cliques within the ruling stratum became even sharper and assumed a new dimension. A faction arose, made up almost entirely of high Chinese officials, among whom the emperor's tutor, Weng T'ung-ho (1830–1904) was especially prominent, which aimed at placing Kuang-hsü in the position of real power and authority, while drastically reducing the role of the Empress Dowager. This group was, however, considerably less influential than Tz'u-hsi's own faction, composed of almost all the Manchu aristocrats and the majority of top officials. In any case, the conflict between these cliques, still largely latent, had as yet no immediate effect on the policies of the Ch'ing government; these were still devoted primarily to the rigid preservation of the status quo. Thus the gap in the rate of development of China and Japan in the 1880s and early 1890s became ever more evident. It was precisely during this period that the Japanese, while proceeding rapidly with economic modernization, also concerned themselves with removing the stigma of inferior status, which had also been imposed on their country by a series of unequal treaties. By 1894, when a new Anglo-Japanese treaty was signed, full success in this respect had been achieved, but simultaneously the rulers of Japan had evolved a programme, harking back to Hideyoshi, which called for inflicting upon its closest neighbours, Korea and China, exactly such a status of inferiority.

The unhappy geographical position of Korea made it a focal point in the expansionist policies of all the foreign powers present in East Asia; the petrified nature of its rigid feudal society, enhanced by consciously adopted seclusion, indicated the probability that the country would be unable to defend itself against determined external

223

aggression. It was the Japanese who chose to play the leading role in the ensuing process of 'opening up' the Hermit Kingdom, which still retained its more than two-century-old status of a Ch'ing vassal. The first attack was launched in 1876, and the Treaty of Kanghwa, signed in February of that year, not only facilitated further Japanese penetration, but also initiated a complete breakdown of Korea's isolation. Diplomatic relations were established, on the advice, for that matter, of the Ch'ing government, in the 1880s with all the major powers, and Korea quickly became the cockpit of heightened international intrigue, which also resulted in intensifying the traditional struggles for power between various cliques of the Korean ruling class. Two main factions emerged from this conflict; a powerful conservative group, usually pro-Ch'ing, and a reformist one, inclined to be pro-Japanese.

Against the background of this domestic strife, the involvement in Korean affairs of the Ch'ing and Japanese governments became still greater after riots in Seoul in 1882. Both countries now stationed troops in the Korean capital, which were to become entangled in the subsequent embroilment, an unsuccessful coup staged in 1884 by the reformist faction, but actually planned and organized by the Japanese minister. This affair almost resulted in a war between China and Japan, but since the Japanese did not consider their preparations sufficient, negotiations were resorted to, which were concluded by the signing of a Sino-Japanese convention on 18 April 1885. On its basis China and Japan were to withdraw their troops from Korea, which now became a co-protectorate of both countries. In effect, the Japanese had gained considerable success in eliminating, for all practical purposes, Ch'ing suzerainty, and the next nine years saw an increasing struggle for influence in Korea between the Ch'ing and Japanese governments. An important role in this conflict was played by Yüan Shih-k'ai (1859–1916), the principal Ch'ing representative in Seoul for the ensuing decade, whose arrogant conduct contributed to a further aggravation of an already sufficiently tense situation which, by 1894, resembled a tinderbox.

The outbreak in March 1894 of the Tonghak rising provided the spark. A syncretic religion, originating in the 1860s, the Tonghak (Eastern Learning) had given rise to a powerful popular movement, with strong anti-feudal and anti-foreign overtones and a remarkable resemblance to the Taipings. The Seoul government, completely incapable of dealing with the insurrection, which had gained much support among the incredibly downtrodden and exploited Korean peasantry, appealed to the Ch'ing for assistance. Although the latter were none too eager to involve themselves, 1500 soldiers were ultimately dispatched to Seoul; the Japanese promptly seized the occasion to send in a 7000-strong force. In the meantime, the Tonghak leaders had suspended their insurrection, and hence the presence of both the Ch'ing and Japanese troops became superfluous. However, the Japanese, already set on utilizing the situation for the realization of their long-standing plans, rejected the Ch'ing proposal for a mutual withdrawal and poured in additional reinforcements.

The Ch'ing government, and in particular Li Hung-chang, the main author of its foreign policy, desired to avoid a war with Japan at any price, and cherished the hope that both Great Britain and Russia would intervene to prevent its outbreak. However, neither power felt that its interests were threatened sufficiently to warrant immediate steps, and the intense rivalry between them also militated against the undertaking of common action to stop the unfolding of Japanese aggression. Hence, the Japanese, who by the end of July had successfully organized a coup d'état and gained complete control of the Seoul government, could proceed with their immediate task of expelling the Ch'ing forces. In characteristic fashion, the Japanese began their military operations without bothering to declare war.

The Sino-Japanese war quickly turned into an unceasing series of humiliating defeats for the Ch'ing regime. By the end of September the Ch'ing armies had been cleared out of Korea, fleeing in panic to take shelter behind the Yalu, while the Ch'ing navy suffered a disastrous debacle on 17 September near the mouth of this river. The two fleets were almost equal in size and both composed solely of foreign-built vessels, but as a result of inferior leadership and the lack of sufficient ammunition, due to peculation, the Chinese lost a third of their ships. For the rest of the war, the Ch'ing fleet was to remain bottled up in Weihaiwei, awaiting its final doom. It should be added that the building up of a modern fleet was supposed to have been one of the greatest achievements of the 'self-strengtheners', boastfully extolled by the navy's main patron, Li Hung-chang. Very considerable sums had been lavished until 1888 on the purchase of ships abroad but, typically for the Ch'ing, afterwards almost no funds were devoted to maintenance and modernization. Instead, almost all the sums allocated for the navy were diverted by Tz'u-hsi for her reconstruction of the Summer Palace.

After its success in Korea, the Japanese army easily routed the Ch'ing forces on the Yalu on 24 October, and began an invasion of Manchuria. Simultaneously, Japanese units landed in Liaotung with the mission of seizing Talien (Dairen) and Lushun (Port Arthur). Prodigious sums had been expended on the fortification of these ports, especially of Port Arthur. But, having earlier captured Talien without losing a single man, the Japanese simply took Port Arthur from the land on 21 November, and celebrated their victory by massacring over 2000 of the civilian population. In January, a strong Japanese force landed unopposed in Shantung, and quickly took the fortifications of Weihaiwei from the rear. The Ch'ing fleet, now completely surrounded, surrendered ignominiously. In March, units of the Hunan Army, thrown into the battle in South Manchuria, were defeated in turn, and the road to Peking lay open. The Japanese succeeded not only in gaining a rapid victory, but also in crushing the Ch'ing government's best equipped and most modern armies. Thus, although only a small part of its total forces had been engaged in the conflict, the military position of the Ch'ing regime seemed hopeless. In fact, it had been trying to initiate peace negotiations ever since November, but the Japanese, wishing to complete their victory, contemptuously rebuffed these efforts until February.

The negotiations finally began on 21 March 1895. The Ch'ing delegation, headed by Li Hung-chang himself, was forced to accept all the Japanese demands; the peace treaty was concluded in Shimonoseki on 17 April, and its main provisions called for the recognition by China, but not by Japan, of the full independence and autonomy of Korea, the cession to Japan of the Pescadore Islands, Taiwan and the Liaotung peninsula, the payment of a 200-million-tael indemnity, the drawing up of a new Sino-Japanese treaty on the same basis as the accords with the Western powers, and the granting to the Japanese of freedom to engage in manufacturing in the Treaty Ports. Politically, the terms were a severe blow, for not only the loss of a vassal state, but also that of incontestably Chinese territory was involved. Economically, the consequences of the last provision, which automatically also accrued to all the other foreign powers, were to prove equally calamitous, since it favoured the growth of foreign-owned enterprises at the expense of Chinese industry.

The Japanese had been able to wage and conclude their war against China without the slightest murmur of opposition or criticism from the Western powers. However, the voracity of their territorial claims did finally arouse some of the powers to a belated reaction. This was particularly true of the Russian government whose own expansion in the direction of Manchuria and Korea could be imperilled by Japan's advance. Thus it was the Tsarist government, prepared to press the issue to the point of war, which took the initiative in organizing the intervention of the powers against the treaty provisions pertaining to Liaotung. For their own reasons, bound up more with European politics than with the problems of East Asia, France and Germany joined Russia in this enterprise while Great Britain, although probably not unhappy with the prospect of having pretensions of the new contender for power cut down to size, preferred to remain comfortably on the sidelines. The three powers were quick to act; already on 23 April their ministers in Tokyo presented an identical *démarche* to the Japanese government, in which the immediate retrocession of Liaotung to China was 'recommended'. The 'friendly advice', accompanied by an explicit implication that force would be used if the Japanese were not to act accordingly, proved sufficient, for, in fact, Japan's military and financial resources had been completely exhausted by the war. In the ensuing talks the Japanese haggled fiercely for an increase of the indemnity, which was finally set at 30 million taels. When the exchange of ratifications of the Shimonoseki Treaty took place in Chefoo on 8 May, the ceremony was witnessed, an act of true subtlety, by numerous naval vessels, including a 17-ship-strong Russian force. The European powers lost little time in presenting the Ch'ing government with an appropriate bill for services rendered, while the Japanese, concealing their rage and humiliation, prepared to take revenge, an aim fully accomplished exactly a decade later.

The disgraceful defeat of the Ch'ing regime was of fundamental significance for the country's development. It had finally revealed the total bankruptcy of policies, followed for the preceding thirty years, of limited modernization and subservience to the foreign powers. It also showed how deeply the rot had set in throughout the entire Ch'ing administration, including its armed forces, thus rendering the country's defence almost impossible. Hence, the debacle placed the Manchu monarchy in a critical situation in which its very existence would begin to be questioned and challenged. Moreover, since the weakness of its rulers had been demonstrated so clearly, China's international position had suffered a further grievous blow precisely at a time when the final transition to rampant imperialism was taking place on a world scale. Thus, the prospect that the foreign powers could complete the subjugation of China and proceed to dismember the country into separate spheres, earmarked for exclusive future penetration and eventual annexation, became ominously imminent.

10. Imperialism and China, 1895–1901

Slicing the Melon

In the aftermath of the Sino-Japanese war, the foreign powers, taking full advantage of the transparently obvious weakness of the Manchu government, immediately joined in a jackal-like pursuit of new political and economic concessions. The pressure exerted on the Ch'ing regime was unprecedented, and in the ensuing process of 'slicing the Chinese melon', all the fundamental features of imperialism were exposed with perhaps an even greater clarity than anywhere else in the world.

The punishing indemnity imposed by Japan furnished an excellent opportunity for further economic penetration. With its annual revenue amounting to only 75 to 80 million taels, it was quite impossible for the Ch'ing government to pay in three years the gigantic sum of 230 million without recourse to foreign loans. While its indebtedness by 1894 had reached the sum of only 40 million, the Peking government borrowed 370 million taels in the years 1895–9, with the result that henceforth most of its annual revenue was diverted to servicing the loans contracted. The furnishing of these funds gave rise to sharp competition between the powers; France and Russia succeeded in arranging the first loan of almost 100 million taels, while Britain and Germany financed the next two, each for 100 million. The terms of the loans were exceptionally extortionate, since their full repayment would have necessitated a sum more than double that obtained. Simultaneously, foreign hold on the finances of the Ch'ing government was considerably extended, for the loans were guaranteed by receipts from the salt monopoly and especially the customs service. As the latter remained under foreign, primarily British, control, almost all the revenue from this vital source was earmarked for interest payments.

The Tsarist government was particularly active in pursuing its expansion at the expense of the Ch'ing empire. Its plans were closely bound up with the building of the Trans-Siberian Railway; in 1895, S. Witte, the finance minister and leading exponent of economic penetration of China, proposed the extension of the line through Manchuria, thus providing a much shorter route to Vladivostok. The economic and political advantages of this concept for the future expansion of Russian imperialism were obvious, and, in order to make it more palatable, the Russians were now ready to offer the Ch'ing a secret treaty of alliance aimed, of course, against the Japanese. Secret negotiations on both these issues were held in Russia in April–June 1896 with Li Hung-chang, whose presence was explained away by his attendance at the Tsar's coronation. Li, whose entire foreign policy had been a complete fiasco, was now inclined to favour an alliance with Russia, and his compliance with both the Russian proposals was secured by the simple device of offering him an appropriate bribe of 3 million roubles. The alliance was concluded on 3 June, and the agreement pertaining to the new railway was signed on 8 September 1896. Thus, the road was clear for the construction of the famous Chinese Eastern Railway; it was begun in 1897 and completed in 1903. The main line running across Manchuria was 970 miles long, the supplementary one from Harbin to Port Arthur 440 miles, and the Russians gained many additional rights in the extensive railroad zone. The significance of the Chinese Eastern was immense, since it facilitated not only the penetration of the entire northeast, but ultimately of North China as well.

France, having completed its brutal pacification of North Vietnam, concentrated her efforts on the southwest, seeking to establish a sphere of influence in this area. The French demanded exclusive mining rights, and were also the first to obtain in 1896 a concession for building a railway on Chinese territory. But French expansionist plans conflicted with those of the British, equally interested in the penetration of Yünnan, Kwangsi and Kwangtung, and this rivalry ultimately prevented a clear demarcation of the zones of influence of these two powers. With the aid of their Russian allies, the French were also successful in obtaining the concession, through the use of a dummy Belgian company, for the construction of the vital Peking–Hankow line. The agreement, concluded in June 1898, was also accomplished by the judicious distribution of sizable bribes to high Ch'ing officials. The British, on the other hand, received the right to build railroads in the Yangtse Valley, such as the Shanghai–Nanking line. In general, the construction of railways was one of the most advantageous forms of imperialist penetration, since not only were large profits gained on the loans granted for this purpose, but practically all the equipment was also imported. Hence, the mad scramble for new concessions; by November 1898 the Ch'ing government had granted rights for the building of 6600 miles of new lines, although some of these were never to be built.

In the last years of the nineteenth century a newcomer, noted for her unparalleled aggressiveness, also entered the fray. Acting on the assumption that 'a gradual but progressive dissolution of the Chinese empire was taking place' (Bülow), the Germans, straining at the leash to get their share of the booty, laid their plans already in 1895, aimed at acquiring a base in China. One of Li Hung-chang's German experts had done a proper job of reconnoitring and recommended that Kiaochow Bay in Shantung, in view of its strategic location, would be an admirable acquisition. Already at the end of November 1896 the German government, having decided to proceed accordingly, since Kiaochow 'was suitable as a starting point for the establishment of a German Colonial Territory', began exerting pressure on the Ch'ing without, however, achieving its aim. But soon fate was to smile on Kaiser Wilhelm's Reich. On 1 November 1897, two German Catholic missionaries were killed by bandits in a Shantung village. Armed with the Kaiser's instruction to proceed 'if necessary, with the most brutal ruthlessness', the German fleet, already in Chinese waters since September, immediately went into action, seizing Tsingtao on 14 November.

The Peking government did not even attempt to offer any serious resistance to this new act of imperialist aggression, hoping only that it might prove possible to utilize the rivalries of the powers to counter the German demands. However, German diplomacy was successful in obtaining the acquiescence of its competitors, and the treaty imposed on the Ch'ing regime on 6 March 1898 satisfied all of the Reich's claims. Germany was granted a 99-year lease on Tsingtao and the entrance to Kiaochow Bay, and the right to railway construction in Shantung, all of which was now considered by her as an exclusive sphere of influence. Incidentally, the case of the two missionaries had been settled two months earlier, and by now was completely forgotten by everyone, except their families.

The Kiaochow affair served to set off a chain reaction. The Tsarist government had not opposed the German acquisition of Tsingtao, primarily because it provided an excellent pretext for a continuation of the Russians' own further imperialist expansion. The immediate goal was to gain control of Port Arthur and Talien, regarded as a vital initial step in the plans of the most adventurist Russian ruling circles, which envisioned the total annexation of Manchuria. The Russian fleet, with troops aboard, sailed into Port Arthur in December 1897. At first a pretence was kept up that its presence there was to serve as a counter to German pressure, but when talks got under way in Peking this was soon dropped. Although he had opposed the entire enterprise as an act of folly, a betrayal of the alliance with the Ch'ing he had concluded, and a flagrant provocation of Japan, Witte, swallowing both honour and pride, conducted the negotiations with his customary flair. Success was easily obtained by reverting once more to bribing Li Hung-chang (only 500,000 taels this time), and a renewable 25-year lease on Port Arthur and Talien was signed on 27 March 1898, with Port Arthur declared to be open only to Russian and Chinese ships.

The successes of Germany and Russia quickly goaded Great Britain into action. Since initial attempts to delimit British and Russian spheres of influence in China had thus far produced no results, the British, having compelled the Ch'ing government to issue a declaration of non-alienation in respect of the entire Yangtse Valley, which was actually tantamount to recognizing it as a British sphere of influence, proceeded to join the 'leasing' game. The choice fell on two areas; the naval base of Weihaiwei Bay in Shantung was acquired on 1 July 1898, and simultaneously the area of Hong Kong was considerably enlarged by a 99-year lease on the remaining, by far the larger, part of the Kowloon peninsula.

Putting forth claims for 'compensation', other powers presented new demands. In April 1898, France received a lease on Kwangchow Bay in Kwangtung, while Japan extorted from the Ch'ing a declaration of non-alienation in respect to Fukien. Only in the case of the weakest claimant, Italy, which demanded a lease on Sanmen

Bay in Chekiang, did the Manchu government, knowing that the Italians would be unable to enforce their bluster with arms, feel strong enough to reject the demand. This solitary success only emphasized the fact that the foreign policy of the Ch'ing regime, based on the premise that its constant capitulations would somehow assure both its survival and the continued support by the foreign powers, had been a complete fiasco and an unmitigated disaster for China.

The United States, largely absorbed in rapid domestic development in the post Civil War decades, was the only major power not to join directly in the earlier phase of the scramble for concessions. However, the acquisition of Hawaii, and then of the Philippines, greatly enhanced America's position in the Pacific and coincided with an increase of American activities in China. The potential possibilities offered by the economic penetration of the Middle Kingdom attracted American capitalism to a no lesser degree, and hence the elaboration of an appropriate China policy became a topical issue. It was to be formulated soon in the Open Door Doctrine, initially enunciated in September 1899. The new American policy concerned itself solely with establishing favourable conditions for future economic expansion, postulating the pious wish that the powers should not infringe on the interests of other countries in their spheres of influence, that customs rates should be equal for all, and that no trade discrimination should be practised. These desiderata obviously implied a full recognition not only of the original unequal treaties, but also of all the concessions that had been wrung from the Ch'ing government in the past two decades, and the fundamental aim of American policy, in many ways similar to that of Great Britain, was to obtain the greatest degree of freedom possible for economic expansion in all of China.

The Reform Movement, 1895–8

The calamitous defeat suffered by the Manchu monarchy in the Sino-Japanese war led not only to the phase of enhanced foreign aggression described above, but also to domestic consequences of equal or perhaps even greater significance. The prospect of imminent partition turned the question as to what should be done to avoid such a fate into a burning issue. It was becoming abundantly clear to a number of educated Chinese that the policies of superficial and limited modernization pursued heretofore had proved to be an utter failure. The victory of the Island Kingdom also constituted a bitter blow to Chinese pride, since there was something especially humiliating in being vanquished by a small Asian country, condescendingly looked upon as China's pupil in the acquirement of its own civilization.

In the five decades since the First Opium War China's isolation had diminished considerably, and the fund of knowledge relating to the outside world increased appreciably. Hence, the elaboration of the programme capable of grappling with the multitude of problems facing China in this moment of mortal peril was already intellectually feasible. However, the great majority of the ruling class, practically the entire Manchu aristocracy and most of the Chinese scholar-officials, was still adamantly opposed to the introduction of any policies which could result in a fundamental alteration of the existing situation. In particular, these groups remained obstinately hostile to any programme entailing consistent modernization which would bring with it a reform of the political and social order, and could thus present a challenge to their position. Nonetheless, it was against this background of overwhelming crisis that a handful of young intellectuals, all of gentry origin, took a stand diametrically opposite to that of the vast majority of their own class, becoming the advocates of a programme of reform and modernization, based precisely on the enlarged knowledge of the Western world. The principal spokesman of this group was K'ang Yu-wei (1858–1927), while his pupils, Liang Ch'i-ch'ao (1873–1929) and T'an Ssu-t'ung (1865–98), were its most prominent members. It was not an accident that most of the group came from Kwangtung, since not only had that province been traditionally anti-Manchu, but it was also one of the parts of the country most affected by the beginnings of capitalist development. While this phenomenon was to be reflected in their ideas, it would be a crude oversimplification to regard these leaders as purely the spokesmen of a nascent bourgeoisie, for they had no direct connections with any capitalist economic activities.

As the intellectual leader of the Reform Movement, K'ang Yu-wei holds a significant place both in political and intellectual history. The scion of a wealthy Kwangtung scholar-gentry family, K'ang received an excellent education in traditional Chinese culture, and by 1895 enjoyed the reputation of an erudite classical scholar. His views, which he expressed both in his teaching and writing, were soon to be regarded as highly unorthodox, since in his early works he undertook a far-reaching reinterpretation of the Confucian tradition. In particular, K'ang, presenting Confucius as fundamentally a great reformer and the creator of all the Classics, sought to use the latter's authority as the justification for the promulgation of a reformist platform. Simultaneously, K'ang developed further the utopian trend of Chinese traditional thought in what is his most interesting work, the *Ta-t'ung shu* ('The Book of the Great Togetherness'). This fascinating and original glimpse of the future also revealed his eclecticism, which is perhaps even more apparent in his other writings. While unacquainted with any European language, K'ang was from his early youth an eager student of Western Learning, and hence his views took the shape of a somewhat confused amalgam of Chinese and Western ideas, with the former still undoubtedly dominant.

Visions of a better future for humanity apart, it was the present to which K'ang Yu-wei and his followers addressed themselves with utmost urgency, in line with the fundamental view that, in his words, 'If we cannot change, we shall perish.' Under the conditions of an absolute monarchy, K'ang believed that a reform programme could be initiated only by the emperor himself. Hence, in order to accomplish this revolution from above, he addressed, from 1880 on, a series of memorials to Kuang-hsü; all the earlier ones were intercepted by court officials, horrified by the views they contained.

The terms of the Shimonoseki Treaty came as a bolt from the blue to the Chinese intellectuals. In May, K'ang Yu-wei and Liang Ch'i-ch'ao, in Peking at the time, wrote their famous 'Ten Thousand Character Petition' to the emperor, and had little difficulty in gaining support for it from around 1200 other scholars also present in the capital for the highest imperial examinations. The petition, a basic document of the Reform Movement, called on the government to reject the treaty, to shift the capital to Sian, and to introduce a reform programme; almost all the points raised in it were, in effect, to be promulgated three years later. Once more, the petition was kept back from the emperor, but a few months later K'ang did succeed in transmitting a memorial in which he paraphrased the views contained therein. Kuang-hsü, although not of strong character, was nevertheless endowed with some intelligence, and potentially an infinitely better ruler than his two degenerate immediate predecessors. However, and this was the crux of the issue, supreme power rested not in his hands, but in those of the Empress Dowager. Thus, it was only after the Ch'ing government had suffered further grievous blows from the foreign powers that Kuang-hsü could manage to try to assert his nominal authority.

In the meantime, the May petition served admirably as an instigating factor for the spread of reformist ideas. In August 1895, K'ang and Liang organized an association for the study of reforms; a similar society was also established in Shanghai. In both cases the members could be counted only in several scores, but the societies did meet with some support from reform-minded high officials and, more importantly, began to publish their own periodicals, a field in which a crucial role was to be played by Liang Ch'i-ch'ao. Also the son of a rich Kwangtung gentry family, Liang, a brilliant scholar, soon demonstrated his outstanding talent as a writer, and was to become the most influential and prolific publicist in the period up to 1911. The organization of such associations of progressive intellectuals and the setting up of publishing houses formed the principal content of the Reform Movement up to June 1898. The spread of reformist views was also considerably facilitated by the greater availability of works representative of the modern West. In this respect the contribution of Yen Fu (1853–1921) was of prime significance. His numerous famous translations which included works by T. Huxley, H. Spencer, A. Smith and J. S. Mill, made a tremendous impact on the impressionable young intellectuals, and his influence equalled that of Liang Ch'i-ch'ao.

Hunan did not produce only inveterate reactionaries, such as Tseng Kuo-fan, but it also gave birth to some of the most famous reformers and revolutionaries in modern Chinese history. In the 1890s Hunan witnessed the formation of a particularly prominent reformist group, whose activity was closely intertwined with that of T'an Ssu-t'ung, the most progressive, and certainly the most appealing, of the reformist leaders. The son of a high official, T'an, exceptionally well read and educated, with a marked inclination for philosophical inquiry, became a follower of K'ang Yu-wei in 1895, and an enthusiastic propagator of reformist ideals. However, in many respects his own views reached significantly further, since not only did he adopt a strong, anti-Manchu position, but also was much more inclined to favour democratic concepts, including the abolition of the monarchy, and to postulate a really far-reaching reform programme, verging on complete 'Westernization'.

In contrast, K'ang Yu-wei's political platform was that of an enlightened absolutism or, at best, of constitutional monarchy. Characteristically, K'ang was attracted by the Petrine reforms and the Meiji Restoration. In 1898 he submitted to the emperor the two books he had written on the subject, which Kuang-hsü studied with care. In his 29 January 1898 memorial, K'ang wrote: 'I beg your Majesty to adopt the purpose of Peter the Great of Russia as our purpose, and to take the Meiji Reform of Japan as the model for our reform.'

The achievement of such a goal, under existing conditions, could also be considered an important step forward, since it could prevent what was uppermost in the reformers' minds, imminent partition and total loss of independence. K'ang often pointed to the fate of India; he also wrote a book entitled 'Notes on the Partition and Fall of Poland', stating in the preface that, 'I cannot read the history of Poland quietly and am impelled from time to time to cease reading, inasmuch as tears pour down from my eyes. I lived through the tragic fate of the Polish nation and king, and thought of the future of China.'

While opposing foreign aggression, the reformers, aware of China's weakness, sought to find allies among the powers, and their choice fell on Britain and Japan, regarded by them as less dangerous than Russia. In this the determining factor was clearly the support which the Tsarist government continued to grant the Ch'ing regime, as personified by Li Hung-chang and the Empress Dowager, after its successful conclusion of the 1896 Treaty. The British and the Japanese did express some sympathy and also offered superciliously some advice, but the reformers' naive expectations were, in their moment of need, to meet with complete disappointment.

In the spring of 1898, the extortion by Germany and Russia of new concessions (the Kiaochow and Port Arthur affairs) roused the reformers to intensify their activities. In April, the leaders met in Peking to organize the 'Pao Kuo Hui' ('Save the Country Society'). Shortly thereafter, with the help of Kuang-hsü's supporters among the high officials, some of them were appointed to junior posts in the government, thus improving their chances for presenting their views to the emperor. Heeding their pleas, on 11 June Kuang-hsü issued his famous edict proclaiming the necessity of reform, thus ushering in one of the most significant episodes in modern Chinese history – the Hundred Days of Reform. The first edict was shortly followed by a series of over sixty-five decrees, prepared by the reformers, in which almost all of their programme was reflected. The edicts postulated, among other things, a change of the examination system and the introduction of modern education, based both on Western Learning and the classical tradition. The central administration was to be reorganized, sinecure posts eliminated, the Manchu Banners reduced in size, and the defence system restructured. A Board for Mining and Railways, and one for Agriculture, Industry and Trade, were to be set up to stimulate economic development. It was planned to follow up these far-reaching measures with a formulation of the reformers' principal political aim – the declaration of a constitution and the calling of parliament, which would thus transform the Ch'ing autocracy into a constitutional monarchy.

It was one thing to proclaim the edicts; their implementation was a different matter. The Ch'ing bureaucrats had not the slightest intention of putting into effect measures which would undermine their own position, and bided their time in the expectation that the Empress Dowager, the real ruler of the empire for over three decades, would soon intervene to put an end to these unprecedented and subversive innovations. These calculations were eminently sound, for Tz'u-hsi and her coterie lost no time in initiating a counteroffensive.

On 15 June, the Empress Dowager brought about the dismissal of Weng T'ung-ho, one of Kuang-hsü's few supporters in the top stratum of Ch'ing officialdom. Simultaneously, she nominated her faithful favourite, Jung-lu (1836–1903), governor-general of Chihli and commander in chief of the armed forces in that province.

Kuang-hsü and the reformers, who were all Chinese, while Tz'u-hsi's henchmen were mostly Manchus, did not disregard the dangers facing them. Considering correctly that the lack of military force was probably their greatest drawback, they sought to gain support of Yüan Shih-k'ai, who since his flight from Seoul in 1894 had become the organizer and commander of the New Army, the only relatively well-trained and equipped force in the country. Yüan's allegedly progressive views seemed to augur well, and on 18 September the emperor dispatched T'an Ssu-t'ung to negotiate with Yüan, requesting the latter to bring his army into Peking, in order to support a coup aimed at depriving Tz'u-hsi of her power. Yüan promised his loyal and obedient assistance, and immediately revealed the entire scheme to Jung-lu.

Three days later, the unsuspecting Kuang-hsü was arrested in the Imperial City by Tz'u-hsi, to remain her prisoner for the rest of his life. An order was issued for the arrest and execution of the reformist leaders; K'ang Yu-wei, saved by the emperor, had already managed to escape Peking, as did Liang Ch'i-ch'ao. Others were not so fortunate. T'an Ssu-t'ung refused to flee, seeking instead to free the emperor from captivity. When this attempt failed, T'an calmly awaited certain death, stating that: 'No one has yet shed his blood for the Reforms – without this there is no hope for a new China; I shall be the first to do so.' On 28 September, T'an and five other young reformers were executed by the Manchus, to become known to posterity as the Six Martyrs of the 1898 Reform. All other participants who had not escaped received heavy sentences or exile. All the reform edicts were repealed, and the Ch'ing autocracy was fully restored on seemingly firm foundations.

The Reform Movement came to its tragic end not only due to the vehement opposition which the measures it proposed aroused in almost all the members of the Ch'ing establishment, but also because of its own limited nature, the conscious effort to effectuate only a 'revolution from above'. There had been no place in the reform programme for obtaining real popular support, and certainly no intention to introduce fundamental changes in the social and economic order, which could have helped to obtain such support. Hence, the reformers found themselves isolated and defenceless against the counterattack of the infinitely more powerful entrenched reactionary forces. Their hopes for support from the foreign powers had also proved to be futile, for a real implementation of an effective programme of modernization did not lie in the interests of the latter. It was much more convenient and beneficial to preserve the Ch'ing regime intact and unchanged, with its 'statesmen' such as Li Hung-chang, playing the role of a Porfirio Diaz, maintaining internal order while safeguarding and facilitating continuous foreign political and economic penetration.

The surviving reformers did not cease their political activity. Having taken refuge in Japan, K'ang Yu-wei and Liang Ch'i-ch'ao, clinging to their constitutional monarchist views, soon established the 'Pao Huang Hui' ('Protect the Emperor Society'), which for a time gained considerable support among the ever growing Chinese diaspora. They also became partially involved in the preparation for an uprising in the Yangtse Valley area in support of Kuang-hsü. The plans for the revolt, scheduled for August 1900, drawn up by a young Hunanese scholar, T'ang Ts'ai-ch'ang (1867–1900), provided also for the participation of secret society members as the main military force. Due to insufficient precautions the plot was discovered on the eve of the rising. T'ang and 19 of his associates were executed, and in the aftermath around 200 progressive intellectuals in Hunan and Hupei met the same fate. Simultaneously, however, the north was in the throes of a colossal popular movement of an entirely different character.

The I Ho T'uan Movement

The suppression of the Reform Movement did nothing to increase the stability of the Ch'ing regime which, on the contrary, soon found its position threatened by a potentially much more dangerous enemy, a new large-scale peasant insurrection. A constant deterioration of the economy, due partially to foreign penetration and reflected in an increase of tax burdens, as well as natural disasters leading to famine conditions, had markedly enhanced peasant discontent, especially in Shantung, and given rise to increased activity of the secret societies, the traditional organizations of peasant revolts. Customarily aimed against the landlord gentry and the authorities, the incipient rebellion this time displayed also an additional trait, for due to intensified foreign encroachment, especially in the 1890s, peasant disaffection assumed a distinctly xenophobic hue. Since, for the overwhelming majority of North China peasants, missionary activity was almost the sole aspect of foreign penetration they came in contact with, the anti-foreign sentiments became inextricably intertwined with hostility to Christianity. Stimulated by the increased scope of missionary activity (by 1898 there were 3900 Protestant and 700 Catholic missionaries; the number of converts was estimated at 500,000 Catholics and 200,000 Protestants), anti-missionary riots had spread like wildfire in many parts of the country. They were always suppressed in a fashion which could only assure their resurgence with greater vigour.

Although the Ch'ing had been successful in putting down earlier revolts initiated by the secret societies, the latter, deeply rooted in the peasant community, preserved their ideology unchanged. This was particularly true of the famous White Lotus sect, whose offshoot, the I Ho Ch'üan ('Fists in the Name of Harmony and Justice'), began to show increasing signs of activity in areas such as Shantung, which had been a traditional stronghold of the parent sect. Its creed was a curious jumble of popular beliefs, mostly of Taoist and Buddhist origin, laced with innumerable superstititions and magical rites. The practice of traditional martial arts, including boxing, and the word 'fist' in the title, accounts for the European name of the movement – the Boxers.

241

In 1899, as its influence spread, especially in Shantung, the I Ho Ch'üan, although remaining basically a peasant movement potentially dangerous to the Manchu dynasty and the Chinese gentry, began to engage increasingly in anti-foreign and especially anti-Christian activities. Initially, the Ch'ing authorities regarded it as but another peasant revolt requiring suppression by force, but relatively quickly the decision was made to take advantage of the movement's anti-foreignism, and seek to channel its hostility exclusively against foreigners and Chinese Christians, thus diverting it from attacking the Manchu dynasty. The majority of the movement's leaders succumbed to these ingenious tactics, and changed their previous anti-dynastic slogans into the ominous 'Support the Ch'ing, Extirpate the Foreigners', while their armed units roamed through the Shantung countryside, burning churches and killing Chinese Christians. Simultaneously, the name of the movement was changed to I Ho T'uan – the word 't'uan' (unit), used to designate gentry-led militia forces, implied official recognition – and its further activities were destined to create almost immediately a critical situation in North China.

The above decision to utilize the I Ho T'uan did not, by any means, represent the views of all the ruling factions of the Ch'ing regime. A considerable number of high officials continued to regard the movement as dangerous and subversive, and demanded its suppression. Nevertheless, Tz'u-hsi and her closest confidants, enraged by the failure of recent schemes aimed at dethroning Kuang-hsü, brought on in part by the objections of the foreign powers, inclined increasingly towards the scheme of favouring the I Ho T'uan. As a result, the Ch'ing government's policies became both contradictory and vacillating. Thus, when, at the end of 1899, the foreign diplomats in Peking, alarmed by the growing scope of the I Ho T'uan's activity, demanded that steps be taken to suppress the movement, Yüan Shih-k'ai was dispatched to Shantung to carry out the appropriate measures. Using his well-armed troops Yüan had not the slightest difficulty in accomplishing his mission; by a liberal employment of machine guns he also promptly deflated the claims of the I Ho T'uan that the incantations they used made them impervious to bullets. However, the decimated insurgents fled Shantung to enter the metropolitan province Chihli, where they quickly grew in strength, ravaging the countryside and soon posing a threat to Peking itself. The number of their victims increased correspondingly, but the fact is that only one foreigner had been killed up to the end of May 1900, by another secret society.

Against this background the demands of the Peking diplomatic corps for the immediate suppression of the I Ho T'uan became still more intense, placing the Ch'ing in an ever greater quandary. By the end of May, when the I Ho T'uan began attacking the Peking–Tientsin Railway, the government had still not undertaken a clear decision, while its troops floundered occasionally into odd conflicts with the rebels. In June, the situation became even more tense, since a number of European railway engineers had been slain, and armed intervention by the foreign powers, rumoured about since March, was quickly becoming a certainty. On 4 June sixteen foreign vessels anchored off Taku, and a week later, in response to the request for aid from the diplomatic corps in Peking, an expeditionary force 2000 strong, composed of men from seven countries (Great Britain, Germany, Russia, France, Japan, the United States and Italy), commanded by E. H. Seymour, a British vice-admiral, set out from Tientsin. Within a week the expeditionary force, having advanced only halfway, was compelled to retreat in face of unceasing attacks by I Ho T'uan units, and succeeded in fighting its way back to Tientsin. According to Seymour, it was only the utter inadequacy of the I Ho T'uan's arms – spears and swords against machine guns and artillery – which saved his force from total annihilation.

Simultaneously, on 13 June, sizable I Ho T'uan forces entered the capital, which soon became the scene for much plunder and slaughter, with Chinese Christians as the principal, though not the sole, victims. Even at this moment the Ch'ing court continued to be at a loss as to its future line of action. All the divergent views were aired in a dramatic debate, until ultimately a forged report that the powers were demanding the Empress Dowager's removal, and the attack on 16 June on the Taku forts by the foreign naval forces, determined the issue. Tz'u-hsi gave her backing to the faction in favour of supporting the I Ho T'uan, even if this move were to entail a war with all the foreign powers. On 19 June, when the news that the foreigners had begun, after taking the Taku forts, to advance on Tientsin, reached Peking, the die was cast. The decision to break diplomatic relations and to declare war was made, and the diplomatic corps requested to leave for Tientsin. But negotiations with the diplomats were broken off the next day during which the German minister, K. von Ketteler, was killed, and the unduly famous fifty-day-long siege of the Legations began. Purcell has aptly referred to it as 'a small incident in the vast history of China', and actually the main historical significance of this curious affair rested in the fact that it illustrated exactly the inconsistent and contradictory nature of the Ch'ing government's policies, since the Legations could have been taken, in Hart's words, in a week or a day, had the will to do so existed.

In fact, the Ch'ing rulers, and Tz'u-hsi in particular, were anxious to extricate themselves from the predicament in which the twofold pressure of the I Ho T'uan and the foreign powers, and their own indulgence in xenophobia, had placed them. The policy which they really wanted to follow was demonstrated in the major part of the country where the governors general, conveniently ignoring the 'declaration of war', quickly suppressed all signs of anti-foreign action, came to an understanding with foreign representatives, collaborated with them and protected foreign property in return for the non-intervention of foreign armies. Thus fighting was restricted primarily to Chihli, while I Ho T'uan actions in Manchuria were immediately pounced upon by the Russians as an excellent pretext for the occupation of the entire northeast.

The defeat of the Seymour expedition exploded the myth of invincibility, according to which a Western regiment could march at will through the length and breadth of China. The organization of an appropriately sizable new expedition was now undertaken, in the course of which all the latent rivalries of the powers quickly surfaced. Formally, the aim was to rescue the Legations, but actually it was to suppress the I Ho T'uan and to bring the Ch'ing regime back to its previous role of a docile servitor of the powers. By 14 July the Allied troops had taken Tientsin; a third of the city was destroyed in the fighting and the rest systematically looted. With Tientsin secured, the Allied force, around 19,000 strong, advanced on Peking at the beginning of August. The technical excellence of Western arms again decided the issue, and the resistance of the I Ho T'uan and the Ch'ing troops was broken with relative ease. On 14 August, the Allies entered the capital, where the bearers of Western civilization, missionaries, diplomats and journalists included, were to prove their great cultural superiority over the heathen of the Middle Kingdom by indulging for many days in an orgy of looting and rapine.

But it was only after the sacking of Peking that the Germans arrived. By the end of October the German force was 19,000 strong, and promptly made certain that the Kaiser's order of instilling a fear of the German name and of giving no quarter and taking no prisoners was scrupulously followed. During the subsequent six months in the course of 45 punitive, actually looting, expeditions, 35 of which were manned exclusively by them, the Germans outdid by far the Tsarist atrocities in Manchuria, and became the most hated of all the foreign interventionists.

In Europe itself, it was only the Marxists, especially the German and Russian Social Democrats, who upheld the honour of true Western culture, speaking out in defence of the Chinese and castigating the greed and brutality of their own imperialist governments.

Within a day of the entry of the expeditionary force, Tz'u-hsi fled Peking, taking along her prisoner, Kuang-hsü. Most of the Ch'ing dignitaries followed her example and the government practically ceased to exist. However, already a month earlier, her faithful servitor, Li Hung-chang, was empowered to begin the inevitable negotiations with the foreigners. His appointment signified that the Ch'ing government was more than ready to revert to its previous role, and was willing to pay any price for the preservation of the Manchu dynasty. To prove this, the Ch'ing carried out a complete volte-face and their troops joined the Allies in campaigns against the I Ho T'uan who, deceived and betrayed, sought to sustain their resistance. The pacification of North China, which lasted into the spring of 1901, turned much of it into a foodless wasteland and caused the death of countless Chinese, thousandfold more than the 242 foreigners who had been slain in the summer of 1900.

During the course of the negotiations, which dragged out to September 1901, the idea of partitioning China was seriously entertained. Nonetheless, it could not be put into effect for two fundamental reasons. On the one hand, although the I Ho T'uan had finally been crushed, the movement had demonstrated the latent power of the Chinese will to resist aggression; thus partition would entail a struggle against the vast population, and was necessarily doomed to ultimate failure. Herein, too, lay the basic significance of the I Ho T'uan. On the other hand, the rivalries of the powers had grown to the point where an agreement on sharing the loot was practically unattainable. This was revealed especially by the acute antagonism of Great Britain and Russia who took totally divergent positions. The Russians, having occupied Manchuria, reverted to their policy of supporting Tz'u-hsi and her clique, concentrating on obtaining the acquiescence of the Ch'ing to their plans, aimed at establishing a protectorate over the entire northeast. The British, who had earlier seriously entertained the idea of partition, now favoured restoring the Manchu regime and using it to frustrate the aspirations of the Russians. For this purpose the British also sought the aid of the Japanese, thoroughly aroused and furious over Russia's actions in Manchuria.

The haggling between the powers over the terms of the punishment to be imposed, in which the Germans proved themselves to be the most vindictive, finally came to an end, and on 7 September the so-called Boxer Protocol was concluded between the Ch'ing and eleven foreign governments (the seven original participants in the intervention and Austria-Hungary which joined them, as well as Spain, the Netherlands and Belgium). It provided, among other things, for payment by China of a colossal crippling indemnity of 450 million taels in gold, actually amounting with interest to over 928 million, the right to station foreign troops in the Peking Legation Quarter and along the Peking–Tientsin Railway, and the obligation of the Ch'ing government to suppress any anti-foreign movements, and to punish those responsible for supporting the I Ho T'uan.

The Manchus, having been assured that they would be left in nominal power, agreed to these terms without a whimper. The Ch'ing government was now to be little more than a debt-collecting agency for the foreigners, while the country it purported to rule had been successfully transformed into a joint semi-colony of all the principal imperialist powers. The scene was thus set for the return of the Manchus to Peking. In Sian, where she had finally taken refuge, Tz'u-hsi had been busy successfully gathering all the attributes of power into her hands. Once the Protocol had been signed, she deemed it safe to proceed leisurely to the capital, with all the fresh plunder which her emissaries had extorted from the provinces. In the meantime, she had heaped all the blame for the recent events on some of her closest collaborators, claiming to have been misled into committing the only political mistake in her entire career. Upon arrival, she smiled graciously at the foreigners gathered to greet her in the Imperial City, and quickly dashed into the palace to dig up her buried treasure which the Germans had not been able to find, though not for want of trying. All was forgotten; complete concord between the Manchus and the powers reigned once again.

11. The 1911 Revolution and the Rule of the Militarists, 1901–18

China During the First Decade of the Twentieth Century

In the aftermath of the I Ho T'uan's defeat the imperialist powers took full advantage of the situation to increase their economic penetration of China on an unprecedented scale. Foreign investments in the 1902–14 period rose from a total of $788 million to $1610 million, with Britain still holding the lion's share ($260 million in 1902, $607 million in 1914). In this process foreign control of China's foreign trade, financed largely by foreign-owned banks, increased substantially. Simultaneously, the Ch'ing government, faced with the problem of paying the horrendous indemnity imposed by the Boxer Protocol, became completely dependent financially on the foreign governments; the latter, in spite of their rivalries, decided to act in unison, a tendency which ultimately gave rise in 1911 to an international consortium which arrogated to itself the sole right to furnish the Ch'ing with further loans. At the same time, continued pressure was successfully exerted to obtain new concessions for railroad and mining rights.

The first decade of the twentieth century also witnessed an intensification of an imperialist struggle for power in East Asia, which affected China most significantly. Against the background of intensified Russo-Japanese rivalry, particularly in respect to Manchuria and Korea, an important realignment of relations between the powers took place on 30 January 1902 with the conclusion of the Anglo-Japanese Treaty. This accord, clearly directed against Russia, greatly strengthened Japan's position, making it now possible for her to contemplate a war against the Tsarist regime. The aggressive plans of the Japanese imperialists were facilitated also by the actions of the Tsarist government, whose failure to carry out in full its promised evacuation of Manchuria added still more fuel to the fire. The Russian rulers, arrogantly confident of victory if a conflict were to ensue, remained quite unperturbed by the possibility of drifting into a war.

Characteristically, once again and not for the last time, the Japanese started the war on 8 February 1904 without bothering to declare it, with a successful and damaging attack on the Russian fleet in Port Arthur. The Russo-Japanese war quickly turned into an unceasing series of heavy and humiliating defeats for the Tsarist autocracy. The miserably led Russian armies suffered serious defeats in Manchuria, and the culminating blow came at the end of May 1905 at Tsushima, with the destruction of the Russian Baltic fleet. The military disasters had even more important consequences, for they served to stimulate the revolutionary movement of the peoples of the Tsarist empire from the summer of 1905 on. Both these factors made the Russian government eager to end the war as soon as possible; the Japanese, completely exhausted by their costly victories, concurred. In the Portsmouth Treaty, signed on 5 September 1905, Russia agreed *inter alia* to turn over her entire Liaotung concession (Port Arthur and Talien), as well as part of the Chinese Eastern Railway, the line from Changchun to Port Arthur. This was reorganized by the Japanese as a South Manchurian Railway company, and developed into a gigantic industrial-military complex, the core of Japanese military aggression in China for the subsequent four decades.

The utterly degraded position of the Ch'ing regime can be deduced from the fact that the Russo-Japanese war had been waged almost exclusively on Chinese soil, and the Manchus could not even lift a finger to prevent their own homeland from being savagely ravaged. While the peace treaty provided for the withdrawal of Russian and Japanese forces from the northeast and the recognition of Chinese 'sovereignty' over the entire area, its principal stipulation called for the Ch'ing government to recognize the transfer of the concessions in Liaotung, which it promptly did. Within two years of their sanguinary military confrontation, Russia and Japan found it advisable to readjust their relations by partitioning, in a secret treaty signed on 30 July 1907, the entire northeast into two exclusive spheres of influence; North Manchuria was recognized as the Russian sphere, South Manchuria as the Japanese. This arrangement proved workable and was confirmed by further secret accords concluded in 1910 and 1916.

While the basic rivalries of the imperialist powers in East Asia had not been and could not be resolved, attempts were made in the years preceding the First World War to establish a *modus vivendi* between them. Thus, for example, Anglo-Russian contention in Asia was alleviated by the agreement reached on 31 August 1907, which also, by recognizing Ch'ing sovereignty, terminated the conflict over Tibet. This accord, as well as other similar ones between France and Japan, and the United States and Japan, which, in effect, were tantamount to a recognition of the existing spheres of influence, resulted in a relative stabilization in the situation in East Asia. Simultaneously, although the Far East continued to remain one of the main focal points of imperialist rivalry, conflicts in other areas were to prove of even greater significance in aggravating international relations.

The marked increase in foreign economic penetration in the 1901–14 period and the country's semi-colonial status continued to present a serious handicap for the development of Chinese national capitalism, as distinct from the development of foreign-owned enterprises in China. Nevertheless, in spite of the almost total incapacity of the Ch'ing government to pursue policies which would stimulate endeavours in this domain, some progress was made regardless of the disadvantageous conditions. An increasing number of Chinese merchants and gentry were willing to invest in industrial enterprises, particularly in light industry. Growth took place especially in the textile industry; some entrepreneurs, such as Chang Chien (1853–1926), were even successful in building entire industrial complexes. However, this new stage of economic development was still quite uneven and restricted primarily to the Treaty Ports and the coastal provinces. Hence, most of the interior remained unaffected, and in the economy as a whole the marked predominance of agriculture continued to prevail, while the inadequacy of communications and the terrible poverty of the countryside militated against the formation of a truly nationwide market. The increased importation of foreign goods and the growth of light industry did have an adverse effect on rural handicrafts, the secondary mainstay of the peasantry, intensifying the latter's pauperization, although not quite as drastically as is sometimes maintained.

The limited growth of capitalist production did not signify that the country had made a transition to the capitalist stage of development since, on the contrary, the old economic forms were still dominant. As a result the economy became, at best, mixed, which was also a reflection of China's semi-colonial status. Nonetheless, the presence of capitalism did have significant social consequences in the formation of new social classes – a Chinese national bourgeoisie, as distinct from a comprador stratum, connected with and serving foreign capital, and an industrial working class. It is clear that this phenomenon was also to be reflected in the political development of this period, but not in as simplistic a fashion as some modern Chinese historians seem to believe. The further penetration of Western ideology and its far-reaching effect on the newly forming Chinese intelligentsia, destined to play a crucial role in determining the country's future, appear to be of at least equal significance. The scope of this influence had increased considerably in these years due to a number of factors, among them the introduction by the Ch'ing government of educational reforms. These resulted in the establishment of a new school system, based on partially modern curriculum, which provided at least some education for a part of the population (by 1900 around 57,000 schools, 89,000 teachers, 1,600,000 pupils, out of 65 million children of school age). Simultaneously, the number of foreign educational institutions increased, and, perhaps most important of all, a large-scale migration of students seeking an education abroad began. Some of them attended European and American universities, but the great majority, for obvious reasons, made their way to Japan.

From a modest beginning of perhaps 100 in 1898, the number of Chinese students in Japan snowballed to 13,000–15,000 by 1905–7. The students, mostly from gentry or merchant families, came from almost every part of China and, while the quality of the education they absorbed was quite uneven, it is hard to exaggerate the significance of this hegira to Japan for future political development. A very large percentage of the leading personalities on the Chinese political arena during the next two to three decades were Japanese-returned students. It was in Japan that many of them made their acquaintance with Western Learning and, joining in fervent debates on the future of China, took their first steps in politics.

The educational innovations referred to above formed a part of a belated reform programme which the Ch'ing government finally began to put into effect in a piecemeal fashion from 1901 on. The deepening political crisis, as evidenced by the growing of ever more vocal discontent, particularly of the new intelligentsia, itself paradoxically largely a product of the educational reform, compelled the Ch'ing authorities to introduce further measures, whose fundamental purpose was the preservation of Manchu rule. The most important of these, undertaken clearly with just this aim in mind, concerned the reorganization of the Ch'ing military establishment. This task was entrusted primarily to Yüan Shih-k'ai, governor-general of Chihli since November 1901, and, with Jung-lu, the most powerful official in the empire. In building up the new modern force, 60,000 strong by 1906 and known as the Peiyang (Northern) Army, Yüan skilfully utilized this oppportunity for promoting his personal followers, thus creating a faithful militarist coterie, which was to form the core of the notorious Peiyang warlord clique, the mainstay of his future rise to power. The majority of Yüan's officers were of gentry origin; retaining close contact with their families they were to take advantage of their position to play the social role, in Lattimore's astute phrase, of landlords with machine guns. The Ch'ing government, while increasing its military strength obviously for internal purposes, also considered it imperative to propose a number of political innovations. In 1905, Tz'u-hsi promised the introduction of constitutional government, and in the next year announced a plan for the establishment of purely consultative assemblies on a national and provincial level. The measures proposed were actually only a time-gaining manoeuvre on the part of the Manchus, since they had not the slightest intention of relinquishing or diminishing their power. The draft of the new constitution, published in September 1908 and scheduled to come into effect in 1918, proved this point clearly, since, although copied almost wholly from Japan, it provided the Manchu emperor with still more extensive power.

On 15 November 1908, the woman who since 1862 had ruled China during the descent into an abyss of catastrophe and degradation, departed to meet her ancestors. Tz'u-hsi's death was preceded a day earlier by that of the ill-fated Kuang-hsü. As one of her last acts she also arranged for the succession to the throne of P'u-i, aged two and a half, the grandson of her favourite Jung-lu and

Kuang-hsü's nephew, whose father, Tsai-feng, now became regent.

The new regent quickly showed himself to be an exceptionally ineffective ruler, totally incapable of dealing with the increasingly critical situation. He did have one accomplishment to his credit; while not fulfilling Kuang-hsü's deathbed request that Yüan Shih-k'ai be executed for his treachery in 1898, it was soon discovered that Yüan suffered from a foot ailment which made the carrying out of his duties impossible. He was therefore permitted to retire to his Honan estate to treat the complaint.

Under constant political pressure the Ch'ing government assented to the establishment in October 1909 of the Provincial Assemblies, and to that of the National Assembly in October 1910. As bodies nominated or elected on a highly restricted franchise, both assemblies, composed mostly of constitutional monarchists, quickly became a useful platform for voicing new demands. Thus the government was compelled to promise the enactment of the new constitution and the calling of parliament for 1913. It also surrendered to the clamour for the introduction of a responsible cabinet in April 1911, but the choice of ministers (eight Manchus, four Mongols and four Chinese) only served to discredit it still more and inflamed the growing anti-Manchu sentiments. The latter were also stimulated by Tsai-feng's inept attempts to strengthen the dynasty's position by placing his brothers in key command posts in the armed forces.

The Rise of the Revolutionary Movement

The cosmetic alterations which the Manchu government was busy introducing did not, of course, signify that any freedom existed for the conduct of political activity aimed against the Ch'ing autocracy. This pertained, even after 1908, to the relatively moderate leaders of the Reform Movement, and thus both K'ang Yu-wei and Liang Ch'i-ch'ao contrived to remain in Japan, seeking to find support for their views among the Chinese abroad. K'ang clung almost unchangeably to his earlier position, remaining a constitutional monarchist, unwilling to accept more advanced ideas. The rapid evolution of the political scene was soon to leave him behind, and he sank relatively quickly into obscurity. Liang, on the other hand, went beyond the views he had adhered to in 1898 to become one of the most influential advocates of modernization. Politically, however, he also remained a constitutional monarchist, opposed to the growing strength of revolutionary ideas. In the years 1901–11 a sharp struggle ensued in Japan between K'ang and Liang and the representatives of the revolutionary trend, and all attempts by their Japanese hosts to reconcile the hostile groups failed. It should be added that the influence of the Japanese on the development of Chinese politics, especially on the actions conducted by the Chinese émigrés, was both considerable and complex in nature. Japanese progressive and early socialist groups were undoubtedly sincere in the support they offered to the Chinese revolutionary movement from its earliest stage. But the Japanese government's policy towards this movement was actually based on the desire to manipulate it for the purposes of its own imperialist expansion.

The son of a family of poor tenant peasants from a village in southwest Kwangtung was destined to become the principal leader and ideologist of the first stage of the modern Chinese revolutionary movement. Born on 12 November 1866, Sun Yat-sen (Sun Wen, Sun Chung-shan) came from a region in which the traditions of the Taiping movement were still strong, and their influence on him was undoubted. Fortunately, having a prosperous elder brother who was an immigrant in Hawaii, Sun was able to acquire a modern secondary education, followed by medical studies in Hong Kong, which he completed with honours in 1892. Sun's acute interest in politics was evident already in his student years, but up to 1895 his advocacy of modernization did not exclude the possibility of effectuating reforms within the framework of the existing order. It was the catastrophic and humiliating defeat of the Ch'ing government which convinced Sun of the indispensability of conducting revolutionary activities for the purpose of overthrowing the Manchu dynasty. He gave up the prospects of a lucrative career as a medical man to devote his entire life to this task.

Sun Yat-sen's first political initiative was the establishment in Hawaii in 1894 of the 'Hsing Chung Hui' (his rendition – 'Association for the Regeneration of China'), whose principal aim was to organize an anti-Ch'ing rising in Kwangtung. The first attempt to accomplish this, made in Canton in October 1895, ended in total failure. While some of the closest of his followers lost their lives in this forlorn enterprise, Sun managed to escape. For the next sixteen years he was to remain abroad as a political exile with a price on his head. Only for a few days in 1907 did he set foot on his native soil. But it was precisely during this period that Sun, having become a professional revolutionary, ultimately emerged as the most eminent leader of the Chinese revolutionary movement. Sun concentrated his activities on political work among the sizable and growing communities of Chinese immigrants, particularly in Southeast Asia, Hawaii and the United States. By 1910 this diaspora numbered around 2,500,000 and the aid offered by it, in money and men, was of utmost importance. For years Sun travelled untiringly from one Chinese community to another, organizing, lecturing, raising funds and instilling among the immigrants an awareness of China's needs. In 1896, the Ch'ing had him kidnapped in London. Sun was rescued from his imprisonment in the Chinese Legation by the intervention of his English friends, in particular by Dr J. Cantlie, his teacher in Hong Kong, and the incident made him a famous figure.

During Sun's years abroad revolutionary activities began to spread in China in spite of the draconic Ch'ing repression. Shanghai became the main centre for revolutionary propaganda conducted by young intellectuals whose publications, in spite of constant hounding by authorities, successfully disseminated revolutionary ideas. An outstanding example was the famous and influential anti-Ch'ing pamphlet, 'The Revolutionary Army', published in 1904. Its author, Tsou Jung (1885–1905), died in prison. The intellectuals in the provinces, often led by Japanese-returned students, also sought to establish revolutionary organizations. In Hunan, Huang Hsing (1874–1916), a schoolteacher's son and later one of the most important revolutionary leaders, founded in December 1903 the 'Hua Hsing Hui' ('Society for the Revival of China'). The society planned an uprising against the Ch'ing to be launched with the help of secret societies, but the attempt ended in failure.

Revolutionary ideas were also making an even greater impact on the Chinese student community in Japan. It was here that under Sun Yat-sen's guidance the first successful attempt to unite a number of separate revolutionary groups was undertaken. August 1905 saw the birth in Tokyo of the famous T'ung Meng Hui ('United League'), the first truly significant modern Chinese revolutionary organization. At the outset Sun Yat-sen was recognized, due to his reputation as the eldest and most experienced revolutionary, as the League's leader, and its programme reflected primarily the views he held at the time. Sun's outlook, shaped largely by his education and study of Western civilization, was summed up by him in his famous 'San Min Chu I' ('The Three People's Principles'). The first principle can be understood as Nationalism which, in this period, denoted above all the struggle against Manchu rule. The second is taken to mean Democracy, interpreted by Sun as the introduction of a republican and constitutional government on the American or French model. The third, People's Livelihood, was referred to by Sun as Socialism; in effect, it signified a desire to face up to China's social problems in the future, bound up with the hope that it would prove possible to avoid the evils inherent in capitalism, of which he was quite aware, by leaping over that stage of historical development. Of these three principles the first was clearly uppermost in the activities of the T'ung Meng Hui, which concentrated on the goal of overthrowing the Manchu monarchy. In the years 1905–10 Sun's young followers devoted much of their efforts to spreading their views, contending with those of the constitutional monarchists, as represented by Liang Ch'i-ch'ao. This ideological struggle filled the pages of the League's most important publication, the *Min pao* ('People's Tribune') which, while published in Japan, was eagerly read by progressive intellectuals in every province of China.

The programme and the activities of the T'ung Meng Hui reflected the marked growth of the political consciousness of the Chinese intellectuals and the increasing ferment within the country. In both these cases the influence of the Russo-Japanese war and the 1905 Russian Revolution was far-reaching, since the political implications of these events, the urgency of modernization and the waging of a revolutionary struggle against an autocratic regime, were grasped without difficulty. However, the actual scope of the United League's activity was circumscribed by a number of factors. Its membership, while larger than that of its predecessors, remained small, probably never exceeding 1000 in the years 1905–7. This was partially the result of the oppressive measures of the Ch'ing regime, which rendered the organizing of a political movement on a mass scale almost impossible and necessitated the use of conspiratorial methods. Under such circumstances, the T'ung Meng Hui chose to pursue a strategy of waging military coups, which, it was hoped, could serve as the spark for setting off a general anti-Manchu insurrection. For this purpose also, League members sought to infiltrate the Ch'ing armed forces and to gain the support of the secret societies. Sun Yat-sen refers in his autobiography to his 'ten unsuccessful revolutionary attempts'. These included the 1895 coup in Canton, another rising in Kwangtung in 1900, and eight coups, all organized in South and Southwest China in the years 1907–11, mostly led by Huang Hsing. The failure of all these attempts, and especially the last one, the famous April 1911 rising in Canton, the best prepared and closest to success of all, and the savage repression which followed in all cases, did not diminish the revolutionary ferment in the country. This was also reflected by other activities unconnected with the League and largely anarchist in inspiration. Hence, it was hoped that a better organized effort could succeed in toppling the ever more obviously rotten and tottering Ch'ing regime.

The 1911 Revolution

In 1911 the tense political situation, already exacerbated by the growing conflict of the Ch'ing government and its political opponents of various hues, was to be inflamed still further by the railway construction problem, an issue with far-reaching economic and political implications. The basic problem was whether future railway building was to be carried out by the central government, completely dependent on foreign loans, or by national capital, subscribed by the Chinese merchants and gentry. The latter, eager to take this potentially profitable endeavour into their own hands, had proceeded to organize appropriate associations and companies, especially in Kwangtung, Hunan, Hupei and Szechuan, the provinces in which the most important ventures, such as the Hankow–Canton and the Hankow–Szechuan lines, were to be undertaken.

257

Against this background the Ch'ing government announced, on 9 May 1911, its new railway nationalization plan which, in reality, was simply a scheme for obtaining fresh loans from the international consortium which would, in effect, place the planned railways under foreign control, while depriving the provincial associations of any participation. The signing on 20 May of contracts for the loan and the construction of the two lines evoked a colossal storm of protest, especially in vast, independently minded Szechuan. By August, disturbances had spread over the entire province, with merchants and students organizing strikes and protest demonstrations. The Ch'ing authorities resorted to brutal repression, which only resulted in provoking uprisings in almost all of Szechuan, thus leading to a still greater political crisis.

The failure of all the risings organized by the T'ung Meng Hui in the south and southwest had led some of its leaders, including one of the most talented, Sung Chiao-jen (1882–1913), to shift their attention to the Yangtse Valley. In this area, and in Wuhan especially, considerable success in infiltrating the Ch'ing armed forces had been attained recently by revolutionary organizations under T'ung Meng Hui influence, making it possible to schedule an insurrection for the late autumn of 1911. The events in Szechuan, to which troops from Hupei were supposed to be sent to quell the revolt, compelled the revolutionaries to set the date for the rising in Wuhan for 6 October, but due to inadequate preparations it was postponed to 16 October. However, all the plans were completely upset by an unfortunate bomb explosion which enabled the Ch'ing to uncover the plot, arrest and execute some of the revolutionary leaders, and supposedly seize a list of all the army conspirators. It was in this setting that a small group of soldiers, members of one of the revolutionary societies, decided to start the uprising themselves. Deprived of their leaders and commanded by a sergeant, the soldiers, soon joined by other units in the Wuchang garrison, succeeded in capturing the entire city on 10 October. By 12 October the revolutionary troops were also in possession of Hanyang, with its important arsenal, and of the great city of Hankow. In their desperate search for experienced leaders, the soldiers also dragged out of hiding a quaking brigade commander, Li Yüan-hung (1864–1928), and compelled him to take command and support a revolution, whose aims he had absolutely nothing in common with.

The Wuchang rising proved to be the spark which Sun Yat-sen and his followers had dreamed of. Within a month Ch'ing authority collapsed like a house of cards in most of Central and South China, with fifteen provinces declaring their independence. Only the northeast, Chihli, Honan and Shantung remained under Manchu control, or rather under that of the Peiyang divisions stationed there. In the Yangtse Valley only Nanking, occupied by the troops of the notorious reactionary, Chang Hsün (1854–1923), still held out; the city was taken by revolutionary units on 2 December. However, although the successes attained were impressive and unexpected, the victory of the revolution was not yet assured by any means, since the Peiyang divisions, the strongest units by far, remained loyal to the government, still more to their creator, Yüan Shih-k'ai, and were readying a drive on Wuhan. Politically, conditions were also not all that favourable, since the numerically inferior and heterogeneous T'ung Meng Hui proved incapable of mastering the situation, and thus almost all the new provincial governments were quickly taken over by constitutional monarchists and former Ch'ing generals and officials, busily masquerading now as ardent advocates of the Chinese Republic.

The Wuhan rising had caught Sun Yat-sen completely unawares in Denver, Colorado, in the midst of still another fund-raising tour. Sun quickly left the States, but he proceeded to China by way of England. While hoping to obtain financial aid for the new revolutionary government and to prevent the Manchus from receiving such assistance, his main intention was to persuade the British to maintain their neutrality. In fact, the rapidity of the Ch'ing collapse had made it unlikely that the British would have followed any other policy, and Sun's long detour, which reflected the fear of foreign intervention gripping most of the Chinese revolutionaries, only meant that his influence on the development of events in this crucial period was minimal.

The disintegration of Ch'ing rule gave rise to a state of chaos and panic in Peking. The Manchus now turned for help to the one man whose influence on the Peiyang Army could possibly bolster their collapsing regime, Yüan Shih-k'ai. However, the initial negotiations produced no results, for Yüan maintained that his foot ailment was still troublesome. Only when all his demands, which were tantamount to placing total power into his hands, were met, did he feel sufficiently well to depart from his Honan estate and assume, on 16 November, his post as Premier of the newly formed, now supposedly constitutional, government. More significantly, Yüan also took command of the military operations of the Peiyang divisions against Wuhan, conducted by two of his closest followers, Feng Kuo-chang (1859–1919) and Tuan Ch'i-jui (1865–1936). Simultaneously, he asserted, with the help of a number of rapidly staged assassinations, complete control of all the military forces in North China, thus assuring the dominance of his Peiyang clique.

The technical superiority of the Peiyang forces soon proved itself; Hankow fell on 1 November, Hanyang on 27 November. However, Yüan Shih-k'ai did not press his army to cross the Great River for an assault on Wuchang, since a quick or easy victory over the revolutionary forces was extremely doubtful. In spite of its initial disorganization, the revolutionary army was being steadily expanded by an unceasing stream of volunteers and its morale remained high. Under these circumstances Yüan preferred to resort to negotiations, and practically all the military operations ceased from the middle of December. Shanghai became the venue for the talks between Yüan's representatives and the delegates of the revolutionary provinces, with the latter offering Yüan the presidency of the future republic for the price of betraying his Manchu masters. He neither rejected nor accepted the offer, but demanded more time, which he deemed necessary to persuade the Ch'ing court of the hopelessness of its position.

In the meantime, Sun Yat-sen arrived in Shanghai on 25 December 1911. His presence did contribute somewhat to lessening the unceasing squabbling among the representatives of the revolutionary provincial governments assembled there. After transferring to Nanking, they proceeded to elect Sun as the Provincial President of the Chinese Republic, which was proclaimed on 1 January 1912. On the same day a provisional government was established, and Li Yüan-hung was the chosen Vice-President. However, the new government had little effective control over the provinces, and its most important initial step was to call for the immediate abdication of the Ch'ing dynasty.

While still in exile, Sun Yat-sen had pondered on the shape which a victorious revolutionary government should take, and his scheme provided for an initial three-year stage of military government, to be followed by six years of provisional government, during which a permanent constitution was to be drafted. Only after these nine years would a Western-type constitutional and parliamentary government be finally established. It is obvious that the first stage of this plan could only be implemented if the country's military forces were under central control, and this was precisely what the Nanking republican government did not possess. Hence, the scheme was doomed to failure from the outset, especially as most of the government was anxious to reach an accord with Yüan Shih-k'ai in order to prevent civil war and foreign intervention, an eventuality which, quite understandably in view of the experiences in the past half century, weighed heavily on everyone's mind. For these reasons too, Sun was persuaded by his colleagues to promise that he would turn over the presidency to Yüan, if the latter brought about the abdication of the Manchu dynasty.

The negotiations between the north and the south continued in an atmosphere of profound and justified mutual distrust. Both sides were also in desperate financial straits, since the country was financially bankrupt, and foreign loans hard to come by in such an unstable situation. The provisional government seized upon the ruinous method of printing an immense quantity of currency, which rapidly resulted in a galloping inflation. Yüan was somewhat more successful in this respect, for assuring the Ch'ing of his eternal loyalty – his Peiyang henchmen sending in streams of publicized telegrams to this effect – he managed to extort some of the court's hoarded treasures.

The Manchu princes still sought to cling to the remnants of their power, and only the further disintegration of the Ch'ing government and constant pressure exerted by Yüan began to weaken their resolve. The final blow came on 28 January; the Peiyang generals, again in a circular telegram, proclaimed the need for the Ch'ing dynasty to abdicate, and announced their devotion to republicanism. Hence, the stage was set for the last scene in the 267-year-long domination of the Manchu monarchy over the Chinese people. The Ch'ing government, betrayed and deceived by the man in whom they had placed their last hope of survival, now surrendered unresistingly. On 12 February,

Lung-yü, Kuang-hsü's widow and regent, weeping bitterly, read out in the presence of the Manchu princes, high court officials and members of Yüan's cabinet, the abdication of P'u-i from the throne of his ancestors. But the abdication edict was an odd document, for the Ch'ing emperor, acknowledging the desire of the majority of the Chinese people for a republic, empowered Yüan Shih-k'ai to undertake the establishment of the provisional republican government. Simultaneously, on the basis of previous secret negotiations between Peking and Nanking, the emperor and his family were to be left in full possession of the Imperial Palace, their wealth and property, becoming pensioners of the Republic.

Yüan Shih-k'ai, as the designated heir of the Ch'ing, now demanded that the Nanking government adhere to its previous promises. It did so immediately; on 13 February, Sun Yat-sen resigned his post – a move which he himself later on was to criticize bitterly – and two days later the Senate in Nanking elected Yüan as the Provisional President. Sun sought to stipulate certain conditions for the transfer of power, including the provision that the seat of government should remain in Nanking, and Yüan's inauguration take place there, but the latter disposed of them by a characteristic manoeuvre. When a delegation of prominent representatives of the Nanking government arrived in Peking to negotiate the above points, a highly dependable Peiyang division promptly staged a well-organized mutiny, enabling Yüan to claim that under such circumstances he could not possibly envisage leaving the troubled Northern Capital. Thus, the republican government was transferred to Peking, where Yüan's inauguration duly took place on 10 March 1912. A new cabinet took office in which four T'ung Meng Hui members held portfolios, but the key posts – the Ministries of the Interior, Army and Finance – were taken over by Yüan's men.

From the vantage point of seventy years after the events it is easy to see that Yüan Shih-k'ai's assumption of the presidency signified at that very moment the defeat of the 1911 Revolution. Its causes rested in the unfavourable alignment of political forces; the revolutionary movement, as represented by the T'ung Meng Hui, proved itself too incompetent and weak to face up to the task of consolidating its initial victory. This weakness, in turn, was derived from the limitations inherent in the League's programme and mode of action, which were only sufficient for accomplishing the overthrow of the Ch'ing autocracy, but inadequate for effectuating a fundamental reconstruction of Chinese society. There was little awareness in the T'ung Meng Hui programme of the magnitude of the political, social and economic problems involved in undertaking such a mission, and of the direction which the necessary transformation should take. Simultaneously, since the League had basically confined itself to conspiratorial activities, no advantage was taken of the large-scale discontent of the population, and hence no thought given to the organization of a mass movement, which could have assured effective popular support for the new Republic. In the ensuing struggle for power, the young and politically inexperienced revolutionaries were quickly swamped by the swarm of former Ch'ing officials and constitutional monarchists, busily jumping on the republican bandwagon, and incapable of dealing with the devious plots of Yüan Shih-k'ai's Peiyang clique. Nevertheless, in spite of its debacle, the 1911 Revolution did have a great accomplishment to its credit – the downfall of the absolute monarchy, an institution with over 2000 years of tradition and prestige. Thus, at least one significant encumbrance on the road to China's renaissance had been cast away.

The outbreak of the revolution had caught the foreign powers quite unawares, for, while the hopeless incapacity of the Ch'ing had become ever more apparent, the Peking diplomatic corps habitually took a hostile and sceptical attitude towards the revolutionary movement, and especially towards Sun Yat-sen, regarded by them as, at best, a futile visionary. The Wuchang uprising did not perturb the powers, for it was felt that the Ch'ing government would be able to suppress it without any trouble. However, when the rule of the Manchus began to show signs of collapsing completely, the imperialists, anxious to preserve the status quo, immediately began to seek the appropriate means, and quickly reached the conclusion that only a new 'strong man' could accomplish this task. Unanimously, their choice fell on Yüan Shih-k'ai.

The cessation of military operations in December, which removed the danger of a large-scale civil war that could prove a threat to foreign interests, obviated the necessity of embarking on direct military intervention, a course which would anyhow have been difficult to pursue in view of the increasing rivalry between the powers, more perhaps on the international arena than in China itself. Moreover, the speed with which Yüan Shih-k'ai had staged the Ch'ing abdication, and his own assumption of the presidency, assured them that power had passed into safe hands. Thus, having previously refused recognition and aid to the Nanking government, the imperialists now quickly rushed to grant both to Yüan in order to bring about the consolidation of his rule.

The Dictatorship of Yüan Shih-k'ai

The assumption of the presidency by Yüan Shih-k'ai, accomplished with such ease, actually marked the beginning of a new stage of sharp political strife over the nature of the future government, in which the forces represented by him, the bulk of the former Ch'ing establishment and especially its military component, were soon to prove much stronger than their confused and disunited opponents, the T'ung Meng Hui intellectuals and other advocates of republicanism. It was in this setting that the formation of political parties, itself a new and most interesting phenomenon, rapidly took place. Ultimately, out of a welter of many various groups, two major parties – the Chinputang and the Kuomintang – appeared. The Chinputang (Progressive Party), formed primarily of former Ch'ing office holders and conservative gentry, and led by Liang Ch'i-ch'ao, soon placed itself completely at the disposal of the new president. The Kuomintang (National Party, KMT), composed of the T'ung Meng Hui and a number of smaller organizations, aimed at endowing the Republic with an appropriate constitutional and parliamentary structure, and put forth for this purpose a purely conventional programme of contesting future elections, neglecting altogether any social measures which could assure it real popular support, especially in the countryside.

By June 1912, it became abundantly clear that the Kuomintang's plans for the creation of a truly constitutional government would be sabotaged by Yüan Shih-k'ai. However, its leaders, including both Sun Yat-sen and Huang Hsing, still harboured some illusions regarding the latter's intentions, and in negotiations in August agreed to support Yüan in exchange for his acquiescence to the holding of parliamentary elections.

The elections, conducted on the basis of a narrow franchise (10 per cent of the population), did take place at the turn of the year and, much to Yüan's chagrin, the Kuomintang, well led by the gifted Sung Chiao-jen, emerged as the undisputed victor with the right to form the next government. Yüan Shih-k'ai's reaction was simplicity itself. Having never bothered to display much finesse in his methods, for he employed only two – gold and bullets – Yüan quickly resorted to the latter. On 20 March 1913, Sung Chiao-jen, the KMT's obvious candidate for premier, was murdered in Shanghai. In no time at all, Yüan's complicity in this crime was established without a trace of doubt. The leaders of the Kuomintang thus faced a crucial choice of either starting a struggle for Yüan's overthrow, or passively awaiting their own annihilation.

Precisely at this moment the powers hurried to aid their 'strong man'. Negotiations for a loan, which had been going on since the previous year, were rapidly concluded, and, on 27 April, a £25-million Reorganization Loan was signed. All the protests of parliament at having been illegally by-passed in the conclusion of the loan were contemptuously brushed off by the Peking diplomatic corps. While the terms were exceptionally usurious, Yüan was only too happy to avail himself of this assistance, which provided him with the indispensable means to pay his armed forces and crush all domestic opposition.

The Kuomintang leaders had by this time reached the conclusion that an armed struggle against Yüan Shih-k'ai was inevitable, but realized that their forces were much weaker than his, since the KMT remained in control of only some provinces, among them Anhwei, Kiangsi and Kwangtung, where the KMT governors were willing to act. In any case, it was Yüan who took the initiative; in June, he ordered the dismissal of these three men, and the Peiyang Army advanced to attack Kiangsi.

The forlorn resistance of the Kuomintang to Yüan Shih-k'ai's aggression, which bears the name of the 'Second Revolution', was probably doomed to defeat from the outset, not only due to the obvious superiority of the latter's military forces, but also to the dispirited fashion with which it was waged and the failure to obtain any appreciable mass support. By mid-September, the KMT forces were completely smashed, and the principal leaders, including Sun Yat-sen and Huang Hsing, compelled to flee abroad. As a result, the authority of Yüan's regime was now extended practically to the entire country.

Having attained his military victory, Yüan Shih-k'ai deemed it advisable to retain the parliamentary facade for a while longer in order to be elected legally as permanent president. This operation was successfully accomplished in October, with the employment of an appropriate combination of intimidation and bribery of the reluctant parliamentarians. As the 'legal' ruler of China, Yüan quickly dispensed with the remaining pretences of constitutionalism. On 4 November 1913, the Kuomintang was outlawed, and all its members deprived of their seats in parliament which, now lacking a quorum, ceased to function. Its formal dissolution took place on 10 January 1914. In May, Yüan took the trouble of proclaiming a new 'Constitutional Compact', which granted him full dictatorial powers, and in December new rules for presidential elections were announced, on the basis of which Yüan's tenure could be lifetime. But all these pieces of paper were in fact meaningless. Yüan Shih-k'ai's real power rested on his full control of the armed forces, and on the efficiency of his appropriately expanded secret police busily tracking down and annihilating his opponents. Supreme power, however, was still not enough, for the megalomania of 'strong men', 'great leaders' and so forth, knows no bounds. Yüan Shih-k'ai longed for one more accolade, the title of emperor, and by the autumn of 1914 the first steps towards a restoration of the monarchy were already being made.

The outbreak of the First World War was also to have immediate repercussions on the situation in China, since it created very favourable conditions for the further pursuit by Japanese imperialism of its far-reaching expansionist plans. Already on 14 August, the Japanese government presented an ultimatum to Germany demanding the surrender of the leased territory of Kiaochow. Shortly thereafter, Japan declared war on Germany, and a brief military campaign ended with the surrender of Tsingtao on 17 November 1914. In this fashion, the Japanese acquired the entire German concession, and quickly converted Shantung into a new base for further aggression against China, in line with the plans formulated by the notorious Black Dragon Society, submitted by it to the Japanese government in the autumn of 1914.

Losing little time, the Japanese proceeded to the next stage of implementing the suggestions contained in the Black Dragon Society's memorial. On 18 January 1915, the Japanese minister presented a note to Yüan Shih-k'ai listing twenty-one demands, composed of five groups, to be accepted without delay by the Chinese government. In the first four groups the Japanese required *inter alia* the recognition of their acquisition of the German concession in Shantung, an extension of their rights in South Manchuria and eastern Inner Mongolia. Their real intentions emerged in the last group which called for the employment of Japanese advisors in political, financial and military affairs, joint Sino-Japanese control of the police force, the establishment of a mutually owned arms industry, and so forth. The aim was transparently obvious, the transformation of China first into a protectorate, and then into an exclusively Japanese colony, all in line with the pattern which the Japanese imperialists had followed in Korea.

It is more than probable that the Japanese government, whose intelligence service always had an excellent, although ultimately self-defeating, grasp of the minutiae of Chinese domestic politics, was well aware of Yüan Shih-k'ai's monarchic aspirations and offered to assist his plans in exchange for a quick acceptance of the Twenty-One Demands. However, this scheme was soon frustrated for, although the Japanese had insisted on absolute secrecy, the news regarding their action leaked out almost immediately, giving rise to such indignant opposition that Yüan's government could not possibly accede to the demands. The reaction of the Japanese was typical; at first, while continuing to negotiate with Yüan, they denied that they had put forth any demands. Subsequently, they published a version in which the fifth group was omitted. After the talks had lasted four months, the Japanese, having sent more troops to Shantung and Manchuria, presented an ultimatum on 7 May with a forty-eight-hour deadline. On 9 May – promptly designated as a 'Day of National Humiliation' – Yüan Shih-k'ai accepted the demands. The first four groups were shortly thereafter embodied in a new treaty, while the fifth was left as the subject of future discussions.

Yüan Shih-k'ai, feeling certain of Japanese support, now

proceeded swiftly with the realization of his plan to restore the monarchy. It was deemed advisable not only to present the restoration as the profound desire of the entire Chinese people, but to buttress it with foreign expertise as well. For this purpose, use was made of an American law professor who, for a suitable fee, furnished an appropriate memorandum in which he proved incontrovertibly that 'it is of course not susceptible to doubt that a monarchy is better suited than a republic to China'. The farcical stage setting, which went on from August to December 1915, also included the organization of an assembly of representatives from the entire country, which astonishingly voted unanimously for the restoration. Even more oddly, all the 1933 members proposed in an identical petition that the President of the Republic should be the new emperor. On 11 December, having first modestly refused, the Great Man graciously acceded to the request of the people.

In spite of the fact that throughout his entire career Yüan Shih-k'ai had shown himself to be a crafty, opportunistic politician, his restoration scheme proved to be a total miscalculation. His regime had become more oppressive and burdensome than that of the Ch'ing, and thus opposition to him could now gain more popular support. Yüan had alienated the backing of some of his closest followers, such as Liang Ch'i-ch'ao, who, for their own reasons, were unwilling to accept the restoration. Liang employed his fluent and persuasive brush to denounce Yüan's scheme, and played a significant role in organizing the political and military opposition to it. Yüan's military supporters, the main prop of his rule, also showed equally little enthusiasm for his endeavours which, in effect, would deprive them of the chance of eventually succeeding him as head of state.

Simultaneously, the expected support of the foreign powers, on which Yüan had banked, failed to materialize, primarily due to the perfidious policy of the Japanese who, after having initially encouraged his plans, turned to opposing them. The devious duplicity of Japanese diplomacy makes it difficult to uncover all the reasons for this volte-face, but it is likely that in view of the growing opposition to Yüan's scheme the Japanese simply wanted to be on the winning side. Thus they gave considerable aid to the anti-Yüan forces, and initiated the diplomatic action of the powers, in which their objections to Yüan's enterprise were expressed.

On 25 December, the first rumble of open opposition to Yüan Shih-k'ai sounded in remote Yünnan. A small group of military commanders, led by the talented Ts'ai Ao (1882–1916), called for the immediate abandonment of the monarchy, and to give force to their demand began to march their troops into Szechuan. By March, the revolt had spread to Kweichow and Kwangsi, and due to it Yüan was forced first to postpone his enthronement, and then to revoke his entire scheme. As additional provinces declared their independence and united to demand Yüan's resignation from the Presidency he had reassumed, it became clear that his closest Peiyang followers, in control of the vital Yangtse Valley, were also unwilling to support him any longer. The final blow came in May, when both Szechuan and Hunan joined the anti-Yüan movement. On 6 June rage and frustration put an end to the dictator's life.

Yüan's death automatically terminated the struggle. Li Yüan-hung succeeded him as President, and the Provisional Constitution was restored. However, the consequences of the four years of his rule were to prove very far-reaching, since it had not only destroyed the initial chance of constructing the new republic, but had also led to a marked corruption of political life and was responsible for the spread of warlordism to every part of the country. The domination of the warlords now became an endemic plague, extremely difficult to eradicate, and under it China's possibilities to resist further foreign aggression, or to recover her full sovereignty, were reduced still further.

China Under Warlord Rule, 1916–18

The political history of the years subsequent to Yüan's dictatorship quickly showed that the heritage was truly disastrous. With the exception of the six provinces of the south and southwest, and the northeast, the rest of China was under the control of the Peiyang warlords. In Peking, Tuan Ch'i-jui, having assumed the post of premier, quickly came to dominate the central government with the aid of his own Peiyang followers. From the outset the militarists proved themselves to be in a much stronger position than the political parties, which now re-emerged together with the newly reassembled parliament, especially in view of the fact that the Progressive Party, led by Liang Ch'i-ch'ao, was only too willing to accommodate itself to Tuan's militarist faction. The Kuomintang, still a majority in parliament, showed itself quite disunited and although, in theory, opposed to warlord rule, incapable of facing up to the task of challenging it. Thus the political situation in Peking quickly deteriorated, with the struggle for power being exacerbated still further by a growing split within the Peiyang clique itself, which ultimately led to the formation of two contending militarist factions. Simultaneously, the hold of the central government on the country was also seriously undermined by the growing strength of already almost completely independent provincial satraps, such as the militarist Yen Hsi-shan (1883–1960) in Shansi, and the former bandit Chang Tso-lin (1876–1928) in the northeast.

Although it was patently clear that there was not the slightest reason why China should in any way take part in the terrible holocaust destroying almost an entire generation of young Europeans, the Allies had shown interest in inveigling China into the war from the outset. However, until the end of 1916, Japan opposed China's entry adamantly, fearing that this could jeopardize the Japanese hold on Shantung. The signing in February 1917 of secret agreements between Japan and the Allies, in which the latter recognized her 'rights' to the former German concession, removed her objections. Under increased pressure from the Allies, and especially from the United States, the Peking government broke diplomatic relations with Germany on 14 March 1917, but the war-entry issue, quite a different problem, still remained unresolved and aroused considerable opposition. Nonetheless, supported and abetted by the Allies, the Tuan military clique clamoured for an immediate declaration of war, in spite of the opposition, backed by a majority in parliament. In May, all the makings of a political crisis were at hand; parliament refused to declare war, Li Yüan-hung dismissed Tuan Ch'i-jui from his post, and Tuan and his followers withdrew to Tientsin to form an independent centre of power.

Under these circumstances, Li Yüan-hung, with no troops of his own, turned for support, oddly enough, to the notorious Chang Hsün, whose ill-famed army had committed countless atrocities during its capture of Nanking in August 1913. Chang Hsün availed himself gladly of this opportunity, and the entry of his queue-wearing soldiers into Peking marked the beginning of a brief, ludicrous farce – the Manchu restoration. On 11 July, the badly frightened eleven-year-old P'u-i was placed once more on the throne, while K'ang Yu-wei emerged for the last time in the shady role of a major participant in the conspiracy. Li Yüan-hung, having to be forced earlier to dissolve parliament, now gave up his office and escaped to the Japanese Legation. However, the crude and brutal Chang Hsün had not taken the necessary precautions to obtain the support of fellow warlords. Tuan Ch'i-jui proclaimed himself the saviour of the Republic, and the Peiyang forces marched on Peking. The bubble burst in a few days. Chang Hsün fled to the Dutch Legation, K'ang Yu-wei to the American, and after some desultory shooting, Chang's troops amicably surrendered their arms for a few dollars each, and, minus their queues, returned peacefully to their Shantung villages. The victor was obviously Tuan, now the complete master of the Peking government.

The assumption by Tuan Ch'i-jui of full power cleared the way for resolving the war-entry issue, and on 14 August 1917 the Peking government declared war on the Central powers. However, China did not dispatch any soldiers to the trenches in Europe, and her role was restricted primarily to the furnishing of labour power. Over 200,000 Chinese workers, including also many students, made their way to Europe, primarily to France, and the real significance of this migration rested in the fact that a number of them were later to form an important nuclear group of the nascent Chinese Communist movement.

Tuan Ch'i-jui's victory soon proved to be only partial for, in effect, it led to a further weakening of the central government. Most of the Kuomintang members of parliament had fled Peking after its dissolution, and by September 1917 reassembled in Canton to join Sun Yat-sen in the forming of a separate regime, which claimed to be the only real government. While Sun was elected Grand Marshal and head of the Canton government, effective power rested not in his hands nor those of parliament, but with the Kwangsi militarists, in control of both Kwangtung and Kwangsi since 1916. This warlord clique soon showed itself to be the real master, and in May 1918 Sun was forced to relinquish his post. Shortly thereafter, he left Canton in disgust, to retire to Shanghai and reflect sadly on the country's and his own future.

Thus the division of China, apparent already during the anti-Yüan movement, was now much more accentuated. The Peiyang clique, in control of Peking, hoped to eliminate this division by force of arms, and military operations were conducted from October 1917 to the spring of 1918, primarily for the control of Hunan, while simultaneously a large number of conflicts between local warlords, especially in Szechuan, also helped to devastate the countryside.

The ineffective struggle of the Peking regime against the south hastened the disintegration of the Peiyang clique, which now split into two distinct groups – the Anfu and Chihli factions. The Anfu clique, headed by Tuan Ch'i-jui and his followers, sought to strengthen its control of the central government against the rival Chihli faction, led by Feng Kuo-chang, President since July 1917, Ts'ao K'un (1862–1938), and the rising new militarist, Wu P'ei-fu (1878–1939), whose troops finally achieved the conquest of Hunan in the summer of 1918. The struggle of these two factions also began to reflect increasingly the rivalry of the powers, since the Chihli warlords became closely associated with British and American interests, while the Anfu clique soon turned itself into an outright tool of the Japanese.

Up to the end of the war the Japanese government continued persistently to pursue its basic expansionist policy, and by granting substantial loans to the Peking government succeeded in extorting extensive new economic rights. Simultaneously, the Japanese markedly increased their political influence by buying up wholesale the corrupt politicians of the Anfu clique, assisting Tuan in strengthening his armed forces, and concluding secret arrangements for future military cooperation.

In the meantime, the facade of republican institutions and parliamentarianism in Peking was wearing thin under the sway of the warlords. In August 1918, Tuan and his political associates of the notorious Anfu Club deemed it advisable to assemble a new, docile parliament. In October, the Tuan faction also installed Hsü Shih-ch'ang (1858–1937), an elder member of the Peiyang clique, in the office of president to replace its rival, Feng Kuo-chang. At the same time, since military operations had temporarily ceased, the Peking government made the empty gesture of expressing its willingness to enter into negotiations with the south for the purpose of achieving peaceful unification.

After the armistice in Europe, the sorry condition of China's international status was soon to be revealed. Since China, as an ally, was to participate in the peace negotiations, high hopes were raised that it would prove possible, especially on the basis of the Wilsonian plans for a new and more just world order, to improve her position considerably. It was believed that China should now succeed in removing all the restrictions on her full sovereignty, which had been imposed by the unequal treaties. In particular, the Chinese felt certain that the Allies would support fully their demand for the reversion to China of all the German rights and concessions in Shantung. The Chinese pinned their hopes above all on the United States, not only due to their faith in Wilsonian diplomacy, but because they still tended to regard America in a different light from the other powers, as a country which had not been in the forefront of foreign aggression, and did not possess a sphere of influence of its own. However, these somewhat naive illusions could have been dispelled, if not the words but the actions of the Americans had been observed with greater care, for already in November 1917 the United States government had concluded an agreement with Japan in which, on the basis of the anomalous doctrine of territorial propinquity, it recognized Japanese 'rights' in China. The stage was, in fact, set for the complete collapse at Versailles of China's great expectations.

12. China in the First Post-war Years, 1919–24

The Cultural Revolution and the May Fourth Movement

The complete absorption of the European powers in four years of mutual slaughter also had a profound effect on Chinese economic and social development. The radical reduction of European economic activities in East Asia created a unique possibility for an upsurge of Chinese capitalism, and the emergent Chinese bourgeoisie availed itself of this opportunity with alacrity, attaining, in spite of intense Japanese rivalry, considerable success. Industrial production increased significantly and Chinese financial institutions also expanded the scope of their activities. However, the progress achieved pertained almost entirely to light industry, and the problem of the country's overall economic backwardness remained largely unresolved, especially in view of the chronic crisis of agriculture, the fundamental domain of the Chinese economy.

The social consequences of the economic changes during this period were also to prove quite significant, since the result was a swift growth of a modern working class which now numbered over two million and actually grew in size more rapidly than the bourgeoisie, for a large part of it was employed in foreign-owned enterprises. This new proletariat was subjected to completely unbridled exploitation, and worked under infinitely worse conditions than those of comparable periods of the Industrial Revolution in Europe. Moreover, it was still totally unorganized for its own defence and, itself mostly of peasant origin, easily replaced and replenished by an incessant flow of villagers from a countryside ravaged by warlord rule. Nonetheless, this new class, still only a small fraction of the total population of perhaps 450 million, was destined soon to play a vital role on the Chinese historical arena.

Simultaneously, the spread of modern education from the beginning of the century not only gave rise to a new, relatively numerous intelligentsia, but also served to set into motion perhaps the most profound intellectual revolution in Chinese history. It is this stirring and inspired movement, and not the sorry travesty of the years 1966–76, which truly deserves the name of Cultural Revolution. Reflecting the marked rise of national consciousness, the intellectuals who participated in this movement sought the solutions to the great multitude of urgent problems facing China, in order to find a proper road to national salvation. Covering the years 1915–20, the Cultural Revolution also constituted a basic component of the May Fourth Movement which was its political manifestation.

A fundamental problem raised in the course of the Cultural Revolution was language reform, the indispensable necessity, if future cultural development was to be assured, of substituting the vernacular for the classical language as the main vehicle of expression. This issue, put forth in the years 1916–18 by a group of brilliant intellectuals, among whom the scholar and writer Ch'en Tu-hsiu (1879–1942) and the philosopher Hu Shih (1891–1962) were perhaps the most prominent, corresponding as it did to the country's needs, found ready acceptance among the great majority of intellectuals and students. Rapid progress was made in the introduction of the vernacular into general education, while its employment made possible not only the flourishing of modern Chinese literature, as exemplified by the splendid work of Lu Hsün (real name, Chou Shu-yen, 1881–1936), but also led to a great increase in the number of newspapers and periodicals, thus opening up the country to the inflow of challenging new ideas. Among these the most influential was the famous 'New Youth' of which Ch'en Tu-hsiu was the chief editor. It was on its pages that the ideas regarding language reform were first advanced and the basic ideological issues of the Cultural Revolution broached.

The principal contention was the urgent need to dispense with the ballast of Confucianism, with its connotation of a moribund and decadent culture, and to replace it by the New Learning, in which the principles of Science and Democracy reigned supreme. Only by employing such an iconoclastic approach to China's cultural heritage could the road be cleared for progress and modernization. In fact, the New Learning advocated so enthusiastically implied a wholesale and rather uncritical acceptance of all the aspects of Western civilization, including its main ideological forms and political structures. However, some of the more serious-minded intellectuals could perceive the startling contradictions between Western ideals and actual practice, as presented by the actions of the Western powers in China, which displayed precious few traits of fraternity, equality and liberty. These doubts regarding the true nature of what the West had to offer were inevitably greatly enhanced by the World War which, of necessity, seemed to signify to many Chinese intellectuals a total bankruptcy of everything that the West had supposedly stood for. This painful disillusionment also undermined the belief that Western principles could and should be employed for the building of a new China; it led as well to a berating, by some, of the West for its 'materialism', and to praising the East for its 'spiritualism', a ridiculous and palpably false dichotomy.

It was against this background of considerable confusion and continuing intellectual ferment that Marxian socialism, destined to exert ultimately a decisive impact on modern Chinese history, made its appearance on the Chinese scene. Many Chinese intellectuals were soon to regard it as an answer to the questions preying on their minds. What was at fault was not Western civilization as such, but the nature of its capitalist stage of development; the solution therefore to the problems of the world, and hence of China as well, was to be found in socialism. The attractive novelty of these ideas was partially due to the simple circumstance that before the October Revolution Marxism had been almost completely unknown in China; only a few fragments of Marxist literature were available in Chinese, while the concepts regarding socialism acquired by some of the Chinese who had studied in Japan were fragmentary and confused.

The propagation of Marxism, in its Leninist form, was to be facilitated not only by the victory of the Bolsheviks, but also by the policy of the Soviet government, which in 1918 proclaimed its decision to renounce all the unequal treaties imposed on China by the Tsarist government, to resign from all the concessions and privileges obtained thereby, and simultaneously called for the establishment of relations between Russia and China on the basis of complete equality. The contrast between these pronouncements and the policies of the West, soon to be manifested once again at Versailles, was both glaring and revealing. The Russians were seen to represent an ideology which, while still eminently Western and perhaps even the most advanced that the West had to offer, appeared to be quite different, since it was not inimical to China, but seemed to provide the key to the solution of the country's fundamental problems. It was in this fashion that the new ideology was to be interpreted by the two principal co-founders of the Chinese Communist movement, Ch'en Tu-hsiu and Li Ta-chao (1889–1927), and the young revolutionary intellectuals who were soon to become their followers. In their view, Marxism-Leninism represented a world outlook which provided them with all the indispensable guiding principles for carrying out what they considered to be the primary tasks facing them – the modernization of China and her re-emergence as a great and mighty country, a status to which, they ardently believed, she was fully entitled on the basis of the splendours of her ancient civilization and thousands of years of culture. It was this ideology which offered them a programme for waging the struggle against imperialism and warlord rule on the basis of a social revolution, which would release the immense potential strength of the Chinese masses. Moreover, Marxism-Leninism appeared to provide an intellectually satisfying philosophy which seemed capable, if applied creatively, of answering numerous troublesome problems relating to both China's past and present. It could show that if Chinese historical development were to be put into a proper world perspective, then the balance sheet would certainly not be in China's disfavour, and could thus dispel the numbing feeling of inferiority gnawing away at the minds of many members of the new intelligentsia.

The spring of 1919 showed that a fertile ground for the reception of the new ideology was being prepared in the shape of the first truly large-scale anti-imperialist and anti-militarist upsurge in modern Chinese history – the May Fourth Movement. While the term is, as noted, a generic one, largely synonymous with the Cultural Revolution, it is derived from the events of May–June, the nationwide demonstrations of protest against the continuing humiliation of China. The campaign was sparked off by the decisions reached by the powers at Versailles on the issues pertaining to China. All the aforementioned great expectations of the Chinese were rudely dashed to the ground; the arguments raised by the Chinese delegation relating to the granting of equal international status, were contemptuously brushed aside as not within the Conference's terms of reference, and the vital issue of the future of Shantung decided in favour of Japan on 30 April 1919. The indignation aroused by the news of this decision in the main urban centres, and especially in Peking, was immense, and stimulated still more by the apprehension that the corrupt, pro-Japanese Anfu clique in control of the central government would more than likely acquiesce and order the Chinese delegation to sign the Versailles Treaty.

The students of Peking were the first to react, and were to remain the leading force of the movement. In their famous demonstration on 4 May they demanded the rejection by the government of the Versailles decision and the dismissal of three ministers notorious for their connections with Japan. The arrests of some of the demonstrators and further government repressions gave rise to national support for the Peking students who, having successfully organized a union, declared a general strike on 19 May. Further brutal police action, including mass arrests of over 1100 students, only aggravated the situation still further, leading to general strikes in other cities. The response in Shanghai was particularly strong, for here the students gained the support of the workers, 60,000 of whom marched out in the first political strike in modern Chinese history. This unexpected turn of events, and the distinct possibility that the protest action would take on a still wider scope, forced the Peking regime to retreat. The arrested students were released, but agreed to leave their prison only after having forced the government to lose all face by apologizing to them; the three ministers were dismissed and the government agreed not to sign the Versailles Treaty. Thus a notable, but of course only temporary, victory had been gained, giving rise to immense elation among the students. However, the road to a real victory over the intertwined forces of imperialism and Chinese reaction was to prove to be long, tortuous and costly for those who were to persist with it.

Political and Military Strife, 1919–24

The process of China's political disintegration, already much advanced in the two years following Yüan Shih-k'ai's death, made further disastrous progress from 1918 on. The split of the former Peiyang clique into two rival warlord factions became definite, and the struggle for power between them was soon to lead to a series of military conflicts, bringing further devastation to the impoverished country. The control of the central government, exercised by Tuan Ch'i-jui and the Anfu clique since 1917, was successfully challenged in 1920 by the rival Chihli faction, led by Ts'ao K'un and Wu P'ei-fu. A brief campaign, known as the Chihli-Anhwei War (14–18 July 1920), ended in the complete defeat of the Anfu faction and the fall of its government. The ease with which this victory had been gained was largely due to the aid given to the Chihli clique by Chang Tso-lin, by now the complete master of the northeast, although his dependence on the Japanese had also grown markedly. Chang's plans foresaw the extension of his power to North China, and thus collided with the identical intentions of the Chihli leaders. Hence, their alliance had been only a temporary arrangement, typical of warlord politics.

The leaders of the Chihli faction, and especially Wu P'ei-fu who now emerged as its dominant personality, utilized their victory for strengthening their position both in Central and North China, but already by the end of 1921 the issue of controlling the Peking government aggravated their relations with Chang Tso-lin. Within a year the political crisis had matured sufficiently for Chang and his Fengtien clique to decide on an armed confrontation with their Chihli rivals. However, Chang's plans misfired badly and the military operations of the First Chihli-Fengtien War (April–May 1922) terminated with the complete defeat of his troops, which were forced to retreat to Manchuria. Nonetheless, the Fengtien army still remained powerful, and Chang's position in the northeast unshaken. The victory now placed the Chihli faction in complete, undivided control of the Peking government; they utilized this for restoring Li

279

Yüan-hung to the presidency he had lost in 1917 and recalling the parliament originally elected in 1912.

During these three years, the conditions in other parts of the country were equally unstable, since the struggle between rival warlords had become truly endemic. This observation applied also to Kwangtung, the scene of Sun Yat-sen's peripatetic appearances. Having been driven out of Canton in May 1918 by the Kwangsi militarists, Sun, refusing to give up his cause as lost, established in October 1919 the Chungkuo Kuomintang to replace the conspiratorial Komingtang (Revolutionary Party) he had set up in 1914. However, the Kuomintang was also a numerically small party, composed primarily of Sun's own personal followers of long standing, and its political influence remained quite limited. Within a year Sun's chances improved when his erstwhile supporter, Ch'en Chiung-ming (1878–1933), a local Kwangtung militarist, succeeded in capturing Canton and driving the Kwangsi warlords back to their own province. Sun returned and in April 1921, having reorganized the government in Canton, was elected by some members of the 1912 parliament as the country's president. It was at this time that Sun Yat-sen developed his cherished concept of accomplishing national unification by military means, i.e., to use Kwangtung as the base for the launching of a Northern Expedition. In actual fact, Sun was never to possess the adequate means for this task throughout the few remaining years of his life. Nonetheless, in May 1922, Sun Yat-sen announced the beginning of the Northern Expedition; its aim was to overthrow the Chihli-dominated government in Peking, and for this purpose Sun was willing to ally himself even with Chang Tso-lin.

Sun Yat-sen's ambitious project soon collapsed disastrously, since local Kwangtung militarists, especially Ch'en Chiung-ming, proved unwilling to support it. Moreover, in June, Ch'en launched a successful revolt which forced Sun once again to retreat to Shanghai. It was clear that Sun's policy of basing himself on unreliable militarists was a complete fiasco, and only his great prestige and indomitable faith in his own historic mission made it possible for him to retain a place on the political arena.

In Peking, the Chihli leaders, relatively secure in their control of the government, began to engage in the customary warlord intrigues. In view of Ts'ao K'un's growing ambition for the presidency, steps were undertaken to remove the decidedly unwilling Li Yüan-hung from his post. The sordid episode ended with his deposition in September 1922, and an appropriately bribed parliament elected Ts'ao K'un as president. A leading part in these goings-on was played by one of Wu P'ei-fu's principal followers, the famed Christian general, Feng Yü-hsiang (1882–1948), undoubtedly one of the most colourful personalities in modern Chinese history.

The kaleidoscopic nature of Chinese politics was soon illustrated by the next turn of the wheel of fortune in Kwangtung. In January 1923, troops loyal to Sun Yat-sen, stationed in Fukien under the command of Hsü Ch'ung-chih (1887–1965), together with units of Kwangsi and Yünnan warlords, drove Ch'en Chiung-ming's soldiers out of Canton without, however, depriving him of his hold on East Kwangtung. Thus, once again, the road was opened and Sun returned to Canton, his basic plans of achieving national unification unaltered. However, a significant change in his general approach soon became apparent. For decades, Sun, always an admirer of the West, had hoped to obtain Western aid for accomplishing his grandiose plans of reconstructing China, only to be repeatedly rebuffed. In January 1923, he made one more attempt in talks held with the American minister in Peking, but his proposals met with complete indifference. By March, Sun was ready to declare that he had 'lost hope of help from America, Britain and France . . . the only country which showed any sign of helping us is Soviet Russia'.

In actual fact, Sun Yat-sen had established contacts with the Soviet government almost from the beginning of its existence. In the summer of 1918 he had sent a message to Lenin expressing his sympathy and support for the new government in Russia. During the next four years he maintained contact with a number of Soviet representatives. The most important were the negotiations conducted in December 1922 with A. A. Joffe, leading to the famous Sun-Joffe communiqué, issued on 27 January 1923, in which the basic conditions for Sun's cooperation with Soviet Russia were established. Concrete measures were soon undertaken, and in August 1923 Sun Yat-sen sent a military delegation to Moscow, whose basic mission was to obtain Soviet aid for the planned struggle against the warlords. The delegation, which accomplished its task successfully, was headed by Chiang Kai-shek (Chiang Chieh-shih, 1887–1975).

The rapprochement with Soviet Russia had another, even more significant, implication for the shaping of Sun Yat-sen's future policy, since it also brought about his increasing cooperation with political forces to the left of his own Kuomintang, with the newly formed Chinese Communist movement. Already in the autumn of 1922 Sun, while initiating a reorganization of the KMT, established close contact with Ch'en Tu-hsiu who participated in this project. However, the truly significant stage of cooperation between the KMT and the Chinese Communists dates from the arrival in Canton in October 1923 of M. I. Borodin (1884–1951). As a representative of the Communist International, sent to China at Sun Yat-sen's own request, the highly gifted Borodin, an experienced revolutionary of long standing, was entrusted with assisting Sun in the task of restructuring the KMT into an effective political organization. He quickly gained Sun's confidence, a feat undoubtedly aided by the existence of a common language, since they conversed in fluent English, and the unfolding of events during the subsequent dramatic years bore to a significant degree the impact of his activity.

The situation in Kwangtung towards the end of 1923 was, however, hardly conducive to a rapid realization of Sun Yat-sen's plans. Some of his older followers objected vehemently to the new policy of cooperation with Soviet Russia, and particularly with the Chinese Communists, since there was no place in their narrowly circumscribed nationalist views for anything that would portend a social revolution. Although Sun overrode this opposition, the group retained its influence within the Kuomintang. Simultaneously, Sun's relations with the Western powers, which refused to recognize the Canton government and continued to regard Sun as, at best, a hopeless troublemaking visionary, deteriorated still further. The immediate cause rested in the refusal of the British-controlled maritime customs to adhere to the arrangements for turning over a part of the receipts to the Canton authorities. Although the incident was ultimately settled to Sun's satisfaction, it had clearly deepened his negative attitude towards the West. On 31 December 1923 he declared: 'We no longer look to the Western powers. Our faces are turned towards Russia.'

The Rise of the Chinese Communist Movement

In the aftermath of the May Fourth Movement a number of its active participants, having adopted Marxism as their vision of the future, sought to master the new ideology and to proceed to the political activity which it called for. It was with this aim in mind that the young intellectuals established as their first step a number of study groups in various urban centres. Thus in the summer of 1920 Li Ta-chao, then a professor at Peking University, organized some of his students into a Society for the Study of Marxism. The majority of them were later to become prominent leaders of the Communist movement, for the group included Chang Kuo-t'ao (1897–1979), Ch'ü Ch'iu-pai (1899–1935), Mao Tse-tung (1896–1976), Teng Chung-hsia (1897–1933) and Yün Tai-ying (1895–1931). In developing his own views Li Ta-chao placed particular stress on the struggle against foreign domination and the role of the peasantry in a future social revolution, while engaging in ardent polemical disputations with such opponents of Marxism as Hu Shih.

Ch'en Tu-hsiu's activities in Shanghai were of equal importance in the spreading of Marxist ideas, especially when the famous periodical he had edited since 1915, 'Chinese Youth', became an organ of the Communist movement. Marxist circles were established also in other cities; in Wuhan by Tung Pi-wu (1886–1975), and in Ch'angsha by Mao Tse-tung. But of at least equal importance was the organization of a numerous group of Marxist sympathizers from among the students in France, for its membership included also such future Communist leaders as Ch'en I (1901–72), Chou En-lai (1898–1976), Li Li-san (1899–1967?), Teng Hsiao-p'ing (b. 1904) and Ts'ai Ho-sen (1890–1931).

From the very outset the Russian Bolsheviks had considered the national and colonial question as crucial, and their concepts relating to it were expressed more fully at the II Congress of the Communist International (July–August 1920). From the point of view of Comintern strategy, China was regarded as of prime importance; no time was lost in establishing contact with the new Marxist movement, and the first Comintern representatives reached China in 1920, when the initial moves to organize a Communist Party were made. These, however, proved premature, and it was only in the summer of 1921 that twelve delegates, representing five groups in China and one in Japan with a total membership of 57, met in Shanghai to hold, with the participation of the two Comintern representatives, the First Congress of the Communist Party of China (incorrectly, but customarily referred to as the Chinese Communist Party – CCP). Both the senior founders of the Communist movement, Li Ta-chao and Ch'en Tu-hsiu, were absent from the meeting, and the future destiny of the delegates can serve as an illustration of the complexity of modern Chinese history. Four of them were to perish in the coming revolutionary struggles, three to abandon the movement, and only two – Mao Tse-tung and Tung Pi-wu – were to remain in leading positions at the time of triumph in 1949. Understandably, the discussions at the First Congress revealed considerable confusion as regards the future, and its basic accomplishment was the establishment, as such, of the CCP.

The new party, composed solely of intellectuals and students, saw its task not only in the propagating of Marxist views but, above all, in establishing contact with the workers in order to transform itself, in line with its ideology, into a proletarian party. In the period up to February 1923 a great amount of effort was devoted to this, and the immense difficulties involved in starting to build a modern labour movement were, on the whole, overcome with considerable success. Trade union activity was conducted, under the auspices of a Labour Secretariat established in Shanghai in 1921, among railwaymen, coal miners and seamen. On 1 May 1922, over 100 unions with a membership of 270,000 joined in holding the First Trade Union Congress in Canton.

However, a direct confrontation of the new labour movement with the realities of warlord rule soon proved disastrous. The plans for a general union of the workers on the Peking–Hankow Railway met with the opposition of Wu P'ei-fu, and a protest strike launched on 4 February 1923 was brutally crushed by his troops, with the killing of over 37 of its participants. Further repressions resulted in the collapse of many unions and two years of intensive work were necessary to repair the damage suffered by the labour movement.

284

In the first two years of its existence the CCP grew slowly, reaching a figure of only 432 members by June 1923. But in the same period the Communists gained much influence among the students, which was reflected in the quicker growth of the Socialist Youth League (SYL); its most prominent leaders included Ts'ai Ho-sen, Teng Chung-hsia and Chang T'ai-lei (1898–1927), and a large number of future CCP leaders were to come from its ranks. Simultaneously, the first significant steps were taken in establishing contact with the peasants. The results obtained were largely due to the activities of P'eng P'ai (1896–1929), the indubitable pioneer in this field. A member of a wealthy Kwangtung gentry clan, P'eng, who had joined the Communist movement while studying in Japan, began in 1922 the difficult task of organizing a peasant union in his native district of Haifeng, which constituted the first stage in the development of the Kwangtung peasant movement.

The basic guidelines of the CCP's programme were clarified within a year from its foundation, and outlined in a manifesto issued on 19 June 1922, which called for an anti-militarist and anti-imperialist democratic revolution. However, a number of tactical problems, especially the question of forming a united front with the Kuomintang for a joint waging of the revolutionary struggle, were resolved only partially.

The World and China, 1919–24

The common front presented by the foreign powers towards China was shattered by the October Revolution, since the Soviet government, as noted, proclaimed an utterly different policy in July 1918. Its basic concepts were recapitulated in the declaration signed by L. M. Karakhan, Vice-Commissar for Foreign Affairs, issued on 25 July 1919. It was on the basis of this famous declaration that the Soviet government proposed to conduct negotiations for the establishment of relations with the Peking government. However, due to a large number of factors, including the unstable situation in the Soviet Far East, the reactionary nature of the Peking regime, and the constant pressure of the Western powers, the dispatch of three

Soviet missions to Peking in the years 1920–2 produced no results. However, the Soviet government, with its position much strengthened by the final fiasco of Japanese intervention in Siberia, renewed its efforts and a new mission headed by Karakhan arrived in Peking in September 1923. After lengthy negotiations, and a concerted attempt by the Western diplomats in Peking to prevent a successful conclusion, the Sino-Soviet Treaty was signed on 31 May 1924 on the basis of the principles outlined in the earlier Soviet proposals. As the first accord since 1840 to be concluded on terms of complete equality between China and a foreign power, its impact on the development of the political situation in China was considerable, especially in view of the fact that the Western powers and Japan had thus far not shown the slightest intention of altering their fundamental policy towards China, or of relinquishing the privileges obtained on the basis of the unequal treaties.

The above contention was fully borne out by the proceedings and results of the Washington Conference (12 November 1921–6 February 1922). The general aim of the Conference, called on the initiative of the United States, was to establish a new balance of power in East Asia which would reduce international friction and preserve the status quo, especially in respect to China. Thus the problem of China became one of the two major topics, and although the Peking government, the only one invited, could hardly have been expected, in view of its dependence on the foreign powers, to conduct an energetic struggle for the recovery of China's rights, it did deem it necessary for domestic purposes to make at least some effort in this direction. Its delegation was composed of the ablest diplomats available; its three leading members were all American-educated, while it also employed as its advisors a number of prominent American former foreign service officials, a reflection possibly of the Peking government's hope that its endeavours would meet with American aid. The Chinese delegation, having prepared itself assiduously, was given the opportunity to present a ten-point declaration of principles which should be applied towards China; although couched in proper diplomatic phraseology it did add up to a programme which, if realized, would have entailed a complete elimination of the country's semi-colonial status. However, since such a step was as far as possible from the intentions of the powers, the Chinese declaration was destined to remain a pathetic listing of pious desiderata.

The principal accord concerning China was signed on 6 February 1922, and was to be known as the Nine Power Treaty (the signatories included the United States, Great Britain, France, Italy, Japan, Portugal, Belgium, the Netherlands and China; characteristically Soviet Russia, obviously a country directly concerned with East Asian affairs, had not been invited to the Conference). While the customary hollow phrases regarding the intentions of the powers 'to respect the sovereignty, the independence, and the territorial and administrative integrity of China' were repeated in the treaty, urgent problems such as the abolition of extraterritoriality or the restoration of tariff autonomy were simply postponed for future discussion. Only one burning issue – the Shantung question – was partially dealt with at this time. In separate bilateral negotiations an accord was reached whereby Japan agreed to restore to China the Tsinan–Tsingtao Railway, the principal German economic asset, in return for a sum of 35 million yen, to be borrowed from Japanese banks. In reality, the Japanese position in Shantung remained basically intact, and the Japanese continued to consider the area as their exclusive sphere of influence.

Thus the position of China had not been affected in any meaningful fashion by the decisions of the Washington Conference, which had also actually contributed nothing to a decrease of imperialist rivalry in East Asia. Hence, the question of waging a struggle against imperialist domination, already raised by the May Fourth Movement, had not lost any of its topicality or urgency.

On the Eve of the Revolution, January 1924–May 1925

A number of steps were undertaken in 1923 by the Kuomintang and the Chinese Communists, which were soon to prove to be of momentous significance. Having decided to adopt the policy of forming a united front with the KMT, the Communists began to join that party on an individual basis, while preserving their own membership in the CCP. In spite of their critical reservations, the Communists agreed on regarding the KMT as the only political party

287

capable of serious revolutionary action, and their primary aim was to assist in reorganizing it into a truly effective force. The decisions of the CCP were shaped largely by the rapid evolution of Sun Yat-sen's position during 1923, and his adoption of what were later referred to as the Three Great Policies, i.e., alliance with the Soviet Union, cooperation with the Communist Party and assistance to the labour and peasant movement. The political implications of the first two points were obvious, while the third signified a radical departure from Sun's previous approach of treating the Kuomintang as his own conspiratorial party, since he now agreed with the need to transform it into a broad organization, intent on seeking and organizing mass support.

The preparations leading to the reorganization of the Kuomintang were culminated by its First Congress held in Canton (20–30 January 1924), in which 165 delegates from the entire country participated, probably 20 of whom were Communists. The Congress passed the famous Manifesto in which the Party's new programme was set forth. It had, in fact, been written in English by Borodin, translated by the American-born Liao Chung-k'ai (1878–1925), one of Sun's closest associates, and edited in both versions by the latter. The Manifesto's basic ideas were a redefinition of Sun Yat-sen's Three People's Principles, with Nationalism now signifying a struggle against imperialist domination, while Democracy was interpreted primarily as the need to abolish warlord rule in order to achieve the country's unification. People's Livelihood was intended to convey an understanding of the indispensability of social reform and concern for the interest of the masses. Sun devoted a series of lectures in 1924 to his new interpretation of the 'San Min Chu I', which revealed the somewhat chaotic and eclectic nature of his views.

While the Manifesto outlined the Kuomintang's fundamental aims, other measures, such as the Party Statute, were concerned with restructuring it into a new political force, largely on the basis of the organizational principles of the Russian Communist Party. In the KMT's new, highly centralized organs, the Central Executive Committee (CEC) was now the most important leading body, but its smaller Standing Committee, often referred to contemporarily as the Political Bureau, soon emerged as the real policy- and decision-making body. The elections to the CEC demonstrated the cooperation of the KMT and the CCP, since 3 of the 24 full members, and 7 of the 17 alternate members, were Communists. At the same time, the Communists were given posts of great importance in the KMT's central party apparatus, especially in sections concerned with the labour and peasant movement. In all, the small but highly dedicated and idealistic group of young Communist intellectuals devoted their untiring efforts, more than likely at the expense of building their own party, to the expansion and strengthening of the KMT, which otherwise would not have been achieved as effectively.

The political and organizational reshaping of the Kuomintang was accompanied by a further very significant measure – the establishment of the famous Whampoa Military Academy. This decision evolved from the conclusion finally drawn by Sun Yat-sen that his heretofore policy of relying on local military forces and warlord alliances had been both futile and calamitous. The aim now was to create a politicized, reliable 'Party Army', and the Academy was to furnish the indispensable officer cadre. It was founded on 5 May 1924, and Chiang Kai-shek was appointed its commander; the post, which he had been reluctant to assume, was to prove to be the turning point of his career. Liao Chung-k'ai, a strong supporter of Sun's Three Great Policies, was nominated political commissar, and a number of young Communists, including Chou En-lai, Yün Tai-ying, Ch'en I and Yeh Chien-ying (b. 1898), also joined the staff. In the establishment of the Whampoa Academy, and the building up of the KMT's new military forces, Soviet aid played a vital role. A sizable group of military advisors began to arrive in the summer of 1924, and, under the command of the highly talented V. K. Blücher (1889–1938), continued its activities for the next two years. The Soviet advisors not only trained the KMT forces but also drew up the plans for and participated in the subsequent military operations. Large quantities of arms and ammunition, as well as financial assistance, were also furnished by the Soviet government.

Although the First Congress of the Kuomintang undoubtedly constituted an important step forward, the political situation remained difficult. A distinct, very meaningful ideological generation gap existed between Sun Yat-sen's older followers, mostly former T'ung Meng Hui members, and the young Marxist intellectuals of the CCP. Hence, among the former there was still much opposition towards Sun Yat-sen's policies of cooperation with the Soviet Union and the Chinese Communists. In some instances such views were openly expressed, in others, as in the case of Chiang Kai-shek, they were carefully camouflaged. At the same time the position of the KMT government left much to be desired, for the territory under its control was limited to a small part of Kwangtung, at moments to Canton itself. Even its hold on Canton was precarious, since its large and wealthy merchant community, fearful of additional financial burdens, was adamantly opposed to Sun Yat-sen's plan of using Kwangtung as the base for undertaking the country's unification by military means. East Kwangtung remained almost completely in the hands of Ch'en Chiung-ming and his 90,000-strong army, while other parts of the province were under the sway of rapacious warlord armies from Kwangsi and Yünnan. The difficulties in Canton were soon to be illustrated by a sharp conflict of the KMT authorities with the city's merchants. The latter, having organized their own armed militia, launched an open revolt against Sun's government on 10 October 1924, which was put down by units of the Whampoa Academy, armed with freshly arrived Soviet weapons.

A fundamental aim of the united front between the KMT and the CCP was to develop a true mass movement, without which a successful outcome of the struggle against warlord rule was deemed unattainable. Hence, in the part of Kwangtung under the sway of the Canton government some progress was made during 1924 in organizing peasant unions. This task was carried out solely by a small group of young Communists, practically in complete charge of the Peasant Department of the KMT. In addition, a Peasant Movement Institute was established in Canton on 30 June 1924, for the purpose of training peasant organizers; it was initially headed by P'eng P'ai, while Mao Tse-tung was in charge of the last of six courses held during the Institute's two years of existence. Of its almost 800 graduates, practically all of whom were active in the peasant movement during the 1925–7 Revolution, the great majority perished in the ensuing struggle, and only a meagre handful survived to 1949.

Conditions for the development of the labour movement were also more favourable in Kwangtung than in other parts of the country, although its growth was partially hampered by sharp distinctions within the working class itself, which made the attaining of complete unity in the trade union field impossible. Nonetheless, sufficient progress was made to provide an adequate foundation for the future upsurge.

In January 1925, the CCP held its Fourth Congress in Shanghai, with the primary aim of assessing its progress and the results of its cooperation with the Kuomintang. It was apparent that, since its membership had increased to only slightly under a thousand, almost all intellectuals and students, the goal of transforming the CCP into a mass working-class party had not been achieved as yet. This shortcoming was considered serious, for it was unanimously held that the revolution could succeed only if it were to be led by the proletariat. The existing form of a united front with the KMT continued to give rise to reservations, but this problem was intimately bound up with the policies pursued by the Communist International, which already then, and still more so during the years 1925–7, were of crucial importance in determining the fate of the Chinese revolutionary movement. The Comintern's role is also a highly controversial subject, and interpretations of it invariably reflect a given writer's own political inclinations. It can be remarked that already in 1922 Lenin noted a significant shortcoming in the Comintern's activity, in its inability to convey Russian experiences in a meaningful way. In relation to China, differing so markedly in her social and political development, the drawing up of directives for the CCP in this fashion would, of necessity, lead to confusion. The directives, often schematic and dogmatic, also displayed a penchant for attaching neat class labels on the groups and individuals appearing on the kaleidoscopic Chinese political arena. Moreover, after 1924, Comintern policy towards China became inextricably intertwined with the growing conflict within the Soviet Party, the Stalin-Trotsky controversy. A thorough examination of the pronouncements on China of these two men must lead to the indisputable conclusion that, in both cases, they were based on inadequate data and insufficient knowledge.

While in the south the Kuomintang and the CCP were mapping out their road for the future, Central and North China were to be convulsed by a new round of warlord conflicts. The increasing rivalry of the Chihli and Fengtien cliques, stimulated by the intense personal antagonism of Wu P'ei-fu and Chang Tso-lin, led in September 1924 to the outbreak of the Second Chihli-Fengtien War. The initial successes of the Chihli faction were quickly terminated by an unexpected coup launched by Feng Yü-hsiang against his superior, Wu P'ei-fu. On 23 October, Feng's troops left the front to occupy Peking, and this move was quickly followed by a complete rout of the Chihli army and Wu's escape with a small remnant of his forces.

As a result of Feng's coup, control of the Peking government now fell into his hands and those of his new temporary ally, Chang Tso-lin. To paper over their obvious rivalry, the discredited Tuan Ch'i-jui was persuaded to leave his haven in Tientsin to become the Chief Executive, a new post combining the function of president and premier. Feng Yü-hsiang also put an end to the presence of the former Ch'ing emperor in the Imperial City. P'u-i succeeded in escaping to the Japanese Legation, thus taking the first step on the road which led him to become Japan's principal puppet in conquered Manchuria.

Shortly after his coup, Feng Yü-hsiang reorganized his three armies and renamed them the Kuominchün (People's or National Army). Only the First Army, 125,000 strong and under his own direct command, constituted a real force to be reckoned with. The fate of the Kuominchün depended largely on the evolution of Feng's political position, which shifted continuously in conformity with the changes in the general situation. Feng now declared himself a supporter of Sun Yat-sen's programme; in 1925 he began his own cooperation with the Soviet Union, primarily for the purpose of obtaining military and financial assistance, and a Soviet military mission was dispatched to his army. In the areas under Feng's rule the KMT and CCP did obtain the chance to function openly and legally, and a number of young Communists, including Teng Hsiao-p'ing, undertook political work in his army.

It was undoubtedly on Feng Yü-hsiang's initiative that, in November 1924, the new Peking government invited Sun Yat-sen to come to the Northern Capital for the purpose of discussing the country's political future. Sun accepted the proposal with alacrity, and advanced the concept of calling into being a new National Assembly, which would determine the nature and composition of the future united government. Considering that warlord rule was still dominant in most of the country, especially the north, the chances of this scheme succeeding were actually quite limited, and the CCP viewed it with much scepticism. Nonetheless, serenely optimistic as usual, Sun Yat-sen departed from Canton for the last time on 13 November 1924, accompanied by some of his closest associates, including Borodin. In Shanghai, Tientsin and Peking he was given a tumultuously enthusiastic welcome as the Father of the Chinese Revolution, but his political plans were quickly frustrated by the machinations of Tuan Ch'i-jui, and it became clear that the negotiations would lead to nothing. Moreover, by the time he reached Peking, Sun was already a dying man. In February, an operation disclosed advanced cancer of the liver. On 12 March 1925, Sun Yat-sen died at the relatively early age of fifty-nine.

On the day before his death Sun signed a message to the Soviet leaders in which he once again stressed his belief in the purposefulness of the alliance between China and the Soviet Union. On the same day he signed his famous testament, in which he called upon his followers to continue the work to which he had devoted his entire life, stating that 'after forty years of experience I am profoundly convinced that in order to reach this aim [the freedom and independence of China] we must wake up the nation and unite with the peoples of the world who treat us as equals'.

The problem of the heritage of Sun Yat-sen was to become a crucial factor in Chinese political development. Death enhanced his stature, for he was to be remembered not for his failures or mistakes, but for his selflessness, integrity and complete devotion to his country. However, the eclectic nature of his ideology made it possible for many aspiring heirs to come forth; all those who seemingly worked together in 1925 under the slogans of National Revolution, claimed fervently to be his faithful followers. But one thing was clear; none of his closest associates possessed a comparable stature which would entitle them to inherit Sun's position as the leader of the Kuomintang and the National Revolution, now to enter a dramatic new stage.

13. The 1925–7 Revolution

The May Thirtieth Movement

In the spring of 1925 the Kuomintang government faced a new challenge when Ch'en Chiung-ming attempted once again to seize Canton itself. However, the forces at its disposal, and particularly the training regiments of the Whampoa Academy, proved more than equal to the task, and in the famous First Eastern Expedition, the plans for which were drawn up by Blücher, Ch'en's army was driven back. The victory emphasized the validity of the decision to develop the KMT's own Party Army, and also contributed to enhancing the reputation of Whampoa's commander – Chiang Kai-shek.

During these months the mass movement in Central and North China began to develop once more at an increasing pace, particularly in the Shanghai and Tientsin textile industries. In February 1925, over 40,000 textile workers staged a strike which, while only partially successful, served as a rehearsal for action in May on a still larger scale. The upsurge of the labour movement was reflected in the increase of trade union membership. The Second Trade Union Congress, held in Canton in May, claimed to represent 540,000 workers. The Congress took the decision to establish an All-China Federation of Trade Unions to guide future activities. The Congress of the Peasant Movement in Kwangtung, held in Canton simultaneously, also showed that progress was being achieved in this difficult domain. Both events constituted a harbinger of the immediate future in which, for the first time in modern Chinese history, with the possible exception of the Taiping Revolution, the 'hundred names', the ordinary people of China, were destined to play an active and crucial role on the political arena. Thus, the stage was set for the dramatic and highly intricate events known to history as the 1925–7 Revolution. Its complexity rested, among other things, in the many alterations of the positions held by its various participants, and in the very specific conjunction of a powerful mass movement with large-scale military operations.

Militant activity of the workers reached a still higher level in May. The murder in Shanghai on 15 May of a young trade union organizer by a Japanese overseer , and the killing of two workers in Tsingtao on 28 May, created an immensely tense atmosphere; protest actions, in which Shanghai students were especially active, became widespread. On 30 May a demonstration of around 10,000 gathered on Nanking Road, one of Shanghai's main thoroughfares, to protest against recent police brutality. The Settlement police, commanded by an Englishman, opened fire; 12 demonstrators were killed and 240 wounded, mostly students.

The massacre aroused the entire Chinese population of Shanghai. A call for a general strike was issued by the newly formed, Communist-led Shanghai Trade Union Federation. On 1 June, around 200,000 workers from all the foreign-owned factories left their jobs; 50,000 university and secondary school students joined the strike, which also gained the support of the great majority of the city's merchants. The sprawling, ugly metropolis, the largest and most important industrial centre in China, ground to an almost complete halt. An immediate boycott of Japanese and British goods, a weapon already used effectively during the past twenty years, was also launched. On 11 June, at a mass meeting attended by over 200,000 people, a declaration was passed listing 17 demands, including the withdrawal of foreign troops, the right to organize trade unions and strike, and the punishment of those guilty of the massacres. The first point was particularly topical for, in fact, the foreign powers quickly increased their military strength, and by 8 June, 26 warships were docked in Shanghai. Simultaneously, the Peking government, largely under Chang Tso-lin's control, reverted to its customary role of 'running dog of imperialism', and fresh Fengtien troops were soon dispatched to Shanghai to crush the mass movement. By September, the severe repressions had produced the desired effect, and the general strike had to be abandoned.

In the wake of the events in Shanghai, the May Thirtieth Movement had spread to a number of other cities, including Peking and Tientsin. Its greatest repercussions, however, were in Hong

Kong, where on 19 June a strike of 100,000 workers began. Four days later, a mass demonstration in Canton was viciously machine-gunned by British and French troops while it was passing the Shameen Concession. Fifty-two people, mostly young students, were killed, and over 178 wounded. The Shameen massacre gave rise to fierce indignation, and the KMT government declared a complete blockade of Hong Kong, where the strike became a general one, with 250,000 workers quitting their jobs. Simultaneously, a boycott of British goods was launched, and its enforcement supervised by a well-organized Hong Kong Strike Committee, based in Canton and almost entirely Communist-led. The general strike became one of the longest of its kind, lasting until October 1926, and had a disastrous effect on Hong Kong's economy.

It was against the background of the intense political ferment of the May Thirtieth Movement, that the Kuomintang government in Canton declared itself on 1 July to be the National Government, thus reaffirming its intention of extending its authority to the entire country, in line with the programme adopted at the First Congress of the KMT. At the same time, a reorganization of its armed forces, now called the National Revolutionary Army, was carried out; by January 1926 six separate and rather heterogeneous armies had been formed. A General Political Department was also established, and this intention to politicize the NRA did differentiate it to some degree from the warlord forces, although it still remained composed mostly of mercenaries. Within a short time of its reorganization the NRA became engaged in a final trial of strength with Ch'en Chiung-ming. On 1 October 1925, the Second Eastern Expedition was launched on the basis of plans drawn up by Blücher, and, after the successful storming of Huichow, Ch'en's main stronghold, all of East Kwangtung was cleared of his troops, while Ch'en himself escaped to his British patrons in Hong Kong. This victory was immediately followed up by a campaign aimed at eliminating the local warlords in other parts of the province. Success was quickly attained, and thus all of Kwangtung could finally serve as a base for the forthcoming Northern Expedition.

During this same period, however, the situation within the Kuomintang, notwithstanding the above military successes, became rapidly more critical, leading to increased factional struggles. The fundamental problem lay in the attitude towards Sun Yat-sen's heritage, particularly towards the Three Great Policies he had adopted during the last years of his life. As noted, a number of his followers on the right wing of the KMT had earlier expressed their objections to them, and in November 1925 this group met in the temple in the Western Hills near Peking, where Sun's remains rested, and, claiming to be Sun's only true successors, organized itself into an open faction. Its principal ideologist was Tai Chi-t'ao (1891–1946), Sun's former secretary, now closely linked to Chiang Kai-shek. Tai's interpretation of Sun's views constituted a total rejection of the Three Great Policies and served as the basis for the reactionary programme proclaimed by the Western Hills faction, which called for the expulsion of the Communists from the KMT, a break with the Soviet Union, and an end of support for the mass movement. While its activities were to be denounced by the KMT CEC in Canton, the Western Hills group simply proclaimed itself to be the true Kuomintang, held its own Party Congress in Shanghai and elected its own CEC.

The schemes of the KMT right wing had already revealed themselves in a more brutal fashion, for on 20 August 1925, Liao Chung-k'ai, Sun's close colleague, the most consistent advocate of cooperation with the Communists and a supporter of both the national and social revolution, was assassinated in Canton. There was no doubt that the crime had been committed at the instigation of the right wing. The crisis created by Liao's murder led to the establishment of a Special Committee, actually a triumvirate composed of Wang Ching-wei, Hsü Ch'ung-chih and Chiang Kai-shek, to whom all power was entrusted. Within a month, however, Hsü was deprived of his post and exiled to Shanghai; thus only two principal contestants for power were left on the arena, Wang, the handsome and eloquent self-proclaimed heir of Sun Yat-sen, and Chiang, busily accumulating more military strength in line with the warlord adage, 'if you have an army, you have power'.

The inner conflicts of the Kuomintang were nonetheless well concealed by a facade of unity. Thus at the Second Congress of the KMT held in Canton (4–19 January 1926) it was still possible to reach an agreement on a programme calling for the continuation of the National Revolution. Over a third of the 250-odd delegates were probably Communists, and the Congress, actually marking the high point of KMT-CCP cooperation, was considered to be a victory for the left-wing forces. The elections of the new CEC seemed to bear this out as well, for 7 of its 36 full members and 6 of the 24 alternate members were Communists. The majority of its KMT members were described as belonging to its left wing, actually a very amorphous group, including primarily the supporters of Wang Ching-wei. The left wing supposedly stood for the full implementation of Sun's Three Great Policies, but then, with the exception of the Western Hills faction, so did the Kuomintang in its entirety. Thus Chiang Kai-shek and his entourage paid lip service to them, while simultaneously working secretly to undermine them completely.

Within two months the March 20th Incident showed that the supposed victory of the left-wing forces had been very hollow indeed. The incident, in fact a crudely staged coup carried out by Chiang Kai-shek, was directed both against the Communists and the Soviet military mission. Over fifty prominent Communists working in the NRA and the Whampoa Academy were arrested, while Chiang demanded the immediate recall of three leading members of the mission, since he considered them an obstacle to the realization of his aim – the establishment of a personal military dictatorship. The Communists, of course, were his only serious political opponents, and his pathological hatred of them now surfaced fully for the first time. The coup came as a complete surprise and shock to its victims, and no less to Wang Ching-wei, the head of the Canton government. But Wang's resolve to rebuff Chiang's action quickly melted away, and within a few days he disappeared from Canton, ultimately to take comfortable refuge in France. Wang's cowardice and political bankruptcy, and the total disarray of his followers, raised some very pertinent questions as to the real nature of the KMT left wing.

The aftermath of the coup was a most curious affair. The Communists were all released, although not restored to their posts, and Chiang Kai-shek, after placing the blame on some of his own subordinates, quickly sought to restore his relations with the Soviet mission, once the three advisors were recalled as he desired, in the expectation of further Soviet aid. While some of the CCP leaders had come to the conclusion that under the circumstances the form of cooperation with the KMT should be changed, the Comintern decided that the existing united front should be preserved. Moreover, in spite of earlier reservations, both the CCP and the Soviet mission now agreed to approve the plans for a speedy launching of the Northern Expedition. The ultimate result was to place the effective power of the Canton government firmly in Chiang Kai-shek's hands. In May, the CEC undertook a number of decisions whose primary purpose was to restrict markedly the position and influence of the Communists within the KMT. Simultaneously, Chiang and his Chekiang clique – for his closest supporters came from his native province – took over the most important posts in the Party's central apparatus, and proceeded to purge it of Communists and left-Kuomintang members. On 5 June 1926, Chiang capped the process of gathering power by having himself nominated commander in chief of the NRA. But, in spite of all these events, both the Chinese Communists and the Soviet leaders accepted the situation, and the facade of the united front was preserved for the sake of the future development of the National Revolution.

The Northern Expedition

During the period when the plans for the Northern Expedition were being prepared, the chronic instability of warlord rule became ever more apparent. The almost inevitable conflict between the rivals for the control of northern China, Feng Yü-hsiang and Chang Tso-lin, came to a head in November 1925. Initially, Feng's chances for victory were considerably enhanced by serious dissension within the Fengtien army itself, the famous revolt of Kuo Sung-ling (1883–1925). One of the highest generals of the Mukden forces, Kuo, a leader of the clique of younger commanders, undoubtedly found Chang Tso-lin's almost total subservience to the Japanese objectionable. Carefully coordinating his plans with Feng Yü-hsiang, and in command of 50,000 troops, the best units of the Fengtien army, Kuo launched his revolt on 22 November, marching straight towards Mukden. Success, which would have made him the new leader of the northeast, seemed assured as his men gained a series of easy victories. However, both Kuo and Feng had failed to take the

Japanese imperialists into full account. With their customary duplicity the Japanese first declared their neutrality but, having reached the conclusion that Kuo's success would be a threat to their domination of Manchuria, they promptly intervened in a decisive fashion at the very moment when Kuo's army was approaching Mukden. Kuo's troops suffered a crushing defeat, and within two days his body and that of his wife were publicly exhibited in Mukden.

Having succeeded in preserving his power, Chang Tso-lin concentrated all his attention on the war with Feng Yü-hsiang, employing also the forces of one of his main subordinates, the notorious Chang Tsung-ch'ang (1881–1932). A former bandit, the elephantine Chang, probably the most brutal and vicious of the warlord breed, had become the governor of Shantung in 1925 and the commander of an army almost 100,000 strong. Moreover, although his position after Feng's coup in October 1924 had seemed almost hopeless, Wu P'ei-fu had managed to make an astounding comeback. By the end of 1925, Wu had gained control of all of Hupei, including the vital triple city of Wuhan, and was busy expanding his power in Honan and Hunan. Wu's hatred for Feng Yü-hsiang knew no bounds, and quickly led to an alliance with his erstwhile bitter enemy, Chang Tso-lin.

In the midst of the fighting against Chang Tso-lin's troops Feng Yü-hsiang took a rather unusual decision. Having turned over the command of his forces to his subordinates, Feng left North China in March 1926 for the Soviet Union, where he was to remain until September. Ultimately, the move turned out to be wise, for during his stay he concluded arrangements for receiving further Soviet aid, which was later to prove crucial. Nevertheless, during his absence, the Kuominchün suffered a number of severe blows; its forces in Honan were almost totally wiped out, while its main core of 90,000 troops evacuated Peking in April 1926 to take up strong positions at the famous Nank'ou Pass northwest of the capital. There, until August, they faced attacks of the united forces of Chang Tso-lin and Wu P'ei-fu, five times their number.

In waging their war against Feng Yü-hsiang, Chang Tso-lin and Wu P'ei-fu did not neglect the opportunity to embellish their campaign with appropriate ideological trimmings, since they proclaimed it to be a struggle against the 'Red Danger' and a crusade against 'Bolshevism'. In 1926, they declared that their alliance was directed against the Kuomintang as well, and in this fashion felt assured that their actions would meet with the approval and assistance of the imperialist powers. However, warlord disunity undermined to a certain degree the effectiveness of this reactionary compact, for although Chang and Wu had by now achieved control of a large part of the country, the vital Lower Yangtse provinces were not under their rule, but under that of Sun Ch'uan-fang (1884–1936). A former subordinate of Wu, Sun had gained control of Shanghai in October 1925, and by 1926 emerged as the strongest warlord in the Lower Yangtse area, with dominant influence over the provincial militarists of Kiangsu, Chekiang, Anhwei, Kiangsi and Fukien. His advantageous strategic position, as well as his control of the most economically developed part of the country, made it possible for Sun to assume a 'neutral' stance towards the ensuing conflict.

As evolved by Sun Yat-sen, the concept of the Northern Expedition was based on two premises: the overthrow of warlord rule by military means would result in national reunification which, in turn, would make feasible the regaining of full independence and the terminating of imperialist domination. In this fashion, the Chinese Revolution would finally achieve the aim it had failed to attain in 1911 and in the subsequent years. But in view of the great discrepancy between the forces of the NRA and those of the northern warlords, it was unthinkable to launch the Northern Expedition without simultaneously obtaining the support of the masses. In spite of the activities of the KMT right wing and of Chiang Kai-shek's striving for dictatorial power, the Canton government could still rely on such support, not only in Kwangtung, where the labour and peasant movement continued to develop at a rapid pace, but in other parts of the country as well. By May 1926 the All-Chinese Federation of Trade Unions claimed to represent 1,240,000 workers, while the membership of the Kwangtung Peasant Union was said to have grown to 600,000.

The position of the Canton government was markedly improved in the spring of 1926 by the adherence to the Kuomintang cause of neighbouring Kwangsi where, after a complex struggle, a triumvirate of young militarists had assumed full power. It was composed of Li Tsung-jen (1890–1969), Pai Ch'ung-hsi (1893–1966) and Huang

301

Shao-hung (1895–1966), all of whom were destined to play a significant role during the next quarter of a century.

The immediate cause which decided the timing of the Northern Expedition arose from an involved struggle for power in rich and strategic Hunan. In March 1926, against the background of much popular discontent, the forces of its governor, Chao Heng-t'i, a hated reactionary and subordinate of Wu P'ei-fu, were expelled from the capital, Ch'angsha, by units of an important local Hunan militarist, T'ang Sheng-chih (1889–1970). Although initially T'ang succeeded in gaining control of the entire province, Wu P'ei-fu intervened, and in May his troops drove T'ang's men back to southern Hunan. Under these circumstances T'ang Sheng-chih quickly announced his adherence to the KMT, and clamoured for aid from Canton. A relief expedition was soon dispatched, spearheaded by the famous Independent Regiment of the Fourth NRA, commanded by Yeh T'ing (1896–1946), one of the earliest and ablest of Communist military leaders.

The formal decision to launch the Northern Expedition was taken on 15 May 1926, and Chiang Kai-shek was appointed its commander in chief. The main forces were directed against Wu P'ei-fu's troops in Hunan, on the assumption that after Wu's defeat it would be easier to deal with the armies of Sun Ch'uan-fang and Chang Tso-lin. Moreover, the initial strategic plan, although the subject of much controversy, envisaged an advance to the Yangtse, and the capture of Wuhan to be followed by a march on Peking, leaving aside temporarily the coastal provinces, where conflict with the imperialist powers would be most likely.

In spite of its numerical inferiority and exceedingly difficult conditions, the NRA succeeded quickly in driving all of Wu P'ei-fu's forces out of Hunan, and by the end of August proceeded to attack the strong positions of his army in southern Hupei. The vanguard, composed of two divisions of the Fourth NRA and Yeh T'ing's Independent Regiment, displayed great valour in crushing the resistance of Wu's troops, gaining for itself the title of 'Ironsides'. The road to the Yangtse lay open, and on 6 and 7 September T'ang's troops succeeded in capturing Hankow and Hanyang. However, due to insufficient coordination, the NRA failed to take strongly fortified Wuchang, and was forced to begin a long siege of the city. This failure was also partially a reflection of conflict within the NRA itself, in particular of the intense rivalry of Chiang Kai-shek and T'ang Sheng-chih, both of whom, equal in their megalomania and striving for power, aspired to the post of undisputed military dictator.

The chronic disunity of the warlords had proved advantageous for the Canton government, since Sun Ch'uan-fang continued to maintain his neutrality during the NRA's successful offensive in Hunan. However, acting on the assumption that Sun would abandon this stance, the NRA unleashed an attack on his forces in Kiangsi, and on 20 September captured the provincial capital, Nanchang. But the victory proved only temporary because Sun's forces quickly retook the city, and it was only after more than a month of further combat that Chiang Kai-shek's forces finally managed to gain full control of Kiangsi. Chiang established his quarters in Nanchang, which soon became the rallying point of all the reactionary forces within the KMT and NRA.

The disaster suffered in Kiangsi by Sun Ch'uan-fang impelled the northern warlords to rally together in order to meet the threat of further NRA offensives. A decision was made to form a joint army over 300,000 strong, still more than double the size of the NRA. Strong units of the Fengtien army, commanded by Chang Tso-lin's eldest son, Chang Hsüeh-liang (b. 1898), were soon dispatched to Honan.

The military operations of the NRA involved also a third campaign against warlord forces in Fukien. The NRA units here were commanded by Ho Ying-ch'in (b. 1890), one of Chiang's closest military collaborators up to 1949, and succeeded by the end of December in gaining control of this province. Thus the possibility arose for an offensive towards the crucial coastal provinces of Chekiang and Kiangsu, but the undertaking of a decision to launch it, contrary to the original strategic plan, depended primarily on the outcome of the growing political strife within the Kuomintang itself.

In undertaking the Northern Expedition the Canton government counted on the support of its only potential ally, Feng Yü-hsiang's Kuominchün. However, the position of Feng's army had worsened considerably in September; new attacks by its enemies had forced it to retreat, while its strength was diminished and its fighting capacity disappeared almost completely. Nonetheless, upon his return from the Soviet Union in September, Feng proved capable of rallying the remnants of his army in Kansu and, with new Soviet aid, restored their military effectiveness. In October, the Kuominchün undertook a successful offensive in Shensi, advancing to capture the historic T'ungkuan Pass, the entry to Honan, thus creating a threat to Wu P'ei-fu's forces in that province.

By the end of 1926, the NRA had achieved remarkable success and increased in size as well. This was a mixed blessing, for the influx of former warlord troops also brought in its train a corresponding change in the army's composition, making it more prone to the political manipulations of Chiang Kai-shek and his coterie. The victories of the NRA were also facilitated to a significant degree by the considerable support it encountered from the population in the areas through which it advanced. The peasants, instead of demonstrating their customary and well-justified fear of soldiers, welcomed the disciplined Canton troops, providing them with food, enlisting for transport work, and furnishing priceless information on the enemy's movements. This invaluable support was also the result of effective propaganda spread earlier in these areas by special units, made up mostly of young Communists, organized and directed by the NRA's Political Department, led by Teng Yen-ta (1899–1931), one of the very few KMT military truly committed to Sun Yat-sen's Three Great Policies.

The success of the NRA also created new conditions for the development of the mass movement. Paradoxically, in Kwangtung itself, the labour and peasant movement began to encounter growing difficulties, but in Hunan, Hupei and Kiangsi it developed with great rapidity. The trade unions in Ch'angsha, and especially in Wuhan, increased their membership markedly, and in the case of the latter became an important source of political support for the KMT government. The growth of the peasant movement was especially impressive in Hunan, where the membership of the peasant associations rose from 300,000 in July to supposedly 1,400,000 by December 1926, a process graphically described in Mao Tse-tung's best-known early work, 'The Investigation of the Peasant Movement in Hunan'. The problems raised by this growth were to prove crucial both for the Chinese Communists and the future course of the revolution. In most cases it had resulted from the intense propaganda and organizational efforts of the young Communist intellectuals, but the peasant movement soon took on its own dynamics, showing many characteristics which had appeared in past peasant rebellions. All things considered, the peasants' demands were moderate, usually limited to the reduction of land rent, and thus could still be contained within the framework of the KMT's own agrarian programme. But the crux of the problem rested in the unwillingness of the KMT to enforce its own postulates, for many of its leaders, especially the higher NRA officers, were themselves of landlord gentry origin. The left wing of the KMT proclaimed their support for land reform, but sought to postpone the entire issue until full victory had been gained.

In this fashion, a basic contradiction arose between the national aspect of the revolution, the striving to regain full independence, and its social goals. But it was obvious that a real victory of the democratic revolution could not be achieved without satisfying the modest demands of the peasants and overthrowing the domination of the countryside by the landlord gentry, who constituted the actual mainstay of warlord rule. This contradiction was certainly not inevitable; it arose primarily from the narrow class egoism of many of the KMT's leaders, and the future was to show, during the anti-Japanese war, that it was possible to link both the national and social aspects, and moreover, to gain victory precisely by doing so. In 1926 and 1927 the young, still relatively inexperienced CCP was probably not in a position to take upon itself the full implementation of such a course. Nonetheless, active involvement in the rise of the mass movement had also resulted in a marked growth of the CCP and the Communist Youth League (CYL); by July 1926 the membership of the former had increased to around 30,000, that of the latter to over 20,000. Thus the Chinese Communist movement had ceased to be represented by a handful of intellectuals, and was well on its way to becoming a serious political force.

During the second half of 1926 the Chinese Communists sought to grapple with the increasingly difficult issues relating to the future course of the revolution, reflected especially in their relations with the Kuomintang. In theory, in order to assure the revolution's victory, its hegemony was supposed to rest in the hands of the working class. But in the existing form of KMT-CCP cooperation, the united front, composed not only of workers and peasants, but also of bourgeois and landlords, it was clearly the latter who held politically, and especially militarily, the dominant position. The machinations of the KMT right wing, as exemplified by Chiang Kai-shek's March coup, caused some Communist leaders to propose changes in the form of the united front, which would give the CCP greater freedom of action. Their apprehensions regarding Chiang's aspirations and future plans were shared to no small degree by Blücher and Borodin, who warned against his boundless ambition. However, the views of these competent observers were ignored, for they did not coincide with Stalin's preconceived desire to maintain the existing form of the united front at practically any cost.

The Crisis of the Revolution

During December 1926 and the first months of 1927 political conflict between the two wings of the Kuomintang became still more acute and apparent; even the question of the government's future location became a subject for controversy. It was generally agreed that to remain in Canton was pointless, but while the majority of the government favoured Wuhan as the new seat, Chiang Kai-shek, already intent on changing the strategy of the Northern Expedition, demanded that Nanchang be chosen instead. Attempts to achieve an accord, undertaken when a Canton government delegation on its way to Wuhan held talks with Chiang, proved fruitless. On 13 December, the government headquarters were established in the triple city which was proclaimed the official capital on 1 January. Thus, two distinct centres of power emerged, and simultaneously the NRA also ceased to be a united entity. T'ang Sheng-chih became the commander of the forces obedient to Wuhan, while Chiang retained his control of the armies recognizing his authority. The situation remained, however, very fluid, with each centre seeking to bring over to its side as many adherents as possible.

The position of the Wuhan government was strengthened to a certain degree by the growth of the labour movement in the triple city, and the success of the workers in taking over the British Concession in Hankow. After an anti-British demonstration had been fired upon by Royal Navy marines, the demonstrators spontaneously occupied the entire concession in response. The Wuhan trade unions, led by Liu Shao-ch'i (1900–69) and Li Li-san, quickly took charge of the action, with the result that complete peace was maintained. The British Concession in Kiukiang was taken over in a similar fashion on 6 January. In both cases, the restoration of Chinese authority was recognized by the British government in subsequent negotiations. This accommodation seemed in surprising contrast with the customary gunboat diplomacy of the foreign powers, which the British themselves had resorted to once again only a while earlier, for in September 1926, in the course of the so-called Wanhsien Incident, units of the British Yangtse Flotilla had bombarded this Szechuanese town causing the death of hundreds of civilians. However, at this stage, the policy of the foreign powers was not to engage immediately in open intervention, while making all preparations to do so, if necessary, in the near future. Military reinforcements were being rapidly dispatched to Shanghai, while the foreign navies strengthened their stranglehold on the Yangtse, with the grey silhouettes of cruisers looming ominously near the Hankow Bund. At the same time, the more far-sighted among the imperialists, noting the factional struggle within the KMT, began to take into account the possibility that the united front might disintegrate, and to ponder on measures which would hasten such a process.

By the end of February, after the capture of Hangchow, it was clear that Chiang Kai-shek and his followers were ready to abandon the plan to march northwards, and would aim first at the takeover of all Chekiang and Kiangsu, in particular of Shanghai. The reasons for reaching such a decision were not hard to discover. Chiang's Chekiang clique had excellent connections with the Shanghai bankers and industrialists, and the possession of the metropolis would provide him with financial support, sufficient to render him independent, both of the Wuhan government and, even more importantly, of heretofore indispensable Soviet aid. Furthermore, Shanghai was an appropriate place to demonstrate to the foreign powers that Chiang's KMT faction was not really a threat to their interests, since it had not the slightest intention of effectuating the anti-imperialist planks of the

307

Kuomintang programme. The rapprochement with the most important Chinese capitalist circles and the foreign powers would make it feasible also to dispense with the aid of the mass movement, at the time when the revolutionary actions of the workers and the peasants were becoming ever more hateful to the KMT right wing.

Shanghai, however, was not only the main centre of Chinese capitalism and the stronghold of imperialist domination; it also constituted the heart of the Chinese labour movement, and was now to witness an undaunted struggle, the finest and ultimately the most tragic page in the history of the Chinese working class. Under the undisputed leadership of the Communists, the Shanghai workers took upon themselves the task of liberating their city from warlord rule. The first of their three risings took place on 3 October 1926. Led by Lo I-nung (1901–28), it was inadequately prepared and was suppressed with considerable losses. The second attempt started on 19 February 1927, with a strike of over 350,000 workers, followed by a two-day-long insurrection. Nonetheless, the lack of sufficient arms and the incredibly brutal measures of the warlord commander brought failure once again. Chiang's troops were not far from the city, but offered no assistance. By now Chiang did not bother to conceal his hatred for the mass movement, and especially for the Communists leading it, whom he regarded, correctly, as his only serious opponents. In numerous speeches, he vehemently attacked the CCP and the labour movement, openly revealing his plans to smash the latter. All of this was scrupulously noted by the imperialists, who began to realize that this 'Red General' was not such a threat after all.

In the meantime, relations between Wuhan and Nanchang deteriorated sharply. At a meeting of the KMT CEC held in Wuhan the left-wing majority deprived Chiang Kai-shek of some of the posts he had accumulated. But he remained in command of the NRA. Simultaneously, the need for the continuance of KMT-CCP cooperation was stressed, and two prominent Communists, T'an P'ing-shan (1887–1956) and Su Chao-cheng (1885–1929), were made ministers of agriculture and labour. The Wuhan KMT also attached much hope to the expected return from France of Wang Ching-wei.

As the intrigues of the KMT right wing increased, the Shanghai working class took up arms once again. At noon on 21 March 1927 the sirens of all the city's factories wailed; a general strike in which

800,000 people, the entire working population, participated had begun. One hour later, the armed insurrection, superbly planned and organized this time, started. By the evening of the following day, all of Shanghai (the parts under Chinese administration, and not the International Settlement and the French Concession) was in the workers' hands. Once again it was the Communists, whose leaders included Chao Shih-yen (1901–27), Ch'en Yün (b. 1900), Chou En-lai, Ch'ü Ch'iu-pai, Lo I-nung, and Wang Shou-hua, who had directed the rising. It was also they who were in charge of the newly established City Council whose authority, however, was not recognized by the KMT army which now finally, under the command of Pai Ch'ung-hsi, entered the city on 23 May without firing a single shot. A tragic dénouement was in the offing. Shanghai was not only the scene of its workers' valour; it was also the gathering place of the most reactionary elements of the Kuomintang, busily concocting their counter-revolutionary plot for the purpose of smashing the labour movement and annihilating its leaders.

Counter-revolution and Debacle

In practically all the areas under the control of NRA generals collaborating with Chiang Kai-shek, actions aimed at suppressing the mass movement were undertaken on an increasing scale from the middle of March 1927. After the entry of NRA units into Shanghai preparations for a counter-revolutionary coup in this vital centre were set into motion almost immediately. On 26 March, Chiang Kai-shek arrived in Shanghai to renew his many connections, which included not only those with the city's bourgeoisie, but also with the secret societies ruling its underworld. The strongest of these was the notorious Green Gang, in control of the opium trade, gambling, prostitution and protection rackets; it is quite likely that Chiang himself had become a member of it during his years as a speculator on the Shanghai stock exchange. The 'Red General' was welcomed joyfully by the city's propertied classes, and this enthusiasm was quickly expressed in very concrete terms, a gift amounting to Ch $10 million.

309

The plans for the coup were quickly coordinated at two crucial secret meetings, chaired by Chiang Kai-shek. The first, attended by some of his closest political collaborators, served to provide the purported formal approval of the Party authorities for the suppression of the mass movement and the expulsion of all Communists from the Kuomintang. At the second, the main military leaders taking part in the conspiracy were present, and specific tasks were assigned to be carried out by NRA units in the coming assault on the Shanghai working class.

The plotting of Chiang and his accomplices was, however, well camouflaged by further political manoeuvres. Every occasion, such as Chiang's meeting with Wang Ching-wei upon the latter's return, was utilized to stress the sincere desire of the Nanchang coterie to preserve KMT unity, and its willingness to recognize the authority of Wuhan. The masquerade was effective, and Chiang's opponents remained largely unaware of his real intentions.

Simultaneously, the threat of direct foreign intervention became more acute in connection with the events which had occurred on 24 March during the occupation of Nanking by the NRA. Disturbances led to the looting of foreign property, and the death of from 6 to 8 foreigners; it is not impossible that these acts were committed by the retreating northern troops. In retaliation, British and American ships bombarded the city, and on 11 April the foreign powers presented an ultimatum to Wuhan and Nanchang, demanding a cessation of all anti-foreign activities, as well as apologies and reparations for the Nanking incident. Numerous foreigners demanded immediate military action, while already over 30,000 troops, mostly British, and 45 naval vessels were concentrated in Shanghai.

The type of action which the foreign powers desired the Chinese authorities to undertake was demonstrated in Peking by Chang Tso-lin. On 6 April, his troops raided the Soviet Embassy, also arresting a group of Chinese Communists and left KMT members who had taken refuge there. After a travesty of a trial, the leader of this group, thirty-eight-year-old Li Ta-chao, the co-founder of the CCP and brilliant visionary of a renascent China, was slowly garrotted to death along with 19 of his comrades. The foreign press in China gloated with joy.

Before dawn on 12 April 1927, the headquarters of the Shanghai Trade Union Federation and of various trade unions were attacked at precisely the same time by armed Green Gang bands and selected units from Pai Ch'ung-hsi's army. The workers, taken completely unawares, put up a desperate resistance, but by noon all the headquarters had been seized and the defenders massacred; over 700 of Shanghai's workers, including many of their leaders, were slain on the first day. A protest demonstration held on the next day was machine-gunned by Chiang's army; over 300 people, mostly women and children, were killed. During the next week the terror continued, and close to 5000 people lost their lives, many disappeared without a trace. The Shanghai massacre set off the counter-revolution in other areas under the control of NRA generals collaborating with Chiang Kai-shek. Thus, on 15 April, Li Chi-shen (1886–1959) ordered his troops to smash the labour movement and the CCP organization in Canton; over 2000 people were arrested and hundreds killed. Similar actions took place in almost every city under the sway of Nanchang.

The 12 April coup put an end to the fiction of Kuomintang unity. On 18 April, Chiang Kai-shek proclaimed the establishment of a new government in Nanking, a move immediately denounced by the KMT leaders in Wuhan, who deprived him of all his posts and expelled him from the Party. However, no attempt was made to follow up this verbal condemnation with political or military measures, aimed at overthrowing or even curtailing the power of Chiang and his neo-militarist clique. The Wuhan KMT did, nonetheless, declare its intention of remaining faithful to Sun Yat-sen's programme, and expressed its determination of continuing to cooperate with the CCP and to support the mass movement.

It was against the background of the grievous disasters suffered from 12 April on that the Chinese Communists met in Wuhan to hold their Fifth Party Congress (27 April–11 May). The 80 delegates were presumed to represent almost 58,000 members, but this was an illusory fiction, for the figure referred to the beginning of April, and since that time hundreds or thousands of Communists had been slain. For the first – and last – time in its history workers were said to make up over half of the Party membership. With the CYL over 35,000 strong, the CCP had come close by now to its goal of transformation into a mass political force, with truly substantial influence in the labour and peasant movements. The KMT rightists had been only too well aware of this in undertaking their decision to opt for a counter-revolution, and the bitter irony of this situation could not escape the delegates at the Congress.

In spite of far-reaching divergences, organizational unity was maintained, and the Congress retained Ch'en Tu-hsiu in his post as the Party's secretary-general, held by him since 1923. The other members of its first Political Bureau, elected now, were Chang Kuo-t'ao, Chou En-lai (who held this post uninterruptedly up to his death in 1976), Ch'ü Ch'iu-pai, Li Li-san, Li Wei-han (b. 1897), Su Chao-cheng, T'an P'ing-shan and Ts'ai Ho-sen.

The Congress was faced with the incredibly complex task of determining a future course of action, rendered still more difficult by the many controversies which had arisen understandably in connection with the 12 April coup and its consequences. Much time was devoted to discussing the form of further cooperation with the Wuhan KMT and the military options which its government had at its disposal. Probably the most vital issue which the CCP deliberated was the stand to be taken towards the peasant movement which, in the areas still under the sway of Wuhan, was assuming, especially in Hunan, the nature of an agrarian revolution. While passing a resolution favouring land reform, the Congress, in line with the Comintern instructions, stipulated that land belonging to families of the officers of the NRA should not be subject to the provisions of the reform. In view of the expanded system of Chinese family relations, this point reduced the programme almost to nil, especially as the Wuhan KMT also had no intention of implementing its own postulates in this domain. Thus, at this critical moment, the Chinese Communists, although they had been its pioneers and principal organizers, did not take the leadership of the agrarian revolution into their own hands.

In the aftermath of the 12 April coup the Wuhan government found itself in an increasingly difficult situation, with the area under its rule surrounded on all sides by superior hostile forces. Its financial position also deteriorated rapidly, due to an economic blockade imposed by the Nanking regime and the sabotage of its measures by the Wuhan bourgeoisie and foreign capitalists. By the end of May, the economic crisis, exacerbated by rampant inflation, became severe, giving rise to mass unemployment among the Wuhan working class, the government's most reliable supporter. Moreover, the threat of imperialist intervention still hung over the triple city; by the end of April the number of foreign warships anchored off the Hankow Bund had increased to 42.

In spite of the above circumstances, the Wuhan government declared its intention on 21 April to continue the Northern Expedition and ordered its troops, under T'ang Sheng-chih's command, to begin an offensive in Honan against the Fengtien army of Chang Hsüeh-liang advancing southwards. The plans called for effecting a junction with Feng Yü-hsiang's Kuominchün, stationed around the T'ungkuan Pass. During May, the Wuhan units, with the famous 'Ironsides' division as their vanguard, fought their way northwards, and in heavy and costly engagements forced the stronger and better equipped Mukden troops to retreat ultimately to the north bank of the Yellow River. On 1 and 2 June, Chengchow and K'aifeng were taken by the Wuhan NRA and the Kuominchün. It was, however, Feng who gained most from the victories, for now he could become an arbiter in the conflict between Wuhan and Nanking.

Paradoxically, at the time when its troops were successfully battling the Mukden army, the position of the Wuhan government in its own capital was imperilled. In May, the forces of the Szechuanese warlord, Yang Sen, began military operations against Wuhan. The critical situation was quickly utilized by a Hupei militarist, Hsia Tou-yin, to launch a revolt and lead his division against the capital. The KMT government fell into a panic in face of this threat, and the situation was saved only by the determined actions of units led by Yeh T'ing and Yün Tai-ying, which quickly smashed Hsia's troops and eliminated the danger to Wuhan.

In the meantime, the peasant movement in the territory controlled by the Wuhan government grew in strength at an amazing pace; by May, the membership of the peasant associations in Hunan had risen supposedly to around 4.5 million, and in Hupei to over 2.5 million. It seemed that an agrarian revolution had truly begun, whose future course could determine China's fate. At this stage the struggle in the countryside took on an appreciably more intense character; the demands of the peasants, especially in Hunan, increased in scope, with a call for redistribution of landlord property also being put forth, while the landlord gentry quickly sought to crush the peasant movement, primarily with the aid of armed force. An unequal battle began to be waged between the new peasant militia, always lacking adequate arms, and the much better equipped landlord bands. The desperate pleas of the peasants to the KMT authorities for aid went unheeded. The attitude of the Wuhan authorities towards this crucial phenomenon was strikingly reflected by the debates in April and May of its special agrarian commission. Although countless hours were devoted to examining all possible policies, the final conclusion taken was to postpone any decision on the issue until final victory in the war against the north had been gained.

The great upsurge of the peasant movement had been clearly the result of the devoted work of thousands of young, mostly Communist, organizers. However, at this critical phase the CCP found itself in an impasse as far as its own policy towards the peasants was concerned, since it was faced with the utterly impossible task of seeking to reconcile two completely contradictory postulates – the preservation of the united front with the Wuhan KMT, and support for the agrarian revolution to which this group was opposed. The Comintern directives on these two issues were explicitly clear, and just as totally contradictory. For the barely six-year-old CCP the authority of the Communist International was overwhelming and unchallengeable, hence its decisions were considered as binding.

The burning urgency of the agrarian question was soon made more apparent by the events in Hunan. On 21 May, Hsü K'o-hsiang, the commander of a regiment in Ch'angsha, launched a revolt and his troops immediately attacked all the headquarters of the trade unions and peasant associations in the city, murdering on the spot over one hundred of their leaders. The Ch'angsha coup served as a signal for an offensive in the entire province by landlord armed bands. However, the peasant associations, still unbroken in the neighbouring districts, sought to mount a counteroffensive to put down Hsü's revolt. Around 300,000 peasants, practically without arms, gathered to storm the city; the Wuhan authorities intervened to call off the assault. But not all the peasants had been notified in time, and when they approached the city they were met with the withering fire of Hsü's machine guns. Hundreds were slaughtered. The counter-revolution in Hunan had begun in earnest, to rage for the subsequent two months. Over 20,000, including all those most active in the peasant associations, were put to death with incredible cruelty, a thousandfold more than the victims of the peasant 'excesses', made much of by the Wuhan KMT. The peasant movement was crushed completely; the gentry families had returned from the towns where they had taken refuge. The old order triumphed. In reality, it had slightly over twenty years of life left.

The events in Hunan inevitably led to an intensive deepening of the political crisis in Wuhan. Both the KMT and the CCP were faced with the immediate need of determining their future policies. At this decisive moment, the arrival on 1 June of a new Comintern directive, contained in the famous Stalin telegram, brought a number of fundamental issues to a head. Briefly, the directive called for the undertaking of a number of radical steps, including support for the agrarian revolution, the formation of new, reliable army units, while preserving the existing forms of KMT-CCP cooperation. Moreover, it was assumed that the Wuhan government would express its approval of the measures recommended. The CCP leaders found the new instructions impossible to implement for, being after all infinitely better informed of the true situation in Wuhan, they saw no reason to assume that the Wang Ching-wei group would change its hostile attitude towards the agrarian revolution. A few days after its arrival, the contents of Stalin's telegram were revealed to Wang Ching-wei by the recently arrived Comintern delegate, M. N. Roy, on his own initiative. Although this odd contretemps did not have a decisive effect, it indubitably hastened the decision of Wang and his followers to break completely with the CCP, since they were most definitely not in favour of the further strengthening of the mass movement. In Wang's own cynical explanation, it was much more preferable to maintain oneself in power by going along with the armed forces, as Chiang Kai-shek had done, than with the workers and peasants.

As a sequel to its undertaken and still unrevealed decision to abandon the united front, and to continue its reliance solely on the military, the Wuhan government hastened to improve its relations with Feng Yü-hsiang. On 10 June, a delegation of Wuhan leaders, headed by Wang Ching-wei, proceeded to Feng's headquarters in Chengchow. In the ensuing negotiations Feng, in view of his advantageous position of holding the balance of power between Wuhan and Nanking, had no difficulty in imposing his proposals, calling for the immediate reconciliation of the two wings of the KMT, which of course implied the adoption by Wuhan of an anti-Communist stance, similar to that of Chiang Kai-shek. Shortly thereafter, Feng Yü-hsiang met in Hsüchow with Chiang and his supporters, and an accord for unity was reached on the basis of the programme he had presented to the Wuhan government. In actual fact, this unity soon proved to be little more than the usual temporary arrangement concluded by rival groups of Chinese warlords.

In Wuhan itself, the government, having accepted Feng Yü-hsiang's demands, prepared the final steps to end its cooperation with the CCP and the mass movement. Simultaneously, a number of its leaders quickly fled the sinking ship, with some joining Feng, while others escaped to Nanking. As a sign of protest, the two Communist ministers resigned from the government, but the CCP had few conceptions for dealing with the rapidly deteriorating situation, and some of its leaders, such as Ch'en Tu-hsiu, succumbed to despair and despondency. The helplessness of their position was reflected also during the meeting of the Fourth Congress of the ACFTU, held in Wuhan from 19–28 June. No viable solution to the immense difficulties of the labour movement, already the object of savage attacks in most of the country, could be advanced either in the report of Liu Shao-ch'i, the Federation's General Secretary, or in the debates. Only on 13 July did the CCP express its position, attacking the Wuhan KMT for its subservience to reactionary generals and its abandonment of Sun Yat-sen's policies.

On 15 July, the Kuomintang in Wuhan announced its final decision to break with the CCP and to oust the Communists from the Party, army and government. Only two of its leaders, Soong Ch'ing-ling (1892–1981) and Teng Yen-ta, opposed the move, denouncing it as a betrayal of the revolution. Both went into exile, but whereas her position as Sun Yat-sen's widow saved Soong Ch'ing-ling from persecution after her return in 1931, Teng was executed in the same year on Chiang Kai-shek's direct orders.

Simultaneously, the Wuhan government put an end to its cooperation with the Soviet Union, and shortly thereafter all the Soviet advisors left China. The valuable experience and knowledge they had acquired was to be dissipated, for the great majority of them, including Borodin and Blücher, fell victim at various periods to Stalin's purges.

Within a few days of the Wuhan government's decisions, the suppression of the labour movement in the triple city began, to be followed by similar actions directed against the peasants and workers in all the areas under its rule. Thus, the labour and peasant movement, built up with so much dedication and effort, was now almost completely crushed in the entire country. In human terms, the costs were still higher, for tens of thousands of the most active revolutionary workers and peasants, including a majority of the almost 100,000 members of the CCP and CYL, were slaughtered by the KMT authorities in the period up to the summer of 1928. Many of the ablest and most promising of the Communist leaders lost their lives during these terrible months. It was a question of pure chance as to who survived. But some did survive to resume the struggle, firm in their belief in the ultimate victory of their cause.

14. The Chinese Communists and the Kuomintang Dictatorship, 1927–37

The Aftermath of Disaster, July–December 1927

In a period when the mass organizations they had created and led were being crushed to bits, and the members of their party exterminated, the Communist leaders desperately sought ways and means which would enable their decimated movement to survive. The decision to resort in self-defence to military struggle evolved logically from the existing circumstances, but the possibilities for waging it were meagre indeed, for, largely due to the united front policy, the Communists had almost no military forces of their own to fall back on.

The few units in which the Communists had some influence were stationed in Kiangsi, and this factor accounted for the decision to gather most of the surviving leadership in Nanchang, in order to prepare an uprising under the slogan of continuing the revolution, now betrayed by both Wuhan and Nanking. Chou En-lai had been delegated as the principal organizer of the rising, while the military forces, between 20,000 to 30,000 strong, to be employed included a part of the famous 'Ironsides' division led by Yeh T'ing, and two units under the command of Chu Te (1886–1976) and Ho Lung (1896–1967). Although Nanchang itself was seized with ease on 1 August, NRA troops soon gathered to attack the city, and on 5 August the insurgents began their ill-fated march southwards to Kwangtung, during which their forces rapidly disintegrated. The surviving troops did manage to capture the port of Swatow in Kwangtung on 23 September, but within a week they were completely defeated by superior KMT forces. Only a detachment of less than 1000 men, led by Ho Lung, escaped from this final disaster to join the peasant insurrection initiated by P'eng P'ai in his native area of Hailufeng (the districts of Haifeng and Lufeng) in eastern Kwangtung. An equally small force, left behind earlier, began its trek to Hunan led by Chu Te.

Thus the first attempt to wage a military struggle ended disastrously. Nonetheless, since 1949, 1 August is celebrated as the holiday of the People's Liberation Army, for it marked the emergence of the first military force under direct Communist leadership, and symbolized the principal form of struggle waged by the Chinese Communists for the subsequent twenty-two years. It was also actually the only feasible one which could assure their physical survival.

Simultaneously with the Nanchang uprising, those CCP leaders who did not participate in it met on 7 August to select a new Political Bureau headed by Ch'ü Ch'iu-pai. The meeting also outlined the policy calling for the launching of insurrections, to be known as the 'Autumn Harvest Uprising', in the four provinces – Hunan, Hupei, Kiangsi and Kwangtung – where the peasant movement had been the strongest. Due to Mao Tse-tung's description of it in his autobiography narrated to Edgar Snow, the rising in Hunan is the best known, but it differed not at all from the others in the complete failure that it suffered. Only a limited force of 8000 men could be assembled, the expected large-scale peasant uprising failed to materialize, and the plan to capture Ch'angsha had to be abandoned. By the end of September, Mao Tse-tung withdrew across the border to Kiangsi, with the remnants of his force of around 1000 men, to seek refuge in the old bandit lair of Chingkangshan.

Although accord between the Wuhan and Nanking regimes had seemingly been reached in July, a complex struggle for power began immediately between the various Kuomintang factions, with the control of the central government as one of the main bones of contention. Having turned its back on Sun Yat-sen's principle of supporting the mass movement, the KMT now took on the unadulterated character of a bourgeois nationalist party in which, however, the military element, represented both by the NRA generals and the even greater number of warlords who had joined it, was definitely the dominant force. Having shed its revolutionary ballast, the KMT now also quickly assumed the role of the indubitable political representative of all the principal groups of the bourgeoisie, and especially of the landlord gentry to whom it entrusted full control of the countryside.

In August, against the background of intense factional conflict in Nanking, Chiang Kai-shek resorted to the useful tactic of resigning from office. The control of the government fell largely into the hands of the Kwangsi clique generals, while the various KMT factions, including the Western Hills group, sought to establish some semblance of Party unity in the shape of the Central Special Committee, formed in September. However, this device, which lasted only until December, was unable to prevent further strife.

It was the instability of the political situation which instilled false hopes among the local CCP leadership that good prospects existed for the launching of a successful insurrection in Canton. The fateful decision to undertake this venture, based also on the Comintern's analysis of the situation in China, according to which an upsurge of the revolutionary situation was supposed to exist, was taken on 26 November. However, the repressions carried on in Canton since April had greatly weakened the labour movement, and, in view of the hurried and inadequate preparations, insufficient effort was made to muster popular support for the rising which broke out on 11 December. The insurgent forces, a 1300-strong officer-training regiment, led by Yeh Chien-ying, and a 2000-strong Red Guard, were able to take the city and establish a new revolutionary government – the famous Canton Commune. They could not hold it against the greatly superior armies of the KMT factions, which quickly ceased their own strife to march in unison on Canton. During the next day furious fighting raged throughout the city in which Chang T'ai-lei, the insurrection's principal leader, and over 2000 of its participants lost their lives. Only around 1500 succeeded in breaking through the cordon of KMT troops; under the leadership of Hsü Hsiang-ch'ien (b. 1902) they joined P'eng P'ai's followers in Hailufeng, the first revolutionary base to be organized by the Chinese Communists, and fought against overwhelming odds until its destruction in March 1928. Sixty of them survived.

The KMT troops celebrated their victory by a massacre of all actual and suspected participants of the insurrection, killing from 4000 to 6000 and committing indescribably horrible atrocities towards the women captured. Five of the six Russian workers of the Soviet Consulate and all six of its Chinese employees were also murdered. Thus, the first attempt to seize power in line with the European pattern of an urban insurrection ended in complete disaster.

The Establishment of the Kuomintang Regime

In January 1928, Chiang Kai-shek reappeared on the confused political arena and quickly regained his dominant position, becoming once again the commander in chief of the Nanking armed forces, as well as the head of its government. The term 'Nanking Decade' is sometimes used to refer to the subsequent years, up to the outbreak of war with Japan, in which the Kuomintang government sought to extend its rule, primarily by military means, to the entire country. The goal was the achievement of national unification, but in many respects there was even less unity and more strife than in the warlord period, especially in the first three years of the Nanking regime. Moreover, while basically it ceased to challenge imperialist domination and failed to resist Japanese aggression, the Nanking government did wage an unrelenting struggle against the Chinese Communists, to which it devoted an ever larger share of its military and financial resources.

At the outset, the territory under direct and effective Nanking control was restricted primarily to the Yangtse Valley. Kiangsu and Chekiang constituted the mainstay of its power, and its authority was also recognized in Kiangsi, Anhwei and Fukien. However, the rest of the country remained under the rule of other militarists, either completely hostile or, even if formally cooperating with Nanking, quite independent of it. It was this situation which impelled the Kuomintang to implement the sole part of Sun Yat-sen's programme which it had not completely jettisoned thus far. The struggle against the northern warlords was to be continued, and on 19 April 1928 the decision to recommence the Northern Expedition was announced.

A huge army, around 700,000 strong, composed of the original NRA units under Chiang Kai-shek's command, the troops of the Kwangsi generals, Feng Yü-hsiang's Kuominchün and the Shansi soldiers of Yen Hsi-shan, was dispatched northwards to deal with the still formidable, 400,000-strong force of Chang Tso-lin and his subordinates. The advance was accomplished on the whole

321

successfully; it was marred nonetheless by the brutal intervention of the Japanese in Shantung, culminating in May in the Tsinan Incident, in which hundreds of Chinese soldiers were killed. By the beginning of June, the position of Chang Tso-lin's army in North China had crumbled, and when Chang finally departed from Peking for Mukden he was soon to perish as his train was blown up by the Japanese militarists. It would seem that they had ceased now to consider him as the amenable and reliable servitor he had been in the past. However, the move soon proved to be a miscalculation, for in the ensuing struggle for power in the northeast it was Chang Hsüeh-liang who was to emerge victorious, and not the generals on whom the Japanese pinned their hopes. In January 1929, Chang disposed of his rivals by means of a favourite warlord gambit – an invitation to a banquet, promptly followed by assassination. Simultaneously, Chang recognized the authority of the Nanking government, although this remained a pure formality, since the control of the northeast rested solely in his own hands.

In spite of the success of the Northern Expedition the country remained, in fact, divided between the victors. Nonetheless, it was considered appropriate to establish, on 10 October 1928, a new National Government in Nanking. An Organic Law relating to the structure and functioning was also passed, which was supposed to embody Sun Yat-sen's concept for government during the period of tutelage before the transition to democratic rule could be effected. The facade of legal and constitutional provisions had, in reality, only one basic aim – to conceal the true essence of the regime which was simply a one-party dictatorship, with the role of the military clearly dominant. Effective power rested largely in the hands of the military headquarters, and thus of Chiang Kai-shek himself. But in view of the complex nature of the forces which had contributed to the formation of the Nanking regime, Chiang, notwithstanding his transparent tendencies towards full dictatorial rule, was compelled to engage in constant manipulation of the strongest military and political factions.

The setting up of a new Nanking government did not in the slightest terminate factional strife between the most prominent leaders of the Kuomintang, nor the rivalries of Chiang Kai-shek, Wang Ching-wei and Hu Han-min, all of whom aspired to the role of indisputable Party leader. While Hu could usually count on the support of his native Kwangtung, Wang proceeded to organize his own faction, known as the Association for the Reorganization of the KMT. However, neither of these men was able to weaken appreciably the position of Chiang Kai-shek, whose supporters were grouped in three main factions, all bitter competitors also in the struggle for the division of spoils. The first of these was the CC clique headed by the brothers Ch'en Li-fu (b. 1900) and Ch'en Kuo-fu (1892–1951), nephews of Chiang's early patron, which came into full control of the KMT central party apparatus, and of one of the regime's two main secret intelligence services. The second, and clearly the most important faction, was composed of the graduates and former instructors of the Whampoa Military Academy. The majority of them held command positions in Nanking's armed forces and remained Chiang Kai-shek's most faithful and reliable followers throughout the whole existence of the KMT regime, the real mainstay of his power. The third, more varied group, usually referred to as the Political Science clique, was made up of influential bureaucrats from the Peking and warlord governments, some military men and individuals connected with large capitalist interests, primarily in Shanghai.

The problem of exercising control over the country's armed forces, grotesquely expanded as a result of warlord domination to probably around two million men, soon brought the alleged unity announced by the Nanking government to naught. It was obvious that the reduction of this tremendous burden was imperative, but no simple solution was available, for the armies remained the only real source of power both of the central government and of individual warlords. In January 1929, a disbandment conference was held at which a decision was reached to reduce the armies to 600,000 regular troops and 200,000 militia. However, none of the participants, all the main military leaders, showed the slightest intention of cutting down the size of their own armies. Thus the ground was prepared for future conflict, made also inevitable by Chiang Kai-shek's policy of achieving 'unity' by means of armed force.

The first attacks of the Nanking regime were launched in February 1929 against the Kwangsi clique. Its armies found themselves isolated and were forced to retreat to their native province where, nonetheless, Li Tsung-jen and Pai Ch'ung-hsi were able to retain full and independent control of the province for the entire Nanking Decade. Shortly thereafter, in May 1929, the growing tension between Chiang Kai-shek and Feng Yü-hsiang, exacerbated by the struggle for the control of Shantung, changed into open conflict. But fighting had hardly begun when Chiang succeeded in subverting with 'silver bullets' two of Feng's main generals who passed over to Nanking's side. Nonetheless, extensive military operations were conducted for two months in the autumn in Honan, with Feng now receiving aid from Yen Hsi-shan.

A new conflict on a much larger scale began in April 1930; while the main battles were waged by the armies of Feng and Yen, defending themselves against an offensive by the Nanking forces, other anti-Chiang militarists, including the Kwangsi generals, also joined the fray. Thus, fighting spread to many parts of the country and lasted until the end of September, having cost the lives of around 300,000 men.

In the course of this bitter strife, almost all of Chiang Kai-shek's opponents, both political and military, sought to establish an effective alliance with the aim of overthrowing the Nanking regime. It was to be known as the Enlarged Conference Movement, which led to the proclamation on 1 September of a rival government in Peiping (the name used for Peking by the KMT during the years 1928–49) in which Wang Ching-wei, Feng Yü-hsiang and Yen Hsi-shan held the most prominent positions. Both the Nanking and Peiping governments now sought to gain the support of the only sizable force still uninvolved in the conflict, the powerful Northeastern Army of Chang Hsüeh-liang. Influenced by recent successes gained by Chiang Kai-shek's troops, Chang made his fateful decision on 17 September in favour of Nanking, and ordered his units to enter North China. This move quickly determined the fate of the Enlarged Conference Movement, which fell apart completely in October. Its defeat also put an end to Feng Yü-hsiang's career as an independent militarist, since he now lost all control over his armed forces.

Although the campaigns in 1930 terminated the main military struggle between the KMT militarists, the authority of the Nanking government still remained very circumscribed in spite of the victory gained. North China was now under the control of Chang Hsüeh-liang; Szechuan, Yünnan and Kweichow remained under the rule of their own warlords, while Sinkiang completely ignored the central government. Kwangtung and Kwangsi also retained full autonomy, which in the case of the former was to be demonstrated in May 1931 by the establishment in Canton of a rival government, composed once again of Chiang Kai-shek's most noted political opponents. Thus, the Kuomintang had proved itself incapable of attaining real unification, and this failure was to weigh heavily on China's future, especially on her ability to defend herself against the next phase of Japanese imperialist aggression, to be inaugurated in September 1931 by the invasion of Manchuria.

The Establishment of Revolutionary Bases and the Chinese Red Army, January 1928–September 1931

In the spring of 1928, the survivors of the disastrous Autumn Harvest Uprising in Hunan, led by Mao Tse-tung, were joined by the remnants of the troops which had participated in the Nanchang uprising, commanded by Chu Te. Their famous meeting was to mark the first crucial steps taken on the long road which, after twenty-one years of unceasing arduous military struggle, was to lead the Chinese Communist movement to its ultimate victory.

The single most important decision undertaken immediately by Mao and Chu pertained to the organization of their forces into the Chinese Red Army, whose primary task was the fulfilment of the political programme of the CCP, while assuring the physical survival of its members. The means at the disposal of these two men were pitifully inadequate, since by August 1928 their troops numbered at most 5000 men, with barely 2000 rifles. From the very outset, the Red Army was engaged in constant struggle against numerically superior provincial forces, and its ability to survive during the difficult initial period was due to a number of specific factors. The country's political decentralization and incessant warlord rivalry undoubtedly contributed to the survival of the Communist forces, which could establish their bases most easily in areas adjacent to provincial boundaries, where the power of the provincial militarists was the weakest.

The fundamental aim of the CCP was to strive for the realization of the unfulfilled tasks of the Chinese Revolution. In view of the nature of Chinese society, the agrarian question remained the most crucial, and from 1928 on the Chinese Communists promoted the agrarian revolution in all the areas under their control, although the methods, usually drastic, and the criteria adopted in effectuating land confiscation and distribution differed widely in various periods. The agrarian revolution could not be carried out, however, without the conquest of power, even if on a local scale, and hence the establishment of a new revolutionary government, which was considered to represent a workers-peasants dictatorship, became a basic and indispensable concern. Both the agrarian revolution and the revolutionary government could continue to exist and develop in the newly founded bases only if they were successfully defended by the Red Army, which thus became the single most important instrument at the disposal of the CCP for implementing its policies. The exceptional role of the military factor confirmed in part the oft-quoted thesis that in China 'armed revolution faced armed counter-revolution', and was destined to become one of the most characteristic features of the Chinese Communist movement and one of the most significant traits of the Chinese Revolution itself.

While the ragged soldiers of Mao Tse-tung and Chu Te were fighting for their lives in the hills of Hunan and Kiangsi, a number of those Communist leaders who had managed to survive the KMT massacres met in Moscow in June 1928 to hold the Sixth Congress of the CCP. The ten-point programme elaborated by the Congress restated the aims of the Chinese Revolution, stressing the need for carrying out the agrarian revolution under the leadership of the working class, but the main emphasis was placed on developing, or rather rebuilding, the completely smashed labour movement. This was an exceedingly difficult task, due both to the great losses which the CCP, now numbering less than 10,000 members, had suffered, and to the relentless measures which the KMT employed against it.

A new Political Bureau was chosen at the Congress, whose composition differed little from that elected in May 1927, or that selected in August 1927. Li Li-san was soon to emerge as the dominant personality in the new leadership. It was decided to maintain the Party headquarters in Shanghai, and attempts were made to establish contacts with the Communists fighting in the countryside, although in view of the circumstances, they were at best tenuous.

In July 1928, a handful of officers, secret CCP members, led by P'eng Te-huai (1898–1974), organized a successful revolt of the KMT troops under their command. Shortly thereafter they were able to join up with the forces of Mao and Chu, thus providing most welcome reinforcements. However, due to the losses suffered by both forces, the whole Red Army at the end of 1928 still numbered only around 5000 men. Heavy fighting during the next three months then reduced its strength to 3000. Nonetheless, at the same time a number of revolutionary bases and local Red armies were being organized by the Communists in other parts of Central and South China. Thus, troops led by Hsü Hsiang-ch'ien established a base in the border areas of Hupei, Honan and Anhwei, while Ho Lung, having survived the disaster in Swatow, returned to his native haunts to continue the struggle in the Hunan-Hupei border area. A particularly successful campaign was waged in Northeast Kiangsi, where a pioneer of the peasant movement, Fang Chih-min (1899–1935), organized a guerrilla movement which led to the formation of the Fukien-Chekiang-Kiangsi base. From 1928 to 1930 the Communists, Teng Hsiao-p'ing among them, were also active in Kwangsi, gaining support among the Chuang peasants. Military struggle was waged and revolutionary governments were set up in other areas as well, and by the spring of 1930 there were 15 bases with a total armed force of around 60,000 armed men. Relatively little contact existed between the various bases, but a common ideology and goals provided the necessary link. In all instances, it was the Red Army, transformed into a highly disciplined and politicized force, with almost a third of its soldiers being CCP or CYL members, which emerged as the main force of the revolution.

In the course of its initial struggles the Red Army developed also a unique code of proper behaviour towards the civilian population, while the relations between its officers and men assumed an unprecedented degree of democracy. Both these factors helped to differentiate it sharply from the mercenary and often bandit-like KMT troops, brutalized by their own commanders and, taken together with the social and political programme implemented, accounted for the support it received from the peasants.

Simultaneously, the strategy and tactics evolved in this period, which made possible the waging of successful operations against always numerically superior enemy forces, were to prove invaluable – not only during the years of expanding and defending the revolutionary bases in Central and South China, but even more during the war against Japan.

While the revolutionary bases were being established and the Red Army waged its ever more successful struggle, the CCP leadership, with its headquarters in Shanghai, sought, in line with its basic tenets, to function primarily as a working-class organization, and to continue activity in the urban centres. Under the incredibly difficult conditions created by the KMT terror which forced the CCP underground, the task of regaining influence among the workers and of expanding the Party in the cities proved ultimately unattainable. The losses sustained by the CCP continued to be heavy; numerous prominent members, such as Lo I-nung and P'eng P'ai, were executed, while the same fate befell countless of their relatives, such as the wife of Chu Te or the wife and sister of Mao Tse-tung.

Nonetheless, in spite of the very unfavourable situation in the cities, the CCP leadership, headed by Li Li-san, proclaimed its intention in 1930 to launch a campaign aimed at gaining power in a number of principal cities and provinces, which would then make it possible to gain victory in the entire country. The final decisions to begin this enterprise were taken in June, and were approved the next month by the Communist International. The plans called for the mobilization of all available Red Army forces, and an offensive against Ch'angsha and Nanchang which, if successful, was to be followed by an assault on Wuhan. In accord with these directives, a part of the Red Army, led by P'eng Te-huai, attacked and captured Ch'angsha on 29 July. However, the victory lasted only a short time, for the city was soon attacked by foreign gunboats and superior KMT units; P'eng's men were forced to evacuate Ch'angsha on 9 August. A simultaneous attempt to take Nanchang ended in a fiasco, as did a second attack on Ch'angsha in September. In view of these failures, the Red Army leaders, Mao Tse-tung, Chu Te and P'eng Te-huai, contravening the directive of the Li Li-san leadership, resolved to give up the entire forlorn enterprise, and ordered their forces to retreat to their mountain fastnesses in southern Kiangsi.

Against the background of this debacle the strong tendency to factionalism within the CCP, apparent already for the past few years, surfaced to give rise to bitter and longlasting disputes. One of the contending factions was made up of a group of twenty-odd former students in Moscow, who returned to China in 1929–30. Its most prominent members were Wang Ming (pseudonym of Ch'en Shao-yü, 1904–74) and Po Ku (psuedonym of Ch'in Pang-hsien, 1907–46). Another faction, led by Ho Meng-hsiung (1903–31), represented those CCP members most actively engaged in the underground labour movement. Both groups attacked the policy of the Li Li-san leadership, although from completely different positions. Ultimately, in November 1930, Li Li-san, saddled with the entire responsibility for the disastrous summer offensive, was removed from all his posts, and sent off to the Soviet Union where he was to remain until 1945. However, Li's disgrace did not put an end to the factional struggles. They were to be reflected also in armed internecine strife in December 1930 in the Kiangsi base, referred to as the Fut'ien Incident. Basically, this was a revolt by some Red Army units against Mao Tse-tung's leadership, quickly put down by troops loyal to him. Subsequently, the whole affair, in which many Communists lost their lives, was ascribed to the machinations of the KMT-sponsored Anti-Bolshevist League, but the existing account is so contradictory that it is difficult to grasp its real course.

The strife within the leadership in Shanghai ended in January 1931 with the complete victory of the Returned Students faction, which now assumed the dominant position in the Political Bureau. Some Western historians simplistically view these conflicts as a mere struggle for power, and in doing so ignore the fact that all those participating in these factional disputes were committed and dedicated Party members, all equally convinced of the unique correctness of their own views. The staunchness of their conviction was largely derived from the supposedly all-embracing and all-elucidating nature of the ideology they professed. They waged their struggle at a time when the victory of the revolution could not be assumed except by an act of faith, thus increasing still more its drama and intensity.

Until the autumn of 1930 the Red Army had fought the overwhelming majority of its battles against provincial troops, for the forces of the Nanking regime had been engaged primarily in the campaigns against other rival KMT armies described earlier. However, from November 1930 on, Chiang Kai-shek directed almost all his efforts against the Communists, embarking on a number of military expeditions with the basic aim of liquidating the revolutionary bases and exterminating their Communist-led forces. Over 100,000 KMT troops took part in the first expedition, which began in November 1930. It was smashed within two months by the 40,000-strong Red Army, which gained valuable new supplies of arms and ammunition and also increased its own strength by enlisting many of the captives, a process it would repeat on numerous future occasions.

Around 200,000 troops, commanded by Ho Ying-ch'in, launched the second expedition in March 1931. By May, it had met with the same fate as its predecessor and withdrew with heavy losses. Once more all the areas lost were regained and the territory of the Central Base in Kiangsi expanded. The defeat of these two expeditions was a heavy blow to Chiang Kai-shek's prestige, and he lost little time in ordering the beginning of the subsequent offensive. Acting on the counsel of his German military advisors, Chiang included this time five of his own divisions in the 300,000-strong army assembled for the new campaign, which he commanded in person, aided by three of the best KMT generals. Although, due to its overwhelming superiority in arms and men, the KMT army was able to penetrate deeply into the Central Base, it too met with a crushing defeat and was forced to retreat by the end of August. Superb leadership, incomparably higher morale, support of the population and the strategy of luring the enemy within the Central Base to destroy his units piecemeal were among the key elements which accounted for the Red Army victory.

The New Stage of Japanese Aggression, 1931–4

In September 1931, the Japanese imperialists set into motion their carefully laid plans for the annexation of Manchuria, which they envisaged as the first crucial stage in the conquest of all China. Within a few days Japanese troops had seized most of Liaoning and Kirin, and by the end of November almost the entire northeast with its immense resources, was under complete Japanese domination. The ease with which the conquest was accomplished was explained by the fact that the Japanese encountered almost no resistance. On Chiang Kai-shek's orders, Chang Hsüeh-liang's sizable army of over 150,000 men withdrew from the northeast without waging a single battle, while the few attempts by other Manchurian units to oppose the Japanese advance were quickly smashed.

Instead of offering resistance and mobilizing all the country's forces to counter Japanese aggression, the Nanking government chose to follow a policy of placing its hopes on the possibility of obtaining the assistance of the Western powers. With this in mind, it made an appeal to the League of Nations, an action which proved to be a classical exercise in futility. The League did dispatch a Commission of Inquiry which reached Manchuria in May 1932. Its report, which curiously enough recognized the Japanese claim that Manchuria should have an 'autonomous' status, was finally accepted in February 1933, by which time the Japanese had thoroughly consolidated their hold on the northeast, and could afford to ignore international opinion by walking out of the League in the subsequent month. The whole sorry affair only served to demonstrate that the Western powers had chosen to follow a policy of complete appeasement, the costliness of which was to be made abundantly clear exactly a decade later.

Not content with the conquest of the northeast itself, the Japanese embarked on an additional campaign for the purpose of intimidating the KMT government still further, and, at the end of January 1932, Japanese forces began large-scale military operations in the Shanghai area. This time, however, their plans miscarried badly, for the attack met with unexpected, strong opposition. In spite of Chiang Kai-shek's orders the Kwangtung troops of the 19th Route Army stationed in Shanghai resisted the Japanese assault for over a month, receiving much assistance from the city's population, and none whatever from Nanking. Their heroic struggle made an immense impression on Chinese public opinion, incensed already since September by the aggression of the Japanese and the appeasement policy of the KMT regime.

The Japanese invasion of Manchuria gave rise to a severe crisis in Nanking and to Chiang Kai-shek's temporary resignation from his leading position. Ultimately, the KMT factions did achieve a semblance of unity, and at the end of January 1932 Wang Ching-wei became premier, while Chiang resumed his control of the armed forces. The new arrangement did not, however, denote any significant alteration in the domestic or foreign policies of the Nanking government.

In the northeast the Japanese, having completed their occupation, proclaimed the foundation of the 'independent' state of Manchukuo, designating P'u-i as its Chief Executive. In spite of its elaborate political and administrative facade, the new creation was obviously only a puppet regime, and the current commander of the Japanese Kwantung army remained the real ruler throughout its existence. In March 1934, the Japanese thought it worth the bother to convert Manchukuo into an empire. Much more significantly, from 1932 on, the Japanese government devoted great efforts to the forcible development of the Manchurian economy, especially of heavy industry, for the purpose of its own future military expansion. In the process, the population of the northeast was subjected to incredibly ruthless and brutal exploitation. Although attempts were made, in particular by the CCP, to organize an armed resistance movement, its scope was limited by the terrorist measures of the Japanese occupiers.

The conquest of the northeast was, as noted, only the first stage of Japanese aggression. In February 1933, the Japanese invaded the Inner Mongolian province of Jehol, annexing it to Manchukuo in the following month. In May, they continued their expansion westward with an attack on Chahar. Simultaneously, the Japanese intensified their efforts to take advantage of the deep discontent of the Mongols in Inner Mongolia with the oppressive rule of the KMT and local Chinese warlords, by seeking to win over some of the nationalistically inclined Mongol leaders. In this endeavour they were at least partially successful, for some of the Mongol princes, such as the famous and controversial Demchukdonggrub (Te Wang, 1902–?), did become important collaborators.

The loss of Manchuria and the unrelenting further pressure of Japanese imperialism created a new political situation in China, in which the problem of national salvation rapidly became uppermost. Increasingly, the vocal part of the population, the intellectuals, students and even bourgeois groups, including also some of the KMT factions and military leaders, demanded that the KMT government abandon its appeasement policy and prepare to resist Japanese aggression. Nonetheless, in spite of this, the Nanking regime showed no inclinations to alter its foreign policy, concentrating all its efforts on trying to consolidate its own power and to suppress all domestic opposition, especially that of the Communists. In the meantime, the factional strife within the KMT continued as usual. In August 1932, Wang Ching-wei resigned from his post as premier, a move which strengthened still further Chiang Kai-shek's hold on the central government.

The victory of the Nazis in Germany served to stimulate markedly Chiang Kai-shek's enthusiastic admiration of fascism, and encouraged him to hasten the measures intended to shape the Nanking regime in the fascist mould. In fact, the first steps aimed at establishing a fascist movement had already been taken in 1931 by a group of Whampoa graduates, Chiang's most faithful praetorians, with his full approval and backing. Characteristically, the fascist organization, usually referred to as the Blue Shirts, was established in secret in the spring of 1932; its leaders, all Chiang's closest military supporters, included the notorious Tai Li (1895–1946), head of one of Nanking's secret police organizations, the Military Statistics Bureau. The Blue Shirts, whose main task was strengthening Chiang Kai-shek's personal dictatorship, specialized also in assassinating outspoken opponents of the KMT regime. One of their many prominent victims was the general secretary of the League for the Protection of Civil Rights, American-educated Yang Ch'uan (1883–1933), gunned down in June 1933.

The growing opposition to the policies of the Nanking government led in November 1933 to a significant new crisis, the famous Fukien Revolt. The military forces engaged in it were primarily the units of the 19th Route Army which had earlier heroically defended Shanghai, while a number of Chiang Kai-shek's more prominent political opponents within the KMT participated in the establishment of a rival government in Fukien, which put forth a programme calling for the resistance to Japan and criticizing the domestic policy of Nanking. However, the leaders of this movement failed to gain the indispensable military support from Chiang's rivals in Kwangsi and Kwangtung; they also did not attain proper cooperation with his bitterest enemies, the Chinese Communists. Thus, the Fukien insurgents found themselves isolated, and in January 1934 Chiang Kai-shek's much stronger forces put down the rebellion with relative ease. In spite of its defeat, the Fukien Revolt showed that in face of the threat of Japanese aggression a new alignment of political forces was imperative if national salvation were to be achieved.

The disastrous political events of the 1931–4 period took place in a setting of further deterioration of China's social and economic development. While the effects of the world depression did not become apparent until 1931, they led to a severe three-year-long crisis, in which agricultural prices fell by around 47 per cent, deepening still further the terrible poverty of the Chinese peasantry which was anyhow, in R. H. Tawney's words, 'constantly on the brink of actual destitution'. The critical position of the peasants, left by the Kuomintang completely at the mercy of the landlords and usurers, was exacerbated still more by the constantly increasing tax burden imposed by the central government and especially by the gentry-run local administration.

The financial position of the Nanking government, which derived most of its revenues from customs and excise taxes, also remained unstable. Its budget deficits, caused primarily by its huge military expenditures, were balanced by the issue of vast quantities of government bonds, which served as a source of profit for the ruling KMT oligarchy. In effect, there were precious few resources left at its disposal for putting into operation the highly advertised modernization plans, which the greatly expanded bureaucracy churned out in profusion. While some progress was made in expanding the infrastructure, most of the construction of roads and railways was undertaken for military purposes. Not a single significant step was made to improve the situation in agriculture, and even the attempt of some individuals to study the crucial social problems of the rural areas met with repression by the KMT authorities.

Simultaneously, the KMT government, in spite of its revolutionary antecedents, quickly reached the level of incompetence and corruption equal to, if not exceeding, the earlier warlord-dominated regimes. Nepotism and graft reached up to the highest levels of the KMT oligarchy, by no means excluding the four most powerful families – the Chiangs, Soongs, K'ungs, and Ch'ens, already well on their way to the accumulation of fabulous fortunes. Hence, in this process of creating bureaucratic capitalism, it was not fortuitous that this arriviste ruling caste was much more concerned with preserving its own power and wealth than in organizing an effective resistance to the Japanese aggression.

The Chinese Soviets and the Long March, September 1931–October 1936

The successes of the Red Army in defeating the first three expeditions of the KMT regime led to a consolidation of the revolutionary bases and especially of the Central Area. The population of all the areas numbered perhaps from 8 to 9 million, while the Red Army increased its strength to around 100,000. Moreover, the victories now made possible the establishment of a government for all the territory under the control of the CCP and the Red Army. It was proclaimed in November 1931 during the First Congress of the Soviet areas held in Juichin, Kiangsi. Mao Tse-tung was elected chairman, and Chang Kuo-t'ao and Hsiang Ying (1898–1941) vice-chairmen of the government's supreme organ. The laws enacted reflected in some respects the aspirations of the Soviet movement more than the actual situation, while the structure of the government, as well as the name itself, revealed the tendency to adhere closely to the Russian model. However, in reality, the Chinese Soviets were purely a peasant movement, and the membership of the CCP also became composed in its overwhelming majority of peasants. Not unaware of this problem, the Communist leadership sought ingeniously to maintain that adherence to Marxism-Leninism automatically safeguarded the proletarian character of the CCP.

The loss of Manchuria and the problems of resisting further Japanese aggression were partially reflected in the policies of the CCP. Thus, on 15 April 1932, the Chinese Soviet government declared war on Japan, and on 10 January 1933, the CCP called for national unity in the struggle against Japan. Nonetheless, the fundamental goal pursued by the Chinese Communists remained the overthrow of the Nanking regime, which was supposed to be accomplished by fighting simultaneously against middle-of-the-road groups, often strongly anti-Japanese, regarded as even more dangerous than the obviously rightist and reactionary KMT leadership. There was nothing original in such formulations, for they were simply a reflection of general policies followed by the Communist International in the years 1928–34, often considered to have been sectarian and dogmatic. As a result, the Chinese Communists were hardly in a position to find the allies necessary for waging a successful struggle for national salvation.

The defeats of his armies only embittered Chiang Kai-shek still further. In June 1932, while continuing his policy of appeasing the Japanese, Chiang gave orders for the launching of a fourth expedition against all the Soviet areas, assigning over 600,000 troops for this purpose. This time the KMT forces achieved at least a partial success, for the sizable Red Army units in the recently expanded Hupei-Honan-Anhwei Soviet Area, led by Chang Kuo-t'ao and Hsü Hsiang-ch'ien, decided to abandon the area and retreat to Szechuan. Nonetheless, the main attack on the Central Area, which continued until April 1933, was beaten back once again by the Red Army. During this period, when the Soviet areas were facing the increasingly intensive and dangerous offensives of the KMT army, the factional struggle within the CCP leadership continued unabated. Due to KMT repressions, which led to the smashing of the Communist underground in many areas, almost all of the surviving leaders had been forced to take refuge in the Central Soviet Area. It was here that the incessant debates on the determination of future policies took place. The main contestants were the members of the Returned Students faction and Mao Tse-tung and his followers, and of the main issues involved the question of the strategy to be employed against the KMT offensives proved ultimately to be the most important. In actual fact, the former group emerged victorious; its representatives took over the leading posts in the CCP and the Red Army, while Mao's political position was appreciably weakened. However, it should be noted that an exact reconstruction of this conflict, whose implications are very far-reaching, for they touched also on the fundamental problem of relations between the CCP and the CPSU, is no easy task. Perhaps the greatest complication arises from the tendentious nature of the data available, and even more from the problem involved in assessing the role and policies of Mao Tse-tung himself. In this respect one is usually faced with two extremes; either hagiographical adulation or vehement denigration which, oddly, do have one trait in common, in that both succumb to the Carlylean interpretation, and vastly exaggerate the role of a prominent individual in history. It would seem preferable to view the history of the Chinese Revolution in the years 1919–49 as shaped by much more significant factors than the actions of any single individual, whose survival in this tragic period was, in any case, determined largely by chance.

Emboldened by the partial successes gained during the fourth expedition, the Nanking regime began its preparations in July 1933 for what it hoped to be the final assault on the Soviet areas. Chiang Kai-shek's large staff of German military advisors drew up the basic strategic plan of the future operations, which envisaged the complete encirclement of the Central Area and its methodical strangulation by means of fortifications and economic blockade. The fifth expedition was started in October 1933, with the bulk of the KMT army, from 800,000 to 1,000,000 men, thrown into action against the 100,000-strong Red Army. However, the outbreak of the Fukien Revolt in November caused a temporary suspension of the assault until the spring of 1934. In spite of all its efforts, the Red Army was unable to stem the advance of the overwhelmingly superior KMT forces; the territory of the Central Area shrank markedly, while the effects of the economic blockade became ever more telling. It is maintained by Mao Tse-tung and his followers that during this period the current CCP leadership altered the strategy heretofore employed, switching largely from mobile to positional warfare. Although this charge is denied by the only non-Chinese direct witness of these events, the Comintern's military advisor to the CCP, Otto Braun, it seems at least partially substantiated by the course of the military operations.

By the summer of 1934, the CCP leadership was compelled to consider the abandonment of the Central Area, and to plan breaking out of the encirclement in order to salvage its remaining forces. To divert the enemy's attention, two separate operations were undertaken. In the first, a 10,000-strong force, led by Fang Chih-min, advanced towards the Yangtse, but was shortly surrounded and almost completely annihilated. Fang himself was executed, and his head in a bamboo cage exhibited triumphantly in Nanchang by his

KMT captors. The remnants of this force, led by Su Yü (b. 1908), returned to the border area of Fukien and Chekiang to continue partisan warfare until the outbreak of the struggle with Japan. A second force, led by Hsiao K'o (b. 1909), Jen Pi-shih (1904–50) and Wang Chen (b. 1909), did succeed in breaking out of the encirclement and joined up with the troops of Ho Lung on the border of Hunan and Szechuan.

The time had now come to abandon the Central Area; the Kiangsi period in the history of the Chinese Communist movement, seven years of incessant struggle, came to a close with the loss of almost everything that had been gained. The disaster facing the CCP was practically as great as that sustained during the 1925–7 Revolution. Nevertheless, there was one vital difference. In 1934 the Party had at least its own armed force; the problem was to preserve this force, and the entire core of the Communist leadership which depended on it for its very survival.

On 16 October 1934, the main forces of the Red Army, between 60 to 80,000 troops, accompanied by 20,000 non-combatants, moved out of the Central Area in Kiangsi to begin the historic Long March, the most dramatic and stirring episode in the eventful history of the Chinese Communist movement. Later versions notwithstanding, there was only one basic goal at the outset – to escape annihilation by breaking out of the clutches of the advancing KMT armies. At the cost of heavy casualties, amounting to half of its total force, the Red Army managed, by the end of November, to break through the four concentric lines surrounding the Central Area. The latter, now occupied totally by the KMT armies, remained the scene of prolonged and bitter partisan fighting waged by the rearguard units of the Red Army, led by Hsiang Ying and Ch'en I. Another prominent Communist leader left behind, Ch'ü Ch'iu-pai, was captured and shortly thereafter ended his life in front of a KMT firing squad.

Having failed to achieve the planned junction with Ho Lung's troops, the Red Army became involved in long and intricate campaigning in Kweichow, capturing Tsun-i on 6 January 1935. It was here that the well-known and highly controversial Party Conference took place. The debates centred on the problem of the future destination of the Red Army and the responsibility for the disasters suffered; the resolutions passed were based on Mao Tse-tung's speech, in which he took to task the previous leadership for the supposedly faulty strategy which it had pursued. It was also at this time that Mao assumed a leading position in the Political Bureau. The long-range plan established now called for advancing to an area where a struggle against the Japanese could be waged, but the immediate task remained to evade the superior and advancing KMT forces.

Once again it proved impossible to unite quickly with other Communist forces, in this case the troops of the Fourth Front Army under Hsü Hsiang-ch'ien and Chang Kuo-t'ao in Szechuan, and the Red Army was impelled to embark on an enormous detour which led it, after weeks of manoeuvring in Kweichow, to an advance through North Yünnan in the direction of the upper reaches of the Yangtse.

After crossing the Golden Sand River – as the Yangtse is called here – the Red Army encountered the almost insuperable task of forcing a passage across the Tatu River, which it accomplished only owing to the indomitable valour of its soldiers. This famous feat made it possible to avoid the fate suffered by Shih Ta-k'ai's Taiping army, surrounded and annihilated precisely in this area.

Continuing an advance through the fiercely difficult mountainous area of western Szechuan, the Red Army, probably only 20,000 men by now, did finally effect a junction with the 40,000-strong Fourth Front Army in June 1935. However, shortly thereafter, divergences between the two Communist-led forces in connection with plans for the future gave rise to a serious political crisis. Chang Kuo-t'ao, the Fourth Front Army's political leader, called for a march westwards in the direction of Sinkiang, while Mao and the majority of the CCP leaders proposed to continue advancing northwards, in order to join up with Red Army units operating in Shensi, under the command of Liu Chih-tan (1902–36) and Kao Kang (1902–54). Ultimately, the decision to follow the majority's proposal was adopted, but during the march northwards a disastrous split of the forces occurred. Only the Red Army's original units, led by Mao, continued the advance to Shensi, overcoming with great difficulties further natural obstacles, while the rest of the troops, under Chang Kuo-t'ao, retreated to winter quarters in remote, Tibetan-inhabited Sikang.

In October 1935, the survivors of the Kiangsi troops, 7–8000 'ragged skeletons', broke through the last barriers to link up with the local Red Army units in Shensi. They had marched 25,000 li (12,500 km), passed through 11 provinces, crossed 18 mountain ranges and 24 major rivers. They had, in P'eng Te-huai's words, 'fought an enormous battle which seemed to have gone on forever', and performed a well-nigh miraculous feat of human endurance.

Shortly thereafter, the last Red Army in South China, led by Ho Lung, Hsiao K'o, Jen Pi-shih and Wang Chen, began its own Long March, leaving Hunan in November 1935. By June 1936, it joined up with the Fourth Front Army, still stranded in Sikang. A decision was taken for both armies to advance to Shensi and rejoin the troops under Mao. By October 1936, this task had been accomplished, but Chang Kuo-t'ao still had sufficient authority with the Fourth Front Army to order the bulk of its surviving units, 20,000 men, to embark on his original plan of proceeding to Sinkiang. This hazardous enterprise ended in total disaster, for the cavalry of the Moslem warlords of the northwest annihilated the Red Army troops during the march through Kansu. Only 700 men, Hsü Hsiang-ch'ien and Li Hsien-nien (b. 1907) among them, survived. The costly debacle indubitably put an end to Chang Kuo-t'ao's aspirations for leadership in the CCP. In 1938 he defected to the KMT.

Thus, by the end of 1936, around 30,000 men of the various Red Army units were finally reunited in one of the poorest and most desolate parts of the country. They had survived against all odds, and were soon destined to lead the CCP and its armed forces in the immense expansion during the war against Japan and to win ultimate victory in 1949. The Long March, in which they had participated, was to become an inspiring saga of unparalleled heroism and indestructibility, for it had saved the Communist movement from annihilation. Almost half a century later, it is still the few survivors of this epic who hold all the highest positions in the CCP and the government of People's China.

The Problem of National Unity, January 1935–July 1937

In 1934 and 1935 the Japanese imperialists, having consolidated their hold on the northeast, proceeded systematically to realize their further expansionist plans, which now envisaged the conversion of North China into a state of dependence similar to that of Manchukuo. The continuing appeasement policy of the KMT regime greatly facilitated the Japanese advances. In June 1935, the Nanking government concluded a secret accord with the Japanese, in which it agreed to withdraw most Chinese troops from Hopei. In November, it acquiesced in the establishment of an 'autonomous' government in East Hopei, which was followed up in the next month by the setting up of a Political Council for Hopei and Chahar. In both cases, the organs were headed by pro-Japanese politicians, including former members of the notorious Anfu clique.

It was against this background that a growing anti-Japanese movement took shape in the main urban centres, whose programme called for national salvation, to be achieved by ending civil war and uniting the country for resistance to Japan. Simultaneously, the CCP had begun to undertake a fundamental reassessment of its policy in relation to the current political situation. On 1 August 1935, the Central Committee of the CCP issued a declaration calling for unity of all the forces desiring national salvation. This was followed, on 13 November, by another appeal on the necessity of resisting further Japanese aggression. Furthermore, at the end of December, the CCP leadership took up the issue of forming an anti-Japanese united front, and determined that henceforth the main task of the Chinese Communists was to organize national anti-Japanese resistance. These steps also coincided fully with the basic shift in the strategy of the Communist International, which at the VII Congress announced its new anti-fascist policies. However, it should be noted that direct contact between the CCP and the Comintern, lost during the Long March, was restored only in 1936.

Intellectuals have played a truly significant role in modern Chinese history, and once again, as in May 1919 and May 1925, it was the

341

students who became the vanguard of the national salvation movement. On 9 December 1935, 6000 students from all the Peiping universities took part in a demonstration, whose main slogan was resistance to Japanese aggression. In spite of police brutality, a still larger meeting was held a week later, and the repercussions of the activities in Peiping were nationwide, giving rise to a new upsurge in the struggle for national salvation, known as the December Ninth Movement. Initially, the action of the students was largely spontaneous, although the influence of the Communist underground organization in North China, led by Liu Shao-ch'i, undoubtedly made itself felt, and ultimately the great majority of the student leaders became active CCP members.

The movement to resist Japan also swiftly embraced many centres of Chinese cultural and intellectual life, leading to the formation of National Salvation associations, in which such personalities as Lu Hsün and other prominent intellectuals participated. By May 1936, a nationwide federation of associations was formed which put forth a call for ending the civil war and for establishing an anti-Japanese united front. From the very outset of the national salvation movement, the Nanking regime regarded it with the utmost hostility, and in November 1936 seven of its leaders were arrested. Their trial in April 1937 only served to cast more odium on the KMT's appeasement policy.

The threat of further Japanese aggression did not put an end to factional strife within the Kuomintang, but actually exacerbated it, for Wang Ching-wei and his followers, always the strongest advocates of appeasement, now embarked on the road which would lead them to national betrayal. Simultaneously, Chiang Kai-shek's attempts to strengthen his dictatorial position had also assumed new dimensions with the launching in 1934 of the New Life movement. The ideology it was supposed to propagate was a weird hotch-potch of Confucian, Christian and fascist elements, with the latter clearly predominating, and the movement, actually run by the Blue Shirts, was intended to provide the Chiang regime with mass support. However, the enterprise, ridiculed by the great majority of the intellectuals, soon proved to be stillborn from the start, and turned into a hollow recitation of meaningless slogans.

After the completion of the Long March, the reunited units of the

Red Army still faced the possibility of further attacks on their positions by the KMT armies, since the Nanking government's determination to exterminate the Communists remained unabated. Nonetheless, the situation in Shensi did not facilitate Chiang Kai-shek's plans for launching a new drive against the Red Army, since the bulk of the forces in Shensi were not central government units, but the Northeast Army of Chang Hsüeh-liang and the provincial troops under the command of Yang Hu-ch'eng (1883–1949). Both these armies, and especially the Manchurians, infinitely more anxious to fight the Japanese and regain their homeland than to kill their own countrymen, showed little enthusiasm for Chiang's projects. By the summer of 1936, all fighting between them and the Red Army had actually ceased, and the negotiations between the CCP and Chang Hsüeh-liang, conducted by Chou En-lai, were in progress.

In the meantime, the Chinese Communists had taken a most significant step forward in the evolution of a united front policy, for in May 1936 they dropped their insistent demand for the overthrow of the KMT regime, proposing instead the cessation of the civil war and the formation of an anti-Japanese united front with the participation of the Chiang Kai-shek government. This initiative, sustained and expanded in further declarations in August and September, coincided with another rise in anti-Japanese sentiment throughout the country, stimulated in November by Chinese workers striking in Japanese-owned factories in Shanghai and Tsingtao, and a new students' demonstration in Peiping in December.

The obvious changes in the country's political atmosphere did not deter Chiang Kai-shek from pursuing his anti-Communist vendetta. On 4 December 1936, he departed for Sian, with the intention of replacing Chang Hsüeh-liang by one of his own reliable Whampoa followers, and compelling all the forces in Shensi to recommence an offensive against the Red Army. However, Chiang's scheme was soon completely frustrated; on 12 December, he was arrested by the troops of Chang Hsüeh-liang and Yang Hu-ch'eng, and presented with two basic demands – the termination of the civil war and the preparation of resistance to Japan. During the next twelve days, intricate negotiations ensued, in which a CCP delegation, including Chou En-lai, Po Ku and Yeh Chien-ying, also participated. At the outset the Communists, who definitely had not been involved in the plot, favoured a public trial for Chiang Kai-shek, whom they hated with boundless bitterness as the man directly responsible for the death of many thousands of their comrades and relatives. But, by 15 December, they changed their stand and successfully exerted all efforts to bring about a peaceful solution for the crisis. The position of the Soviet Union could well have been crucial in this respect, for it considered the arrest of Chiang as a blow to the formation of an anti-Japanese united front.

Although no written accord is said to exist, the negotiations did end with Chiang Kai-shek agreeing to terminate military operations against the Red Army, to reconstruct the KMT government and eliminate the pro-Japanese elements in it, to free the leaders of the National Salvation movement and other political prisoners, and to take measures aimed at preparing the country for resistance to Japan. On this basis, the famous Sian Incident ended on 25 December with Chiang's release and departure by plane to Nanking. While Chiang Kai-shek failed to adhere to most of the points in the agreement, the principal one was observed. The civil war was not resumed, and a lengthy period of negotiations relating to the formation of the new united front between the KMT and the CCP ensued. The prospect of the Chinese achieving unity faced the Japanese imperialists with the choice of either discarding their consistent policy of aggression, or launching quickly a war of colonial conquest. By 7 July 1937 they had made their decision.

15. The War with Japan, 1937–45

The Initial Phase of Japanese Aggression, July 1937–October 1938

The time had come for the Japanese imperialists to seek to accomplish their fundamental, long-cherished goal – the total subjugation of China. In pursuing this aim during eight years of war, they were to inflict unforgettable and unforgivable suffering on the Chinese people on an even greater scale than the many cataclysmic invasions which had been inflicted on the unfortunate inhabitants of the Middle Kingdom during previous centuries. This time, however, foreign aggression was to give rise to profound domestic changes which were to determine the country's future.

While it is possible to assume that the military operations launched by the Japanese in North China, which began on 7 July with the trifling incident near the beautiful Lukouch'iao (Marco Polo) Bridge near Peiping, were to be primarily a part of the earlier process of expanding Japanese control, it is more probable that the Japanese felt impelled to embark on a general campaign, aimed at bringing about a total collapse of China, before a further consolidation of Chinese unity and resistance would render the achievement of such a result much more difficult. In starting the war, the Japanese counted on gaining a quick and decisive victory, basing this calculation on the undoubted superiority of their armed forces in equipment, training and organization. Simultaneously, they banked on utilizing the political divisions of the Chinese, and especially on the presence within the Kuomintang itself of influential pro-Japanese elements, willing to collaborate with the potential victors. The international situation also seemed favourable, for there was no indication that the Western powers would abandon the policy of appeasement, which they had followed so persistently during the Japanese conquest of

345

Manchuria. Actually, there was only one factor which the Japanese had failed to take into full account – the will of the Chinese to resist, and their unwillingness to be turned into colonial slaves.

Within days of the Lukouch'iao Incident, the Japanese poured a large number of troops into North China, and since the Nanking government had failed to organize effective resistance in this area, they were able to occupy Peiping on 28 July, and Tientsin on 30 July, with the greatest of ease. Although its troops were busily overrunning Chinese soil, the Japanese government did not consider it necessary to declare war, referring to it simply as the China Incident. Since, for reasons of its own, the Nanking government also did not proclaim war, this anomalous state of affairs was to continue until December 1941.

The Japanese lost no time in following up their successes in the north by embarking on a new campaign in the Yangtse Valley. On 13 August, they began operations against Shanghai, and within a few weeks assembled a powerful force of 150,000 men in this area. However, much to their surprise, they encountered a staunch resistance from the Chinese troops here, for the KMT government had decided to preserve, at almost any price, control of the territory which had always been the principal base of its power. On 17 July, Chiang Kai-shek expressed the Nanking government's determination to resist Japan, and now his best divisions, over 300,000 men, were thrown into the bitter three-month-long struggle for Shanghai. The battle was decided by the superior fire power of the Japanese who, having wiped out almost the entire Chinese air force, also ruled the skies. On 2 November, the Chinese, having lost at least a third of their troops, were forced to retreat from Shanghai.

After the loss of Shanghai, Chiang Kai-shek sought the help of the Nazis to end the conflict, with the German ambassadors in Nanking and Tokyo acting as mediators. The Japanese, while willing to negotiate, decided to inflict further blows on the Chinese army to assure the acceptance of their onerous terms, which included the recognition of all their conquests. Within a few weeks, Japanese troops, now over 300,000 strong, began their drive towards Nanking. The Kuomintang capital fell on 13 December 1937, and immediately became the scene for one of the most infamous episodes in modern world history – the Rape of Nanking. The Japanese soldiery went on

346

a barbarous rampage, with the full permission of its commanders, raping and killing countless thousands of women, and slaughtering in a ghastly fashion tens of thousands of civilians and captured soldiers. The estimate of casualties ranged from 200,000 to 300,000 Chinese killed. The massacre was largely premeditated and intended to break the Chinese will to resist. Its effect was just the opposite.

Having taken Nanking the Japanese stiffened their conditions for a peaceful settlement, demanding also an indemnity to cover the cost of their military operations. On this, the negotiations reached an impasse, for the KMT regime was unable to accept the new terms, since such a surrender would have jeopardized its very existence. At the time when their armies had been advancing to take Nanking, the Japanese also carried out a number of successful operations in North China, extending their control of the main communication lines, and capturing such strategic centres as Kalgan, Kweisui and Paotow. Simultaneously, Japanese troops invaded Shansi, taking both Tat'ung and T'aiyüan, while other units swept southwards on the Peiping–Hankow line. Similar successes were gained in Shantung, where Tsinan fell to the Japanese on 25 December. All in all, the defeats suffered by the KMT armies in North China were as disastrous as those in the Yangtse Valley. In both areas the losses were immense; it was officially claimed that by 1 January 1938 Chinese casualties had amounted to 800,000 or 40 per cent of the total strength. Twenty-two out of 23 air squadrons and 50 per cent of all the artillery and tanks had also been lost. It seemed that only its vastness could prevent the Japanese from overrunning the entire country.

Although the victories of the Japanese, described above, were resounding, the basic aim of forcing China to surrender had not been achieved. Moreover, by their actions the Japanese imperialists had brought into existence the very factor which they had dreaded, the national unity, albeit only temporary, of the Chinese. In face of Japanese aggression, the Chinese Communists immediately called for resistance and the organization of a united front of all forces, including the KMT government, ready to struggle against Japan. On 15 July the CCP issued a manifesto, reiterating its willingness to cooperate with the KMT, promising to abandon its campaign for the overthrow of the Nanking government, to terminate its land reform policy, to reorganize the Soviet area in the northwest into a special

347

region, and to redesignate the Red Army as a National Revolutionary Army. Simultaneously, the Communists called for a reorganization of the central government on a democratic basis, and the full mobilization of all forces for the war against Japan. In August, the CCP announced a more elaborate, ten-point programme of national salvation, outlining the policies it deemed indispensable for a successful waging of the war.

On 22 September, the Nanking government published the 15 July declaration of the CCP, a measure which actually signified the formation of the new united front, which nonetheless was to differ in a number of essential respects from the earlier one in 1924–7. This time, the Chinese Communists did not enter the Kuomintang as members, or participate in the government it controlled. No common programme was established at any time. The possession of their own armed forces and territory, though both still very limited, made it possible for the Communists to preserve their complete political and military independence. Mindful of the heavy price they paid in 1927, they were determined never to abandon it.

On the basis of the new accord with the Nanking government, the Red Army, redesignated now as the Eighth Route Army, was reorganized. Chu Te remained its commander in chief, with P'eng Te-huai as his deputy. Three divisions were established: the 115th, commander, Lin Piao (1907–71?), deputy commander, Nieh Jung-chen (b. 1899); the 120th, commander, Ho Lung, deputy commander, Hsiao K'o, and the 129th, commander, Liu Po-ch'eng (b. 1892), deputy commander, Hsü Hsiang-ch'ien. Their total strength probably did not exceed 30,000 men, but within a year it had grown to around 150,000. The reorganization did not in the slightest way affect the basic nature of the army, as a highly politicized force led solely by the CCP. In the autumn of 1937, units of the three new divisions started their advance into Shansi, Hopei, Honan and Shantung, soon to penetrate behind the positions of the Japanese and engage in guerrilla warfare, the type of military operations they were superbly suited for. Thus began the lengthy and difficult process of building up Liberated Areas in territories abandoned by the KMT and nominally under Japanese occupation.

The establishment of KMT-CCP cooperation also put an end to the military operations of the Nanking forces against the remnants of

Communist partisans in the former Soviet areas in South China. The KMT government now agreed to their reorganization into the New Fourth Army; Yeh T'ing was its commander, with Hsiang Ying as his deputy. The new unit went into action in the rear of Japanese armies in the areas south of the Yangtse. By August 1938, it had increased in size from 12,000 to around 30,000 men.

The constantly expanding activities of the Eighth Route Army and the New Fourth Army were guided throughout by the CCP leadership from its headquarters in the small and dreary central Shensi town of Yenan, the capital of the Shensi-Kansu-Ninghsia Border Region (Shen-Kan-Ning), itself one of the poorest parts of the country, with a population of barely 1,500,000. Nonetheless, having set themselves the goal of becoming the leading force in the nation's resistance, the Communists soon converted their capital into a magnet, which drew to itself tens of thousands of the most active young people from the whole country and Chinese communities overseas. Increasingly, Yenan became for them the only centre dedicated to waging an effective struggle against the Japanese invaders.

The first stage of the Japanese invasion was concluded with the fall of Nanking; the second phase began immediately thereafter, to continue until the middle of May 1938. Since their victories had, in spite of their scope, proved insufficient to bring the war to a satisfactory end, the Japanese now aimed at smashing the remaining Chinese armies, by linking up the North and Central China fronts, and preparing operations for the capture of Wuhan. The KMT High Command, and most of its government, was now located in this vital centre. In the course of this immense campaign the seemingly invincible Japanese army met with a serious reverse in March, when a group of Chinese divisions, seeking to avoid encirclement, launched a successful counterattack in the area of T'aierhchuang, inflicting considerable casualties on the Japanese. However, the Chinese command was unable to utilize its rare victory properly, and by May the Japanese achieved their basic goals, reaching the positions required for the assault on Wuhan. In June, to stem the Japanese advance in Honan, the KMT High Command ordered the blowing up of numerous dykes to divert the course of the Yellow River; the Japanese were stopped, but hundreds of thousands of Chinese peasants lost their lives in the ensuing inundation.

In July 1938, the great battle for Wuhan was waged by a quarter of a million Japanese troops against Chinese armies twice the size. Once again, in spite of the staunch defence of the Chinese infantrymen, the superior arms and tactics of the Japanese won the day. In mid-October, the KMT armies evacuated Wuhan, while the government took refuge in remote Chungking. Simultaneously, the Japanese captured Canton, the last major port still in Chinese hands and the main entry for military supplies from abroad.

In the period up to the fall of Wuhan, the united front between the Kuomintang and the Chinese Communists did function after a fashion, although the actions of the KMT showed clearly that it had no intentions of relinquishing its monopoly on political power, or of granting democratic rights. The problem of the role of the CCP within the united front remained also the subject of controversy within the Communist leadership. Wang Ming, having returned to China in 1937 after six years in Moscow as the chief CCP representative in the Communist International, called for strengthening the united front at practically all costs, and his views were sharply criticized, although in a veiled fashion, by Mao Tse-tung, who stressed the indispensability of maintaining the CCP's independent position, necessary for assuring it the role of the leader in the national liberation struggle. The progressive weakening of cooperation between the KMT and the CCP and then the disintegration of the united front decided this issue in Mao's favour.

By the end of 1938, the Japanese imperialists had made immense gains; almost all of China's major cities, all the principal industrial areas, and most of the main lines of communication were now in their hands. The KMT government, having taken refuge in the backward hinterland, adopted a policy of passive defence, and henceforth, up to 1944, the Japanese were content to cease serious military operations against it, and to concentrate their efforts on consolidating their rule over the vast territory they had overrun. For this purpose they proceeded to set up a number of separate puppet governments in the various parts of the country. By the end of 1937, the Japanese had established, with the aid of such Mongol collaborators as Te Wang, an administration for the Mongol-inhabited areas of the north and northwest. In December 1937, a Provisional Government was formed in Peiping, composed mostly of former members of the Anfu clique, which was supposed to administer the Japanese-occupied areas in Hopei, Honan and Shantung. A Reformed Government, allegedly representing the KMT, was established in Nanking in March 1938, to rule over Kiangsu, Anhwei and Chekiang. In all instances power rested obviously in the hands of the Japanese military and officials assigned to these regimes, and the Japanese planned to link them up eventually into a more effective central government. For this purpose the Japanese intelligence service, which thought it knew the price of every Chinese politician and militarist, began negotiations already in November 1938 with Wang Ching-wei, with the aim of securing his services.

Polish patriotism notwithstanding, it can be argued that the Second World War began not on 1 September 1939, but on 7 July 1937, since undoubtedly the total failure of the Western powers to aid China and to oppose Japanese aggression, which constituted part and parcel of their general appeasement policy, greatly encouraged Nazi Germany to embark on her first campaign. In spite of the threat to the still considerable British interests, the policies pursued by the Chamberlain government in East Asia were practically identical with its European measures, apart from the additional trait of racist-tinged arrogance and smugness. American policy did not differ in any significant respect, and the United States remained up to 1940 the principal purveyor to Japan of indispensable war materials, especially oil, scrap iron and steel. Thus, throughout the entire period up to the beginning of the war in Europe, the Japanese were able to conduct their offensive in China with complete impunity and without the slightest fear that their activities would meet with countermeasures by the Western powers.

Only the Soviet Union, for a number of sound strategic reasons including its own security, followed a different policy towards Japanese aggression. Diplomatic relations with the KMT government, broken off in 1928, had been restored in 1932 after the Japanese invasion of Manchuria, and negotiations, begun in 1937, led in August to the signing of the Sino-Soviet Non-aggression Treaty. The granting of substantial aid to China began immediately, and during the first eighteen months of the Sino-Japanese war the Soviet Union became the only major source of assistance. Two loans of $50 million each were granted in March and July 1938, followed by a $150 million loan in 1939. Large quantities of war supplies were shipped first by sea and, after the fall of Canton, by land over the incredibly difficult route across Sinkiang. In addition to artillery, ammunition and tanks, the Soviet government also provided almost 1300 military aircraft. All the equipment was delivered solely to the KMT government, and none of it ever reached the Communist-led armies. A Soviet military mission of advisors was also dispatched, in which some of the few survivors of the group which had been in China in the years 1924–7 also served.

More significantly, over 2000 Soviet aviators, many of them experienced veterans from the Spanish Civil War, participated directly in the fighting against the Japanese from the beginning of 1938. Their role in depriving the Japanese of their complete mastery of the skies was crucial, especially during the great battle for Wuhan, and the struggle they waged with great success was the largest before the outbreak of the European war. The price was heavy – the remains of over 200 Soviet flyers lay buried in Chinese soil.

At the same time, the presence in the area adjacent to Japanese-occupied Manchuria of the powerful Soviet Far Eastern Army, led by Blücher until his tragic death in 1938, also provided indirect aid to the Chinese, for it tied down the forces of the Japanese Kwantung army. In July and August 1938, having resolved to try out Soviet defences, this army suffered a heavy and humiliating defeat. Direct Soviet assistance, however, came to a complete end in July 1941 in the wake of the Nazi invasion.

China Before the Outbreak of the War in the Pacific, November 1938–December 1941

The Japanese, having established the puppet regimes and embarked on the consolidation of their immense gains, soon became involved in an insuperable conflict with the population of the areas they had overrun. The initially spontaneous resistance by the Chinese to the rule of the Japanese invaders, brought on largely by the latters' atrocities and rapacious greed, was quickly taken in hand by the

Chinese Communists, who endowed it with an appropriate organization and military shape. Thus, while a stalemate prevailed on most of the lengthy frontline separating the Japanese and the Chungking armies, the struggle in the Japanese-occupied areas, especially in North China, was to assume an ever greater intensity.

It was the initially numerically insignificant Eighth Route Army which became the leading military force of the resistance movement. Small detachments were dispatched to various parts of North China to become the organizing cadres for the establishing of Liberated Areas and the building up of their armed forces. The successes gained under unbelievably difficult conditions were quite astonishing. By August 1940, the population of the Liberated Areas in North China had grown, according to Chu Te, to over 40 million, while the strength of the Eighth Route Army had increased from 30,000 to 400,000 men. In Central China, the Liberated Areas had a population of 13 million, and the strength of the New Fourth Army had gone up from 12,000 to 100,000.

The key to this amazing achievement lay in the ability of the Communists to gain the support of the population and to mobilize it for the struggle against the Japanese, in line with P'eng Te-huai's memorable phrase 'the people are the sea, while the guerrillas are the fish swimming in it'. The mobilization did not apply only to the military aspects of the struggle, but entailed also a far-reaching transformation of life in the Liberated Areas which, in effect, was tantamount to a social revolution. This was particularly true of the local governments established here, which soon won the deserved reputation of being probably the first truly honest administration in Chinese history. But the most significant measures pursued by the CCP pertained to social relations in the Liberated Areas. While abandoning the radical methods employed during the Soviet period, the Communists nonetheless untiringly pursued the goal of land reform for the purpose of obtaining the support of the peasants and solving the economic problems. A flexible tax policy, and the employment of existing and heretofore unenforced legislation to carry out rent reduction, led to marked changes in rural social conditions.

The tremendous expansion of the CCP's activities up to 1940 would have been totally impossible without the influx of new cadres provided by the tens of thousands of educated youth who arduously made their way to the Liberated Areas, and especially to Yenan. It was here that they received their training in the new institutions established for this purpose, in particular the famous K'ang-ta – the Anti-Japanese Military and Political Academy – to be delegated after its completion to the Liberated Areas for the vital task of building up their military and political forces. This task could not possibly have been accomplished by the surviving membership of the CCP, which did not exceed 30,000 in 1937. It was this new intellectual cadre, along with the most active participants in the Liberated Areas administration and the soldiers of the Communist-led armies, who now swelled the ranks of the Party to 800,000 by 1940. They had joined the CCP primarily to fight for their country's national liberation, and their belief in the necessity of social revolution was acquired later, from the training they received, and the education and experience gained in working among the peasants. In a few years, the leaders of People's China will be drawn exclusively from this generation.

Up to the summer of 1940, the Eighth Route Army adhered to the strategy of guerrilla warfare, thus utilizing its past experiences, and taking advantage of the country's vast territory and immense population. However, the famous Hundred Regiments campaign, conducted from August to December 1940, seems to have been a departure from this mode of warfare. In this offensive, launched by 400,000 troops, almost the entire strength of the Eighth Route Army, considerable casualties were inflicted on the unsuspecting Japanese, but at a heavy cost. In reprisal, the Japanese embarked on their notorious 'Three-all' (Kill all, burn all, destroy all) campaign which, waged with unparalleled brutality for almost a year, caused severe losses to the Liberated Areas and their armed forces. Nonetheless, the barbaric methods of the invaders ultimately proved counter-productive, for they increased the hatred of the peasants, facilitating their mobilization for further struggle.

The Japanese conquests in North and Central China had not only forced the KMT government to take refuge in Szechuan, but also gave rise to an immense migration of millions of Chinese fleeing from the occupied areas. The staff and students of some of the country's best universities also joined in this exodus, to resume their activity in such cities as Kunming, Chungking and Ch'engtu. At the same time, attempts were made to salvage as much vital industrial equipment as possible, and entire factories were dismantled and shipped westward. In both instances, the Japanese plans for a quick victory were frustrated thereby, and the possibility of further Chinese resistance enhanced. Nonetheless, the transfer to the west marked the beginning of significant changes in the character of the KMT regime. Deprived of one of its bases of power, the support of the Kiangsu and Chekiang bourgeoisie, the Chungking government became increasingly dependent on the reactionary landed gentry of Szechuan, while its military component became even more dominant. Its fundamental nature as a police state became still more apparent with the marked increase of the activities of Tai Li's notorious secret police. At the same time the KMT's attitude towards the united front became increasingly negative, and its determination to continue the War of Resistance considerably weakened.

The stalemate on the front led to a steady deterioration of the KMT armed forces, a process hastened by the barbarous practices employed in conscripting recruits, the brutal treatment meted out to the soldiers, and the endemic corruption of much of its officer corps. Hence, the army's mortality rate from disease and starvation became increasingly higher than combat casualties and, as an astute observer noted, its greatest victory was staying alive. Only the fact that the Japanese refrained from any large-scale operations until 1944 prevented the KMT army from suffering a further debacle.

Although the majority of the KMT persisted in its determination to continue resistance, one part of its leadership, including Chiang Kai-shek and his closest followers, began to assume a more vacillating position, while another group, led by Wang Ching-wei, was ready to capitulate outright to the enemy. The Japanese intelligence service concluded its negotiations with Wang's representatives in November 1938, reaching a full agreement regarding the terms of his collaboration. In December, Wang effected with surprising ease an 'escape' from Chungking to Hanoi, where the self-proclaimed heir of Sun Yat-sen shortly announced his support for the newest Japanese proposals for terminating the war, which were actually tantamount to the acceptance by China of the status of a Japanese colony. In the summer of 1939, negotiations between Wang Ching-wei and the Japanese government were continued in Tokyo. The slowness with which the Japanese proceeded to establish him as their principal puppet could be explained partially by the fact that they had by no means relinquished the hope that the Chungking government could also be compelled or persuaded to capitulate. The terror bombings of Chungking, started in May 1939, were undoubtedly intended to serve the attainment of this end.

On 30 March 1940, the Wang Ching-wei regime was finally inaugurated in Nanking as the only authentic Kuomintang government, in line with Wang's claim to be the sole genuine representative of the Party's programme and ideology. His rabid anti-Communism accounted partially for Wang's decision to betray his country, but a no lesser role was played by his vanity, ambition and the frustrations he suffered in his rivalry for leadership with Chiang Kai-shek. Wang had preceded both Laval and Quisling, but fate, blind as usual, was kinder to him, for he died in Nagoya on 10 November 1944, thus evading the settling of accounts with the nation that he had betrayed.

The Japanese, still engaged in secret negotiations with Chungking, finally recognized their own creation in November 1940. The existence of the Nanking regime did undoubtedly benefit them to a certain degree, for it signified a definite split within the ruling strata of Chinese society. Although they allowed their puppet regime to possess large armed forces, around 800,000 men by 1945, used primarily against the Liberated Areas, the Japanese exercised stringent control over every aspect of its activity. Moreover, while theoretically the authority of Nanking was supposed to have extended to all the Japanese-occupied areas of the country, it was additionally circumscribed by the rivalries between the commands of the Japanese armies in North and Central China, each anxious to preserve its own control. At the same time, the terror, brutality and unbridled exploitation only served to stimulate still greater resistance to the invader.

The cooperation between the Kuomintang and the Communists began to deteriorate markedly after the fall of Wuhan. The rapid expansion of Communist activity aroused an increasing apprehension in the Chiang Kai-shek regime which, by 1939, had reached the decision that the struggle against the CCP was of greater importance than the continuation of resistance against Japan. Thus, in May 1939, the first steps were taken to blockade the Shen-Kan-Ning Border Region in order to isolate the CCP's main headquarters from the other Liberated Areas; at least 200,000 of the Chungking government's best troops were assigned to this task, with the number increasing steadily in the following years. Simultaneously, armed conflicts between KMT units and Communist-led forces became more frequent in the period between December 1939 and March 1940, referred to by the CCP as Chiang Kai-shek's first 'anti-Communist campaign'. However, since the Chungking forces had few successes in this fratricidal fighting, the KMT regime embarked on a second campaign, lasting from October 1940 to March 1941, which was to lead to even more serious consequences. The principal aim was to eliminate the growing activities of the New Fourth Army south of the Yangtse, and the high point of the campaign came in January 1941, with the treacherous attack in South Anhwei by 80,000 KMT troops on the 10,000-strong headquarters unit of the New Fourth Army. Only 1000 men escaped, 2000 were killed, the remainder taken prisoner and shipped to KMT concentration camps; Yeh T'ing, the New Fourth Army commander, was taken prisoner, while his deputy, Hsiang Ying, was murdered.

The South Anhwei incident actually signified the end of the united front. The CCP, while castigating the KMT for its action, rejected Chiang Kai-shek's demand for the dissolution of the New Fourth Army, and quickly appointed Ch'en I as its acting commander and assigned Liu Shao-ch'i as the army's new political commissar. In spite of its losses, the New Fourth Army was shortly to expand its activities on a still larger scale. Thus, even before the Nazi attacks on the Soviet Union and Pearl Harbor, both of which were to influence the future development of events, the threat of civil war in China had become perilously imminent.

Japan's position had obviously been strengthened by the Nazi invasion of Poland, but it was the fall of the Low Countries and France which made it possible for her not only to exert more pressure on the European powers, but to seek to isolate China still further. Thus, in July 1940, the Japanese were able to force the British to close for three months the Burma Road which, apart from the Sinkiang route, was the only remaining line of communication with the outside world. In September, the Japanese had no trouble in compelling the

Vichy government to grant them air bases, and to agree to the entry of their troops into North Vietnam. The desire of Japan to gain control of the British and Dutch possessions in Southeast Asia was becoming ever more apparent, and hence the possibility of a confrontation with the United States also increased. However, it was only after the Nazi invasion of the Soviet Union that the course of future Japanese aggression was to be determined. The decision to ignore Germany's proposals for joining her in the assault against the Soviet Union, and to proceed with expansion in Southeast Asia, was taken in July, and Japanese troops marched into South Vietnam, a move to which the United States responded by freezing Japanese assets.

Since the end of 1938, and especially after the outbreak of the war in Europe, the United States began to play the leading role in determining the attitude of the West towards the Sino-Japanese conflict. The first American loan to China, for the sum of $25 million, was signed in February 1939, but no restrictions were placed as yet on American trade with Japan. A second loan of $20 million was granted in March 1940, a third, of $25 million, in September, followed by a credit of $100 million in November. In each case, the timing was clearly motivated by current political needs, and the basic aim throughout was to bolster the KMT government's willingness to continue its resistance to Japan. However, the Chiang Kai-shek regime, whose appetite for American aid grew steadily, increasingly employed the funds received primarily for strengthening its own position. Simultaneously, more and more convinced that war between the United States and Japan was inevitable, the Chungking government began to employ the unsubtle tactics of blackmailing the Americans with the threat that the failure to grant more aid could lead to its abandonment of the struggle against the Japanese. In March 1941, Roosevelt extended the provisions of the new Lend-Lease Act to China, which was to serve as the basis for furnishing the bulk of future aid. While the demands presented by the KMT government were quite elaborate, the realities of the war in Europe, to which top priority was assigned, limited the quantity of material shipped to China to a small fraction of the total granted under Lend-Lease.

The Chinese Communist Movement During the War in the Pacific, December 1941–August 1945

The outbreak of the War in the Pacific did not diminish the intensity of the struggle of the Liberated Areas against the Japanese invaders, especially in North China where the latter continued their barbarous 'Three-all' campaign. Although the losses suffered were severe, in 1943 the armed forces of the Liberated Areas were able to resume their slow but steady expansion. By the end of 1944, the population had grown to 80 million, and close to 100 million by the spring of 1945, in nineteen different Liberated Areas, scattered throughout the entire country, from North Hopei to Hainan Island. The Communists maintained that by April 1944 the regular forces of the Eighth Route Army numbered 320,000 men, while the New Fourth Army had grown to 150,000. Both were said to be backed by local militia units of over two million men. Exactly a year later, Chu Te claimed that both armies had almost doubled in size, numbering 910,000, and were responsible for tying down 56 per cent of all the Japanese troops in China and 95 per cent of their puppet forces. The qualitative difference between the Communist-led forces and the KMT army was even more significant, for it was shortly to prove a crucial factor in determining the country's fate. Composed almost entirely of peasant volunteers, the Eighth Route Army and the New Fourth Army were organized on the principles of the Red Army. Hence, as much attention was paid to political and ideological education as to military training, with the result that almost a third of its officers and men became CCP members. In this highly motivated force the soldiers were treated as human beings, and their behaviour towards the population also differed radically from the practices of the Chungking army, in which the habits of the warlord era still largely prevailed. Thus, the peasants of the Liberated Areas came to regard the Communist-led armies as their own defenders against the depredations of the Japanese and puppet forces. One important drawback did exist. The arms and equipment available, acquired mostly by capture from the enemy, were woefully inadequate and hence, apart from its advantages against a technically superior foe, guerrilla warfare remained the only mode of struggle that could be pursued with success.

The great expansion of the Liberated Areas and their armed forces led, as noted, also to the phenomenal growth of the CCP. While the Communists also conducted underground activities in the main Japanese-occupied cities and in the areas under the rule of the Chungking government, it is clear that the great majority of the members were recruited in the Liberated Areas. It was probably the rapidity of this growth, and the heterogeneous composition of the new membership, which inclined the CCP leadership to embark in the spring of 1942 on a prolonged educational campaign known as the Rectification Movement. Its main aim was to achieve the ideological, political and organizational consolidation of the CCP, and the principal method employed was an intensive study of the Party programme on the basis of 22 selected documents, combined with criticism and self-criticism at interminable meetings. Mao Tse-tung's well-known talks on art and literature, given in May 1942, were characteristic of the main direction of the Rectification Movement. Much stress was placed on the supposed proletarian nature of the Party's ideological and political programme, which did not in the least alter the fact that the CCP was composed overwhelmingly of peasants, led by intellectuals of various origins, and that the working class had ceased since 1927 to play a significant role in it.

One of the results of the Rectification Movement, which actually was carried well into 1944, was to strengthen the position in the CCP leadership of Mao Tse-tung and his closest followers, since it was in this period that they emerged victorious from the factional struggle with the group represented by Wang Ming. The principal issue at stake was the proper assessment of the national factor in the Chinese Revolution, in purported counterposition to the interests of the international Communist movement, as interpreted by the Soviet Communist Party. The dichotomy, always completely false, nevertheless lay at the foundation of all the debates from 1927 to 1938, continuously stimulated by basic differences in the approach to and the evaluation of the situation in China, and the policies to be pursued. Wang Ming and some of his colleagues, defeated in this round of embittered disputations, were subsequently removed from all important leadership posts. They retained their Party cards and their heads, for the Chinese Communist leaders showed no inclination, at this time, of instituting Stalin-style purges of their own comrades.

Although political consolidation was undoubtedly the greatest concern of the CCP leadership it was also compelled to devote much of its attention to the very serious economic difficulties besetting the Liberated Areas. A consistent and successful campaign was undertaken to lessen the burdens on the rural population by decreasing the size of the administration and making the armed forces largely self-supporting. To achieve the latter the army units engaged in large-scale agricultural production, and it seems almost certain that in this endeavour the historically minded Chinese Communists were simply drawing on the past, on the well-known examples of the military colonies, established already during the Han. Much effort was also devoted to expanding agricultural and handicraft production in the Liberated Areas in order to improve living conditions.

From the outset of the Sino-Japanese war, the Chinese Communists had assigned primacy to the task of national liberation, subordinating to it the social and political transformation of the country, which they continued to deem indispensable as soon as victory could be achieved. But the war in China had become, since 1 September 1939, and even more after 21 June and 7 December 1941, only a part of the immense conflict to which the term 'the Second World War' is applied – an inexact catch-all, since it actually embraced a number of distinct wars, waged very differently by its participants. In the case of China, it became patently obvious from 1942 on that her liberation would depend increasingly on the success of the anti-fascist coalition on other fronts. Thus, the slow but steady progress in 1943 and 1944, the costly but crucial success of the Soviet armies, particularly at Stalingrad, the North African campaign, and finally the opening of the Second Front in Europe in June 1944, decided the issue in the more important European theatre. At the same time, the great Japanese successes in the War of the Pacific had come to an end in the Battle of Midway in June 1942, and by the summer of 1944 the capture of the Marianas pointed to the victory in East Asia as well.

It was against this background of certitude in the ultimate victory that the CCP held its long-delayed Seventh Party Congress in Yenan.

The sessions lasted from 23 April to 11 June 1945, and were attended by 544 delegates, representing 1,210,000 members. Mao Tse-tung delivered the main political report, Chu Te summed up the achievements of the armed forces, while Liu Shao-ch'i dealt with the problems of the Party's organization. The latter paid fulsome praise to Mao, referring to his works as the 'Thought of Mao Tse-tung'. The Congress did actually constitute an important stage in the process of creating the personality cult of Mao; it is possible that this resulted, at least in part, from the conscious decision of the CCP leaders that such a cult, in which Mao Tse-tung was to be a charismatic symbol of the Party's achievements and aspirations, would prove advantageous. In any case, in 1945 it had not yet reached the sickening proportions of the years 1966–9.

The principal goal of the CCP, as outlined at the Congress, was to strive to put an end to the dictatorship of the Kuomintang, to be replaced by a democratic coalition government, in which the Communists would participate. It was maintained that such a government could finally carry out the anti-feudal and anti-imperialist tasks of the Chinese Revolution, in line with the concept put forth in June 1940 by Mao Tse-tung in his 'On New Democracy'. In this work Mao envisaged a lengthy period of transition, in which such a government, led by the proletariat, would implement fundamental changes, the land reform and the nationalization of the key sectors of the economy. However, all such plans were predicated partially on the unlikely premise that the KMT would abandon its monopoly of political power.

Assuredly, the Communists also took into account the distinct possibility that, after the termination of the war, the Chiang Kai-shek regime would try to recover control of the entire country, and thus plunge China once more into civil war, and made the appropriate preparations for such an eventuality. Japan's final downfall still remained to be achieved, and the greatly increased involvement of the United States in Chinese affairs added a vital factor to complicate still further the sufficiently intricate domestic situation.

Kuomintang China, 1942–5

The entry of the United States into the war was greeted with relief by the Chungking government, since it could now envisage the prospect of victory over Japan, attained primarily, if not exclusively, by the efforts of China's new ally. Hence, from the outset of the War in the Pacific, the Chiang Kai-shek regime took an increasingly passive attitude towards the War of Resistance, while the process of its general demoralization made significant and steady progress. Corruption, profiteering and trade with the Japanese-occupied areas increased on an immense scale. Among those participating in these practices were many prominent members of the top ruling strata of the Kuomintang.

Simultaneously, the newly acquired assurance of survival and the hope of bountiful American aid served to bolster the KMT regime's determination to preserve its monopoly of political power and helped to enhance still further its reactionary nature. The latter was illustrated quite clearly in 1943 by the appearance of 'China's Destiny', a work ascribed to Chiang Kai-shek, which could be considered as the Kuomintang's fundamental programme for the future. The book's utterly obscurantist and xenophobic character was so obvious that the Chungking government tried its best for four years to prevent an English translation from appearing. The ideas represented in 'China's Destiny' actually reflected accurately the policies which the Chiang regime was busily implementing, and especially its rigid suppression of any opposition or criticism of its rule.

In line also with the policies adopted by the Chungking government after Pearl Harbor, the stalemate on the fronts, existing since the end of 1938, was maintained, contributing to a further marked deterioration of the KMT armed forces, which by now were, in the words of the American general J. W. Stilwell, the best expert on the subject, 'in desperate conditions, underfed, unpaid, untrained, neglected, and rotten with corruption'. However, a goodly part of these forces ceased to be the direct concern of Chungking, for the simple reason that by 1944 at least 56 KMT generals had gone over with their troops to serve Wang Ching-wei's Nanking regime, and thus well over half of the puppet army was composed of Chiang Kai-shek's former soldiers. It is quite probable that this strange phenomenon formed a part of what was referred to then as the Kuomintang's 'curved path of national salvation', for the main task of the puppet army was to fight the Communist-led guerrilla forces, and after Japan's defeat they were to revert to their previous allegiance and assist the Chungking regime in recovering the territory it had lost. After VJ Day, this is exactly what did happen.

The economic position of the Chungking government, exacerbated by the loss of the most highly developed areas, also declined steadily from 1942 on. The KMT authorities proved totally incapable of preventing the emergence of a fatal inflationary spiral; the annual rate of inflation increased from 160 per cent in the years 1939–41, to 300 per cent in the 1942–5 period. Actually, the process was stimulated by the government's recourse to the printing presses for covering its expenditures, and thus while in 1937 the amount of currency issued was Ch $2060 million, it reached in 1945 the astronomic sum of Ch $1,031,900 million. The economic crisis produced thus affected the living standards of almost the entire population, but the rural areas suffered the most, for after the outset of the war the KMT government initiated a new grain tax, the collection of which, accompanied by incredible corruption, led to a further impoverishment of the peasants. Moreover, the ruthless methods employed were also responsible for causing one of the greatest disasters of the war years, the Honan famine. By their refusal to remit taxation after a drought and their failure to furnish relief aid, the KMT authorities brought about a man-made famine, lasting from the summer of 1942 to the spring of 1943, in which between 2 to 3 million men, women and children died of starvation. The Honan famine was only one illustration of the utter callousness of the Kuomintang towards the peasants, for which it was soon to pay an appropriate price.

The Chiang Kai-shek regime lost little time after Pearl Harbor in stretching out its hands for American aid. In January 1942, it requested the granting of a $500 million loan, then a huge sum, and quickly succeeded in obtaining it. This incident was but the first in the long series of Sino-American contacts, for the United States quickly became involved in all the aspects of the situation in China, and hence American policy also became an important factor in shaping the future course of Chinese development. After Pearl Harbor, it was based primarily on the desire to keep China in the war for the dual purpose of tying up Japanese forces and serving as a future base for operations against Japan. This military view was of prime importance, while the political aspects were relegated rather to the post-war future. As envisaged by Roosevelt, whose personal influence in formulating American policy towards China was considerable, China was to be treated as a potential Great Power and a reliable future United States ally – in fact, a partner, a very junior one to be sure, in the reconstruction of East Asia.

The course of events was soon to prove that both the military and political premises of American policy were based on an inaccurate assessment of the situation in KMT China. In particular, insufficient account was taken of the Chungking regime's obvious tendency to concern itself only with its own political survival. Thus, from the outset, the American aid it was to receive in increasing quantity was employed not for conducting military operations against the Japanese, but stored up to be used in the coming civil war against the Communists, which was being systematically prepared for since the New Fourth Army Incident of January 1941. It was largely the question of how American aid was utilized by the KMT government which was later to lead to innumerable controversies between Washington and Chungking, culminating in the well-known Stilwell Incident.

The seemingly endless succession of Japanese victories in the first three months of the War in the Pacific dampened the expectations of the Chungking government, and the debacle in Burma, which entailed the loss of its last major land supply route, dramatically worsened its position. While the American Air Corps did succeed in organizing a replacement – the famous Hump from Ledo to Kunming – the new air route could never be more than a palliative, and hence the problem of the reconquest of Burma and the reopening of the Burma Road became a constant demand of Chungking. It was, however, only one of the many controversial issues which were to arise in the relations between KMT China and the United States.

From 1942 on, Chiang Kai-shek pressed constantly for an increase in the delivery of supplies, particularly of aircraft, in connection with the plans of his air advisor, C. Chennault, that Japan's defeat could be attained simply by the destruction of her air force and the bombardment of the home islands. This scheme was opposed by Stilwell, holding the anomalous position of Chiang's chief of staff and supervisor of Lend-Lease supplies, who favoured the concept of radically reorganizing the KMT armies into an effective fighting force, to be trained and equipped by the Americans. The implementation of this idea was, in fact, begun by Stilwell, and Chinese divisions were organized in India, earmarked for use in the planned reconquest of Burma. Stilwell, politically a conservative Republican, gave vent to his resentment at the endless tribulations encountered in his contacts with Chiang and the KMT regime in his private diary. His characterization of the Chungking government was pertinent: 'A gang of fascists under a one party government, similar in many respects to our German enemies . . . sympathy here for the Nazis. Same type government, same outlook, same gangsterism.' Couched in a more restrained language, the reports of the American diplomats in Chungking conveyed much the same picture of conditions in KMT China and of the nature of the Chiang regime. Hence, it would be difficult to claim that the Washington administration was unaware of the real situation in China. Nonetheless, its efforts to bolster the prestige of the Chungking government went on apace.

The high point of the Rooseveltian policy of seeking to convert the moribund KMT regime into a 'Great Power' came during the Cairo Conference (22–26 November 1943), to which Chiang Kai-shek was invited. One positive result was at least achieved, since, for the above purpose, the intention of restoring to China all the territory seized by Japan – Taiwan, the Pescadores and Manchuria – was unequivocally affirmed by the United States and Britain. The Teheran Conference, held a month later, was nonetheless of still greater significance, for, in the negotiations with Roosevelt and Churchill, Stalin confirmed the promise that the Soviet Union would enter into the war against Japan after the conclusion of military operations against Germany. Such an eventuality obviously affected the role to be assigned to KMT China in the final stage of the War in the Pacific. Moreover, within a few months, the negligible value of the Chungking regime as a military factor was to be revealed in a dramatic fashion.

The Final Stage of the War in the Pacific, June 1944–August 1945

In the spring of 1944, the Japanese embarked on the first large-scale campaign in China since the end of 1938, known as the Ichigo offensive. The basic plan was to take over the parts of the north–south railways still in Chinese hands, to establish complete control of a communication zone from Manchuria to Vietnam, and to destroy the recently expanded American air bases in Southwest China. In April, the Japanese quickly succeeded in routing completely the KMT armies in Honan, and in May they began their assault in Hunan, the first phase of which culminated with the fall of Ch'angsha on 18 June. Upon resuming their offensive, the Japanese not only took the remainder of Hunan, but also advanced into Kwangsi, terminating their drive with the capture of Kweilin on 10 November. In the course of the Japanese offensive, the Americans were forced to demolish all their bases but one, destroying huge quantities of equipment and fuel.

In view of the above disaster the prospect of using Kuomintang China as a base for future operations against Japan became exceedingly dubious. Nonetheless, American involvement in China increased still more, partially due to the fear of the US government that a complete collapse of the Chungking regime was imminent. Already in July 1944, the Roosevelt administration proposed the appointment of Stilwell as commander in chief of all the Chinese armies, including the Communist-led forces. Such a concept, which also called for the furnishing of arms and equipment to the latter, was obviously anathema to Chiang Kai-shek. The tense and critical negotiations between Washington and Chungking on the issue continued to the beginning of October and ended, due to his still effective blackmailing tactics, in a victory for Chiang and the recall of Stilwell, his hated antagonist.

In the course of the War in the Pacific the United States government became increasingly aware of the growing importance of the struggle waged by the CCP and the Liberated Areas against Japan. From the American point of view, the desirability of establishing direct contact with the Communist leadership, both for political and military purposes, was obvious. In the summer of 1944, Washington succeeded in obtaining the reluctant acquiescence of Chungking to the dispatch of an American mission to Yenan. Its arrival there on 4 July initiated a series of intricate negotiations between the CCP and the Roosevelt administration, while the material gathered by the mission, whose members included some of the best American China experts, provided Washington with an accurate assessment of the situation in the Liberated Areas. In particular, note was taken of the striking contrast between the conditions in the Liberated Areas and Kuomintang China, between, in Tsou Tang's words, 'the dynamism, hopefulness, self-reliance and dedication of the Communist areas . . . and the gloom, stagnation, despair and selfishness in Nationalist China'. The information collected by the mission, both from its own reconnaissance and the data furnished by the principal Communist leaders, also fully substantiated the claims of the Chinese Communists regarding the scope of the activities of their armed forces and the extent of the Liberated Areas.

The presence of the mission was utilized by the CCP leadership for presenting to the Roosevelt administration its basic domestic and foreign policies. Such was the purport of the unusual six-hour conversation between Mao Tse-tung and Szechuan-born J. Service, held on 23 August 1944. In obvious expectation of a greatly heightened presence and markedly increased influence of America on developments in China, Mao stressed the CCP's desire for cooperation with the United States in all aspects, including the military, extending this idyllic prospect also to the post-war period. His assumption was that America would become the primary source of desperately required economic aid, which the war-devastated Soviet Union would not be in a position to provide. Mao's appeal for aid was accompanied by an appropriately derogatory appraisal of the Kuomintang, which he characterized as fascist, and of Chiang Kai-shek, to whom he referred simply as a gangster and blackmailer. According to Mao, the Chungking regime was bent on unleashing a civil war, but strong American pressure could compel it to agree to the only possible peaceful solution – the establishment of a coalition government. Thus the Communist leadership accepted American involvement in Chinese affairs as an inevitable phenomenon; Mao Tse-tung stated in March 1945 that 'there is no such thing as America not intervening in China! You are here as China's greatest ally. The fact of your presence is tremendous.' It certainly was, but the question remained as to which forces on the Chinese political arena were to benefit from it.

The attempts of the CCP to establish a rapprochement with the Roosevelt administration were conducted at a time when its relations with the KMT regime had reached a truly critical stage. Since the New Fourth Army Incident, the further deterioration of the Chungking government's position and the rapidly growing strength of the Communists had exacerbated still more the bitter enmity and rivalry between them. All attempts at negotiations from 1942 on had ended in a complete impasse, for while the CCP called for the replacement of the KMT dictatorship by a democratic coalition government, the Chiang regime countered with the demand that the Communists give up their armed forces and recognize the authority of Chungking. This was the crucial issue, recognized as such by all astute observers. Stilwell noted that 'the Communists *cannot* compromise; if they give up their military organization, they'll be massacred', while another Szechuan-born American diplomat, J. P. Davies, remarked that 'the Communists dared not accept the Central Government's invitation that they disband their armies . . . to do so would be to invite extinction'. In reality, the CCP had not the slightest intention of repeating the costly errors of 1927, and of depriving itself of the ability to survive.

By the autumn of 1944, the deadlock in KMT-CCP relations was complete. It was at this time that US involvement took on a new aspect, partly in connection with the activities of P. J. Hurley, Roosevelt's personal representative. On 7 November, Hurley flew to Yenan to embark on the first of a series of ill-conceived and ill-fated American attempts to mediate the KMT-CCP conflict. The discussions with the CCP leaders led to the elaboration of a draft agreement, which provided for the establishment of a democratic coalition government, and was countersigned by Mao Tse-tung and Hurley. Chou En-lai returned with the latter to Chungking for negotiations, aimed at bringing about the KMT's acceptance of the proposed accord. This, of course, proved completely illusory, the talks broke down and in the meantime Hurley altered his position, now devoting all his efforts to supporting the Chiang regime.

In spite of the above, the CCP leadership did not resign from its desire to cooperate with the Washington administration. On 9 January 1945, a message was transmitted directly to Washington requesting Roosevelt to receive Mao Tse-tung and Chou En-lai. The proposal was rejected on Hurley's urging, and sustaining the Chungking government at almost any price became increasingly the dominant American policy. By June, the Communist leaders were beginning to realize that their hopes for assistance and recognition by the Roosevelt administration were ephemeral; the first attacks on the United States for its policy of supporting the KMT government and 'aggravating the civil war crisis' were made in June and July.

As the prospect of the victory in Europe grew closer, the question of Soviet policy towards China became increasingly topical. Since the spring of 1943, Soviet relations with the Chungking government had worsened appreciably, especially after the success of the KMT in reducing Soviet influence in Sinkiang. From August 1943, the Soviet press began to print critical comments on the situation in China. However, the total involvement in the struggle with Germany necessarily relegated the problem of China to a position of lesser importance. The main pronouncements on this subject by the Soviet leaders were made in the course of talks with a number of American representatives, and while the verisimilitude of this material may give rise to some doubts, it would appear that Stalin sought to create an impression of being unconcerned with the Chinese problem, speaking disparagingly of the Chinese Communists, and expressing his approval of American efforts to bolster Chiang Kai-shek. The only reliable account of Stalin's policy is to be found in the report on his talk with the Yugoslav leader, Kardelj, in 1948. Indulging in unique self-criticism, Stalin admitted advising the CCP leaders in 1945 to seek a *modus vivendi* with Chiang Kai-shek,

join the KMT government and dissolve their army; he concluded that, having agreed with his views, the Chinese returned
to their country to act otherwise, thus proving themselves to be
right.

Although completely intertwined with Soviet policy towards
China, the question of Soviet participation in the war against Japan
was a separate issue. During a talk with Churchill in October 1944,
Stalin specified that the Soviet Union would enter the war three
months after the conclusion of the conflict in Europe. In the course
of the Yalta Conference (4–12 February, 1945) the political issues
involved were settled. The terms were tantamount to a restoration
of Tsarist Russia's position in Manchuria before her humiliating
defeat in the Russo-Japanese war of 1904–5, and hence required
further negotiations, aimed at obtaining their acceptance by
the KMT government. However, in order to prevent a leakage to
the Japanese, the Yalta decisions were not revealed to Chungking
until June.

Since the planned invasion of Japan would involve immense
casualties, the United States government continued to attach vital
importance to the question of Soviet entry. It was the main purpose
of Hopkins's trip to Moscow at the end of May 1945, and during his
talks with Stalin he obtained the latter's assurance that the Soviet
offensive against the formidable Japanese Kwantung army in
Manchuria would begin on 8 August. The issue was raised once again
at the Potsdam Conference, where Truman obtained Stalin's
reaffirmation, which he considered as the most urgent reason for
attending the meeting.

Thus, it was against the background of the certainty of Soviet
participation in the last stage of the war against Japan that the
negotiations between the Soviet and Chungking governments were
conducted. Ultimately, the complex problems involved, including
joint Sino-Soviet control of the principal railroads in the northeast,
and Soviet rights in Port Arthur and Talien, were settled, and on 14
August a Sino-Soviet Treaty of Friendship and Alliance was
concluded. The accord implied the continued recognition by the
Soviet Union of the Chiang Kai-shek regime as the central
government of China, but, in any case, the course of events in that
country was to be determined ultimately this time not by the policies

or actions either of the United States or the Soviet Union, but by the Chinese themselves.

16. The Victory of the Chinese Revolution, 1945–9

The End of World War II and its Aftermath, August–December 1945

The unexpectedly quick conclusion of the War in the Pacific gave rise almost immediately to an intricate political struggle between the contending parties in China, in which the issue of who was to take the surrender of the Japanese forces, and liberate the territory occupied by them, became the most urgent. Although the KMT armies had an immense superiority in strength and equipment, their best units were remote from the areas in question, while the Communist-led forces were but a few miles from such vital centres as Shanghai and Nanking.

In the ensuing tug of war the Chungking regime proved able to take over most of the areas held by the Japanese and especially the major cities, an achievement due almost exclusively to the actions of the United States government. The Americans not only embarked on an immense operation of transporting the KMT troops by air to strategic centres in Central and North China, but also brought their own units into China, purportedly for the purpose of rendering assistance in accepting the surrender of the Japanese. By the end of September, over 140,000 KMT soldiers had been flown in, while by October 53,000 US marines were busy occupying Tientsin, Peiping and other important points. As a result, the bulk of the 1,200,000-strong Japanese army in China surrendered and turned its arms over to the Chungking government, while practically all the Nanking puppet forces returned to their previous allegiance to the KMT.

At the same time as the race to take over the Japanese-held areas continued, political negotiations between the KMT and CCP were resumed. The Chiang Kai-shek regime, convinced that in view of its overwhelming military superiority and American assistance it would succeed in extending its power to the entire country, thus crushing the Communist-led forces and eliminating the Liberated Areas, nonetheless thought it advisable to employ political measures also, in order to avoid the responsibility for initiating civil strife. The CCP leadership, convinced that the KMT was intent on civil war, agreed to negotiations precisely because it desired to place the onus for the eventual outbreak of the conflict squarely on Chiang and his followers.

On 28 August, having accepted Chiang Kai-shek's invitation, the CCP delegation, headed by Mao Tse-tung and Chou En-lai, arrived in Chungking. The negotiations lasted until 10 October and ended with an agreement which was supposed to prevent the outbreak of civil war. The Chungking government promised to introduce a number of democratic reforms, to legalize the existence of other political parties, and to call a Political Consultative Conference whose aim was to establish a programme for a reorganized democratic government. However, two crucial issues remained unresolved – the question of the administration in the Liberated Areas and the control of the Communist-led armed forces.

In actual fact, the Chiang regime had no intention of honouring the 10 October accord which, in its view, was only a useful smoke screen to hide its further preparations of large-scale military actions against the Liberated Areas, scheduled to begin almost immediately. Thus, by the end of October, around 800,000 KMT troops were already engaged in offensive operations, which nonetheless did not achieve the main objective – the taking over of the principal lines of communication between Central and North China. The failure of this campaign convinced the Chungking government that more time was required for adequate preparations to launch a full-scale civil war.

From August onwards, the struggle for the control of the most important contested area, the vital northeast, also began. In the case of Manchuria the pretext of disarming the Japanese could not be employed, since this had already been accomplished by the Soviet army. At the time when the Chiang regime was winning, due to crucial American aid, the battle for mastery of the urban centres in the Yangtse Valley and North China, the CCP leadership undertook a brilliant decision. Having resolved not to compete with the KMT in the struggle for Central China, it pulled out some of its troops from this area and dispatched them, along with numerous political cadres, to the northeast, still a no-man's-land. While in September the various units supporting the Communists in Manchuria numbered from 30,000 to 50,000 men, by January 1946 the newly organized United Democratic Army, commanded by Lin Piao, was already 300,000 strong. It seems certain that the UDA was able to obtain from the Soviet army a good part of the arms and equipment of the Japanese Kwantung army which, nonetheless, was considerably less than the quantity taken over by the KMT, or handed to them by the Americans, in Central and North China. The contest between the KMT and the CCP for Manchuria would have been practically impossible had not the United States intervened once again. In October and November 1945 the American air force and navy transported 150,000 KMT troops to South Manchuria, thus enabling Chiang Kai-shek to start an offensive towards Mukden, which was taken on 12 December.

The plans of Chungking to effect a speedy occupation of the entire northeast were complicated by the continuing presence there of the Soviet army, whose withdrawal had been planned for December 1945. However, the KMT government, fearing that such a schedule would result in the taking over of Manchuria by the UDA, entered into negotiations with the Soviet authorities, with the result that the withdrawal was rescheduled, and took place finally in April 1946. At the same time, the departure of American troops, which had increased to 113,000, scheduled for the end of 1945, was also delayed, since they were still engaged in assisting the KMT to gain control of North China. The United States also expanded its large-scale programme of reorganizing the Chungking army; by the summer of 1946, 58 KMT divisions, numbering 747,000 men, had received American training as well as arms and equipment.

By the end of November 1945, American policy of granting unlimited support to the Chiang Kai-shek government had become the source of considerable controversy in the United States itself, brought to a head by the resignation of Hurley, its main protagonist. In the wake of this affair, the Washington administration was forced to restate its policy towards China, and on 15 December Truman issued a statement in which he expressed his government's desire to see the arising of a 'strong, united and democratic China', the cessation of hostilities, and the employment of political means to achieve unification by broadening the existing 'one-party' government. Simultaneously, G. C. Marshall, the wartime chief of staff, was appointed the President's Special Representative in China, with the mission of mediating the conflict in that country. Although the aims proclaimed by Truman seemed unobjectionable, the United States continued to furnish large-scale military assistance to the Chungking regime, thus strengthening its resolve to launch the civil war at an appropriate moment. In reformulating its policy the Washington administration had to take into account that an increase in the size of the American forces in China and, even more, direct involvement in military struggle was unthinkable for a number of reasons, including a factor seldom appreciated or mentioned – the amazingly rapid demobilization of the American armed forces in the months following the end of the war. The CCP leadership, increasingly apprehensive over American actions, nonetheless took a position of not opposing the Marshall mission, awaiting anxiously a further clarification of the supposedly new policies it was said to represent.

Mediation and Preparation for Civil War, January–June 1946

An uneasy situation of neither war nor peace prevailed in China in mid-December. In line with its strategy of seeking to place the responsibility for the civil war on the KMT government, the CCP agreed to resume negotiations once again, and on 17 December its delegation, headed by Chou En-lai, arrived in Chungking. Three days later, Marshall flew in to begin his ill-fated mission of mediation. Initially, some success was obtained, for on 10 January 1946 an agreement on the cessation of military operations and the movement of troops was signed, and an Executive Headquarters, representing the Chungking government, the CCP and the US, was established in Peiping for the purpose of implementing the accord. Simultaneously, the PCC, in which not only the KMT and the Communists but also representatives of middle-of-the-road parties participated, started its deliberations in Chungking; they were culminated on 31 January by the adoption of a series of accords on the fundamental political problems relating to the country's peaceful future development. It is clear that had the KMT regime honoured its word and adhered to the PCC accords, such a peaceful road could have been assured. However, within less than a month it became apparent that it had no intentions of doing so. In March, the KMT CEC met to discuss the PCC accords, and its final approval was hemmed in by so many reservations and amendments as to be tantamount to a rejection, thus demonstrating that the Kuomintang would not relinquish its monopoly of political power.

The ceasefire agreement also covered the northeast, but it did permit the movement of troops into this area, and this exception was seized upon eagerly by the Chiang Kai-shek government, seeking to extend its control to all of Manchuria. From December on, a steady flow of Chungking troops was directed to the northeast, almost all of them transported once again by American ships and planes. The units dispatched were the flower of Chiang's forces, the elite American-trained and equipped divisions of his own Central Army. While the Communists did not object to the entry of KMT troops as such, they did demand that the UDA and the local governments they had established be recognized. The Chungking government ignored this completely, and from the beginning of February attacks on Communist-led troops became common, leading by mid-March to considerable strife in the area of Mukden. The UDA responded to the KMT offensive by occupying the strategic town of Ssup'ingkai, halfway between Mukden and Changchun, and on 14 April a bitter month-long battle for its control began. Shortly thereafter, UDA forces also occupied Changchun, Harbin and Tsitsihar. The war for the northeast was on.

In launching its Manchurian offensive the KMT government committed what Chiang Kai-shek himself later characterized as its biggest fatal mistake. Although almost half a million troops had been sent to the northeast, they had been unable by May to conquer more than one-fifth of this vast land. Only the arrival of further reinforcements and equipment brought in by the Americans finally broke the resistance of the UDA in Ssup'ingkai and enabled the KMT armies to continue their advance. Finally, on 6 June, the KMT, in view of the fact that its forces were now strung out on dangerously long lines, agreed to a truce in the northeast.

The fighting in Manchuria obviously constituted a peril to the maintenance of peace in other parts of the country. Moreover, in view of the vital aid which the US was furnishing the KMT armies in their Manchurian operations, a distinct worsening in the relations between the Communists and the Americans took place, with the former coming rapidly to the conclusion that the principal role of the Marshall mission was to serve as a smoke screen for the further propping up of the Chiang regime. On 22 June Mao Tse-tung made his first public declaration on US policy since the end of the war; he castigated American aid to the Chungking regime as active, armed intervention in Chinese domestic affairs, resulting in civil war, and a threat to China's security, independence and territorial integrity. He demanded the immediate termination of American assistance and the withdrawal of the American armed forces.

The many warnings of the CCP and its proposals to confirm the truce in the entire country were ignored by the Chungking government, which interpreted them as a sign of weakness. Thus the conditions presented by Chiang Kai-shek for an extension of the ceasefire in the northeast were tantamount to demanding that the Communist-led forces agree to being pushed away from all the cities and railway lines, and scattered in the countryside, to be liquidated later at an appropriate time. The stage was being prepared for a new holocaust for the Chinese people, as if its sufferings during the war with Japan had not been sufficient.

The First Year of the Civil War, July 1946–June 1947

By the end of June 1946, the Chungking government's preparations for embarking on the civil war were completed. The superiority of its armed forces was overwhelming, for they were said to number 4,300,000 as against the 1,200,000 Communist-led troops. The advantage in equipment was also striking, since only the Chiang armies had sizable quantities of tanks and heavy artillery at their disposal, while the KMT air force, with a thousand American planes, was the unchallenged master of the skies. Moreover, the KMT

378

government ruled over much the greater part of the country with a population of 300 million, while the territory under Communist control, split up into separate Liberated Areas, held around 130 million people.

The strategic plan of the KMT High Command called for a series of offensives by almost two million of its troops against the main Liberated Areas, with the basic aim of destroying the Communist-led forces (referred to by the CCP now as the People's Liberation Army – PLA) to be achieved within three to six months. Initially, thanks to their marked superiority, the KMT armies did gain a number of successes, occupying much territory in most of the Liberated Areas and taking a number of important towns. However, neither the goal of destroying the PLA, nor the lesser but still important aim of restoring control of the principal north–south railway lines, was achieved, and the victories were bought at a heavy price. The PLA claimed to have inflicted during the first year losses of 1,120,000 men on the KMT armies, over half of whom were captured. At the same time, instead of being annihilated, the PLA maintained that its forces had grown to 2,000,000 men, the increase largely drawn from KMT prisoners. The Communist-led armies also claimed to have captured immense quantities of arms and equipment, in line with their earlier boast that the KMT troops always served as their supply train.

The successes of the KMT armies in Central and North China were also counterbalanced by the deterioration of the position of the Chungking troops in the northeast. As in other parts of the country, the KMT forces, strung out on long communication lines and forced to garrison strategic centres, became increasingly exposed to PLA attacks, which assumed the greatest intensity in the Manchurian area. By May 1947, the initiative in this vital battleground had definitely passed to the PLA, while the effect of the Kuomintang's misrule of the northeast, especially the mismanagement of the economy, exacerbated by the carpetbagging of rapacious officials, also helped to hasten its political collapse.

The KMT onslaught did not cause the Chinese Communists to lose their confidence and unshakeable faith in ultimate victory. But faith in itself would have been insufficient. The Communist-led armies also adhered to a well-tested strategy of concentrating superior forces against the enemy, avoiding disadvantageous actions and destroying the enemy's strength, instead of seeking to retain territory at all costs. In this fashion, by waging mobile warfare, the PLA could and did achieve a progressive annihilation of the enemy's forces, while strengthening itself by gaining arms, equipment and manpower.

The conduct of successful military operations by the above means was, nevertheless, only one aspect of the struggle waged by the CCP. The sociopolitical measures adopted at this time were of equal significance. The most important of these was the decision, undertaken on 4 May 1946, to revert to radical agrarian reform, replacing the policy of reducing rent by the confiscation of landlord property and its redistribution among the peasants. In carrying out this measure the Communists intended to rely on the poor peasants, always in the majority in the countryside, while gaining also the support of the middle peasants. The systematic implementation of the land reform, from the second half of 1946, on in a series of dramatic campaigns resulted ultimately in a social and political consolidation of the Liberated Areas, which proved to be of considerable value in the struggle against the Kuomintang. In the final analysis, it was the backing of the 'lao pai hsing' – the common people of China – which made the victory of the Communists possible.

The oddity of the political situation in China was revealed by the fact that while the civil war raged with full force from the end of June 1946, negotiations between the KMT government, now back in Nanking, and the CCP continued until mid-November, as did Marshall's efforts. The Communists, represented in the talks by Chou En-lai, demanded an immediate cessation of the KMT offensives, especially of the drive on Kalgan, as a condition for their participation in the proposed National Assembly. However, Kalgan was taken on 11 October and, elated by the seeming successes of his army, Chiang Kai-shek announced his unilateral decision to convene the National Assembly in violation of the PCC accord, a move which finally put paid to the negotiations.

In seeking to preserve its monopoly of political power, the Nanking regime did not limit itself to embarking on military operations against its main opponent, the CCP, but simultaneously sought to suppress all other opponents or critics of its rule. In July 1946, two leading members of the middle-of-the-road Democratic League, Li Kung-p'u and Wen I-to, were assassinated by the KMT secret police in

Kunming. The attempt to terrorize the intellectuals proved nonetheless to be a failure, for from December 1946 the student movement grew in scope, expressing its opposition to the Kuomintang's instigation of civil war. A series of large-scale anti-government student demonstrations swept the main urban centres in May and June 1947; the Nanking regime replied with brutal and ultimately ineffective repression. The main result was to accentuate its growing alienation from the Chinese intellectuals and the middle class. The convening of the National Assembly, the enactment of a new constitution in December 1946, and the formation of a new government in April 1947 with the participation of some non-KMT ministers, were all measures primarily for the benefit of American public opinion, and contributed almost nothing to alleviating the growing political isolation of the KMT regime.

The decision to embark on the civil war was undertaken by the Nanking government with a total disregard of the perilous economic situation of the country, ravaged by eight years of war and Japanese occupation. The policies pursued by it in 1945 and 1946, when the great bulk of the immense quantity of Japanese-held property ended up in the hands of the KMT oligarchy, had already created the makings of a crisis, which the civil war was to heighten. Close to 80 per cent of the budget was consumed by the expenses of the armed forces, and, since the government resources were insufficient to cover this immense drain, the printing press was resorted to again. The result was a galloping hyper-inflation. The paper currency in circulation increased from Ch $500,000 million in July 1945 to Ch $16,000,000 million in April 1947, while the ratio between the US $ and the Ch $ rose from 400 to 1 in 1945 to 50,000 to 1 in June 1947. The price index showed even more that inflation 'soared like a kite whose string had broken', for from 1800 in July 1945 (100 in 1937) it reached 60,000 in April 1947.

The financial catastrophe inevitably disrupted the economy still further. Both industrial and agricultural production slumped dismally. By December 1946, 60 per cent of Shanghai's factories were idle, while by July 1947 agricultural production had fallen by 10 to 40 per cent depending on the area. Under these circumstances the social base of the KMT regime, always a narrow one, especially in the countryside, shrank still more, since even the urban middle class, its erstwhile supporter, suffered from the effects of the crisis it had produced.

The beginning of the KMT offensives in July 1946 terminated the increasingly dubious American mediation effort. It did not end, however, the involvement of the United States in Chinese domestic affairs or Marshall's activities. The latter remained in China until January 1947, participating together with the new American ambassador, J. L. Stuart, the China-born former president of Yenching University, in the political manipulations of the Nanking regime. At the same time, the policy of furnishing substantial aid to the Chiang government for the purpose of waging the civil war continued apace. American military supplies, especially so-called surplus stocks sold to the KMT for a fraction of their original cost, poured generously into China, while sizable American military missions continued their training of KMT personnel of all services. By August 1946, the value of US aid furnished to the Nanking government since VJ Day was estimated at around $4 billion, a calculation on the low side, since it did not include the cost of training nor of transporting the KMT armies to the fronts. There is no doubt that the assurance of continued American aid was a prime factor in emboldening the Chiang regime to launch the civil war.

By July 1946, the CCP leadership had received enough proof to dispel whatever doubts it might have cherished as to the basic nature of American policy. On 29 September 1946, Mao Tse-tung noted that, 'The policy of the US government is to use the so-called mediation as a smoke screen for strengthening Chiang Kai-shek in every way and suppressing the democratic forces in China through Chiang Kai-shek's policy of slaughter so as to reduce China virtually to a US colony.' This was to remain the fundamental CCP position for the duration of the civil war; it was to be expressed with mounting vehemence for, in actual fact, the beginning of the civil war did not put an end to American involvement. Having washed its hands of the mediation episode, the Washington administration continued its untiring efforts to prop up the Nanking regime, while minimizing the scope of American aid and denying any responsibility for the course of events in China. The proclamation of the Truman Doctrine in March 1947, which only confirmed what the United States had been doing in China since the end of the war, reaffirmed the Chiang Kai-shek regime in its belief that, as a faithful and reliable American ally, it would continue to receive all the assistance it needed. It was this belief, and the assumption that its overwhelming military superiority would prove decisive, which set the Kuomintang off on the road to its doom.

The Turning Point – the Second Year of the Civil War, July 1947–June 1948

July 1947 marked the beginning of a decisive shift of the civil war with the People's Liberation Army going over from strategic defence to a strategic offensive. It was soon to prove to be the turning point not only in the war itself but also in the history of the Chinese Revolution.

At the end of June, troops under Liu Po-ch'eng and Teng Hsiao-p'ing, known later as the Second Field Army, began their march south of the Yellow River. Their successful operations led ultimately to the establishment of an extensive new base, the Central Plains Liberated Area, which constituted a direct threat to Wuhan and Nanking. Other Communist-led units went on the offensive in Shantung, Honan and Shensi, with the result that by the end of the year the main theatre of operations had been shifted by the PLA from North China to the limitless plains between the Yellow River and the Yangtse. Simultaneously, the Communist troops in the northeast under Lin Piao, the future Fourth Field Army, succeeded in a number of offensive actions in reducing the area held by the KMT army, squeezing the latter into increasingly narrow zones on the main railway lines. Similar results were obtained in North China by the PLA troops led by Nieh Jung-chen, and in the northwest by P'eng Te-huai's army, later the First Field Army. In the six months between July and December 1947, the Communists claimed to have eliminated over 750,000 KMT troops, thus reducing the enemy's armed forces at a still faster rate, while simultaneously capturing immense quantities of arms and equipment.

The above successes were immediately followed up by a large-scale winter offensive, lasting three months, in Manchuria. By the end of March 1948, the PLA claimed to have gained control of 98 per cent of the northeast, and completed the isolation of the still sizable KMT garrisons in Mukden and Changchun. In the spring of 1948 new PLA offensives in all the main theatres led to the regaining of considerable territory in Shensi, Shansi and Honan. The Communists claimed to have eliminated during the second year of the war more than 1,500,000 KMT troops (two-thirds taken prisoner); the size of the PLA had increased to 2,800,000, but the KMT army still remained larger, with a force of 3,650,000. By inference, it can be calculated that the PLA's losses in the two years amounted to at least 800,000 men. In spite of their great successes, the Communists did not succumb to euphoria, and cautiously estimated that at least three more years of warfare would be necessary to achieve complete victory.

When launching their strategic offensive, the Chinese Communists restated the fundamental aims of their struggle. On 10 October 1947, the PLA issued a manifesto setting out the CCP's political programme in eight points, which could be summed up in a single phrase – the complete overthrow of the Kuomintang regime and its replacement by a new democratic coalition government. At the same time, the CCP continued to implement the agrarian reform, and a new Outline Land Law was published on the same day as the PLA Manifesto, thus emphasizing the significance of the land reform as the most important instrument for bringing about the defeat of the Kuomintang. In effect, by June 1948, more than 100 million peasants in the Liberated Areas, had received land, in what was but the first stage of one of the most far-reaching social revolutions in world history.

In order to increase the political isolation of the Chiang Kai-shek regime the CCP reverted also to the tactics of a united front, designed to rally all the anti-KMT forces. In May 1948, the concept was put forth of convening a People's Political Consultative Conference for the purpose of establishing the new democratic coalition government. Almost all the non-Communist opposition groups responded favourably, agreeing to participate in the proposed body.

It was only in July 1947 that the Nanking government finally acknowledged that it was at war, and proclaimed a general mobilization, while Chiang called for the extermination of the Communists. However, the KMT army was not particularly successful in achieving this aim, and it was simpler to deal with such of the regime's opponents and critics who did not have an armed force at their disposal. Thus, in October 1947, the Democratic League was outlawed, but some of its leaders succeeded in escaping, and its activities were continued in Hong Kong. The island also served as a rallying point for a number of prominent KMT members, such as Soong Ch'ing-ling and Feng Yü-hsiang, opposed to the Chiang regime, who established a new organization, the Revolutionary Committee of the Kuomintang.

At the same time, the Nanking regime went through the motions, recommended by the Americans, of demonstrating its purported democratization by the holding of elections to the National Assembly in November 1947. The CC clique, still in charge of the KMT party apparatus, emerged not unexpectedly as the victor. The election in April 1948 of Chiang Kai-shek as the new 'Constitutional' president was equally unsurprising, but the contest for the vice-presidency, ultimately won by Li Tsung-jen against Chiang's wishes, revealed that the factional strife within the KMT oligarchy had increased even more during this critical period.

The failure of the Nanking government to gain the promised victory over the Communists and the rapid deterioration of its position placed the American government in a quandary in respect to its future policy towards China. Having no intention of resigning from its basic premise of bolstering the Chiang Kai-shek regime, the Truman administration was faced with the problem of determining the scope of further assistance to be granted to its moribund client. It was for this purpose that in July 1947, A. C. Wedemeyer, formerly Stilwell's successor as the main American military representative in China, was dispatched on a month-long inspection mission. After upbraiding in a proper vice-regal fashion the KMT elite for its failure 'to stamp out' the Chinese Communists, Wedemeyer demanded the implementation of a far-reaching series of reforms for the purpose of endowing the regime with the indispensable viability. After his return to Washington, although fully aware that his proposals would not be carried out, Wedemeyer recommended the granting of further large-scale aid to Nanking. Nonetheless, the question of how much assistance should be given, in view of the defeats being sustained by the KMT, became increasingly difficult to resolve, and also gave rise to a great amount of controversy. In November 1947, Marshall, Secretary of State since his return from China, announced a new programme of aid to Nanking, which was to cost the American tax-payer $300 million. The sum was supplemented in April 1948 by $463 million, and through this largesse the value of American aid for the Chiang Kai-shek regime had reached a total of at least $6 billion. By this time, however, the Truman administration had reached the unwelcome conclusion that the defeat of the Chinese Communists could be attained only by, in Marshall's words, 'virtually taking over the Chinese government and administering its economic, military and governmental affairs'. This was something that Washington did not dare to undertake.

The granting of additional American aid to Nanking exacerbated the hostility of the Chinese Communists to the US still more. They viewed it as 'an open declaration of war by US imperialism against the Chinese nation', and it is probable that many non-Communist Chinese were inclined to share this outlook, for further American assistance to the Chiang regime led to a prolongation of the civil war. This growth of anti-American sentiments was revealed by the upsurge of the student movement in April–June 1948. Thus the policy of the Washington administration led not only to the further alienation of the Chinese intellectuals and middle class, normally the most pro-American strata in Chinese society, but was to have a decisively negative effect on Sino-American relations for the next three decades.

The Final Victory, September 1948–September 1949

The successes gained during the second year of the civil war made it possible for the CCP leadership to order its armies to embark on three decisive campaigns – the Liaohsi-Shenyang (2 September–2 November 1948), the Huai-Hai (7 November 1948–10 January 1949) and the Peiping-Tientsin (5 December 1948–31 January 1949). By the beginning of these immense operations, the PLA had achieved a slight numerical superiority over the still much better equipped KMT army. It was not this factor which was to bring victory, but the superb generalship of the Communist commanders and the high morale of the PLA, counterposed to the ineptitude of the KMT generals and the growing demoralization of their forces.

The PLA forces under Lin Piao in the northeast, now already around 700,000 strong, equipped with large quantities of captured American arms and backed by 1.6 million peasants engaged in logistic support, began their campaign by capturing on 15 October the vital strategic town of Chinchou, thus completely isolating all the KMT forces in Manchuria from North China. The position of the main KMT garrisons in Changchun and Shenyang (Mukden) became hopeless. Changchun fell on 20 October; the desperate attempts of the KMT force in Shenyang to break out of encirclement were smashed, and the city was captured on 1 November. Thus, the entire northeast was now in the hands of the Communists, while the Nanking regime had lost an army of almost half a million, including the majority of its best American-trained and -equipped divisions. The northeast PLA, reinforced with huge quantities of newly captured heavy equipment, was now free to take part in the struggle for North China. Within two weeks of the fall of Shenyang, its soldiers, riding in their American trucks and jeeps, were pouring through the passes in the Great Wall.

The Huai-Hai campaign, waged by 600,000 men of the Central Plains Field Army and the East China Field Army (the future Second Field Army), under the supervision of a special CCP Front Committee headed by Teng Hsiao-p'ing, turned into a classic battle of annihilation. The half-million-strong KMT army, commanded by the top generals of the Whampoa clique and including what was left of Chiang Kai-shek's elite divisions and the rest of his armoured force, was split up into separate fragments and destroyed piecemeal in three stages on the vast plains of East China. Once again, the successful mobilization by the Communists of over two million peasants who dug the trenches around the encircled KMT troops and pushed the barrow loads of food, ammunition and fuel, proved to be a vital factor in gaining victory.

In the last campaign, the North China Field Army and the Northeast Field Army faced the 600,000-strong army of Fu Tso-i, concentrated in the three centres of Kalgan, Peiping and Tientsin. The PLA's principal aim was to prevent the escape of this force to Central China; due to the rapidity of its movement the PLA was able to accomplish this. Once again, the PLA succeeded in dividing the enemy forces into separate segments. Kalgan was taken on 24

December, while Tientsin surrendered on 14 January. With his forces isolated in Peiping, Fu Tso-i accepted the ultimatum to evacuate the city and turn his army over to the PLA. On 31 January, the Communist soldiers marched peacefully into the happily untouched historic city to which the proper name of Northern Capital – Peking – was soon restored.

As a result of the above three campaigns the Chiang Kai-shek regime lost over 1,500,000 men, and its military viability was reduced to almost nil. Although military operations, in which many thousands of Chinese were still to lose their lives, were to continue until the end of 1949, the issue of the civil war had been determined.

Even before its armies were to suffer the crushing defeats described above, the position of the KMT government, still in control of the major part of the country, deteriorated further, with the economy on the verge of complete collapse. Inflation continued on its mad spiral; the ratio between the value of the Ch $ and the US $ increased from 220,000 to 1 in January 1948 to 12,000,000 to 1 in August. The Nanking banknotes became worth less than the paper they were printed on. In August 1948, in a desperate attempt to remedy the situation, a new currency, the gold yuan, was established, and a number of special economic regulations introduced. However, since the fundamental problems of the economy had not been dealt with, all the stopgap measures failed totally. Inflation quickly recommenced, and by April 1949 the gold yuan had fallen from its original rate of 4 to US $1 to over 5,000,000 to 1.

Simultaneously, the KMT regime clamoured to Washington for increased aid. In November 1948 Chiang Kai-shek appealed to Truman for 'speedy and increased military assistance', and in December his wife, Soong Mei-ling (b. 1897), the KMT's most persuasive lobbyist, presented a request for $3 billion of new aid. Nonetheless, the US government, although still dispatching considerable quantities of military supplies to Nanking, was unwilling to commit itself to a new aid programme, for it had reached the conclusion that only direct American intervention could prevent the inevitable, complete defeat of the KMT armed forces. In 1948 and 1949, although the Cold War had set in already, such an enterprise could not be undertaken for the reasons already referred to. All that could be done at the time was, in Stuart's words, to scheme how 'to save what we can from the wreckage', and various futile plans, including the jettisoning of Chiang Kai-shek, were being elaborated in Washington. Without intervening with its own military forces there was simply nothing that the United States, for all its vaunted wealth and might, could do to prevent the total collapse of the Nanking regime.

As the great battles of the Huai-Hai campaign were nearing their conclusion, the Nanking government proposed on 1 January 1949 the initiation of peace negotiations. The primary purpose of this move was to gain time for building up its defences south of the Yangtse against the inevitable new PLA offensives. Having earlier proclaimed its intention to continue the struggle to the very end, the CCP leadership rejected the KMT proposals, putting forth on 11 January its own terms of negotiations. Basically, they were tantamount to demanding the complete surrender and dismantling of the KMT regime, which was to be replaced by a democratic coalition government.

Under these circumstances Chiang Kai-shek, leading the list of war criminals recently published by the CCP, announced on 21 January his decision to 'retire', and turned over his office to Li Tsung-jen. A three-month-long period of intricate political manoeuvres and negotiations ensued. During this time fighting ceased almost completely on all fronts; no small matter in terms of human suffering. The PLA utilized this interval to regroup its forces north of the Yangtse in preparation, if necessary, for a new offensive. Chiang Kai-shek, still of course in real control of the KMT regime, busied himself with turning Taiwan into his final lair, shipping troops, arms, as well as all the gold, silver and foreign currency reserves of the Nanking government to the island.

The peace negotiations finally got under way in April in Peiping, the new headquarters of the CCP. Although the KMT delegation was willing to accept the terms, the Nanking government refused to accept the final version and ignored the ultimatum that the accord be signed by 20 April. In response to this, Mao Tse-tung and Chu Te ordered the PLA to cross the Yangtse and achieve final victory.

By the early morning of 21 April the crossing of the Great River had been successfully accomplished, and 300,000 men from Liu Po-ch'eng's Third Field Army and Ch'en I's Second Field Army advanced swiftly towards the main cities still under KMT rule. Within two days the Communist soldiers had entered Nanking and begun their pursuit of the fleeing KMT troops. On 27 May, after a skilful encirclement, Shanghai was taken with all its industrial plants intact. In July, the PLA claimed that during the third year of the civil war the KMT army had lost over 3 million men, 2,500,000 of whom had been either taken prisoner or had themselves crossed over to the PLA. Furthermore, the Communists listed the capture of an immense quantity of war materials, most of which had been furnished to the KMT by the United States.

In the summer and autumn, the PLA, now more invincible than ever, continued its advance. By the end of 1949 practically all of continental China had been cleared of the enemy; the final battle was fought at the end of December near Ch'engtu. Only the width of the Taiwan Straits and the Communists' lack of naval forces made it possible for Chiang Kai-shek and his last followers to remain on Chinese soil.

The victory of the Chinese Revolution had been achieved primarily by military means, the only ones possible in view of the political and socioeconomic conditions prevailing in China for the preceding three decades. The dominance of this factor did not signify that other elements were not also present. The oppressive nature of the Kuomintang regime had given rise to large-scale opposition and resistance to its rule in the areas under its control, which also contributed to its downfall. Nonetheless, this was a secondary phenomenon, and the fundamental strategy of the CCP of seeking a military victory, by first gaining mastery of the countryside and then liberating the cities, based on its twenty years' experience of unceasing struggle, proved to be eminently sound and successful. Although the course of events in China was determined fundamentally by domestic causes, the influence of external elements was far from negligible, and the CCP leadership did not hesitate at the time to admit that were it not for the existence of the Soviet Union and the defeat of the fascist powers, the victory of the Chinese Revolution could not have been attained.

The above favourable factors had been, nonetheless, counterbalanced to a significant degree by the far-reaching involvement of the United States in its desperate efforts to uphold the

KMT regime. In the summer of 1949, when the fiasco of these efforts was obvious, the Truman administration found it advisable to vindicate the past actions of the US government by publishing its famous White Paper on American policy towards China. This voluminous compendium, a curious mélange of truths, half-truths and falsifications, actually constituted an unintentional confession of impotence and of the inability of the United States to alter the course of Chinese history. No lessons, however, were ever drawn in Washington from this admission of complete bankruptcy; within fifteen years the American government was to plunge into an ever greater and costlier catastrophe in Vietnam.

With the complete victory already assured, the Chinese Communists turned their attention to the establishment of the new government. After initial preparations in June, the Chinese People's Political Consultative Conference, representing all the organizations cooperating with the CCP, assembled on 21 September in Peiping. During a ten-day session, having adopted a Common Programme, the CPPCC enacted the Organic Law of the Central People's Government of the People's Republic of China, and elected the new government. On 1 October, Mao Tse-tung, as its chairman, proclaimed the establishment of the new government at a mass meeting on T'ien An Men Square.

The fundamental aspirations which guided the Chinese Communists during their long struggle were summarized by Mao.

The Chinese have always been a great, courageous and industrious nation; it is only in modern times that they have fallen behind. And that was due entirely to oppression and exploitation by foreign imperialism and domestic reactionary governments . . . Ours will no longer be a nation subject to insult and humiliation. We have stood up.

17. People's China: In Search of a Future, 1949–65

The Establishment and Consolidation of the PRC, 1949–52

The proclamation of the People's Republic on 1 October 1949 marked not only the victory of the Chinese Communists, one of the most significant events in twentieth-century history, but constituted as well the first step in the series of transformations which were to affect the world's most populous country. A multitude of tasks still faced the CCP; its armed forces had to complete their operations against the sizable remnants of the Kuomintang troops and, most important of all, a truly effective government, capable of administering the entire country and undertaking the restoration of the economy, had to be established. For the accomplishment of these aims the Communist leadership had at its disposal basically two closely interlinked forces, the CCP, around 4 million strong by May 1950, and the People's Liberation Army.

The military operations were concluded without any particular difficulty by the spring of 1950, and a considerable part of the CCP cadres working in the PLA could now be transferred to the task of building up the civilian administration. The entire country was divided into six large administrative areas, under the supervision of local special bureaus of the CCP, but directed in all important respects centrally from Peking by the Communist leadership in its dual character of leaders of the Party and the new government. While the united front principle was maintained and a large number of non-Communists received posts in the central government, the dominant and decisive role of the CCP was apparent from the outset. Within three years the Communists succeeded in creating a viable administrative structure, the first truly unified government in modern Chinese history, while simultaneously extending the functioning of the Party to the entire country, in most cases down to the village level.

The CCP established its rule under very unfavourable and difficult conditions. The backward economy, suffering from the effects of twelve years of war, was a shambles. Industrial production in 1949 was barely half the pre-war level, while the state of agriculture was only slightly better. Communications, and especially the railway network, had been destroyed to a considerable extent. Moreover, the country was desperately poor, with a GNP estimated in 1950 at US $50 *per capita*. The rampant inflation inherited from the KMT regime completed the picture of economic chaos. Nonetheless, by the end of 1952, the new government had succeeded in achieving a recovery in all basic fields, thus enabling it to proceed to the implementation of its plans for a fundamental reconstruction of the economy.

Although land reform had been launched in the Liberated Areas already in 1946, the agrarian system had remained intact in the major part of the country. The CCP, convinced of the necessity of carrying out the agrarian revolution to the fullest extent, pressed almost immediately for its accomplishment. On 28 June 1950, a new Agrarian Reform Law was enacted, and an immense systematic campaign was begun, which during the subsequent two years resulted not only in the confiscation and redistribution of landlord property, but also in the elimination of the landlord gentry as a class. In numerous cases this elimination was pursued relentlessly, leading to large-scale physical extermination as well. Both in the rural and urban areas a 'settling of accounts' took place, and often deeds committed in the 1920s were recalled and punished. The ruthlessness of this campaign, which partially coincided with the general movement to suppress counter-revolutionaries, exacerbated from October 1950 by the Korean War, left a heritage of dubious value, as demonstrated by the propensity to violence to be revealed later during the tragic decade of the 1966–76 'cultural revolution'. The agrarian reform, while satisfying in part the demand of the peasants for land, could not by itself constitute the basis for a development and modernization of agriculture, and it is clear that the CCP leadership envisaged even then a rapid transition to collectivization.

The total bankruptcy of the KMT regime had created a situation in which the establishment of a new government by the Chinese Communists was greeted with relief by a good part of the urban population, while the land reform gained it the support of the peasantry. The most enthusiastic response came from educated youth, and thousands of students were to be quickly enlisted for training as new cadres for the growing Party and government bureaucracy. Although the CCP had considerable experience in administering the countryside and dealing with the peasants, the task of ruling the cities and operating industry posed a serious problem and necessitated the adoption of appropriate policies towards the bourgeoisie and the intellectuals. Thus, in the initial period of reconstruction, nationalization was limited to the largest enterprises, and a relatively considerable sector, around 30 per cent of industry, was left in private hands, although under increasing state supervision. The banking system, on the other hand, was immediately placed under total state control. A large amount of private trade and artisan production was also tolerated initially. In this fashion the new authorities sought to utilize as fully as possible the limited resources of existing trained personnel. However, if any of the capitalists harboured illusions as to their position and the fundamental policies of the government, these were assuredly dispelled by the 'Five Anti' campaign (versus bribery, tax evasion, fraud, theft of government property and stealing of state economic secrets) waged with much intensity from February to June 1952 in the main urban centres, especially in Shanghai. It showed clearly not only the government's determination to exercise strict control over the privately owned enterprises, but also that the process of extending state ownership to all of industry would be speedily completed.

The building up of an effectively functioning administration, extending in the towns to neighbourhood committees and in the countryside to the natural villages, was accompanied also by the expansion of mass organizations of different types, all of which were intended to play an important auxiliary role of strengthening the influence of the new authorities. In some cases, such as the Women's Federation, they were assigned the additional task of working for the implementation of the new social policies being introduced, such as the very significant Marriage Law (passed on 30 April 1950) which had the basic and far-reaching aim of putting an end to the inferior position, upheld by many centuries of tradition, of half of the country's population. In other instances, as in the case of the trade unions, they were to be utilized primarily as a transmission belt in the

Party's efforts to disseminate its programme and ideology. While a complete control of all the media, existing from the outset, facilitated this task, the sad heritage of the past, and especially the shockingly high illiteracy rate (over 80 per cent), presented great problems and necessitated the undertaking of mass education in various forms. This aim coincided of course with the CCP's goal of ideological and political indoctrination of the country as a whole, in which special attention was to be paid to what was referred to as the remoulding of the intellectuals. The vital importance of this small but crucial stratum of Chinese society was certainly recognized by the Chinese Communists, and an entire series of ideological campaigns was waged for the purpose of inducing the intellectuals, some of them Western-educated, to adopt the Party's ideology.

All the endeavours of the new government in Peking were to be vitally affected within less than a year of its establishment by an external factor, the outbreak in June 1950 of the war in Korea. Whatever the origins of this conflict, the one thing that can be ascertained with complete certainty is that the Chinese Communists did not initiate it. In view of their domestic tasks it can also be safely assumed that they were not at all eager to participate in it. Nonetheless, when in October 1950 Chou En-lai's repeated warnings to the Americans not to advance to the Yalu were contemptuously dismissed by MacArthur, PLA units 400,000 strong, having sewed on their uniforms a small oblong patch with the inscription 'Chinese People's Volunteers', crossed the Yalu unperceived, and in a series of rapid offensives smashed the Americans back across the 38th parallel, capturing Seoul in January 1951. However, the overwhelming technical superiority of the enemy, particularly in the air, brought about the loss of Seoul in March, and the conflict settled down to a see-saw struggle on the 38th parallel, in which the CPV, commanded by P'eng Te-huai, proved capable, although at the cost of heavy casualties, of struggling on an equal basis against the world's strongest power. The China of the Opium Wars and the I Ho T'uan era had truly receded into a remote past. Having fought the Americans to a standstill, the Chinese agreed in July 1951 to begin negotiations which were finally concluded in July 1953 with the signing of an armistice.

The Korean War contributed markedly to closer relations between

395

the PRC and the Soviet Union. Even earlier, on 16 December 1949, Mao Tse-tung had departed for Moscow for his first official meeting with Stalin, and the somewhat peculiar negotiations which ensued led ultimately to the signing on 12 February 1950 of a Sino-Soviet Treaty of Friendship and Alliance, while on the basis of separate economic talks the Chinese obtained credits for the sum of $300 million. In the course of the conflict in Korea the Soviet government extended considerable military assistance to the CPV, all of which was later paid for in full by the Chinese. It was also logical that the Chinese Communists in the first years after coming to power not only counted on Soviet aid, but were also anxious to utilize Soviet experience in practically all fields, especially the economic. This attitude gave rise in many cases to a tendency towards mechanically copying Soviet features, to the point that when the PLA introduced a system of regular ranks it adopted for its officers' uniforms the Tsarist epaulettes which had been reintroduced in the Soviet army during the war with Germany.

The initial closeness of Sino-Soviet relations resulted also from the need of the PRC to bolster its international position in view of the continuing hostility of the Washington administration towards the new government in Peking. This was manifested not only by the American policy of blocking the entry of the PRC into the United Nations but also, perhaps more significantly, by the decision undertaken on 27 June 1950 of assigning to the US Seventh Fleet the task of 'neutralizing' the Taiwan Straits, which, in effect, meant extending full American protection to the Kuomintang remnants on the island.

Economic Reconstruction, 1953–7

The successful completion by the end of 1952 of basic economic rehabilitation enabled the CCP leadership to embark on a far-reaching programme of reconstruction, envisaged by them as a transition to socialism. The fundamental aim was to achieve a comprehensive modernization of the backward country by restructuring the entire economy on the basis of overall planning. In September 1953, the principles of the First Five Year Plan were published, but its final version was not to be adopted until April 1955. The basic premises of the plan, which was to cover the years 1953–7, were largely modelled on Soviet experience, and called for an appropriate industrialization, in which priority was assigned to the development of heavy industry. Simultaneously, the extension of state ownership to the entire industrial sector was envisaged and, in effect, achieved by the beginning of 1956. While Soviet assistance was of importance in the industrialization programme, since 147 key plants were furnished, its total value amounted to only 3 per cent of the sums assigned to the fulfilment of the Five Year Plan. Hence, the problem of the source of accumulation for the ambitious programme outlined in it remained crucial, and the inevitable conclusion drawn was that Chinese agriculture, in itself backward, would have to provide the main funds required.

It was the above factor which largely determined the decisions of the CCP to proceed with the radical transformation of the rural economy only two years after the completion of the agrarian reform. While the initial proposals for cooperativization were adopted in December 1951, relatively little progress was achieved during the next two years, with the number of cooperatives in December 1953 amounting to only around 14,000. By October 1954, it had risen to 100,000, at which time the intensity of the drive was increased by the Party, with the result that by June 1955 650,000 cooperatives had been formed, embracing 16.9 million peasant households out of a total of 110 million. On this basis of only partial success, the CCP leadership, Mao Tse-tung in particular, decided in October 1955 to speed up the process still further, setting a schedule for a completion of the collectivization by April 1958. In fact, the pressure exerted was so great that by December 1956 already 88 per cent of the peasants were enrolled in the cooperatives, and practically all of them by the end of 1957.

The initial collectivization of agriculture in the PRC, although carried out at such a rapid pace, did not entail as calamitous a disorganization and loss of production as had been the case in the Soviet Union, nor did it bring with it comparable hardships and sufferings for the majority of those involved. However, in view of the low level of the country's industrialization (in June 1954, Mao remarked 'We can't make a single motor car, plane, tank or tractor'), the newly formed cooperatives could not be provided with the indispensable equipment which would make it possible to take full advantage of the organizational changes and to proceed to a large-scale mechanization of agricultural production. This problem had given rise from the outset to considerable differences of opinion among the Chinese Communist leaders as to the speed with which collectivization should be effectuated, and these divergences were to be increased at the subsequent stage due to the strivings of one group, led by Mao Tse-tung, to carry out a further restructuring of the rural areas by the introduction of the people's communes. It should be noted that these debates, which in fact led to much exacerbation of relations within the top CCP leadership, were on the whole carefully concealed from public view, and a facade of complete monolithic unity preserved.

The rapid consolidation of the administrative machinery, and the successful extension of control over the entire country by the end of 1951, made it also possible to prepare for a transition from a provisional form of government adopted in 1949 to a more permanent structure. In November 1952 work on the drafting of the new constitution was begun; the pace followed was rather leisurely, for the final version was not completed until June 1954. It was adopted on 22 September 1954 during the first session of the new formal governing body, the National People's Congress. A larger degree of centralization now prevailed, the Greater Administrative Areas had been abolished in June, while the functioning of their equivalent, the regional CCP bureaus, came to an end in December 1954. The establishment of the government on the basis of the new constitution did not involve, however, a significant change in any respect, since the great majority of the incumbent ministers and officials, led by Chou En-lai (Prime Minister from 1949 to his death in 1976) continued to hold their previous posts, while all the fundamental policy-making decisions rested in the hands of the CCP Political Bureau.

It was in this period that the first sign of dissension within the Communist leadership was revealed in connection with the official condemnation of two prominent officials, the Shensi guerrilla leader, Kao Kang, former top CCP representative in Manchuria and subsequently head of the State Planning Commission, and Jao Shu-shih (1901–?), the previous head of the Party's East China Bureau. In February 1954, both men were accused of forming an 'anti-Party alliance' with the aim of splitting the Party and seizing power, and removed from all their posts. Over a year later in March 1955, the affair was made public; there is little possibility of determining the validity of the charges, maintained up to the present, but it should be noted that some of those accused of being Kao Kang's 'accomplices' have recently been restored to high Party positions. There are some indications that the episode could have been connected with the problem of Sino-Soviet relations. The latter remained outwardly still apparently harmonious until the spring of 1956, when the issues raised by Khrushchev in his 'secret' speech at the 20th Congress of the CPSU brought out into the open for the first time important divergences between the Soviet and Chinese Parties. On 5 April 1956, the CCP published its own evaluation of these issues in its 'On the Historical Experiences of the Dictatorship of the Proletariat', destined to become the first salvo in a long series of increasingly embittered polemical disputations. The range of problems involved was extremely broad, but undoubtedly the assessment of Stalin's role and the question of the cult of the individual connected therewith became one of the most important points of divergence. Although their own experiences with him had not been the easiest, to say the least, the Chinese Communist leaders, and especially Mao Tse-tung himself, refused to accept as valid Khrushchev's indictment of Stalin, which revealed only an infinitesimal part of the sufferings of the Soviet people during his reign. Instead, they continued to present Stalin as an 'outstanding Marxist-Leninist fighter' who had, however, committed some serious mistakes. In April 1956, Mao, with the typical Chinese penchant for using numerical comparisons, portrayed Stalin's achievements as outweighing his mistakes on a 7 to 3 ratio. The reasons for doing so were many and complex, but the prime cause rested in the discomforting resemblance between the means associated with Stalin's name and those which Mao himself was soon to employ. While the CCP did seek to draw some conclusions from the negative example of the cult of the individual, its failure to deal with the problem adequately was to be demonstrated with dramatic clarity within exactly ten years, when Mao launched his disastrous 'cultural revolution'.

In September 1956, the CCP held its 8th Congress, the main purpose of which was to sum up the experiences of the previous eleven years and to determine the main features of the country's future development. The Party had increased in size almost tenfold since 1945, for it now numbered 10.9 million members, 60 per cent of whom had joined it after 1949. Not surprisingly, in view of the composition of the country's population – the census conducted in June 1953 showed that 80 per cent of China's 583 million lived in rural areas – 69 per cent of the CCP members were peasants, 14 per cent were workers and 12 per cent intellectuals.

A considerable part of the Congress was devoted to a pragmatic and realistic appraisal of the achievements of the post-1949 period. This was particularly true of the principal report delivered by Liu Shao-ch'i; it pertained also to the approach to the future, as shown in the discussions concerning the Second Five Year Plan, scheduled for the years 1958–62. While the goals set in it were quite ambitious, they were on the whole realistic and feasible. Its basic premises remained similar to its predecessor's, with emphasis still placed primarily on heavy industry as the indispensable foundation for general industrialization, the country's modernization and the escape from the heritage of backwardness and poverty, still obviously prevalent. Politically, a tendency towards collective leadership was displayed, which in itself reflected the effects of the changes in the Soviet Union. Thus, while Mao Tse-tung remained Chairman of the Central Committee, a Standing Committee of the Political Bureau was established, whose members included, apart from Mao, the four vice-chairmen – Liu Shao-ch'i, Chou En-lai, Chu Te and Ch'en Yün – as well as Teng Hsiao-p'ing, appointed to the newly created post of Secretary-General. Simultaneously, the reference to Mao Tse-tung's Thought contained in the 1945 Party Constitution was deleted in the new Constitution passed by the new Congress.

The Hundred Flowers

The concern of the CCP leadership to bring about an ideological reeducation of the intellectuals, while simultaneously gaining the support of this almost four-million-strong stratum, indispensable for carrying out the planned transformation of the country, was demonstrated once again by Chou En-lai in a policy-setting speech on 14 January 1956. It followed a period of intensive attempts at indoctrination, which reached a high point in 1955 with the vociferous drive against the literary critic Hu Feng (1903–?). The ruthlessness of this campaign (based on false charges, for Hu Feng was to be fully rehabilitated in 1980) undoubtedly perturbed the intellectuals to a great extent, and no one was better suited than Chou En-lai to pour oil on troubled waters and to assure them of proper treatment and respect in the future in return for the loyal performance of their tasks. He had already in the preceding year played an important role in formulating the guidelines for the fifteen-year plan of the newly established Academy of Sciences.

It was this problem of the intelligentsia which rested at the core of Mao Tse-tung's slogan, voiced on 2 May 1956, 'Let a hundred flowers bloom, let a hundred schools contend.' The speech in which this sentiment was proclaimed was never made public, but it can be assumed that its basic content was reflected in the pronouncement made on 26 May by Lu Ting-i (b. 1904), then head of the Central Committee's Propaganda Department. The general purport of Lu's speech was to advocate a relatively large degree of independence and freedom of thought in the sciences and arts as a prerequisite for their development. The Hundred Flowers approach was of course also a component part of the CCP's reactions to the 20th Congress of the CPSU, but in the autumn of 1956 the turbulent events in Poland and Hungary provided the Chinese Communist leadership with much additional food for thought regarding the problems of exercising power. It is abundantly clear that Mao Tse-tung's speech 'On the Correct Handling of Contradictions Among the People', delivered on 27 February 1957, but published in a substantially altered version only on 19 June, was conceived as an attempt to answer the vital questions involved. While stressing the non-antagonistic nature of contradictions among the people, including the principal one – between the rulers and the ruled – and thus implying that they could be resolved by non-coercive political means, Mao also advanced the concept that a class struggle between the proletariat and the bourgeoisie continued to exist in the ideological field. It was this thesis which, in an exaggerated and distorted form, was later to serve as the supposed theoretical basis for the 1966–76 'cultural revolution'. However, in the spring of 1957, the main concern was to bring about an alleviation of tension by creating the possibility for expressing criticism of existing conditions, and, with this in mind, Mao renewed his Hundred Flowers appeal on 12 March, combining it with the simultaneous inauguration of a new Party rectification movement.

Within a few weeks the flowers really did begin to bloom, and although the authorities carefully restricted the movement to the intelligentsia, penetrating criticism of the fashion in which the CCP was running the country became ever more widespread, with the students becoming particularly active. Some of the leaders of the small, numerically insignificant, democratic parties, which had aided the CCP in establishing the PRC in 1949, also joined in the fray, with trenchant remarks on the way in which the Communists had completely monopolized all political power. By the end of May, a sharp frost nipped the blossoms before they could unfold further; some of the Communist leaders, feeling that the dominant role of the CCP was being challenged, although there is little evidence to substantiate this fear, now tended to regard the blossoms not as potential fragrant flowers, but as poisonous weeds to be uprooted as quickly as possible. On 8 June, a campaign against alleged rightists was announced, which turned into a counterattack by the CCP on many of those who had voiced their critical views in the preceding three months. A large number of these 'rightists' were compelled to go through the humiliating ritual of public recantation. In line with the tendency to preserve the image of the Party's infallibility, it was maintained that the criticism had been encouraged initially for the purpose of bringing the enemies of the new government out into the open, so as to facilitate their identification and political elimination. This line of reasoning was largely false for, in fact, the Communist leaders had not expected that the rule of the CCP, with many undoubted achievements to its credit, should have given rise to as much resentment and disaffection as the criticism during this period revealed. Nonetheless, in contrast to what the future had in store, the years 1949–57 were a period of relative stability and marked progress in practically all fields.

402

The Great Leap Forward, 1958–9

The intensive efforts exerted during the First Five Year Plan had produced substantial results in building up an industrial base, with production increasing at an annual rate of 18 per cent. The production of steel had grown from 1.3 million tons in 1952 to 4.5 million in 1957; the output of coal had risen from 66 million tons in 1952 to 130 million in 1957; electrical power increased from 7.2 billion kwh in 1952 to 19.3 billion in 1957. However, the development of agriculture lagged considerably behind that of industry, with a rate of annual increase of less than 4 per cent, and thus grain production rose from 150 million tons in 1952 to 182 million in 1957, at a time when population kept growing at a rapid pace, having reached an estimated 656 million in 1957 as compared with 583 million in 1953. The disparity between the progress achieved in industry and the relative stagnation of agriculture presented a large number of serious problems, especially when the latter had to serve as the principal source of accumulation for the development of the economy as a whole, while simultaneously being burdened with the task of feeding almost a quarter of the world's population.

It was against the above background that a part of the Chinese leadership, and Mao Tse-tung in particular, began to question increasingly the validity of the economic strategy pursued up to 1957, largely based on a faithful and unduly mechanical application of the Soviet model. In a number of speeches made at the beginning of 1958, Mao unveiled a fundamentally different approach to the problems of economic reconstruction, based more on political and ideological assumptions than on a realistic assessment of economic factors. The key element in his scheme was the desire to harness the one resource that China had in great abundance, the labour power of its vast population, especially of its 500 million peasants, whose potential was only partially being utilized. The task was to be achieved by a total mobilization of the entire nation with the aid primarily of ideological and political means. It was further assumed that such a mobilization would make possible a simultaneously rapid and equal progress of all

403

branches of the economy, industry as well as agriculture, and eliminate the dangers inherent in the widening gap in the development of the cities and the rural areas.

Mao Tse-tung's vision of such a Chinese road to socialism was partially derived from his belief in the necessity of regarding the revolution as a permanent phenomenon in which 'one revolution must follow the other, the revolution must continuously advance'. In fact, the course of events in the 1949–56 period, especially the rapidity with which total collectivization had been carried out, resembled such a permanent revolution to a remarkable degree, and the considerable successes achieved encouraged Mao in his advocacy of continuing such a course. It has become customary to refer to Mao's concepts as voluntaristic, with the implication that insufficient attention was paid in their elaboration to objective factors, while stress was placed above all on the decisive role of human consciousness. But the entire history of the Chinese Revolution from 1927 to 1949 was conducive to precisely such an emphasis, since its victory had certainly not been predetermined by objective causes, but brought about by a supreme exertion of human will and intelligence. It would seem more advisable to pose the question as to whether this victory did not give rise among some of the Chinese Communist leaders to a hubristic self-confidence and a belief in the almost infinite possibilities of manipulating the Chinese people. In April 1958, Mao Tse-tung stated that: 'China's 600 million people have two remarkable peculiarities; they are, first of all poor, and secondly blank. That may seem like a bad thing, but it is really a good thing . . . a clean sheet of paper has no blotches and so the newest and most beautiful words can be written on it, the newest and most beautiful pictures can be painted on it.' These words show that the above question may well be answered in the affirmative.

It was under these circumstances that the Chinese people were impelled into one of the most painful episodes of their long history – the Great Leap Forward. A propaganda campaign of unparalleled intensity, even by Chinese standards, called on the nation to engage in three years' hard work to be followed by eternal well-being, in line with the slogan of 'more, better, faster and cheaper', which would lead to a rapid transformation of the backward economy and to such huge increases in both agricultural and industrial production as to make possible the surpassing of the economic level of Great Britain within fifteen years. Economic decision-making was largely decentralized, while the premises of the Second Five Year Plan were set aside and much higher targets set.

The most important single element in the Great Leap Forward programme was the further transformation of agriculture and the countryside by the establishment of the people's communes. The rural commune was to be created by the fusion of the existing production cooperatives, and while the primary purpose was to facilitate an increase in production, at a time when it was still impossible for industry to furnish the required equipment for mechanization, it was to embrace, according to the original concept, every aspect of peasant life. Moreover, the commune movement was proclaimed as the basic solution of all the problems arising from China's backwardness, and as a form of rapid transition to communism. The first commune was organized on an experimental basis in Honan in April 1958, and the venture received its official blessing during the Second Session of the CCP's 8th Congress (5–23 May 1958), which actually marked the formal beginning of the Great Leap Forward. During the summer the entire Party apparatus concentrated practically all its efforts on the further establishment of the rural communes, with the result that by the end of the year the previously existing 740,000 production cooperatives, embracing over 123 million peasant households, had been reorganized into slightly over 26,000 communes. In the feverish process many of the peasants' meagre personal possessions and, most important, their private plots, were converted into communal property. Simultaneously, tens of millions of people in the entire country were mobilized to engage in local and small-scale smelting of iron and steel, which was expected to increase national production at least fourfold. This particular scheme, which ended dismally in a vast wastage of resources and labour power, was linked with the general concept aiming at the decentralization of industrialization.

In the autumn of 1958 the Chinese media were putting forth grandiose statements of colossal achievements in all fields; under the impact of the Great Leap both agricultural and industrial production were said to have almost doubled. Within less than a year it became apparent that all these statistics were spurious. Luckily for the

Chinese, exceptionally favourable weather conditions did result in a bumper crop of 210 million tons of grain for 1958, much less of course than the 370 million claimed. In 1959, production plummeted down to around 165 million tons. Actually, by the end of 1958, the signs that the country was approaching a severe and largely self-inflicted crisis, caused primarily by the chaotic disorganization and disruption of the economy and the hastiness of the organization of the communes, were becoming apparent. At the Sixth Plenum of the Central Committee (28 November–10 December) held in Wuhan, while the completely false data for the economic results of 1958 were endorsed and equally unrealistic targets were set for 1959, an initial attempt was made to curb the utopian excesses of the commune movement and to introduce a modicum of rationality into their organization and functioning. At the same time it was announced that Mao Tse-tung would not continue to hold the office of PRC Chairman, a decision which went into effect in April 1959, when Liu Shao-ch'i assumed this largely ceremonial post of head of state. It is difficult to ascertain to what degree this move resulted from factional dissension which was soon to surface within the CCP leadership. However, it did partially mark the beginning of the process during which fundamental policy-making decisions were taken more and more out of Mao's hands, while full outward reverence to his role as the Party's leader continued to be rendered. Mao himself is said to have stated that henceforth he was 'treated with respect as a dead parent at his own funeral'.

In the spring of 1959 the signs of an oncoming crisis were obvious and undeniable, although claims of gigantic successes were still being trumpeted. The faults of the Great Leap Forward programme were many, and perhaps the principal one rested in the mechanical application of political and ideological mobilization, which had proved successful in attaining victory by 1949, to a different set of problems and circumstances. Oddly enough, it would seem that a number of the Communist leaders, and Mao Tse-tung in particular, had forgotten some of the basic elements of their previously applied strategy, especially the need to prepare a campaign with the utmost care and with full calculation of all the factors involved. In 1958 their actions were characterized by an overwhelming impatience, psychologically comprehensible but no less harmful, derived from their intense desire to drag China out of the mire of poverty and backwardness during their own lifetime. It was this subjective approach which led them to the cherishing of totally unrealistic expectations and the formulation of grandiose, but badly planned and clumsily implemented schemes, the execution of which heaped immense, almost insupportable burdens on the Chinese people. By November 1959, the Great Leap Forward ended with a whimper, to be followed by the Great Economic Crisis of 1960–2. The clean sheet of paper had been inscribed not with a most beautiful picture, but with an ugly, distorted daub.

With the exception of main addresses delivered at such gala occasions as the 8th Party Congress, the Chinese Communists have not practised the publication of speeches or stenographic records of discussions at such vital gatherings as Central Committee Plenums. Hence it is very difficult to reconstruct a true picture of the debates of the Communist leaders on all the really crucial issues in the post-1949 period. However, a certain amount of material of this type was leaked on purpose, usually for quite reprehensible reasons, during the first years of the 'cultural revolution', and eagerly pounced upon by Western *soi-disant* China experts. Unfortunately, it is these publications, whose authenticity and reliability are open to question, which constitute the main source of data on the inner-Party disputes in connection with the Great Leap. The chief protagonists in the debates were Mao Tse-tung and P'eng Te-huai, and the confrontation between the two men began during the 7th Plenum, held in April 1959. On 14 July, P'eng submitted a Letter of Opinion, listing his criticisms of the current policies, and it can be assumed that he repeated them at greater length at the tumultuous 8th Plenum, held in Lushan (2–16 August). P'eng charged Mao with responsibility for the chaos which had been created, and characterized the Great Leap Forward as a manifestation of 'petty bourgeois fanaticism'. At the end of the session, Mao, with full use of his prestige and authority, launched a successful counterattack against P'eng, with the result that the latter's political career and that of a number of his associates came to a complete end. (In 1981, the Lushan decision was declared to be 'entirely wrong'.) A month later P'eng was also removed from his post of Minister of Defence, which was taken over by Lin Piao. For having dared to challenge the Great Leader, P'eng Te-huai was humiliated, beaten and finally hounded to death by the Red Guards during the 'cultural revolution'.

The Great Economic Crisis, 1960–2

The disruption caused by the breakneck pace of the commune movement dealt agriculture a serious blow, which was further worsened by severe natural calamities in 1960 and 1961. As a result grain production fell to a catastrophic 150 million tons in 1960. Near-famine conditions now prevailed in many parts of the country, and only the effective functioning of the strict rationing system prevented a disaster on the scale similar to that of the 1930s. But the rations were cut to the bone, and by September 1961 amounted probably to not more than 1500 calories a day. One of the new government's greatest and most proudly acclaimed achievements – its ability to keep the population nourished on a relatively adequate and equitable level – had been shattered. In a bitter speech in January 1962 Liu Shao-ch'i claimed that the food crisis had been 70 per cent man-made, with the natural conditions accounting for the remainder. There was little doubt as to who was the principal author of the Great Leap Forward, and while Mao Tse-tung admitted his responsibility, he sought, at the same time, to shift most of the blame on to the lower level of CCP cadres, whose blind enthusiasm had supposedly helped to wreck the economy.

At the cost of prodigious efforts and with the aid of a number of administrative measures, the food crisis was alleviated. Grain production rose to an estimated 160 million tons in 1961 and probably 170 million in 1962. From 1961 on sizable quantities of grain were also imported, both for current consumption and to build up almost totally depleted reserves. The rural communes were systematically reorganized and reduced in size, with the original 26,000 divided into more viable 74,000 units. Most of the initial far-fetched projects, such as commune canteens, were eliminated. Gradually, the production team, grouping 20 to 30 households, became the basic unit for determining production plans. Private plots, amounting to around 6 per cent of the land under cultivation but furnishing a much higher share of the peasants' income, were also restored. A Central Committee Conference held in Peitaho (July–August 1960) established the guidelines for a new economic policy, in which agriculture was proclaimed the foundation of the economy, and industry its leading factor. The latter was entrusted with the imperative task of furnishing the former with the products indispensable for its further development, such as chemical fertilizers and farm equipment. By and large, the situation in agriculture was successfully stabilized by the end of 1962, and henceforth grain production continued to rise. It should be noted in passing that in the years 1959–76 the PRC authorities published only very fragmentary statistics, and most of the data pertaining to this period are foreign estimates.

While in 1958 and 1959 industrial production had also increased, in some cases very sharply due to the lavish and wasteful use of labour power, the effects of excessive decentralization, mismanagement, the general chaos of the Great Leap Forward, and especially of the agricultural crisis, soon brought about a slump whose dimensions were almost as calamitous as those of the agrarian sector. Hence, the authorities were faced with the necessity of carrying out a programme of reorganization and retrenchment. This led to the closing down of countless new enterprises which had sprung up during the Great Leap and to a sizable reduction of investment in industry. The problem of large-scale unemployment, which now emerged in the urban centres, was dealt with radically by means of sending the redundant labour force, partially peasants who had flocked to the cities earlier, down to the hungry countryside. By the spring of 1962 probably close to 20 million people had been affected by this policy. At the same time a concerted effort was made to restore central economic planning, to reintroduce material incentives in order to stimulate production. With the help of these measures a considerable degree of stabilization was also achieved in industry by the end of 1962.

The critical situation of Chinese industry in 1960 was further exacerbated in July by the abrupt withdrawal of all the nearly 1400 Soviet experts, engaged on the 147 key projects, mostly large and crucial installations in various stages of completion. The move came as a complete surprise and shock to the Chinese, for while the polemics between the CCP and the CPSU had become increasingly sharp, reaching a high point in June 1960 with a vitriolic exchange in Bucharest between Khrushchev and P'eng Chen (b. 1902), state relations had seemed, at least outwardly, to remain proper. In reality, however, they had deteriorated significantly earlier, when in June 1959 the Soviet government had made its decision not to implement the October 1957 Sino-Soviet agreement on furnishing the PRC with atomic military technology. Both of these measures were to become important milestones on the road leading to the transformation of the Sino-Soviet alliance into bitter hostility between the two neighbouring states, both of which considered themselves socialist, to the great delight of all the world's anti-Communist forces.

The ignominious collapse of the Great Leap Forward undoubtedly constituted a severe political setback for Mao Tse-tung. Having assumed a position of partial retreat from day-to-day matters concerned with the running of the country, Mao theoretically was to busy himself with the formulation of fundamental Party policies. It would appear, however, that one of his main concerns from 1960 on was to strengthen his influence over the PLA, and in this endeavour he availed himself of the eager assistance of Lin Piao, whose willingness to extol Mao and his thoughts to the skies was constantly being demonstrated. In October 1960 Lin Piao inaugurated a programme of strengthening the indoctrination of the PLA under the main slogan of 'become a good soldier of Mao Tse-tung', stressing simultaneously the primacy of politics and ideology over any other factor. In this fashion the PLA was being groomed to play a decisive political role, whose true nature was to be revealed fully only in 1966.

It is clear that the grave problems produced by the Great Crisis had to be the subject of infinite concern for the CCP leadership and were discussed profusely at the 9th Plenum (14–18 January 1961), at four special work conferences held in 1961 and 1962, and at the 10th Plenum (24–27 September 1962). However, once again there is a paucity of truly reliable material which would show what views were voiced and what policies advocated by the participants, who now represented a CCP of over 17 million members, 80 per cent of whom had joined the movement after 1949. From the fragments available it can be assumed that there existed a considerable swell of resentment against the top leadership for the irresponsible introduction of ultimately disastrous policies. Quite in accord with Chinese literary tradition and existing circumstances, these sentiments were to be voiced in an appropriately esoteric and Aesopian form by three talented writers, the eminent historian Wu Han (1909–66), the journalist Teng T'o (1911–66) and the writer Liao Mo-sha (b. 1907). In January 1961, Wu Han published his play, 'The Dismissal of Han Jui', in which the allusion to P'eng Te-huai's fall was easily perceived. In March Teng T'o began to write a special column in a Peking newspaper and his sarcastic essays were interpreted by the Peking cognoscenti as a subtle assault on Mao's penchant for verbosity. In October, Wu, Teng and Liao joined forces to produce a series of devastating satirical articles entitled 'Notes from the Three Family Village'. Although by 1963 the three men had ceased this activity, all of it had been carefully recorded. In the first stage of the 'cultural revolution', Wu Han and Teng T'o were either killed or driven to suicide; Liao was imprisoned for over eight years, surviving to testify at the famous trial in November 1980.

Respite Before the Storm, 1963–5

A slow but steady recovery from the consequences of the Great Leap Forward debacle commenced from the beginning of 1963 to continue until the outbreak of the 'cultural revolution' in the summer of 1966. Grain production rose from around 185 million tons in 1963 to perhaps 200 million in 1965, aided in part by a marked increase in the production of chemical fertilizers (2.8 million tons in 1963; 7.2 million in 1965). Steel production increased from 9–12 million tons in 1963 to 11–15 million in 1965, while coal extraction reached a level of 210–270 million tons in 1963 to rise to 230–300 million by 1965. The first important steps were also taken to develop oil production which rose from a relatively insignificant 1.4 million tons in 1957 to 7.5 million in 1963 and 10 million in 1965.

Against this background an improvement of living conditions took place and a somewhat more relaxed atmosphere prevailed. In some ways the situation resembled that of the 1950s – a land full of promise, a China with no opium, no beggars, no flies and very little crime. Significant progress continued to be made in the two vital fields of education and health. In 1949 the illiteracy rate had stood at over 80 per cent, with only 24 million children attending primary schools. Enrolment had risen to 64 million in 1957 and 80 million by 1964, and adult education had also aided in the substantial reduction of illiteracy. The number of students in university level schools rose from 117,000 in 1949 to 440,000 in 1957 and 700,000 in 1964. The advance in health, sanitation and hygiene aided by mass propaganda campaigns was equally impressive. The number of doctors trained in modern medicine increased from 40,000 in 1949 to 150,000 by 1965, while the number of graduates in medicine rose from 1300 in 1949 to 6200 in 1957 and 25,000 in 1963. However, there was one fundamental drawback in these remarkable achievements; the urban areas benefited from them to a much larger degree than the rural ones, thus accentuating a disturbing and growing gap in the development of the towns and the countryside.

The progress attained in these years was largely due not only to the ever present and infinite capacity of the Chinese for hard work, but also to the relatively moderate and realistic domestic policies pursued by the majority of the Chinese Communist leadership, headed by Liu Shao-ch'i, directly in charge of running the country. Nonetheless, while a facade of seeming unity was successfully preserved until 1966, divergences within the top CCP leadership concerning both current and future policies grew in intensity. They were already apparent during the 10th Plenum, at which Mao Tse-tung began to develop still further his concept regarding the existence of a growing class struggle. It is quite likely that the increase in these differences accounted for the failure to hold another plenum for the subsequent four years.

One of the principal issues at stake pertained to the Party's activities in the countryside. In the aftermath of the Great Leap catastrophe, the need to revitalize the functioning of the Party rural organization and to improve the existing structure of agriculture was to be met by the launching of a new political campaign, to be known as the Socialist Education Movement. From May 1963 to January 1965 an intricate inner-Party struggle was waged over the aims of this movement and the methods to be employed. The programme initially formulated by Mao Tse-tung, envisaging a further round of political strife in the countryside, was challenged, on the whole effectively, by the Party apparatus under Liu Shao-ch'i and Teng Hsiao-p'ing, who succeeded partially in keeping the movement within bounds, thus preventing a likely new disruption of agricultural production.

The inability to force through his own concepts increased Mao Tse-tung's dissatisfaction with the Party apparatus and its leaders, and led him to seek new allies for a planned and foreseen political struggle. For this purpose Mao had turned to the PLA, which remained under his direct authority as the Chairman of the Party's vital Military Affairs Commission, the real decision-making body in all military affairs, and to its commander, Lin Piao. There are sufficient grounds to maintain that by 1963 Mao Tse-tung had come to regard the highly politicized PLA as the only truly reliable component of the CCP, and there is no doubt at all as to Lin Piao's willingness to aid in transforming the PLA into Mao's principal political base and to glorify the Party's Chairman and his ideology. Thus, according to Lin, Mao was 'the greatest Marxist-Leninist of our era', while his thought constituted an 'inexhaustive source of strength and a spiritual atom bomb of infinite power'. In May 1964, the first edition appeared of what was to become the famous Little Red Book – 'Quotations from Mao Tse-tung' – prefaced by Lin Piao's admonition to study Mao's writings, follow his teaching and act according to his instructions. The building up of the cult of Mao increased at a frenetic pace, reaching already gigantic proportions by 1965, with busts and statues scattered and pictures plastered over the length and breadth of China.

A crucial role in the ideological elaboration and dissemination of the Mao cult was also played by Ch'en Po-ta (b. 1905), the editor of the 'Red Flag', the CCP's main theoretical organ. An intimate associate of Mao's since the 1940s, Ch'en had made by far the most concerted effort in propagandizing the latter's views, seeking to present them as a meaningful and significant contribution to the further development of Marxism-Leninism. Having reached by 1969 the highest pinnacle of power, Ch'en fell into disfavour during the next year, to reappear on the Chinese political arena only in 1981 when he received a sentence of eighteen years' imprisonment for his actions during the 'cultural revolution'. It is quite clear that the strivings of Lin Piao and Ch'en Po-ta met in this period with Mao Tse-tung's wholehearted approval and support, for he viewed the cult as a politically advantageous instrument. After the fall of Khrushchev,

Mao remarked ironically to his American Boswell, Edgar Snow, that the Soviet leader could have avoided such a fate, had he created an appropriate cult for himself.

The glorification of Mao Tse-tung and the extolling of his thought carried on by the PLA was also utilized for strengthening the latter's political importance. At the beginning of 1964, when the media were still at least partially amenable to Mao's directives, an intensive propaganda campaign was launched, aimed at presenting the PLA as the 'great school of Mao Tse-tung's Thought', as a prime example of the principle of 'politics in command', worthy of emulation by the entire country. At the same time, PLA representatives were increasingly shifted to key strategic posts in the political departments of the state administration, which were now being rapidly expanded and strengthened. In the history of the CCP it had been axiomatic that, as Mao himself had stated in 1938, 'the Party commands the gun, and the gun must never be allowed to command the Party'. Nonetheless, by the end of 1965, a situation had been created in which the future observance of this salutary provision was by no means assured. Matters were complicated additionally by the simple fact that a large part of the PLA, practically all of its officer corps and certainly its entire commanding staff, was composed of loyal Party members. Thus, to envisage the employment of the PLA as an instrument of struggle in an attack against the majority of the CCP leadership called for very thorough preparation and much ingenious and devious political manoeuvring, in which the fullest use was made of Mao Tse-tung's immense prestige and authority. In fact, plans to utilize the PLA for precisely such a purpose were carefully made ready by the spring of 1966, and it was the complete assurance that he would be able to rely on this formidable force which did much to embolden Mao Tse-tung to launch the 'cultural revolution'.

It was in this period that relations between the CCP and the CPSU continued to deteriorate, reaching by the beginning of 1964 practically a point of no return. The problems involved ran the whole gamut, from far-reaching divergences in ideological interpretation to basic differences in assessing the world situation. But perhaps the most crucial issue at stake was the respective role of the two parties in determining the overall strategy of the international Communist movement. With each side adamantly convinced of the sole correctness of its views, the dialogue became increasingly embittered. For a while, the protagonists attacked each other by proxy, with the Chinese Party castigating the supposed revisionist sins of Yugoslavia, and the CPSU inveighing against dogmatic Albania. But this transparent device was soon discarded, and the polemics became more obvious and open. It is clear that by the beginning of 1962 Mao Tse-tung had written off the Soviet leaders as revisionists aiming at the restoration of capitalism – a term employed by him to denote anything not in accord with his own version of socialism – while the latter were more and more inclined to regard their Chinese opponents as incorrigibly insubordinate, nationalistically minded, sectarian adventurists.

An attempt to prevent a complete split was undertaken in the summer of 1963 during a meeting held in Moscow between the Soviet delegation, headed by M. Suslov, and the Chinese, led by Teng Hsiao-p'ing (5–20 July). Since the divergences had been already allowed to develop to such an extreme, it proved impossible to attain any results. On 14 July, the CPSU published an Open Letter stating at very great length its critical assessment of the Chinese position. The Chinese replied in a series of their own nine Open Letters, the first appearing in September 1963, the last in July 1964. From the breakdown of the July 1963 talks, relations between the two parties formally ceased to exist. The pot and kettle recriminations continued, however, and the damage inflicted on the international Communist movement was undoubtedly substantial. The CPSU was able to retain the support of the majority of the non-ruling Communist parties, for in its intransigence, the CCP managed to antagonize even the polycentrically inclined Italian Party. Thus Mao Tse-tung was left with the sorry tyrant of Tirana as his sole ally, and was soon to proclaim Albania as the 'shining beacon light of Marxism-Leninism' in Europe.

18. The 'Cultural Revolution' and Its Aftermath, 1966–82

The First Stage of the 'Cultural Revolution', May 1966–April 1969

By the beginning of 1965, Mao Tse-tung had reached the conclusion that the power to formulate fundamental Party decisions no longer rested fully in his hands. It was this factor, above all, which impelled him to initiate the series of measures which were to culminate in the 'cultural revolution' of 1966–76. The principal aim was to regain control of the Party apparatus and of the media, but the achievement of this was to be gained by a direct assault on those members of the CCP leadership who were actually in charge of these domains.

Underlying Mao's thoughts was his theory of permanent revolution and the thesis that class struggle must necessarily become sharper as the process of the building of socialism unfolds. He regarded all his political opponents, and in particular Liu Shao-ch'i, the second most prominent personality in the CCP leadership, as revisionists, aiming at the restoration of capitalism. Hence, their overthrow was deemed indispensable, and it was to be accomplished by the launching of a great cultural and political revolution in which supposedly one class would overthrow another.

Two principal forces were to be employed in the planned attack on the Party and state establishment. The PLA under Lin Piao had already been carefully prepared for this task; the second, China's youth, was now to be mobilized for this purpose, under the seemingly innocuous and commendable desire of endowing it with the requisite revolutionary experience. Actually, this manoeuvre proved to be nothing more than a cynical exploitation of the inherent idealism of young people, with dire consequences for the moral development of an entire generation.

In January 1965, Mao Tse-tung proclaimed the necessity of launching a new ideological campaign, designed supposedly to

416

further a revolutionization of culture, and a special five-man group, led by P'eng Chen, the head of the Peking Party Committee and the city's mayor, was established to elaborate its programme. It was later maintained that this cultural revolution group took up its task with a marked lack of enthusiasm, for its members were themselves the leaders of the Peking cultural establishment. Thus the first salvo of the 'cultural revolution' had to be fired on 10 November 1965, not in the nation's capital but in Shanghai, and it took the shape of a carefully prepared, vitriolic attack on Wu Han and his play, purportedly written by a young literary critic, Yao Wen-yüan (b. 1931).

By the spring of 1966, after Yao's article had finally been reprinted in Peking, and the PLA's 'Liberation Daily' had bestowed upon the planned ideological campaign the grandiloquent title of the Great Proletarian Cultural Revolution, the political infighting in the capital reached a new pitch. Mao's adherents launched a bitter attack on the five-man group for the alleged inadequacies of its activities, thus setting the scene for its disbandment in May, and replacement by a new group, composed primarily of Mao Tse-tung's most intimate collaborators. Its actual leaders were Chiang Ch'ing (b. 1914), Mao's wife since 1937, the Shanghai propagandist Chang Ch'un-ch'iao (b. 1917), Ch'en Po-ta, Yao Wen-yüan and K'ang Sheng (1899–1975), the grey eminence of the CCP's security organization, expelled posthumously from the Party in 1980. Within a few months the new group, acting directly under Mao's orders, became the real ruling force in Peking, while the Party's Political Bureau was rendered powerless.

The establishment of the new cultural revolution group was accompanied on 16 May by the issuance of a Central Committee Circular in which the call for a far-reaching purge of the Party and state apparatus was clearly made. The struggle was to be waged against the representatives of the bourgeoisie who had allegedly infiltrated the Party, and were headed by China's Khrushchev, a transparent reference to the Chinese head of state – Liu Shao-ch'i. At the same time, the country's youth was now mobilized to be used as the vanguard of this struggle, and on 29 May the first Red Guard unit was formed from the students of Tsinghua University in Peking. Within two months the Red Guard had spread, although by no means only spontaneously, to practically every major urban centre, and especially to all the universities. It was actually a very complex social movement, in which many different tendencies and trends could be observed. Its members included a multitude of starry-eyed youngsters, full of the purest idealism, setting off with packs on their backs to Chingkangshan to retrace the route of a glorious revolutionary past. But it also had within its ranks such vicious thugs, as those of the Peking Aeronautical Institute, whose behaviour forcibly brought to an eyewitness's mind their startling and shocking resemblance to Nazi stormtroopers.

By the beginning of June, the new cultural revolution group had succeeded in taking over control of the central propaganda media, and an editorial in the 'People's Daily', written by Ch'en Po-ta, set the tone for launching the attacks on the 'ghosts and monsters' of the Party and state establishment. This theme was also taken up by the immense flood of wall posters plastered throughout Peking. The most prominent of these was of course Mao Tse-tung's own contribution, revealingly entitled 'Bomb the Headquarters'. In Mao's own phrase, the country was now being thrown into turmoil. The feeble attempts of Liu Shao-ch'i and his associates to control the situation in Peking by the sending of work teams to the universities in June and July ended quickly in a fiasco, for the Red Guards, assured of Mao's support, grew more vociferous in their attacks. In June, a number of top leaders, including P'eng Chen and Lu Ting-i, were removed from their posts.

During the period from November 1965 to April 1966 Mao Tse-tung had made an unpublicized tour of the provinces, and then spent May and June in one of his favourite residences in Hangchow; subsequently he made a spectacular re-entry into public view in July with his much advertised swim in the Yangtse. He then returned to Peking for the next crucial move, the holding of the 11th Plenum (1–12 August). The meeting was packed with non-members, Mao and Lin supporters, and its principal significance rested in the sixteen-point decision it adopted, which constituted the basic programme of the 'cultural revolution', expressing Mao Tse-tung's aforementioned concepts. A week after the plenum the enormous hegira to Peking of Red Guards from the entire country began, which led to the staging of eight gigantic parades and rallies on T'ien An Men Square, during which the Red Guards paid homage to the Great Leader. The first was held on 18 August, the last on 25 November; it could easily be observed that the entire enterprise was under the complete control and management, rather skilful at that, of the PLA. In the process around 11 million young Chinese underwent an exhilarating experience, since for many, if not most of them, it was probably their first and last trip to Peking.

Inspired by the heady slogans, especially by the call to destroy all vestiges of the Four Olds (culture, ideas, habits and customs), the Red Guards, soon to be joined by equally numerous older 'revolutionary rebels' among the workers in the factories and offices, on returning home went on a wild rampage of vandalism. Immense and incalculable damage was inflicted on cultural relics by this 'cultural revolution', throughout the length and breadth of China, from the historic statues in Confucius' shrine in Ch'ü-fu in Shantung, to the despoiled monasteries of Tibet. But statues can be copied and temples rebuilt. Cut-off heads do not grow back again, as Mao Tse-tung astutely observed, and the human costs were infinitely more shocking. The data revealed in November 1980, during the trial of Mao Tse-tung's and Lin Piao's surviving closest associates – an account which should be obligatory reading for all Western admirers of the 'cultural revolution' – portray only a fragment of the horrors and atrocities inflicted on the Chinese people during this terrible decade. 729,000 people were 'framed and persecuted', of whom 34,800 were 'persecuted to death'. As could be expected, the intellectuals and old Party cadres were in the forefront of those victimized, and suicides – the traditional Chinese form of protest against oppression – soon followed on a vast scale. Among these thousands of victims, either killed or driven to suicide, was the economist Li Ta, a participant of the CCP's First Congress, the famous novelist Lao She, the eminent historian Chien Po-tsan and the legendary Red Army leader Ho Lung. All this in the name of ideological purity.

In October and November the propaganda campaign against the alleged capitalist-roaders within the CCP leadership intensified still further. An additional touch of colour was provided by the hate-filled, distorted caricatures of Liu Shao-ch'i and Teng Hsiao-p'ing (capitalist-roaders number one and two) with their heads pierced by the pens of the righteous artists. In December, P'eng Chen, Lu Ting-i and two more prominent CCP leaders were arrested and next month dragged out by the Red Guards to a Peking stadium, after being hung up by their hands and feet, for a kangaroo trial in front of a howling crowd of thousands of spectators. Nonetheless, except for Peking, the campaign aimed at overthrowing the establishment had made relatively little progress, and on 1 January 1967, Mao Tse-tung gave the order for a general attack, which was speedily acted upon, especially in Shanghai. The successes now obtained were largely the result of the direct involvement of the PLA, which was ordered into the fray in February with the task of supporting the Red Guards and the 'revolutionary rebels'. However, the best-laid plans often go astray, and it was becoming transparently obvious during the first two months of 1967 that the 'cultural revolution' was getting out of hand, revealing simultaneously a large number of unsuspected severe conflicts and tensions within post-1949 Chinese society, including serious contradictions within the working class itself. All of these were seized upon and utilized by the countless demagogic careerists and opportunists busily jumping on the 'cultural revolution' bandwagon.

It was against this background that a group of vice-premiers, including Yeh Chien-ying, Ch'en I, Li Hsien-nien, Nieh Jung-chen and Hsü Hsiang-ch'ien, strove in February 1967 to aid Chou En-lai in his herculean attempts to preserve a modicum of viability and sanity in face of the threatened collapse of the entire state administration, which remained under incessant attack. Chou's indefatigability in this period was truly astounding, and, in his dealing with the loutish Red Guard leaders and even more in his negotiations with Chiang Ch'ing's group, he was constantly faced with the problem of preserving his own personal integrity. Nonetheless, the efforts of Chou and his colleagues were of no avail and the situation in the provinces rapidly deteriorated. By the spring of 1967, a complex struggle between various groups contending for power in Szechuan, Kwangsi and Yünnan degenerated into armed conflict with thousands of casualties. But, luckily for China, the 'cultural revolution' remained throughout most of its existence primarily an urban phenomenon, although it did overflow occasionally to the suburban rural areas. Had it been otherwise, the calamity would have been severely magnified. In the cities, as the turmoil increased, all the previously existing mass organizations, including the Communist

420

Youth League and the trade unions, were dissolved, while the Party committees and the municipal administration had, in most cases, ceased to function. It was under these circumstances that the ruling group in Peking, after a few weeks of loose talk of utilizing the democratic model of the Paris Commune, opted in February 1967 for the creation of a new governmental structure – the Revolutionary Committee. It was to be formed on the basis of three forces; the PLA, former Party cadres recognized as politically reliable, and representatives of the new revolutionary organizations, with the first clearly playing the dominant role. In the meantime, however, the effectiveness of the central authority in Peking had been extensively undermined. Gone were the days when instructions relayed simultaneously by telephone to all the first secretaries of the provincial Party committees could ensure a more or less uniform implementation of general policy. Thus, one of the greatest achievements of the PRC, the country's real unification, was seriously jeopardized.

In the muggy evening hours of May Day 1967, Mao Tse-tung stood on the terrace of the Gate of Heavenly Peace, gazing down on the surging mass of half a million of his fellow citizens, gathered on the immense square. At his side were Chiang Ch'ing, the 'standard-bearer of the Great Proletarian Cultural Revolution', and Lin Piao, his 'closest comrade-in-arms'. The densely packed crowd held up coloured banners which read 'Ten thousand years to the Great Leader, Great Teacher, Great Supreme Commander and Great Helmsman'. A dazzling display of fireworks seemed to symbolize the Chairman's deification in his own lifetime. Things looked promising. Liu Shao-ch'i, regarded by Mao as his most prominent opponent, was soon to be placed under house arrest. In October 1968, he was to be drummed out of the Party, to which he had devoted his entire life, as a 'counter-revolutionary, renegade, hidden traitor and scab', to perish miserably by November 1969 in a K'aifeng prison.

Within six months of Mao's appearance on T'ien An Men everyone in China, even if quite illiterate, could perceive how the Chairman viewed his place in world history. On 7 November 1967, gigantic posters were displayed everywhere; the content of the message was abundantly clear, for over the dates 1917–1967, five portraits in profile were superimposed on each other, the last being that of Mao

Tse-tung. But in the country ruled by him the situation continued to deteriorate sharply, as the conflict in the provinces increased in force. By the summer of 1967 even the PLA, not quite as monolithic as had been assumed, was finding it difficult to maintain its position as the mainstay of the 'cultural revolution' in view of the intensity of the struggles between rival Red Guard groups. In July, the principal PLA commanders in strategic Wuhan, having thrown their support to a majority rebel faction, composed mostly of workers, took the unprecedented step of arresting a central government mission dispatched to the city, headed by the Minister of Security, Hsieh Fu-chih (1898–1972, posthumously expelled from the Party in 1980). The incident was soon resolved, but it served to illustrate the serious nature of the political crisis which was also demonstrated by the marked lack of progress achieved in establishing the new Revolutionary Committees.

In the meantime, in Peking itself, a number of the most violent Red Guard units turned their attention as well to the foreign diplomatic missions. In January, the Soviet Embassy underwent a lengthy and raucous siege, and in February the French met with a similar fate. These attacks culminated in August with the physical assault on the British chargé d'affaires and the devastation of his chancery and residence. During the same month a group of 'revolutionary rebels' seized the Chinese Ministry of Foreign Affairs, with the slogan of 'smash Ch'en I's dog's head'. Most of his assailants had been, at best, in split pants at the time when the valiant marshal was leading the guerrillas in South China.

In spite of the attempts to restore stability, the general situation did not improve appreciably in the early months of 1968, while a complex factional struggle continued to be conducted in Peking, affecting both the cultural revolution group, some of whose secondary members were removed from power, and the PLA. By the summer, a state of near-anarchy again prevailed, as fighting in the provinces once more grew intensive, particularly in Canton, and even more so in Kwangsi, where the contending groups were employing large quantities of arms pilfered from transports earmarked for Vietnam. In July, the rival Red Guard outfits at Tsinghua University in Peking, comprising, to be sure, only a small minority of the student body, were taking full advantage of the suspension of studies since May 1966, and were again busily devastating the campus and killing each other. By this time, Mao Tse-tung had had enough of his 'little red generals'. At the end of August 1968 the PLA was commanded to restore complete order in the entire country, a decision which was not unaffected by the events in Europe and the situation on the Sino-Soviet border. Within the next six months close to 20 million of the erstwhile Red Guards found themselves sent down to the countryside. The process of setting up the provincial Revolutionary Committees was hastened and completed by September. In October, the 12th Plenum was held, attended by only a small part of the original members elected in 1956. Its task was to be the reconstruction of the shattered Party and the preparation of a new Party Congress.

Scheduled originally for 1967, the 9th Congress met in the spring of 1969 (1–24 April). Its delegates had been carefully selected and not elected, and only a small part of its proceedings was made public. Lin Piao delivered the main report, and was designated officially as Mao Tse-tung's successor in the new Constitution adopted by the Congress. The PLA emerged with 45 per cent of the members of the new Central Committee, while only 30 per cent of those elected in 1956 retained their seats. The new Political Bureau's Standing Committee was composed of Mao Tse-tung, Lin Piao, Chou En-lai, Ch'en Po-ta and K'ang Sheng. A revealing light on CCP history in this period is cast by the fact that of the 21 full members of this Bureau, by 1981, 8 had died and 8 were in prison. In 1981, the guidelines adopted by the 9th Congress were written off officially by the CCP as 'wrong, ideologically, politically and organizationally'. But the truly interesting problem is whether and to what degree the CCP really existed in 1969 as a functioning and viable organization.

If problems concerning the economy were raised at the Congress (not a single word was devoted to this subject in Lin Piao's report), then certainly nothing of the discussion was revealed, probably for the sound reason that the first stage of the 'cultural revolution' had resulted in 'tremendous losses'. Industrial production fell in 1967 by around 20 per cent, and by at least 10 per cent in 1968. Fortunately, grain production did not decline but remained at an annual level of probably 180 million tons in 1967 and 1968. Some progress was made at least in one domain, for the defence industry and especially nuclear technology was out of bounds for the 'cultural revolution', and thus in September 1969 the first hydrogen bomb was tested.

The Intermediate Stage of the 'Cultural Revolution', April 1969–August 1973

Mao Tse-tung once observed that 'three thousand years of history weigh heavily on our heads'. How very true. Events during the early 1970s showed that the heritage of feudal autocracy could still exert a baneful influence, and the style of politics pursued by the current CCP leadership had an uncanny resemblance to that which prevailed in the imperial palaces of Ch'in Shih-huang, Liu Pang and Chu Yüan-chang. Certainly the participation of the 800 million Chinese in the formulation of decisions affecting the fate of their country had been reduced to nil.

Although Mao had proclaimed the 9th Congress as 'a congress of unity and victory', an intense factional struggle soon developed within the CCP leadership. Two rival cliques, one headed by Chiang Ch'ing and Chang Ch'un-ch'iao, and the other by Lin Piao, strove to grasp power into their own hands, while a third group, led by Chou En-lai, manoeuvred cautiously on the sidelines. The conflict was well concealed from public view, and only the sudden disappearance of Ch'en Po-ta after the 2nd Plenum held in Lushan (23 August–6 September 1970) provided an inkling of what was going on. It is now maintained that the rift between Mao Tse-tung and his designated successor Lin Piao had begun during this meeting. Formally, an attempt was being made to rebuild the Party from the top down, in accordance with the political line established at the 9th Congress. By August 1971, all the provincial Party committees had been reconstructed, and characteristically 20 of the 29 first secretaries came from the PLA. However, the functioning of the Party apparatus at lower levels had not yet been restored.

From the outset of the 'cultural revolution', Sino-Soviet relations had undergone a further drastic deterioration, culminating in March 1969 in a military confrontation on the Ussuri. It was partially against this background of mounting hostility towards the Soviet 'social imperialists' that the CCP leadership undertook a reassessment of its policy towards the United States, notwithstanding increased American involvement and intervention in Vietnam. In January 1970, Sino-American ambassadorial talks were resumed after a two-year suspension, and at the end of the year Mao Tse-tung extended his invitation to Nixon to come to China. Kissinger's trip to Peking in July 1971 laid the groundwork for the Nixon visit which, postponed due to the Lin Piao affair, finally took place in February 1972 and resulted ultimately in the normalization of PRC-US relations. An earlier by-product of this Sino-American rapprochement was the withdrawal of the American veto, which for 22 years had blocked the entry of China into the United Nations. In October 1971, the PRC took its place in this organization.

The re-establishment of Sino-American relations led to the creation of the Moscow-Peking-Washington triangle. Throughout the entire decade of the 1970s, the absence of any meaningful dialogue between the Soviet Union and the PRC signified that in this peculiar formation the US had gratuitously been granted the most advantageous position. It remains to be seen whether in the 1980s, Moscow and Peking, having handed Washington such a present on a silver platter, will continue to leave this situation unaltered. The PRC, having resumed in 1970 the conduct of foreign affairs, almost completely abandoned during the 1966–9 period, has sought to regain its place on the international arena by establishing diplomatic relations with almost the entire world. Since 1978, the principal effort has been to stress China's role as a potential spokesman for the developing countries of the Third World.

In September 1971, a political crisis of great magnitude affected the CCP. According to the official version, first released in July 1972, the Chairman's designated successor had concocted an intricate plot to kill his patron and usurp all power. Having failed to accomplish this aim, Lin Piao purportedly fled on 13 September, to meet his death when his plane crashed in the Mongolian People's Republic. No explanation is offered as to the motives of Lin's actions. It is not clear why the anointed successor was not content to await his promised inheritance. It is also puzzling that this brilliant strategist should have proved such an ineffective, fumbling conspirator. The credit for foiling Lin's alleged plot is officially assigned to Mao Tse-tung and

Chou En-lai. Whatever the case, Lin and his faction disappeared from the Chinese arena, but five of his closest surviving associates were to resurface in November 1980, to face trial for their actions during the 'cultural revolution', including their involvement in Lin's supposed schemes. It is obvious that the repercussions of the Lin Piao case were immense, and that the partially rebuilt political stability was thereby shattered once again. It might be assumed that the increasing dominance of the PLA had given rise to a situation in which the sacrosanct principle of the Party controlling the gun had become imperilled. If so, the fashion in which the problem was resolved, and the aura of imperial palace intrigues surrounding the Lin Piao affair could only lead to diminishing the credibility of the CCP leadership.

The Last Years of the 'Cultural Revolution', August 1973–September 1976

During the last phase of the 'cultural revolution' the weary population continued to be bombarded by its threadbare exhortations, while a new series of propaganda campaigns was launched, including one against the departed Lin Piao. No appreciable diminution could be noted in the propagation of the cult of Mao Tse-tung, and his occasional, ever rarer and briefer pronouncements, were immediately endowed with transcendental significance.

The disgrace of Lin Piao created the necessity of revising once again the Party Constitution, but almost two years were to pass after his fall before the 10th Congress was finally held (24–28 August 1973). At this meeting a new candidate for the unenviable role of successor was revealed in the person of a certain Wang Hung-wen (b. 1935), a former Shanghai security official, whose rapid rise to prominence caused him to be referred to as the 'helicopter'. Wang was entrusted with delivering the main report; its principal claim was that the functioning of the CCP had been completely restored and its leadership role once more reasserted. In fact, the struggle within the leadership had by no means disappeared with the elimination of Lin Piao and his followers. While the almost eighty-year-old Chairman nominally retained his dominant position, an ever greater role was being played by Chiang Ch'ing's faction, which gained almost complete control of the Party's ideological and propaganda activities. However, it was partially counterbalanced in the Political Bureau by a strong group of regional PLA commanders and first secretaries, while Chou En-lai utilized his considerable authority to seek to strengthen the state administration. It is thought likely that Chou was responsible for the surprising re-emergence in April 1973 of Teng Hsiao-p'ing in the role of vice-premier, and it is quite clear that Chou, desperately ill with cancer, was grooming Teng as his successor, for the latter was appointed first vice-premier during the 2nd Plenum (7 January 1975), becoming simultaneously one of the Central Committee's vice-chairmen. It was at this meeting that Chou En-lai, reverting to what was really essential, presented the programme of the Four Modernizations (agriculture, industry, national defence, science and technology) which the 'cultural revolution' had done so much to delay. But Chou's plans met with the opposition of Chiang Ch'ing's faction, which had been utilizing the current anti-Confucius campaign for assaulting the prime minister by means of quite obvious innuendoes. All of this, of course, constituted the initial steps in the struggle for the succession, expected to take place after the Chairman had departed to meet his Maker.

On 8 January 1976, Chou En-lai succumbed to his fatal disease. Characteristically, he specified in his testament that no mausoleum should hold his remains, but requested that his ashes be scattered over the countryside. On 15 January, Teng Hsiao-p'ing delivered the eulogy for Chou; this was to be his last political act during this dramatic year, for on 7 February it was not he, but the relatively unknown Hua Kuo-feng (b. 1921), formerly first secretary of the Hunan Party Committee, who was appointed acting prime minister.

A unique occurrence in the history of the PRC took place on T'ien An Men on 4 April 1976, for in what was indubitably a truly spontaneous manifestation, the populace of Peking assembled on the traditional day of mourning by the hundreds of thousands to show their respect and esteem for Chou En-lai, and to place countless wreaths at the obelisk commemorating the martyrs of the revolution. The mysterious disappearance of these wreaths led to a tumultuous mass riot the next day which, after suppression, was declared to be a counter-revolutionary plot. Within days Teng Hsiao-p'ing was charged with responsibility for the incident and removed from all his Party and state posts. On 7 April, Hua Kuo-feng was nominated the Party's first vice-chairman and prime minister. According to Hua, his appointment was made by Mao Tse-tung himself. But the Chairman was sinking rapidly. On 9 September 1976, Mao Tse-tung died, and with his death an entire era in the history of the Chinese Revolution came to an end. Ultimately, his life and deeds might well appear, in the immense span of Chinese history, to be but a moment, as brief, in Ssu-ma Ch'ien's memorable phrase, 'as the glimpse through a crack in the wall of a running white colt'.

China After the 'Cultural Revolution', September 1976–October 1982

The 'cultural revolution' died with its creator. On 6 October, its most prominent luminaries – Chiang Ch'ing, Chang Ch'un-ch'iao, Yao Wen-yüan and Wang Hung-wen, all Political Bureau members, henceforth known as the Gang of Four – were arrested. Those who organized this action included the chief representatives of the PLA, Party and state apparatus – Yeh Chien-ying, Hua Kuo-feng and Li Hsien-nien, all also Political Bureau members. The accounts of observers agree that when the news of the arrest of the Gang of Four was made public on 21 October it was greeted with a widespread, authentic demonstration of joy and unalloyed relief.

On 7 October, the assumption by Hua Kuo-feng of Mao Tse-tung's two key posts – the chairmanship of the Central Committee and of the Military Affairs Committee – was announced. In the subsequent months a concerted attempt was made to preserve a seeming political continuity with the recent past. The programme of the 'cultural revolution' was still extolled, while final touches were applied to the apotheosis of the Chairman, whose remains were to be placed in an elaborate mausoleum on T'ien An Men Square. In February 1977, Hua Kuo-feng pronounced the thesis that all of Mao Tse-tung's thoughts and actions had been infallible and should be rigorously followed; simultaneously, Hua attempted to create a parallel cult of his own person as the 'wise leader'. At the 3rd Plenum (12–21 July

1977) the return of Teng Hsiao-p'ing to top Party and state posts was formally recognized.

Within less than a year from Mao Tse-tung's death the 11th Congress met (12–18 August 1977) in an attempt to formulate policies for tackling anew the problems of China's modernization. However, the programme, announced within a few months, was regarded by 1982 as having been over-ambitious and responsible for a further aggravation of the country's economic difficulties. While eliminating most of the Gang of Four's followers from their positions, the Congress did not undertake an appraisal of the 'cultural revolution' decade, which rendered the elaboration of a truly constructive programme practically impossible. It can be assumed that, as a result, much ideological confusion must have prevailed in the Party, since a fourth of its 35 million membership was composed of those who had joined it during precisely this period. The new Standing Committee chosen at the Congress actually consisted of the leaders who had been instrumental in bringing about the downfall of the Chiang Ch'ing faction, but it is clear that these five men – Hua Kuo-feng, Yeh Chien-ying, Li Hsien-nien, Teng Hsiao-p'ing and Wang Tung-hsing – represented diametrically different views as to the future course of policy, and that a political struggle continued at the very apex of power.

The beginning in December 1977 of the rehabilitation on a large scale of the victims of the 'cultural revolution' served as the first sign of the direction in which the political struggle was tending. The fundamental issues were largely decided during the 3rd Plenum (18–22 December 1978), now referred to as a 'great turning point'. It was resolved to undertake seriously an assessment of the 'cultural revolution' and the inextricably intertwined problem of Mao Tse-tung's legacy, stating clearly that at least one of its elements, the thesis regarding 'class struggle as the key link', was to be rejected. These conclusions were a victory for the views represented by Teng Hsiao-p'ing, and the 3rd Plenum marked his rise to the position of the dominant personality within the CCP leadership. A number of the 'cultural revolution's' most prominent victims, including P'eng Te-huai, were also fully rehabilitated, albeit posthumously.

The above political line was further strengthened at the 5th Plenum (23–29 February 1980), during which two of Teng's close younger

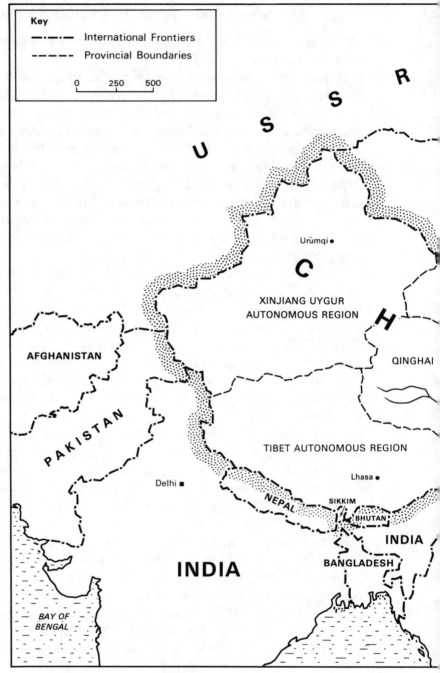

U S S R

U

S

S

R

C

H

Urümqi •

XINJIANG UYGUR
AUTONOMOUS REGION

QINGHAI

AFGHANISTAN

PAKISTAN

TIBET AUTONOMOUS REGION

Lhasa •

Delhi ■

NEPAL   SIKKIM

BHUTAN

INDIA

BANGLADESH

INDIA

BAY OF
BENGAL

20. China in 1983

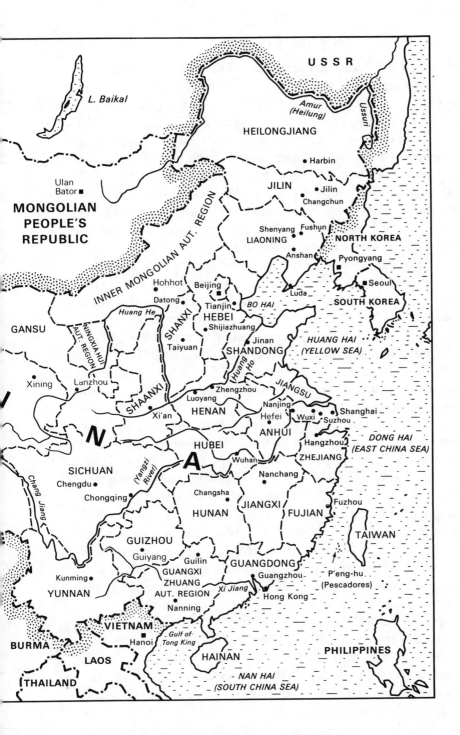

colleagues joined the Standing Committee. These were Hu Yao-pang (b. 1915), now designated the Party's Secretary-General, and Chao Tzu-yang (b. 1919), who replaced Hua Kuo-feng as prime minister in September 1980. Now, finally, eleven years after his tragic death, Liu Shao-ch'i was completely exonerated from all the vile charges that had been heaped upon him. At least a part of the means employed against Liu and other victims was to be revealed at the end of 1980 during the extensively publicized trial of Mao Tse-tung's surviving associates in the two rival factions headed by Chiang Ch'ing and Lin Piao, both of which were designated as composed of 'counter-revolutionary careerists and conspirators'.

The post-'cultural revolution' period, and in particular the years 1979–82, witnessed the continuation of intensive efforts to rebuild the country and to make up for the self-inflicted damage of the tragic 1966–76 decade. By the end of 1981 production of steel stood at 35.6 million tons (1952 – 1.3 million), the extraction of coal at 620 million tons (1952 – 60 million), electric power at 305 billion kwh (1952 – 7.2 billion), oil production at 101 million tons (1952 – under 1 million), the railway network had been extended to 50,000 km (1949 – 21,000 km). In general, it was claimed that an 'independent and fairly comprehensive industrial base' had been created, with industrial assets in 1980 amounting to 27 times those of 1952. The production of grain attained the level of 325 million tons as against 150 million in 1952. However, this figure revealed the continued existence of what is perhaps the PRC's most serious single problem, for in these thirty years its population has also almost doubled (1953 – 583 million; 1982 – 1031 million). Hence the intensity with which the authorities are promoting the idea of population control, a problem completely ignored in some of the previous periods of euphoria. Taken as a whole, the above achievements in the economic field do constitute a great tribute to the 'enormous vitality' of the Chinese people.

The years 1981–2 witnessed two political events of considerable political significance. At the 6th Plenum (27–29 June 1981) a resolution on CCP history in the years 1949–81 was adopted. In this carefully prepared and on the whole cogently reasoned document, the 'cultural revolution' decade is characterized as 'a comprehensive, long-drawn-out and grave blunder . . . responsible for the most severe setbacks and the heaviest losses suffered by the Party, the state and the people since the founding of the PRC'. At the same time a strenuous and not unskilful attempt is made to deal with the vexing problem of Mao Tse-tung's place in history. The chief responsibility for the 'cultural revolution' is squarely placed on Mao, and his actions in connection with it are viewed as resulting subjectively from the mounting arrogance and arbitrariness he had displayed in the preceding years. Moreover, they are regarded as Mao's personal tragedy, since, although undertaken in the belief that they were in accord with the Party's ideology, they were in fact a negation of his own previous achievements. The resolution laid primary stress on Mao's role in the era up to 1956, when he was the 'most prominent' of the Party's 'many outstanding leaders', an assessment which is historically accurate. The basic conclusion drawn up by the present CCP leadership, all of whom were, after all, Mao Tse-tung's close followers for half a century, is that his 'contributions to the Chinese revolution far outweigh his mistakes', and that he should be viewed as 'a great Marxist, great proletarian revolutionary, theorist and strategist'. At the same time, the Thought of Mao Tse-tung has been redefined as the 'crystallization of the collective wisdom of the CCP'. The fundamental aim of the resolution is of course to leave intact as much as possible of the undoubted achievements of the CCP and PRC. The extent to which the argumentation employed will be found convincing by a non-Chinese observer will, however, ultimately depend on his own political inclinations.

The 12th Congress of the CCP (1–11 September 1982) reaffirmed completely the political line established at the 6th Plenum, and in the main report, delivered by Hu Yao-pang, Chairman of the Central Committee since June 1981, attention was focused primarily on future tasks, on finally accomplishing China's full-scale modernization. In organizational matters, an ingenious innovation was introduced by the establishment of a Central Advisory Commission, whose membership includes a large number of the Party's most prominent veteran members. While a sizable part of the new Central Committee membership comes from a younger generation, it should be noted that of the 28 Political Bureau members, 19 had participated in the Long March, while most of the others were also active in the movement at that time. The Congress confirmed the complete political eclipse of Hua Kuo-feng and Wang Tung-hsing, and the present Standing Committee is composed of Teng Hsiao-p'ing, Hu Yao-pang, Chao Tzu-yang, Yeh Chien-ying, Ch'en Yün and Li Hsien-nien.

The balance sheet of the PRC is something which only the Chinese themselves are entitled to draw. A non-Chinese observer might well be inclined to estimate that almost twenty of its thirty-four years had been largely wasted. However, a visitor at present must be forcibly struck by the determination of the Chinese intellectuals, particularly those of the older generation, who, fully mindful of their bitter experiences, especially during the appallingly catastrophic 1966–76 decade, are ready to pick up the pieces and are striving, motivated largely by their well-justified national pride, to make up by their ambitious endeavours for the time lost.

Only time will tell whether the Chinese Communists will prove capable of fulfilling their pledge 'to turn China step by step into a modern socialist country which is highly democratic and highly cultured'. There can certainly be no doubt that the Chinese people fully deserve such a future.

Suggested Reading

The reader might wish to consult other surveys of Chinese history. Those available in English include the following:

Bai Shouyi (ed.), *An Outline History of China* (Beijing, 1982).

Dawson, R., *Imperial China* (London, 1972).

Eberhard, W., *A History of China* (London, 1950; 4th ed., 1977).

Fairbank, J. K., Reischauer, E. O. and Craig, A. M., *East Asia: The Modern Transformation* (Boston, 1965).

Fitzgerald, C. P., *China: A Short Cultural History* (London, 1935; 4th ed., 1976).

Gernet, J., *A History of Chinese Civilization* (Cambridge, 1982).

Goodrich, L. C., *A Short History of the Chinese People* (New York, 1943; 3rd ed., 1960).

Hucker, C. O., *China's Imperial Past* (Stanford, 1975).

Jian Bozan, Shao Xunzheng and Hu Hua, *A Concise History of China* (Beijing, 1964, 1981).

Loewe, M., *Imperial China* (London, 1966).

Meskill, J. (ed.), *An Introduction to Chinese Civilization* (New York, 1972).

Reischauer, E. O. and Fairbank, J. K., *East Asia: The Great Tradition* (Boston, 1958).

Most of the above works, as well as the author's *A History of China*, vols. I and II (Oxford, 1979, 1983), contain extensive selected bibliographies, and list the most significant monographic studies. Mention should also be made of the *Cambridge History of China*, of which volumes 3, 10, 11 and 12 have been published to date, and of J. Needham's *Science and Civilization in China*: nine tomes have appeared thus far.

Chronological Table of Dynasties

Hsia Era	2000 (?)–1766 (?) BC	
Shang	1766 (?)–1122 (?)	
Chou	1122 (?)–256	
1. Western Chou	1122 (?)–771	
2. Eastern Chou	771–256	
(a) Spring and Autumn period	722–481	
(b) Warring States period	403–221	
Ch'in	221–207	
Han (Western)	202 BC–AD 9	
Hsin (Wang Mang)	9–23	
Han (Eastern)	25–220	
Three Kingdoms Era	220–280	
1. Wei	220–266	
2. Shu Han	221–263	
3. Wu	222–280	
Chin (Western)	266–316	
Chin (Eastern)	317–420	
Northern and Southern Dynasties period	420–589	
Southern Dynasties		
Liu Sung	420–479	
Southern Ch'i	479–502	
Liang	502–557	
Ch'en	557–589	
Northern Dynasties		
Wei (Northern)	386–534	
Eastern Wei	534–550	Western Wei 534–557
Northern Ch'i	550–577	Northern Chou 557–581
Sui	581–618	
T'ang	618–907	
Five Dynasties Era	907–960	
1. Later Liang	907–923	Nomad dynasties in
2. Later T'ang	923–936	North China
3. Later Chin	936–947	Liao 916–1125

Chronological Table of Dynasties

4. Later Han	947–950		Hsi Hsia	990–1227
5. Later Chou	951–960		Chin	1125–1234
Sung (Northern)	960–1226			
Sung (Southern)	1127–1279			
Yüan	1279–1368			
Ming	1368–1644			
Ch'ing	1644–1912			

Index

Abahai, 157
Afghanistan, 51, 82
Africa, 150
Agrarian revolution, 312–14, 326, 393
Agriculture, 13, 16, 19, 21, 23, 26, 31, 37, 42, 48, 53, 58, 65, 67, 73, 75, 86, 94–5, 99, 115, 119–21, 126–7, 138, 147, 150–2, 156, 166, 169, 250, 274, 334, 361, 381, 393, 397–8, 403–5, 408–9, 427
Aigun Treaty, 203, 205
Aisin Gioro, 156
Akuta, 123
Albania, 415
Albazin, 167
Albigensians, 80
Alchemy, 83, 102
All-China Federation of Trade Unions, 294, 301, 316
Amherst, Lord, 178
Amitabha Buddha, 81
Amoy, 165, 183
Amur River, 157, 167, 203
An Lu-shan, 100–2, 106
Analects, 34–5
Anfu clique, 272–3, 278–9, 341, 351
Anglo-Japanese Treaty (1894), 223
Anglo-Japanese Treaty (1902), 248
Anhwei, 29, 44, 74, 115, 142, 195–6, 265, 301, 321, 327, 336, 351, 357
Anking, 190, 194
Anti-Bolshevist League, 329
Anyang, 17
Apaochi, 114
Arabs, 99–100, 104, 127, 153
Archaeology, 13, 15–17, 19, 42, 45, 52, 65
Architecture, 66, 81, 97, 110, 147, 162
Argun River, 167
Aristocracy, 17, 23, 27, 31, 34, 44–5, 77, 86, 90, 94–5, 98, 117, 140–1, 208, 210, 223, 234
Art, 20, 65, 81–5, 97, 109, 133–5, 144, 175–6
Asia, 95, 129, 199, 207, 234
Assyrians, 32
Atlach, 100
Austria, 247
Autumn Harvest Uprising, 319, 325
Avars, 75

Bactria, 51
Balázs, E., 108
Banners, Manchu, 156, 164, 169, 191, 238

Belgium, 230, 246, 287, 357
Black Dragon Society, 267
Black Flags, 221
Blue Shirts, 333, 342
Blücher, V. K., 289, 294, 296, 306, 316, 352
Bogue, Treaty of the, 184
'Book of History', see Shu ching
'Book of Odes', see Shih ching
Borodin, M. M., 282, 288, 293, 306, 316
Boxer Protocol, 246, 248
Boxers, see I Ho Ch'üan
Braun, O., 337
Bronze, 19–22, 25, 65–6, 135
Bucharest, 410
Buddhism, 21, 79–84, 94, 97–8, 103, 107, 109–10, 136–7, 140, 142–3, 149, 159–60, 175, 241
Bukhara, 96
Bülow, B. von, 231
Bureaucracy, 17, 23, 48–9, 55, 57–8, 78, 86, 91, 93, 95, 98, 102–4, 106, 117, 120–2, 128, 148, 152, 155, 168, 195, 208, 212, 238, 323, 334
Burma, 165, 170, 220–1, 365–6
Burma Road, 357
Byzantine Empire, 97

Cairo Conference, 366
Calligraphy, 84, 134, 136, 144, 166
Cambaluc, 132
Canals, 87–8
Cantlie, J., 255
Canton, 104, 153, 177, 179–83, 186, 200, 202–3, 255, 257, 271–2, 280–2, 284, 288, 290, 293–4, 296–9, 301–4, 306, 320, 325, 350, 352, 422
Canton Commune, 320
Canton-Hankow Railway, 258
Capitalism, 127, 152, 211–12, 235, 250–1, 256, 274, 335, 394, 416
Capua, 190
Carlyle, T., 337
Caspian Sea, 59, 87
Catholics, Roman, 153, 171, 185, 219, 231, 241
CC clique, 323, 385
Central Asia, 51, 59–60, 79, 82, 96, 100, 102, 107, 119, 123, 127, 130, 138, 140, 145
Ceramics, 162, 175
Ceylon, 82, 97
Chahar, 332, 341

Index

Chamberlain, N., 351
Champa, 89
Chan kuo ts'e, 39
Ch'an Buddhism, 81–2, 135, 175
Chang Chien, 250
Chang Ch'ien, 51
Chang Chüeh, 60
Chang Ch'un-ch'iao, 417, 424, 428
Chang Hsien-chung, 157, 165
Chang Hsüan, 110
Chang Hsüeh-liang, 303, 313, 322, 324, 331, 343
Chang Hsün, 259, 270–1
Chang Kuo-t'ao, 283, 312, 335–6, 339–40
Chang T'ai-lei, 285, 320
Chang Tsai, 137
Chang Tso-lin, 270, 279–80, 291–2, 295, 299–303, 310, 321–2
Chang Tsung-ch'ang, 300
Changchun, 249, 377, 384, 387
Ch'ang-an, 46, 56–7, 65, 72, 90, 95, 100–2, 111, 162
Ch'angchou, 207
Ch'angsha, 190, 283, 302, 304, 314, 319, 328, 367
Chao, state (Chou), 29, 32, 40
Chao Heng-t'i, 302
Chao Kao, 43
Chao K'uang-yin, 115, 117–18
Chao Meng-fu, 144
Chao Shih-yen, 309
Chao Tzu-yang, 432, 434
Chefoo, 222
Chefoo Convention, 220
Chekiang, 13, 31, 51, 73, 103, 122, 152–3, 183, 194–6, 198, 201, 206–7, 233, 299, 301, 303, 307, 321, 327, 338, 355
Ch'en dynasty, 78, 86
Ch'en Chiung-ming, 280–1, 290, 294, 296
Ch'en I, 283, 289, 338, 357, 389, 420, 422
Ch'en Kuo-fu, 323
Ch'en Li-fu, 323
Ch'en Po-ta, 413, 417–18, 423–4
Ch'en Shao-yü, *see* Wang Ming
Ch'en Sheng, 44
Ch'en Tu-hsiu, 275, 277, 282–4, 312, 316
Ch'en Yü-ch'eng, 194
Ch'en Yün, 309, 400, 434
Cheng, king, *see* Ch'in Shih-huang
Cheng, Ch'eng-kung, *see* Koxinga
Cheng Ho, 150
Chengchow, 313, 315
Ch'eng, king (Chou), 22
Ch'eng, Hao, 137
Ch'eng, I, 137
Ch'engtu, 69, 354, 390
Chennault, C. L., 366
Ch'i, state (Chou), 27, 29, 32, 40
Ch'i (Huang Ch'ao's dynasty), 105
Ch'i Pai-shih, 175
Ch'i-shan, 182
Ch'i-ying, 183
Chia-ch'ing, 169, 177
Chiang Ch'ing, 417, 420–1, 424, 427–9, 432
Chiang Kai-shek, 215, 281, 289–90, 294, 297–

9, 301–3, 305–11, 316, 320–5, 330–4, 336–7, 342–4, 346, 355–8, 362–4, 366–8, 370–1, 373–5, 377–8, 382, 384–90
Ch'iang tribes, 71
Chieh (Hsia ruler), 22
Chieh tribes, 71
Chien Po-tsan, 419
Ch'ien-lung, 168–70, 173–4
Chihli (Hopei), 208, 216, 239, 242, 244, 252, 259
Chihli clique, 272, 279–80, 291–2
Chihli-Anhwei war, 279
Chihli-Fengtien wars, 279, 292
Ch'ih-pi, 69
Chin, state (Chou), 27, 29
Chin dynasty (266–420), 70–3, 84
Chin dynasty (Jurchen), 123, 125–6, 130–1, 156
Chin (Sha-t'o state) 114
Chin-chi-pao, 214
Chinchow, 387
Chin-ch'uan tribes, 170
Chin P'ing Mei, 160
Ch'in, state and dynasty, 26–7, 31–2, 35–8, 40–51, 62, 66, 87, 90
Ch'in Kuei, 125
Ch'in Pang-hsien, *see* Po Ku
Ch'in Shih-huang, 40, 42–4, 50, 424
Ch'in-tsung, 125
Chinese Communist Party (CCP), 271, 277, 282–5, 287–93, 295–9, 302, 304–6, 308–12, 314–21, 325–30, 332–3, 335–43, 347–50, 352–4, 356–7, 359–62, 364–5, 368–70, 373–80, 382–402, 404–10, 412–21, 423–9, 432–4
Chinese Eastern Railway, 230
Chinese People's Political Consultative Conference, 384, 391
Chinese People's Volunteers, 395–6
Chingghis Khan, 129–31, 167
Chingkangshan, 319, 418
Chingshih, 147
Chingtechen, 152, 162
Chinkiang, 183, 190
Chinputang, 264, 270
Ch'ing, dynasty and era, 135, 145, 157–8, 163–83, 185–6, 188–98, 200–8, 210–17, 219–33, 236, 238–46, 248–55, 257–64, 268, 292
Ch'iu Fu, 103
Ch'iu Ying, 161
Chou, duke of, 22
Chou, dynasty and era, 15, 21–3, 25–7, 29, 32–4, 38–40, 57, 62, 65–7
Chou dynasty (7th cent. AD), 98
Chou En-lai, 283, 289, 309, 312, 318, 343, 370, 374, 376, 380, 395, 397, 400–1, 420, 423–7
Chou Fang, 110
Chou Hsin, 22
Chou Tun-i, 137
Chouk'outien, 11
Christianity, 79, 104, 154, 171, 188–9, 192, 198, 200–1, 219, 241–3, 342
Chu Hsi, 137, 148, 159, 171–2
Chu-ko Liang, 169
Chu Ta, 175

Index

Chu Te, 218–19, 325–8, 348, 353, 359, 362, 389, 400
Chu Wen, 105, 112
Chu Yüan-chang, 143, 145, 147–50, 424
Ch'u, state (Chou), 27, 29, 32, 38–40, 44
Ch'u tz'u, 38
Ch'uan-pi Convention, 182
Ch'un-ch'iu, 34, 39
Chuang, nationality, 327
Chuang Chou, 36
Chuang-tzu, 36
Ch'üanchou, 153
Chungking, 350, 353–60, 363–71, 373–9
Chungkuo, 13
Chung-tsung, 98
Ch'ung-cheng, 155
Churchill, W., 366, 371
Ch'ü Ch'iu-pai, 283, 309, 312, 319, 338
Ch'ü Yüan, 38
Ch'ü-fu, 419
Classics, Confucian, 38–9, 64, 93, 137, 148, 235
Coal, 212, 403, 411, 432
Cohong, 177, 183
Communist International (Comintern), 282–4, 291, 298, 312, 314–15, 320, 328, 336–7, 341, 350
Communist Youth League, 305, 317, 327, 420–1
Confucianism, 34–8, 49, 53–4, 58, 62, 64, 79–83, 93, 107–8, 136–7, 171, 189, 192, 235, 275, 342
Confucius, 33–5, 48, 235, 419, 427
Corvée, 23, 27, 43, 46, 80, 87, 94, 121
Cotton, 127, 152
Couplet, P., 171
Crimean War, 201
Cultural Revolution (1915–20), 275, 277
Cushing, C., 185

Davies, J. P., 369
December Ninth Movement, 342
Demchukdonggrub (Te Wang), 332, 335
Democratic League, 380, 385
Dennett, T., 184
Denver, 259
Derby, Lord, 202
Diaz, P., 240
Dorgon, 157
Drama, 144–5, 160
Dubs, H. H., 63
du Halde, J. D., 171
Dzungaria, 214, 221

Earlier Ch'in, 73–4
East Asia, 11, 32, 63, 87, 153, 171, 177, 185, 223, 248, 250, 274, 286–7, 351, 361, 365
East India Company, 178
Eastern Chin, 72–3, 75, 78
Eastern Chou, 25–6, 32, 34, 67
Eastern Expeditions, 294, 296
Eastern Han, 57–61, 79, 99, 102, 112
Eastern Mongols, 167
Eastern Turks, 87, 89, 91, 95–6
Eastern Wei, 77

Eberhard, W., 43, 70
Egypt, 11
Eighth Route Army, 348–9, 353–4, 359
Eleuths, 167, 170
Elgin, Lord, 202, 204–6
Elliot, C., 180–1
England, 153, 177–85, 199–207, 212, 214, 217, 220, 225, 227, 229–33, 237–8, 243, 246, 248, 250, 255, 259, 272, 281–2, 287, 295–6, 307, 310, 351, 357–8, 366, 405, 422
Enlarged Conference Movement, 324
Esen, 151
Eunuchs, 54, 58, 61, 102, 104, 107, 150–1, 155, 168, 210
Europe, 16, 20, 34–5, 38, 65, 77, 79–80, 85, 106, 129, 131, 133, 150, 153–4, 165, 167, 169–71, 176, 178, 182, 200, 207, 216, 227, 235, 243, 245, 251, 270–1, 273–4, 320, 351–2, 357–8, 361, 370–1, 415, 423
Ever Victorious Army, 207
Examination System, 48, 93, 95, 117, 122, 148, 176, 198, 238
Extraterritoriality, 185, 287

Fa-hsien, 82
Fan Chung-yen, 121
Fan K'uan, 134
Fan Wen-lan, 198
Fanch'eng, 132
Fang Chih-min, 327, 337
Fang, Ch'ung, 56
Fang La, 122
Far East, 250
Fascism, 333, 342, 368
Fei River, 74
Feng Kuo-chang, 260, 272
Feng Yü-hsiang, 281, 292, 299–300, 303–4, 313, 315–16, 321, 324, 385
Feng, Yün-shan, 188, 190
Fengtien clique, 279, 291, 295, 303, 313
Ferghana, 96
Feudalism, 16, 23, 25, 36, 52–3, 55–6, 99, 155, 186, 198
Fitzgerald, C. P., 37, 128
Five Bushels sect, 60, 73
Five Dynasties, 112, 115
Five Elements theory, 38, 49
Five Hu (nomads), 71
Foochow, 133, 183, 212, 222
Four Books, 35
France, 185, 201–7, 219, 221–3, 227, 229–30, 232, 243, 250, 256, 271, 281, 283, 287, 296, 298, 308, 357, 422
Franco-Prussian war, 219
French Concession 201, 309
Fu Chien, 73–4
Fu Tso-i, 387–8
Fukien, 51, 104, 152–3, 166, 201, 232, 281, 301, 303, 321, 327, 333, 338
Fukien Revolt, 333–4, 337
Fu-lin, 157–8, 166
Fung Yu-lan, 83
Fut'ien, 329

Galdan, 167

Gang of Four, 428–9
Gautama, 81
Gentry, 117, 121, 128, 138, 141–3, 152, 157–9, 164, 166, 174, 188–9, 191–2, 195, 197–8, 208, 210, 215, 219, 234–5, 241–2, 250–2, 257, 264, 305, 313, 315, 319, 334, 355, 393
Germanic tribes, 16, 71
Germany, 227, 229, 231, 243–7, 266–7, 270, 273, 287, 330, 333, 337, 346, 351, 358, 366, 370, 396
Ghurkas, 170
Gibbon, E., 171
Gladstone, W. E., 179, 181
Gobi, 50, 128, 143
God Worshippers' Society, 188
Golden Sand River, 339
Goodrich, L. C., 72, 82
Gorbitsa River, 167
Gordon, C. G., 207
Grand Canal, 183
Granet, M., 38
Great Britain, *see* England
Great Leap Forward, 404–11, 413
Great Wall, 42–3, 75, 88, 152, 157–8, 387
Green Forest Army, 56
Green Gang, 309, 311
Gros, Baron, 202
Gutenberg, J., 108

Haifeng, 285, 318
Hailufeng, 318, 320
Hainan, 359
Hakka, 186, 188
Han River, 29, 44, 132
Han, dynasty and era, 17, 44–6, 48–52, 54, 60–5, 69–70, 78, 82, 91, 93, 95, 118, 128, 137, 145, 361
Han, state (Chou), 29, 32, 40
Han (Hun state), 72
Han Fei, 37
Han fei tzu, 37
Han Hsin, 46
Han Kan, 110
Han School of Learning, 172
Han shu 63–4
Han Yü, 107
Hangchow, 88, 125, 195, 307, 418
Hankow, 191, 259–60, 302, 307, 313
Hanlin Academy, 160
Hanoi, 355
Hanyang, 191, 258, 260, 302
Hao, 21, 25
Harbin, 230, 377
Hart, R., 217, 219, 222, 244
Hawaii, 233, 254–5
Hideyoshi, 154–5, 223
Himalayas, 170
Historical Writing, 22, 62–4, 71–2, 87, 90–1, 104, 112, 126, 135–6, 165, 172–3, 215
Ho Lung, 318, 327, 338, 340, 348
Ho Meng-hsiung, 329
Ho Ying-ch'in, 303, 330
Holland, 153, 165, 178, 246, 271, 287, 357–8
Honan, 13, 17, 27, 29, 56–8, 105, 142, 157,

177, 196, 232, 253, 259–60, 300, 303–4, 313, 324, 327
Hong Kong, 182–4, 199, 254–5, 385
Hopei, 29, 58, 71, 77, 90, 104, 142, 147, 177, 341, 348, 351, 359
Hopkins, H., 371
Ho-shen, 168
Hsi K'ang, 83
Hsia dynasty, 15–17, 22, 37
Hsia Kuei, 135
Hsia, Tou-yin, 313
Hsiang Ying, 335, 338, 349, 357
Hsiang Yü, 44
Hsiangyang, 132
Hsiao, duke of Ch'in, 31
Hsiao Ch'ao-kuei, 188, 190
Hsiao K'o, 338, 340, 348
Hsieh Fu-chih, 422
Hsieh Ho, 84
Hsien-feng, 204–5, 209
Hsien-pi, 59, 71, 75, 77, 114
Hsien-tsung, 101–2
Hsienyang, 42, 44
Hsi Hsia, 119, 130
Hsin dynasty, 54
Hsing Chung Hui, 254
Hsiung-nu, 42, 50–1, 56, 59, 71, 129
Hsi-yu chi, 160
Hsü Ch'ung-chih, 281, 297
Hsü Hsiang-ch'ien, 320, 327, 336, 339–40, 348, 420
Hsü K'o-hsiang, 314
Hsü Shen, 64
Hsü Shih-ch'ang, 272
Hsü Ta, 143
Hsüan-tsang, 107
Hsüan-tsung, 98–102, 105–6
Hsüchow, 317
Hsün Ch'ing, 35, 37–8
Hu Feng, 401
Hu Han-min, 322–3
Hu Shih, 55, 275, 283
Hu Yao-pang, 432–4
Hua Hsing Hui, 255
Hua Kuo-feng, 427–9, 432–3
Huai Army, 195, 208
Huai River, 125
Huai-Hai Campaign, 386–7, 389
Huai-nan, 64
Huai-nan tzu, 64
Huan, duke of Ch'i, 29
Huang, Ch'ao, 104–5
Huang Hsing, 255, 257, 264, 266
Huang Kung-wang, 144
Huang Shao-hung, 302–3
Huang Ti, 15
Huang Tsung-hsi, 172
Hui (Han emperor), 49
Huichow, 296
Hui-ti, 149
Hui-tsung, 125, 134, 142, 175
Hunan, 147, 190, 192, 195, 213, 237, 240, 255, 258, 269, 300, 302–4, 312–15, 319, 325–7, 338, 340, 367, 427
Hunan Army, 192, 194, 208, 226

Index

Hundred Regiments Campaign, 354
Hung Fu, 196
Hung Hsiu-ch'üan, 186, 188–9, 193, 196
Hung Jen-kan, 193, 196
Hung-lou meng, 176
Hung-wu, *see* Chu Yüan-chang
Hungary, 401
Huns, 42, 71, 73
Hupei, 17, 147, 190, 240, 258, 300, 302, 313, 319, 327, 336
Hurley, P. J., 369–70, 375
Huxley, T. H., 236

I tribes, 25
Ichigo Offensive, 367
I ching, 39
I Ho Ch'üan, 241–2
I Ho T'uan, 242–6, 248, 395
Ili, 170, 182, 214, 221
Imperial City, 149, 162, 239, 247, 292
Imperial University, 49, 58, 93
India, 11, 81–2, 97, 107, 178–9, 181, 183, 197, 202, 237, 366
Indians, North American, 185
Indochina, 221
Indo-European languages, 51, 59, 82
Industrialization, 211–12, 215, 250, 397, 402, 404
Inflation, 261, 312, 364, 381, 388, 393
International Settlement, 201, 309
Iron, 26, 45, 52, 55, 119
Irrigation, 26–7, 45, 115, 119, 126–7, 140, 147, 151
Islam, 97
Italy, 153, 232–3, 243, 287, 415

Jao Shu-shih, 399
Japan, 52, 81, 97, 110, 127, 140, 148, 152–5, 211, 216, 220, 223–5, 229–30, 232, 237–8, 240, 243, 246, 248–52, 254, 256, 266, 274, 276, 278–9, 284–7, 292, 295, 299–300, 321–2, 325, 328, 330–6, 338–68, 371, 373–5, 378, 381
Japan, Sea of, 203, 205
Java, 82
Jehol, city, 205
Jehol, province, 332
Jen Pi-shih, 338, 340
Jesuits, 141, 153–4, 170, 174
Jesus, 188
Jews, 104
Joffe, A. A., 281
Jou-jan, *see* Avars
Ju-lin wai-shih, 176
Jui-tsung, 98
Juichin, 335
Jung tribes, 25
Jung Hung, 215
Jung-lu, 239, 252
Jurchen, 123, 125–6, 129–31, 133, 135, 138, 141, 156

K'aifeng, 114, 123, 130–1, 135, 313, 421
K'aip'ing, 212
Kalgan, 347, 380, 387

Kanghwa, Treaty of, 224
Kansu, 22, 42, 51, 71, 84, 89, 102, 119, 213–14, 304, 340
K'ang-hsi, 166–9, 173–4, 176
K'ang Sheng, 417, 423
K'ang-ta, 354
K'ang, Yu-wei, 234–7, 239–40, 253–4, 271
Kao Kang, 339, 398
Kao K'o-kung, 144
Kao-tsu, *see* Liu Pang
Kao-tsu (618–26), *see* Li Yüan
Kao-tsung (650–83), 97–8
Kao-tsung (1127–62), 125
Karakhan, L. M., 285–6
Karakorum, 130, 132
Kardelj, E., 370
Karlgren, B., 38
Kemingtang, 280
Ketteler, K. von, 245
Khatmandu, 170
Khingan, 57
Khitan, 100, 114–15, 117, 123, 125–6, 129, 131, 133, 138, 141
Khrushchev, N. S., 399, 410, 413
Kiakhta, 167–8
Kiangnan Arsenal, 211
Kiangsi, 115, 121, 152, 162, 265, 301, 303–4, 318–19, 321, 327–30, 335, 338–9
Kiangsu, 29, 103, 115, 194–6, 201, 206–7, 301, 303, 307, 321, 351, 355
Kiaochow, 231–2, 238, 266
Kirghizia, 100
Kirin, 330
Kissinger, H., 425
Kiukiang, 190, 194, 307
Ko Hung, 83
Koguryo, 89, 96
Korea, 52, 81, 89–90, 96–7, 127, 140, 154–5, 157, 223–7, 248, 267, 395–6
Kowloon (Chiulung), 205, 232
Koxinga, 153, 165
Ku K'ai-chih, 84
Ku Yen-wu, 172
Ku-chin t'u-shu chi-ch'eng, 173
Kuan Chung, 29
Kuang-hsü, 210, 223, 235–40, 242, 245, 252–3, 262
Kuang Wu, *see* Liu Hsiu
Kuan Han-cheng, 144
Kuan T'ung, 134
Kubilai, 132, 141
Kumarajiva, 82
Kunming, 354, 365, 381
K'ung, family, 334
K'ung fu-tzu, *see* Confucius
Kuo Sung-ling, 299–300
Kuo Sung-tao, 216
Kuo Tzu-i, 101
Kuo Wei, 114
Kuo yü, 39
Kuominchün, 292, 300, 303–4, 313, 321
Kuomintang (KMT), 264–6, 270–1, 280, 282, 285, 287–94, 301–15, 318–21, 323–8, 330–4, 336–51, 354–9, 362–71, 373–93, 396
Kwangchow Bay, 232

Kwangsi, 43, 51, 188, 194, 202, 230, 269, 271, 280–1, 290, 301, 320–1, 323–5, 327, 333, 367, 420
Kwangtung, 43, 51, 104, 107, 132, 200–1, 230, 232, 235–6, 254–5, 257–8, 265, 271, 280–2, 285, 290, 294, 301, 304, 318–19, 324, 331, 333
Kwantung Army, 332, 352, 371, 375
Kweichow, 69, 103, 145, 213, 269, 324, 338–9
Kweilin, 190, 367
Kweisui, 347

Labour movement, 284, 288–90, 294, 301, 304, 306–9, 311, 316–17, 320, 326, 329
Lacquer, 65
Lamaism, 140
Land equalization, 75, 86, 94, 99, 120, 157
Land reform, 312, 347, 353, 362, 380, 384, 393, 397
Lant'ien, 11
Lao She, 419
Lao Tzu, 35–6
Late Chin, 157
Later Chin, 114
Later Chou, 115
Later Han, 114
Later Liang, state, 86
Later Liang, dynasty, 105, 112, 114
Later T'ang, 114
Lattimore, O., 43, 252
Laval, P., 356
League of Nations, 331
Ledo, 365
Legalism, 31, 35, 37–8, 40, 42, 49
Leibniz, G. W., 171
Lenin, V. I., 276, 281, 291
Lhasa, 167
Li, T'ang imperial clan, 90, 95, 98, 112
Li Chen, 110
Li Ch'eng, 134
Li chi, 39
Li Chi-shen, 311
Li Hsien-nien, 340, 420, 428–9, 434
Li Hsiu-ch'eng, 193–4, 196, 206
Li Hung-chang, 195, 207–8, 211–13, 216, 220, 222, 225–6, 230–2, 238, 240, 245
Li K'o-yung, 105, 114
Li Kung-p'u, 330
Li Li-san, 283, 307, 312, 326, 329–30
Li Lin-fu, 99–100
Li Lung-chi, *see* Hsüan-tsung
Li Lung-mien, 134
Li Po (Li T'ai-po), 106
Li sao, 38
Li Shih-min, 91, 94, 96–8, 100, 109
Li Ssu, 38, 42–3
Li Ssu-hsün, 111
Li Ta, 419
Li Ta-chao, 277, 283–4, 310
Li Tsung-jen, 301, 323, 385, 389
Li Tzu-ch'eng, 156–8, 164
Li Wang, 25
Li Wei-han, 312
Li Yüan, 90–1

Li Yüan-hung, 259–61, 269–71, 279–81
Liang Ch'i-ch'ao, 234, 236–7, 239–40, 253–4, 256, 264, 268, 270
Liang dynasty, 78
Liang family, 58
Liang K'ai, 135
Liao Chung-k'ai, 288–9, 297
Liao dynasty, 114, 117–19, 123, 126
Liao Mo-sha, 411
Liao River, 157
Liaohsi-Shenyang Campaign, 386
Liaoning, 22, 42, 71, 114, 330
Liaotung, 89, 145, 157–8, 226, 249
Liberated Areas, 348, 353–4, 356–7, 359–61, 368, 374, 379–80, 383–4
Lin Piao, 348, 375, 383, 387, 407, 410, 413, 416, 418–19, 423–6, 432
Lin Tse-hsü, 180–2
Lin-an, 125, 127, 132, 135
Literature, 17, 20, 42, 61, 64–5, 106–7, 160, 176, 276
Liu, Han imperial clan, 46, 50, 56
Liu An, 64
Liu, Chih-chi, 109
Liu Chih-tan, 339
Liu Chin, 151
Liu, Hsiu, 56–7
Liu Hsüan, 56–7
Liu, J. T., 106
Liu Pang, 44–6, 49–50, 143, 424
Liu Pei, 69
Liu Po-ch'eng, 348, 383, 389
Liu Shao-ch'i, 307, 316, 343, 357, 363, 400, 406, 408, 412–13, 416–19, 421, 432
Liu Sung dynasty, 73, 78
Liu Ts'ung, 72
Liu Tsung-yüan, 107
Liu Yü, 73, 78
Liu Yüan, 71–3
Liu-ch'iu Islands, 220
Livadia, Treaty of, 221
Lo I-nung, 308–9, 328
Lo-lang, 52, 65
London, 216, 255
Long March, 338, 340–2, 433
Loyang, 22, 25–6, 57, 60, 65, 67, 72, 77, 84, 88, 90, 101, 104, 111, 131, 157
Lu, state (Chou), 33–4
Lu Chia, 49
Lu Hsün (Chou Shou-jen), 275, 342
Lu Ting-i, 401, 418–19
Lufeng, 318
Lukouch'iao, 345–6
Lü, empress, 49–50
Lü Pu-wei, 40
Lun heng, 64
Lun yü, 34
Lung-men, 84, 109
Lung-shan, 13
Lung-yü, 262
Lushan, 407, 424
Lushun, *see* Port Arthur

Ma Hua-lung, 214
Ma Yüan, 135

Index

Macao, 153, 185
MacArthur, D., 395
Macartney, Lord, 179
Mahayana Buddhism, 81
Mailla, J. de, 171
Maitreya Buddha, 81, 142
Man tribes, 29
Manch'eng, 65
Manchu, people and empire, 100, 155–9, 164–7, 169–79, 181, 186, 188–92, 197, 200–1, 203–6, 208, 210, 213, 215–16, 219–23, 228–9, 233–5, 239, 242, 245–7, 249, 252–4, 256–7, 260–2, 271
Manchuria, 123, 156, 226–7, 230, 244–6, 248–9, 267, 279, 292, 300, 325, 330–1, 335, 343, 346, 351, 366–7, 371, 374–5, 377–9, 383, 387, 398
Mangu, 132
Manichaeism, 97, 103, 122
Manufactures, 95, 128
Mao Tse-tung, 283–4, 290, 304, 319, 325–9, 335–7, 339–40, 350, 360, 362, 368–70, 374, 378, 382, 389, 391, 395–404, 406–8, 410–21, 423–9, 432–3
March 20th Incident, 298
Margary, A. R., 220
Mariana Islands, 361
Marshall, G. C., 376, 378, 380, 383, 385–6
Marxism, 16, 141, 159, 198, 276–7, 283–4, 289, 335, 413, 415
Maspero, H., 22, 79
Massachusetts, 185
Mawangtui, 65
Mawei, 212
May Fourth Movement, 275, 277, 283, 287
May Thirtieth Movement, 295–6
Mediterranean, 16, 97
Mei Tei (Mao Tun), 50
Meiji Restoration, 211, 220, 237
Melbourne, Lord, 181
Mencius, 34–5, 49
Meng T'ien, 42–3
Merchants, 27, 40, 52, 95, 97, 104, 127–8, 140–1, 147, 212, 250–1, 257, 290
Mesopotamia, 11
Miao people, 213
Mi Fu, 134
Midway, 361
Mill, J. S., 236
Min pao, 256
Ming, dynasty and era, 54, 67, 135, 143, 147–52, 154–62, 164–6, 168, 172, 174–5, 186, 220
Missionaries, 153, 171, 185–6, 202, 204, 219, 231–2, 241, 245
Modernization, 184, 211–12, 216–17, 220, 223, 227, 234, 240, 254, 256, 276–7, 334, 393, 396, 400, 427, 429, 431
Mohism, 37
Money, 26, 55, 70, 78, 94, 120, 140
Mongolia, 96, 148, 167, 221
Mongolia, Inner, 114, 157, 267, 332
Mongolia, Outer, 167
Mongolian People's Republic, 129, 168, 425
Mongols, 59, 71–2, 99, 114, 123, 126, 128–33,

140–5, 147–9, 151–2, 169, 253, 332, 350
Mon-khmer 43
Moscow, 281, 326, 329, 371, 396, 415, 425
Moslems, 104, 123, 130, 140, 150, 213–14, 221, 340
Most-favourite-nation principle, 184–5, 203, 205
Mo Ti, 36–7
Mo-tzu, 36
Mu Ch'i, 135
Mu-jung clan, 75
Mukden, 299–300, 313, 322, 375, 377, 384, 387
Muraviev, N. N., 203
Muscovy, 147

Nagoya, 356
Nanchang, 303, 306, 308, 310–11, 328, 337
Nanchang Uprising, 318–19, 325
Nan-chao, 100
Nanking, 70, 72–3, 84, 143, 147, 149, 152, 164–5, 183, 190–7, 200, 207, 259–62, 264, 271, 310–13, 315–16, 318–24, 329, 331–5, 337, 341–4, 346–9, 351, 356, 373, 380–90
Nanking Treaty, 183–5, 199–200
Nank'ou, 300
Napier, Lord, 180
National Revolutionary Army (NRA), 296, 298–9, 301–6, 308–13, 318–19, 321, 348
National Salvation movement, 342, 344
Naturalists, 38
Nazis, 333, 346, 351–2, 357–8, 366, 418
Needham, J., 36, 38, 64, 83
Neo-Confucianism, 107, 136–7, 159, 172–3
Neolithic, 11, 19
Neo-Taoism, 83
Nepal, 170
Nerchinsk Treaty, 167, 203
Nestorianism, 97, 103, 123
New Fourth Army, 349, 353, 357, 359, 365, 369
New Life Movement, 342
Ni Tsan, 144–5
Nieh Jung-chen, 348, 383, 420
Nien, 196, 213
Nine Power Treaty, 287
Ningpo, 153, 183, 207
Nixon, R., 425
Nobility, see Aristocracy
Nomads, 25, 31, 42–3, 50, 59, 67, 71–5, 77, 80, 86, 90, 99–100, 103, 114, 118, 122, 128–9, 138, 157, 174
North Africa, 361
Northern Ch'i, 77–8
Northern Chou, 77–8, 86, 90
Northern Expedition, 280, 296, 299, 301–3, 306, 313, 321–2
Northern Sung, 125, 134, 145, 160–1, 175
Northern Wei, 74–5, 77, 80, 86
Novel, 160, 176
Nurhachi, 156–7

October Revolution, 276, 285
Ogodei, 130–1
Oil, 411, 432

Open Door Doctrine, 233
Opium, 178–81, 184, 200
Opium Wars, 180–1, 185–6, 199, 202, 206, 208, 215, 217, 234, 395
Oracle bones, 19–20
Ordos, 42, 50, 96
Ou-yang Hsiu, 136

Pa, state (Chou), 31
Pacific Ocean, 13, 233
Pacific, War in the, 359, 361, 363, 365–6, 368, 373
Paekche, 96
Pai Ch'ung-hsi, 301, 309, 311, 323
Painting, 36, 66, 82–3, 106, 110–11, 133–6, 144–5, 161–2, 169, 174–5
Palmerston, Lord, 202
Pamir Mountains, 42, 59, 96, 170
Pan Chao, 63
Pan Ch'ao, 59–60, 63
Pan Ku, 59, 63, 108–9
Pan Piao, 63
P'ang Hsün, 103
Pao Huang Hui, 240
Pao Kuo Hui, 238
Paotow, 347
Paper, 65, 95, 97, 120, 133
Paris, 222
Pearl Harbor, 357, 363–5
Pearl River, 181
Peasant movement, 285, 288–90, 295, 301, 304, 311–15, 317, 319, 327
Peasant rebellions, 44, 53, 56–7, 60, 73, 81, 90, 103–4, 122, 142, 145, 155–8, 169, 186, 192, 197, 199, 213, 241–2, 305
Peiping (Peking), 324, 342–3, 345–6, 351, 373, 376, 387–9, 391
Peiping-Tientsin Campaign, 386–7
Peitaho, 409
Peiyang Army, 252, 259–63, 265, 269–73, 279
Peking, 88, 100, 130, 143, 149, 151–2, 154, 158, 162, 164, 166, 168, 177–8, 182–3, 191, 200, 202, 204–5, 216, 220–1, 226, 231–2, 236, 239, 242–5, 260, 262–3, 265, 269–73, 278–81, 285–6, 292–3, 295, 297, 300, 302, 310, 322–4, 388, 395–6, 411, 417–22, 425, 427
Peking Convention, 205
Peking Man, 11
Peking University, 283
Peking-Hankow Railway, 230, 284, 347
Peking-Tientsin Railway, 243, 246
P'eng Chen, 410, 417–19
P'eng P'ai, 285, 290, 318, 320, 328
P'eng Te-huai, 327–8, 340, 348, 353, 383, 395, 407, 411, 429
People's Liberation Army, 319, 379–80, 383–4, 386–90, 392, 395–6, 410, 413–14, 416–24, 426–8
Persia, 97, 127, 153
Persian Gulf, 150
Pescadore Islands, 226, 366
Peter I, 237
Philippines, 233

Philosophy, 32, 35–6, 62, 64, 81, 83, 136–7, 159, 172–3, 277
P'ingch'eng, 77
P'ing Wang, 25
Plato, 35
Po Chü-i, 101, 106–7
Po Ku, 329, 343
Poetry, 36, 38, 63, 65, 84–5, 106–7, 121, 136
P'ohai, Gulf of, 118
Poland, 237, 351, 357, 401
Political Consultative Conference (PCC), 374, 376–7, 380
Political Science clique, 323
Polo, M., 127, 141
Population, 23, 26, 45, 53, 57, 70–1, 78, 87, 101, 119, 127, 140, 147, 152, 166, 169, 186, 403, 432
Porcelain, 65, 95, 127, 152, 162, 176–8
Port Arthur, 226, 230, 232, 238, 249, 371
Portsmouth Treaty, 249
Portugal, 153, 287
Potsdam Conference, 371
Pottery, 13, 21, 109
Printing, 65, 107–8, 135
Prospect Hill, 149, 158
Protestants, 193, 198, 201, 219, 241
Purcell, V., 244
P'u-i, 252, 262, 271, 292
P'yongyang, 89

Quisling, V., 356

Railroads, 212, 230–1, 248, 257–8, 393, 432
Rectification Movement, 360
Red Army, 325–30, 335–40, 342–4, 348, 359
Red Eyebrows, 56–7, 64
Red Guard, 408, 417–20
Red Turbans, 142–3
Reform Movement, 173, 235–6, 238–9, 253
Reischauer, E. O., 48, 127
Religion, 21, 32–3, 37, 64, 79, 81–4, 94, 97, 110, 153–4, 188
Returned Students group, 329, 336
Ricci, M., 153–4
Rice, 65, 127
Roman Empire, 48, 53, 59, 67, 71–2, 115
Romance languages, 20
Romance of the Three Kingdoms, 67, 160
Roosevelt, F. D., 358, 365–70
Roy, M. N., 315
Russia, Tsarist, 167, 203, 205–6, 214, 221, 225, 227, 229–30, 232, 237–8, 243–6, 248–50, 276, 371
Russian Revolution (1905), 256
Russo-Japanese war, 249, 256, 371

Salt, 29, 52, 55, 229
Samarkand, 96
San-kuo chih yen-i, 160
Sanmen Bay, 232
San Min Chu I, 256, 288
Sanskrit, 82
Script, 20, 42, 61
Sculpture, 65, 83, 109–10
Secret societies, 56, 60, 81, 143–4, 169, 186, 240–1, 255–7, 309

Seoul, 154, 224–5, 239, 395
Service, J. S., 368
Seven Sages of the Bamboo Grove, 83
Seymour, E. H., 243–4
Shameen, 296
Shang dynasty, 13, 15–17, 19–23, 25, 33, 65
Shang Yang, 31, 37
Shanghai, 183, 195, 199, 201–4, 206, 212, 236, 255, 260, 265, 272, 278, 280, 283–4, 291, 293–5, 297, 301, 307–11, 323, 326, 328–9, 331, 333, 343, 346, 373, 390, 394, 417, 420, 426
Shanghai-Nanking Railway, 231
Shanhaikuan, 158
Shansi, 17, 29, 71, 77, 89, 110, 114, 270, 321, 347–8, 384
Shantung, 13, 17, 29, 33–4, 56–8, 65, 82, 105, 142, 177, 196, 226, 231–2, 259, 266–7, 270–1, 273, 287, 300, 324, 347, 351, 383, 419
Shao Yung, 137
Sha-t'o Turks, 105, 112, 114
Shen Chou, 161
Shen-tsung, 121
Shensi, 11, 21, 29, 31, 42, 44, 46, 58, 69, 71, 90, 102, 119, 126, 155–6, 158, 213–14, 304, 339–40, 343, 349, 383–4, 398
Shensi-Kansu-Ninghsia Border Region (Shen-Kan-Ning), 249, 357
Shenyang, *see* Mukden
Shih chi, 62–3
Shih ching, 34, 38
Shih Ching-t'ang 114
Shih K'o-fa, 165
Shih Le, 72–3
Shih Ssu-ming, 101
Shih Ta-k'ai, 188, 193, 339
Shih-t'ung, 109
Shimonoseki Treaty, 226–7, 235
Shu, state (Chou), 31
Shu (Three Kingdoms), 67, 69–70
Shu ching, 34, 39
Shui-hu chuan, 160
Shun, 15
Shun (Li Tzu-ch'eng's dynasty), 158
Shuo wen, 64
Siam, 222
Sian, 46, 236, 246, 343
Sian Incident, 343–4
Siberia, 167, 203, 286
Sikang, 339–40
Silk, 13, 45, 50, 65, 87, 95–6, 111, 118–19, 123, 125, 133, 149, 152, 177–9, 199
Silk Route, 51, 59, 96
Silla, 96
Sinkiang, 51, 170, 215, 221, 325, 339–40, 352, 357, 370
Sino-French war, 221–2
Sino-Japanese war (1894–5), 223, 225–9, 234
Sino-Japanese war (1937–45), 345–72
Sino-Russian Treaty (1858), 203
Sino-Soviet Treaty (1924), 286
Sino-Soviet Treaty (1937), 351
Sino-Soviet Treaty (1945), 371
Sino-Soviet Treaty (1950), 396
Slav peoples, 16, 20

Slavery, 16, 19, 23, 48, 55
Small Swords Society, 201
Smith, A., 236
Snow, E., 319, 414
Social Democrats, 245
Socialism, 198, 256, 276, 396, 404, 415–16
Socialist Youth League, 285
Sogdiana, 100
Soochow, 152, 194–5, 207
South Manchuria Railway, 249
South Yüeh, 43, 51
Southeast Asia, 97, 127, 140, 150, 221–2, 255, 358
Southern Ch'i, 78
Southern Ming, 165, 172
Southern Sung, 125–8, 135, 162
Southern T'ang, 115
Soviet Communist Party, 276, 283, 288, 291, 336, 360, 399, 401, 409, 414–15
Soviet Russia, 276–7, 281–2, 285–7
Soviet Union, 168, 288–90, 292–3, 297–8, 300, 304, 307, 310, 316, 320, 329, 335, 344, 351–2, 357–8, 361, 366, 368, 370–2, 374–5, 390, 395–7, 400, 403, 410, 422, 424–5
Spain, 246, 352
Spencer, H., 236
Spring and Autumn Period, 26–7, 31
Srong-btsan-sgam-po, 96
Ssu-k'u ch'üan-shu, 174
Ssu-ma family (Chin), 69
Ssu-ma Ch'ien, 17, 32, 42–3, 45, 51, 62–3, 109, 428
Ssu-ma Hsiang-ju, 65
Ssu-ma Kuang, 121, 135–6
Ssu-ma T'an, 62
Ssu-ma Yen, 70
Ssup'ingkai, 377
St Bartholomew's Day, 80
St Paul, 35
St Petersburg, Treaty of, 221
Stalin, J. V., 291, 306, 315–16, 361, 366, 370–1, 396, 399
Stalingrad, 361
Steel, 403, 411, 432
Stilwell, J. W., 363, 365–7, 369, 385
Stuart, J. L., 382, 388
Su Chao-cheng, 308, 312
Su Shih (Su Tung-p'o), 136
Su Yü, 338
Su-tsung, 101
Suchou, 214
Sui dynasty, 78, 86–7, 89–91, 95
Sun Ch'uan-fang, 301–3
Sun Ch'üan, 70
Sun En, 73, 78
Sun Wu-kung, 160
Sun Yat-sen, 254–7, 259–64, 266, 271–2, 280–2, 288–90, 292–3, 301, 304, 311, 313, 319, 321–2, 355
Sung dynasty and era, 65, 93, 108, 110–11, 115, 117–23, 125–7, 132–8, 142, 144, 152, 162, 170, 173–4
Sung Chiao-jen, 258, 265
Sung Ch'ing-ling (Soong Ching Ling), 316, 385

Sung Mei-ling, 388
Sungkiang, 152
Suslov, M., 415
Swatow, 318, 327
Sweden, 38
Syria, 97
Szechuan, 29, 31, 44, 60, 69, 100–1, 132,
    158, 170, 193, 258, 269, 272, 307, 313, 324,
    336, 338–9, 354–5, 368–9, 420

Tai, state, 74
Tai Chen, 173
Tai Chi-t'ao, 297
Tai Li, 333, 355
Taipings, 156, 186, 188–98, 200–1, 206–8,
    211–13, 217, 221, 225, 254, 294, 339
T'aierhchuang, 347
T'ai-p'ing Tao, 60
T'ai P'ing T'ien, Kuo, 189, 196, 198
T'ai-tsu, *see* Chao K'uang-yin
T'ai-tsung, *see* Li Shih-min
T'ai-tsung (976–92). 117–18
Taiwan, 89, 153, 165, 220, 226, 366, 389
Taiwan Straits, 390, 396
T'aiyüan, 90, 347
Taku, 181, 203–6, 243
Talass River, 100
Tali, city, 213
Tali, kingdom, 132
Talien, 226, 231–2, 249, 371
T'an P'ing-shan, 308, 312
T'an Ssu-t'ung, 234, 237, 239
Tangut, 119
T'ang dynasty and era, 48, 54, 65, 90–1, 93–8,
    100–10, 112, 118, 120, 133–4, 136, 145, 147,
    151, 153, 159, 162, 174
T'ang Sheng-chih, 302–3, 306, 313
T'ang Ts'ai-ch'ang, 240
T'ang, Yin, 161
Tao te ching, 35, 83
Tao-chi (Shih-t'ao), 175
Tao-kuang, 177, 180, 182
Taoism, 21, 35–6, 56, 60, 64, 79–83, 85, 102,
    106, 137, 144, 241
T'ao Yüan-ming (T'ao Ch'ien), 85
Tariff autonomy, 183, 287
Tarim Basin, 59, 214
Tatu River, 339
Tat'ung, 77, 84, 347
Ta-t'ung shu, 235
Tawney, R. H., 334
Taxation, 27, 43, 45–6, 52–3, 57–8, 60, 77, 80,
    87, 94, 99, 102–3, 115, 119–20, 122,
    126–7, 140, 147, 152, 198, 241, 334, 353,
    364
Te Wang, *see* Demchukdonggrub
Tea, 85, 119, 127, 149, 177–9, 199
Teheran Conference, 366
Temujin, *see* Chingghis Khan
Ten Kingdoms, 112, 115
Teng Chung-hsia, 283, 285
Teng Hsiao-p'ing, 283, 292, 327, 383, 387, 400,
    413, 415, 419, 427, 429, 434
Teng T'o, 411
Teng Yen-ta, 304, 316

Thai people, 43, 100
Three Kingdoms, 67, 69–70
Ti tribes, 25, 71
Tibet, 71, 73, 96, 102, 119, 132, 167, 170, 250,
    339, 419
T'ien Li sect, 177
T'ien Shan, 51, 118, 214
Tientsin, 181, 191, 202, 205, 216, 222, 243–4,
    271, 291–2, 294–5, 346, 373, 387–8
Tientsin Incident, 219
Tientsin Treaty (1860), 204–6, 217
Tientsin Treaty (1871), 220
T'ien An Men, 391, 418, 421, 427–8
Tirana, 415
Toba (T'opa), 74, 77, 80
Tokyo, 227, 256, 346, 355
Tonghak, 224
Tongking, 221
Trade, 26–7, 50, 59, 95–7, 119–20, 127–8, 140,
    150, 153, 177–8, 202, 204
Trans-Siberian Railway, 230
Triad, 186, 201
Tripitaka, 82
Trotsky, L. D., 291
Truman, H. S., 375–6, 383, 385–6, 388, 391
Tsai-feng, 253
Ts'ai Ao, 269
Ts'ai Ho-sen, 283, 285, 312
Ts'ao family, 70
Ts'ao Chan, 176
Ts'ao K'un, 272, 279–81
Ts'ao Pei, 69
Ts'ao Ts'ao, 67, 69
Tseng Kuo-fan, 192, 194–6, 208, 211, 215,
    237
Tsinan, 322, 347
Tsinan-Tsingtao Railway, 287
Tsinghua University, 417, 422
Tsingtao, 231–2, 266, 295, 343
Tsitsihar, 377
Tso chuan, 29, 39, 136
Tso Tsung-t'ang, 195, 208, 213–14
Tsou, 34
Tsou Jung, 255
Tsou Tang, 368
Tsou Yen, 38
Tsun-i, 338
Tsungli Yamen, 216
Tsushima, 249
Tu Fu, 107
Tuan Ch'i-jui, 260, 269–72, 279, 291–2
Tung Ch'i-ch'ang, 161–2, 174
Tung Cho, 61
Tung Chung-shu, 49
Tung Pi-wu, 283–4
Tung Yüan, 134
Tung-lin, 155, 172
Tungus, 59, 74, 123, 156
Tunhuang, 84, 110
T'ung-chih, 210
T'ung-chih Restoration, 210, 212, 215
T'ungkuan, 104, 303, 313
T'ung Meng Hui, 256–9, 262–4, 289
T'ung-tien, 109
Turkestan, 170, 214